Beautiful

Beautiful

The Story of Julian Eltinge, America's Greatest Female Impersonator

ANDREW L. ERDMAN

OXFORD
UNIVERSITY PRESS

Oxford University Press is a department of the University of Oxford.
It furthers the University's objective of excellence in research, scholarship,
and education by publishing worldwide. Oxford is a registered trade mark of
Oxford University Press in the UK and in certain other countries.

Published in the United States of America by Oxford University Press
198 Madison Avenue, New York, NY 10016, United States of America.

© Oxford University Press 2024

All rights reserved. No part of this publication may be reproduced, stored in
a retrieval system, or transmitted, in any form or by any means, without the
prior permission in writing of Oxford University Press, or as expressly permitted
by law, by license or under terms agreed with the appropriate reprographics
rights organization. Inquiries concerning reproduction outside the scope of the
above should be sent to the Rights Department, Oxford University Press, at the
address above.

You must not circulate this work in any other form and
you must impose this same condition on any acquirer

Library of Congress Cataloging-in-Publication Data
Names: Erdman, Andrew L., 1965– author.
Title: Beautiful : the story of Julian Eltinge, America's greatest female
impersonator / Andrew L. Erdman.
Description: New York : Oxford University Press, 2024. |
Includes bibliographical references and index.
Identifiers: LCCN 2023058804 | ISBN 9780197696330 (hardback) |
ISBN 9780197696354 (epub) | ISBN 9780197696361 (ebook)
Subjects: LCSH: Eltinge, Julian, 1883–1941. |
Female impersonators—United States—Biography.
Classification: LCC PN2287.E5215 E73 2024 | DDC 792.702/8092 [B]—dc23/eng/20240110
LC record available at https://lccn.loc.gov/2023058804

DOI: 10.1093/9780197696361.001.0001

Printed by Sheridan Books, Inc., United States of America

For Judi

"What he was doing was in no sense parody; it was too simple and too restrained. It wasn't even theatrical. This dark young man with his thin, hairless arms and soft, rounded shoulders, who rocked an imaginary cradle as he crooned, was really a woman."

—*The Day of the Locust* by Nathanael West (1933)

"It costs me all but the breath of life to be a woman."

—Julian Eltinge (1912)

Contents

Acknowledgments	ix
A Note about Citations	xi
Introduction: "Merely a Man"	1
1. A "Cute Little Beaute from Butte, Montana" (But actually, from Boston)	28
2. Mr. Simplicity, or a Cadet-Turned-Chorus-Girl	44
3. Mr. Wix of . . . Vaudeville	68
4. "George M." Is for Minstrel	93
5. Fascinating Stardom	122
6. From Crinoline to Celluloid	152
7. Impersonating in the USA, 1919	178
8. The Twenties	202
9. The Velvet Inquisition	222
Epilogue	249
Notes	257
Select Bibliography	315
Index	341

Acknowledgments

I am deeply grateful to the following people for helping me with this book: Norm Hirschy and Zara Cannon-Mohammed, my editors at Oxford University Press; Jeremy Wang-Iverson, formerly of OUP; Anne Alison Barnet for her assistance with Julian Eltinge's tenure in the Cadets in Boston; Lou Lumenick for his guidance on college musicals; Terry Reid, Caitlyn Shea, and (formerly) Ceylan Swensen of the Northport Historical Society; Peter and Kathy Sullivan, for their assistance with Julian Eltinge's Fort Salonga, Long Island, property; Kim Kohn of the Butte-Silver Bow Public Archive in Montana; Prof. Emeritus Laurance Senelick of Tufts University; Suzanne Lipkin and the entire staff of the New York Public Library's Billy Rose Theatre Collection; Gregor Benko of the JulianEltingeProject.com website; Matthew Wittmann of the Harvard Theatre Collection; the Alpine Historical Society (San Diego County, CA); Sylvia Wang of the Shubert Archive (New York); Lisett Chavarela of the L.A. Conservancy; Miles Kreuger and Eric Davis of the Institute of the American Musical, Inc. (Los Angeles); Anthony Roth of Montana Technological University; Jacob Bloomfield, author of *Drag: A British History*, for help with images; Tony Castaneda and Charles Knill of Villa Capistrano; Daniel Miller of the *Los Angeles Times*; Craig Rayle and Earl Ganz for background on Butte and its history; Heidi David of Moxie Mayhem Marketing; the writer Benjamin Cheever for his perusal of early iterations of this book; the writer Andy Corren for his feedback; and my dear and loving friends Mary Birdsong, Tracy Cochrane, Carlos Dengler, Judi Friedman, Ellen Paltiel, Michael Rogers, Allen Salkin, Shana Sobel, Tony Stiker, Melissa Schulz, Tracy Cochrane, and Hugh Taylor. Also, my brother, the playwright, librettist, and theatre scholar Harley Erdman. Plus, all the rest of you. You know who you are.

# # #

A Note about Citations

Some newspaper articles cited in the sources were accessed via Newspapers. com. Sometimes, there was a discrepancy between the "page number" exhibited on the Newspapers.com website and the page number printed on a publication's actual page. In such cases, *the historical, printed number is provided first and the Newspapers.com pagination, second, in brackets*. For example: "Amusement Notes," *Brooklyn Daily Eagle*, July 30, 1907, 4 [22]. This approach is used with other, similarly discrepant online sources (e.g., Lantern.MediaHist.org).

Periodical sources are titled per *exactly what appeared on the print edition itself on the day the article was first published*. Thus, for example, if it read *Boston Daily Globe* on a paper's header, then the publication is cited as *Boston Daily Globe* rather than *Boston Globe*. In cases where geographical location might be unclear, misleading, or redundant, I have included a two-letter, postal-style state or provincial shorthand in parenthesis, for example *Richmond Item* (IN), and *Evening Free Press* (Winfield, KS). Place names are also written as they appeared in original publication as well even if spellings have since changed (e.g., "Pittsburg").

The Select Bibliography contains the vast majority of Endnote sources but not all of them. Brief or marginal articles, books, and chapters in Endnotes may be excluded from the Select Bibliography. Hence, "Select."

When complete citational information was not available—because, say, it refers to a fragment of an article or document from an archival resource—I have made my best effort to indicate the partial nature of the source, where I saw it, and why it appears that way.

# # #

Introduction

"Merely a Man"

A beautiful woman steps out of the wings and onto the stage at Keith's vaudeville theatre in Boston in 1910. She stands on the edge of the playing area, the apron, in front of a curtain and gestures gracefully, fluidly, the picture of a refined lady—a middle-class white lady, to be sure—but the former is synonymous with the latter and vice versa in most patrons' minds. The woman onstage is dainty yet self-possessed. Spontaneous and natural, yet self-controlled. She harmonizes nicely with her surroundings. The theatre lobby has marble floors, aisles that descend at just the right angle, cushiony seats, Louis XV–style furniture in the lounges, and China vases and jardinières in the lobby, all of it scrubbed and dusted to a shine each day. The audience members hold playbills whose pages are bordered in lavender and gold-leaf. Even the boiler room is finished in gleaming brass.[1]

This woman, on whom all eyes are trained, wears a plush, velvet gown of turquoise-blue. It is décolleté with a plunging back revealing her flawless, porcelain shoulders and "enviable bust," according to one theatergoer. The curtain behind her now rises; she walks upstage under the glow of the spotlights. As she does so, the audience gets a glimpse of her fashionable "French heels," a new style in which the ankle is heightened to accentuate the bustline and derriere. American women aren't quite ready for it, but they will be soon enough. The nation, after all, is expanding abroad, finding new markets and dominating new realms. So, getting in-sync with the latest fashions from abroad seems right. The audience recognizes that this woman, with her hands on her hips, thumbs pointed forward, is a Gibson Girl, a female archetype created by *Life* magazine artist Charles Dana Gibson in 1890 and all the rage by 1900. Tall, voluptuous, neckline plunging, hair swept up in a glorious pompadour, the Gibson Girl was an evolutionary step before the boyish "1914 Girl," and two steps behind the skinny, glamorously-a-bit-unkempt "flapper" who would later dominate American style and fashion. But still: the Gibson Girl ventured outside her home much more than the

Beautiful. Andrew L. Erdman, Oxford University Press. © Oxford University Press 2024.
DOI: 10.1093/9780197696361.003.0001

domesticated, Victorian housewife before her who was bogged down by skirts, laces, brocades, and crinolines. Tennis and beachgoing were out of the question for the Gibson Girl with her long dress and high-piled globe of hair. But she could ride a bike, at least for a while, then spread out on a blanket for a picnic in Central Park or Boston Common. That was activity enough. An audience member finds the woman onstage "as charming a piece of feminine loveliness as can be found in the confines of the States." Many agree.[2]

Now center-stage, the velvet-gowned wonder sings "I'm Getting Fond of You" in a soft yet rich contralto. Her voice is dulcet-toned but substantial. As soon as she finishes, though, she disappears backstage! When she comes back, the Gibson Girl is gone. In her place, it's a dead-on impression of vaudeville superstar Elsie Janis. Another song, a few fancy dance steps, and then off again, and on again! Now she wears a filmy, pseudo-Eastern costume, all the rage these days, as she gives a rendition of contemporary dancer Ruth St. Denis's "Cobra Dance," with its snakelike sways and gyrations. It's actually pretty good. Not a mocking version as some others might do. This woman can dance. She can even do a split.[3]

Figure I.1 Eltinge as the Gibson Girl, a female archetype created by illustrator Charles Dana Gibson in the early 1890s. The Gibson Girl was less confined and more mobile than her Victorian precursors. But with that huge pompadour and long dress, she was still a few evolutionary steps shy of the modern flapper.
Credit: *Copyright reserved, Northport Historical Society (Long Island, NY).*

Finally, the performer comes out in a bathing suit, singing "Take a Dip in the Ocean." The crowd gapes at her exposed, alabaster neck. The song ends. She curtsies politely. The audience explodes in applause. Encores are demanded.[4]

The lady demurs as her mouth curls into a smile. Of course she'll give the crowd what it wants. She knows she's the best thing on the bill. Thirteen minutes of sheer joy. It's customary to give a short curtain speech in these situations, so she steps forward, footlights accentuating her ivory legs.[5]

Then she removes her wig.

And it turns out this woman is no woman, but a man.

His name is Julian Eltinge. Strapping. In his twenties but more like a teen somehow. Many in the crowd had no idea that all these *women* were in fact *this young man*. Or maybe they did not want to know. After all, how could a man so completely become a woman? And not just one woman at that! Perhaps some in the audience felt a secret delight, a never-to-be-spoken pleasure at knowing all along that beneath these skirts resided a male anatomy. Even those who knew—or insisted they had, afterward—loved the pleasure of being fooled. They loved the reveal as much as the illusion. They were, after all, accustomed to master illusionists and magicians, from the authentic ones like Houdini to the countless sleight-of-hand conjurers, all favorites of American amusement-seekers.[6]

Some men in the crowd admit that they'd fallen for her, this perfect vision of womanhood. "I was quite in love with her," says one. "That's a woman al-right, and a very fine one too!" says another. Women were fooled as well. "He's prettier than any girl I ever saw," says one. "I never saw a more beau-tiful woman's face on the stage than his, not even Mrs. Langtry's in her palmy days," says another, comparing Julian Eltinge to famed actress Lily Langtry. Even the house manager, who knows full-well it was a put-on, writes that Eltinge "makes a handsome girl" in his notes to the head office. Were there some in the audience, perchance, who were even *more excited* to discover that "a man's heart" pulsed under the swirling silk and whitewashed skin, making them want to "steal a kiss" all the more? Were there a few gents who wondered what it might be like to try on such attire themselves? (In private of course, not on stage.) Were there women who, while oohing and aahing over the lovely dresses wondered, if a man can play women's parts so skillfully, mightn't they themselves play roles that were supposed to be "men's": professionals, executives, politicians, and entrepreneurs? Julian Eltinge's female impersonations were so perfectly executed, so pure, that in a

4   BEAUTIFUL

sense, theatergoers could project virtually limitless fantasies, wishes, curiosities, and judgments onto them. "If only he were a girl, I should straightaway lose my heart to him," sighs a lifelong bachelor. Sir, you're allowed to lose your heart to him even if he *weren't*—and that can be our little secret for now.[7] Plus, you will have plenty of other chances to see men playing women. For this is the golden age of female impersonation on amateur and professional stage alike. But no one is better than Julian Eltinge. He's the top of the heap. The platinum standard. "He is the best ever seen on any stage," concludes the manager in his report to the Keith vaudeville company's head office, happy that he booked this crowd-pleasing, crackerjack entertainer.[8]

* * *

What follows is the story of Julian Eltinge and his rise to the apex of a highly competitive and popular profession (and avocation) in his day: dragging-up as women for the purposes of entertainment. Eltinge's long tenure atop the female-impersonation boom—a boom he effectively cocreated—tells us a great deal about ideas and concepts that continue to stoke strong feelings and arguments, and serve as touchpoints for battles over the cultural terrain, both in the performer's day and ours. These ideas and concepts include what we might now call proper gender behavior; acceptable sexual attitudes; the role of men in society; the role of women; how and why groups and individuals act as they do amid economic and political shifts; the significance of white skin and white values in determining what is beautiful, what is clownish, what is masculine, and what is feminine; and how all of these things came together within, and were affected by, a new era of mass-market commerce—and vice versa. At the center of the maelstrom was an emerging, white middle class who, along with its plutocratic allies, were fighting to define what it meant to be "normal"—and, by extension, *healthy* and *successful*—and what it therefore meant to be, well, *ab*normal, which therefore suggested illness and/or failure. As we will see, an allegedly abnormal individual could be labeled an "invert," or their behaviors "inversive," the opposite or upside-down of what was thought desirable and therefore natural and expectable. They were, or did things that were, "contrary." Inverted. Such people literally upended cultural norms and were often punished. A new breed of scientific thinkers was trying to unlock the secrets of people whose sexual and gender activities were at apparent odds with the norm. Was their behavior willful? Compulsive? Did it come from within, or was it learned and repeated?

A number of things could lead to suspicions or accusations of being an invert. A man who dressed as a woman, for example, could under certain circumstances be thought the opposite of a man. Though as we will see, many men, Julian Eltinge chief among them, could also freely engage in such dress-up behaviors and even make a decent amount of money doing so if they adhered to certain parameters. In fact, in many settings, crossdressing, if executed properly, could be considered not only acceptable but downright manly. Natural, expectable. Men who were principally sexually attracted to other men could be called inverts (or "perverts"), though in some settings, a guy who enjoyed anonymous sexual encounters with other men but otherwise passed for "masculine" might still be regarded as "normal." Some of the rigid binaries, notably "hetero" and "homo," hadn't yet been normalized in the way they would later come to be, even if in our present moment, that binary is again up for debate, as gender fluidity supplants homosexuality in the eyes of many an inversion-worrier. Men who spoke or gestured in a manner normally associated with women, or dressed in ways more colorful and stylish than, say, a quotidian lawyer or businessman, could be open to charges of inversion. The artists who practiced female impersonation for money onstage employed a range of styles, some more naturalistic, others what we might call campy or satirical.

In Julian Eltinge's day, men who were able to pull off the most precise impressions of women were often freer from charges of inversion than their more cartoonish or carnivalesque peers, who were vulnerable to charges of degeneracy. Eltinge was never called a degenerate or an invert, not despite but in many ways (as we will see) *because* he so completely and seamlessly inhabited his female portrayals. He was an "artist," of course, though also just as important, he framed himself as a *technician*, a dedicated *professional* who comported himself onstage and off "without suggestion." While other performers seemed to mix or confuse the sexes, or make fun of gender uptightness, Eltinge so utterly submerged himself in his womanly renditions as to leave even potential critics in stunned silence. As we shall see, Julian Eltinge was just as thorough in his gender depictions *offstage* as on it, making his "real" life so often seem an extension of his act. At the time, female impersonators who seemed to prefer the opposite sex erotically offstage and depicted women naturalistically onstage were "perfectly acceptable," according to a modern historian, while male artists who veered too far from these parameters faced censure and imprisonment.[9] While things were somewhat more complicated, and while

6 BEAUTIFUL

that equation changed over the course of Julian Eltinge's life and career from the late 1890s to the early 1940s, few performers in his genre depicted both polarities—conventional manhood and womanhood, respectively—with such attention to detail. That is why Eltinge reinforced what women and men were supposed to look like, respectively, while at the same time demonstrating how people could effectively become both—or neither. In that sense, Eltinge, for the most part unwittingly, showed the mainstream American public that it prized *fidelity* more than a singular, unchanging notion of manhood or womanhood.[10]

While few in our day know the name Julian Eltinge, some who do consider his artistry to have been a "radical" subversion of cultural norms. In a sense that's true. But as we have glimpsed, the situation was much more complicated. On the one hand, the actor's precise and compelling impersonations could not but upset the idea, held by many at the time, that gender was inherent and immutable. Eltinge's act was thus, in the words of one modern writer, "undeniably queer." By its very nature, his work showed the seemingly indissoluble barrier between "man" and "woman" to be rather porous after all. Yet the women he played onstage and to a large extent, the man he played off it, in fact reinforced "rigid gender conventions." Only late in his career, and under extreme circumstances, did Julian Eltinge ever do otherwise, and that was but one time and briefly at that. In fact, cisgender women and men were often accused of contravening sexual and gender norms without ever trying to imitate the opposite sex. Usually, these were people whose ethnicities and/or bodily features, from complexion to proportion, marked them as outsiders from the Caucasian, Anglo-European mainstream. Jewish immigrant, vaudevillian, and cabaret star Sophie Tucker, famously called the "last of the Red-hot Mamas," belted-out racy songs in tight dresses stretched over her full, Rubenesque form, neck and fingers decked out in garish gems and baubles. "I got a jeweler to make me four rings of bright green stones," she'd tell crowds while running her hands "snakily up and down" her curves. Legal and moral enforcers attacked Tucker as they never did Eltinge. It was Julian Eltinge who dutifully reinforced cultural rules and wishes, not Sophie Tucker. Just as important, Eltinge and Tucker both were both members of that strange human petting zoo known as the theatre, a world apart, able to play by some of its own rules, in fact expected to do so, and within its ranks, permitted certain inversions and agreements that civilians on the outside would never understand. In some ways, Eltinge's only true home and community was among his fellow thespians and clowns, though he also bristled

Figure I.2 Both the press and Eltinge's PR machine loved using trick double shots like this, with the performer superimposed next to or interacting with his female characters. It reinforced the duality of gender while undermining it at the same time. Ever personable, Eltinge gave out as many autographed photos and publicity cards as he could, such as this one for comedian/songwriter Fred Hillebrand.
Credit: *Billy Rose Theatre Division, The New York Public Library for the Performing Arts.*

at fully fitting in because no group—and no individual—is monolithic and uncomplicated.[11]

Sophie Tucker sang about "liquid-fire lovin'" and her desire for men. Julian Eltinge's women, on the other hand, were often marked by

8   BEAUTIFUL

restraint. As social mores loosened, so too did his aesthetics. But Eltinge's unironic depictions of women, whether in "a ball gown, as a chorus girl, [or] in female street attire," made others see him as simply a man with a "professional's ability to play every part he undertakes," as the *Philadelphia Inquirer* put it in 1901.[12] That gave him more leeway than some of his peers who, despite being very talented at what they did, were never regarded as expert renderers of the "beautiful." These other artists were often open to accusations of inversion or perversion because they failed to play the proper role *when not in drag* or in their so-called personal lives. One example was Bert Savoy, one of Julian Eltinge's best-known contemporaries and a counterpoint against whom Eltinge could define himself. Savoy was just as enthusiastic and dedicated as Eltinge, but considered "parodic" because of his campy approach, his inflation of some details and dismissal of others, which usually resulted in a cartoonish mockery of masculinity and femininity. He was an exemplar of what popular culture author Simon Doonan has recently termed the "comedy drag" subgenre. A journalist writing in the early 1940s not long after Julian Eltinge's death conceded Eltinge was indeed the "greatest female impersonator" of all time but that Savoy "was the funniest." While most audiences laughed at Savoy's "bawdy harlot" character, who was eccentric but "good-natured," he would not reach the heights of commercial entertainment that Eltinge did. Perhaps that is partly due to the fact that Savoy was okay with being seen as (and called) an "overt fairy," not caring as much to fit in to conventional life with its rights, privileges, and rewards—and its abundant constraints, compromises, and chronic suffocations.

Bert Savoy, who teamed up with another impersonator, Jay Brennan, has sometimes been called the first modern "drag queen." But recent research reveals that, in fact, a man named Dorsey Swann, a Black performer and political organizer born in Maryland in 1860, deserves the title, his contributions having been obscured by a white-focused history. Swann, born in enslavement, organized parties where he and other men wore impressive ballgowns and finery. Convicted of "keeping a disorderly house" by Washington, DC, police in 1888, Swann wrote to President Grover Cleveland asking for clemency and arguing he'd done nothing wrong. (Swann didn't get pardoned.) Bert Savoy, Jay Brennan, and Dorsey Swann were the kind of impersonators often accused of blighting the stage with "the simpering and disgusting antics of the she-man," in the words of an especially agitated journalist from 1911 who set Julian Eltinge aside as the only acceptable drag artist. While most journalists of the day saw female impersonation as largely unproblematic, those who felt otherwise spared no hyperbole, like a Nashville newspaperman who believed most impersonators were "highly unattractive to the average theatergoer," triggering "feeling[s] of revulsion which cannot be kept in check throughout" a performance. Of course, if he looked at the bills in vaudeville houses and other venues, from college stages to men's clubs, he'd know the opposite was true—or in all likelihood, he already did, triggering his frantic outrage.[13]

Julian Eltinge steered clear of being a brassy camp queen. He also avoided getting lumped in with other subspecies of female impersonators, notably the intentionally grotesque or strange sort, whose chief exemplar was the lumbering Harry Lehr. Lehr, who had little interest in conformity or convention, was unpredictable and hard to pin down. Like Tartuffe or Rasputin, Lehr insinuated himself into the ranks of East Coast society, a rarefied realm that delighted in his eccentricities. The swell set liked female impersonators. They needed pets, court jesters, to rouse them from their social entombment. Above the common fray, they had room for odd specimens. In fact, such oddities reinforced the socialites' lofty status, just like cultivating a new strain of hothouse flower or exhibiting fashions from the exotic East. Harry Lehr, a "social arbiter of New York, Newport, and Baltimore," kept things lively for the swells. It was a pretty good gig for a drag artist. Society icons Mrs. Stuyvesant Fish and Mrs. William Astor made Lehr a confidant, hiring him to emcee their galas, perhaps to keep the millionaires from dozing off in their tuxedos. Mamie Fish, ever bored with elite stuffiness, loved pranking her prim and proper peers, usually with Lehr's assistance. On one occasion, Lehr forwent the ballgown and accompanied Fish to a gala as the Czar of Russia. Lehr was known to wade into fountains in expensive dresses and tiaras, and he once thew a dinner party in toney Newport, Rhode Island, at which the guest of honor was a monkey. (The poor simian, forced to wear a tuxedo, unsurprisingly began hurling champagne glasses around the place.) In contradistinction to Harry Lehr's "burlesque"—code for a cartoonish and inherently unmasculine, if not exactly feminine, aesthetic—Julian Eltinge was hailed for his "counterfeit presentment of a well-bred young woman," rendered in "a really artistic manner," with "grace and ease" in the words of a 1904 *Boston Globe* article that featured the impersonator as a sinuous "Spanish Dancing Girl" in décolleté halter and cascading skirt. In 1901, Harry Lehr married Elizabeth Drexel, heiress to a Philadelphia banking dynasty, effectively marking his retirement and leaving open the job of crossdressing pet

10 BEAUTIFUL

of the wealthy. Julian Eltinge would soon fill the position, to Mamie Fish's delight, even if his whole approach was quite different indeed.[14]

* * *

Julian Eltinge crafted his offstage renditions, in this case of *manhood*, by making clear that he spent his leisure hours and downtime just like any conventional fellow, doing the things they did, looking the way they did. In that sense, he curated his civilian look as brilliantly as he did that of his stage women. He was no "fairy" and wouldn't be caught dead throwing a dinner party for a monkey or jumping into a fountain in a ballgown. In fact, especially early in his career, Julian Eltinge made it clear that his favorite offstage activity was beating up anyone who questioned his masculinity. Yes, Julian Eltinge was marvelous "as a 'she'," according to Tin Pan Alley composer L. Wolfe Gilbert. But, Gilbert hastened to add, "many a tough long-shoreman and hoodlum" learned the hard way just what a "he-man" Eltinge really was when they called him names. Especially at the time, boxing and brawling were unquestioned markers of rough manhood, even if the moneyed set were learning to leave ugly scuffles to their lawyers and spokespeople, for actually to punch and kick was beneath them.[15]

Tales of Julian Eltinge's hot-tempered fisticuffs spread virally, taking on a life of their own. When a "husky" stagehand in Denver "sneeringly" called Eltinge "Mamie!," the actor launched a lightning attack: "Biff! Biff! Bang!" "I guess you won't call me 'Mamie' again, will you Bright Eyes?," asked Eltinge, before gathering up the train of his evening gown and heading to his dressing room.[16] He whipped up such good PR that the impersonator had to occasionally remind his industry peers that it was mostly fiction, hoping they'd understand and keep it under wraps. When it was reported that he had decked a guy who called him "Cissie," the actor wrote to the theatrical trade paper *Variety*, "If I tried to thrash every one [*sic*] who made remarks I would have a perpetually sprained wrist and bruised knuckles."[17] For the time being, though, he'd at least have to attack the *notion* that he might be a "cissie." Originating in the 1840s as a term of endearment for one's sister, by Eltinge's day, "cissy" or "sissy" referred to "spineless" males, cowards seemingly bereft of drive, willpower, and self-agency. The actor claimed he hated them. A few other impersonation artists similarly pretended to be bruisers, like Francis Renault who promised to clobber a "kidder," though Eltinge led the pack by far in this rhetorical sparring match.[18]

"MERELY A MAN" 11

In addition to playing the brawler, Julian Eltinge also fashioned himself a former college footballer, boxer, and wrestler, a "broad-shouldered, muscular fellow" who had to give up those sports because they led to the development of muscles, and muscles "are not feminine," which hardly needed to be said at the time. Wrestling, boxing, and a willingness to aggressively compete showed one's "rough" manliness, an essential survival trait in an increasingly competitive business world. Because he had to give up muscle-building sports, Eltinge eventually allowed that he enjoyed horseback riding in their stead. In general, he lived in a "manly and strenuous" way, according to a news article that pictured him in a lovely "sheath gown," as a bathing beauty, and in a bejeweled bra top as the biblical temptress Salome.[19]

As many men, not just Julian Eltinge, were learning, to be a man meant trumpeting your individuality while also straining to conform, a paradox best handled by walking a middle line between the two, dipping to each side, respectively, as the situation required. Few were more agile at navigating this tightwire than this stage artist. "Off the stage I do not have to try to be a man," he said, revealing how perfectly he understood what to say and do, what attitude to strike, when not in women's dresses. To be "a man" was of course to *try to be a man*, the first task of which was reinforcing how effortless and natural certain things were for you, like fighting, competing, and near-constant exertion. Who could better apprehend all this than an individual who succeeded so well at trying to be a woman?[20]

* * *

Julian Eltinge's efforts onstage and off allowed him to lead a profession consisting of not a few, but rather hundreds if not thousands of impersonation artists, from top-tier professionals to aspiring amateurs, and everything in between. He came so fully to define female impersonation that virtually all others, even those from vastly different cultural settings and traditions, were likened to him.

The first decades of the twentieth century have been called the "high water mark" of sex impersonation, its "heyday." "Never before or since have impersonators achieved such prominence or stature," notes entertainment historian Robert Toll. Informed by drag practices in different entertainment settings, crossdressing had emerged as a viable, commercial art form, though as we will see, dragging-up onstage goes back thousands of years. In particular, *female* impersonation—that is, men skirting-up as women—was

12 BEAUTIFUL

significantly more popular than its counterpart, though some *male imper-sonators*, so-called He-She's like Vesta Tilley and Ella Shields, enjoyed large followings. Toll discovered fifty-five news-clipping files of male-to-female performers in the archives of the New York Public Library for the Performing Arts, perhaps North America's leading repository of such resources, but only fifteen for women who played men. While hardly scientific proof, and taking into account any number of cultural and historiographic reasons why an institution might pay greater attention to one group versus another, there does seem to be some face validity to the finding. Other sources, like the *Encyclopedia of Vaudeville*, corroborate this datum.[21]

A lot had changed since the middle of the 1800s, when few men dared practice the art of dragging-up, and the idea of a man in a dress bred but brutal mockery. When word leaked out that Confederate leader Jefferson Davis had tried to escape Union capture by dressing as a woman, northern newspapers delighted in depicting Davis in drag, "emasculated, more than merely defeated." When the War Department refused to sell Davis's alleged petticoats to P. T. Barnum—the latter offered the feds $500—the famed showman settled instead on a realistic, life-size replica of the Confederate ex-president in skirts. Even characters in an 1877 pro-Klan "comedy" titled *The Ku-Klux Klan; or, The Carpetbagger in New Orleans*, make fun of the "female toggery"—that is, long, white robes—worn by one character, an outfit that would of course later become standard issue for many an enthusiastic white supremacist.[22]

But by 1900, when Julian Eltinge and many other men, professional and amateur, were putting on dresses in myriad performances, the American stage was rich in female impersonators, or "imps" as they were sometimes termed. Among the most famous was Danish-born Bothwell Browne. Browne deployed brilliant mannerisms and sensuous costuming, and was regarded Eltinge's "close rival."[23] Englishman Bert Errol was regarded "the Julian Eltinge of London" in part because his voice so closely imitated that of Italian opera soprano Luisa Tetrazzini.[24] Another Brit, Henry Schaefer, won acclaim on both sides of the Atlantic impersonating women as the "Great Lafayette," though he eventually left the drag for conventional melodrama, a goal Julian Eltinge long dreamed of.[25]

Many female-impersonation artists went by one name, typically some-thing quirky, glamorous, or mystical, not unlike rap and pop stars in our era. These sobriquets conveyed drag's playful, plastic qualities just by appearing in newspaper ads or columns. The talented Vardalan, for example, emphasized his "beautiful gowns of rich texture" and was briefly heralded "a second Eltinge" like others including Lucian, a Floridian artist and yet one more "second Julian Eltinge." The names may seem odd or even humorous, but they were an important part of many impersonators' tradecraft, artisanal stamps that subtly rebuked hetero-patriarchal naming conventions. Julian Eltinge had even briefly billed himself as just "Eltinge" to "give his act an air of mystery," and another time experimented with "Julian," before deciding it would serve him better not to look the outlier.[26]

Single-named impersonators were also paying homage to one of drag's pioneering figures, an artist who called himself simply "Leon." Born about 1840, Leon's real name was Patrick Francis Glassey. He was a gifted singer whose youthful soprano "never altered." Leon sometimes went by Leon Wa Delle, or Wa Dele, but he eventually settled on just "Leon." Leon was a talented "prima donna" in blackface minstrel troupes, a common training ground where many, including Julian Eltinge, cultivated their gender artistry. Leon danced with "gentility and delicacy" and could ably sing both Mozart and Gilbert & Sullivan. His sincere, non-burlesque aesthetic paved the way for Eltinge. Eugene, Ricardo, Stuart, and the curious "Lind?" (or sometimes "?Lind?," though also just plain "Lind.") followed in Leon's artistic footsteps.[27]

Playing with nomenclature, nicknames, and fanciful monikers reflected the impersonators' inherent shaping and unmaking of gender itself, as in the case of Oriano the Cameo, who dragged-up in an act titled "An Artist's Dream." Vaudeville routines in which performers, particularly women (or woman-impersonators) wore white, skintight fleshings to resemble nude statuaries, sanitized erotic content under the guise of highbrow culture.[28] Like Oriano the Cameo, Georgie Paduzzi also took a fanciful stage name, the "Creole Fashion Plate." He later became Karyl Norman when briefly challenging Julian Eltinge's primacy in the early 1920s. Like Eltinge, Norman was a gifted vocalist with an ability to sing both soprano and baritone, similar to "double-voiced" specialists like James Hollis and Tacianu ("deep baritone and a high soprano") who could toggle between conventionally female and male vocal ranges, respectively. As a teen, Norman had been inspired by Eltinge. But when the former starred in the 1927 transvestic musical *Lady Do*, the *New York Times* shrugged, "he just doesn't look like a girl," something never said of Eltinge in his prime.[29]

China enjoyed a centuries-long tradition of female impersonation in its famed operas and dramas. While that of course existed in its own unique cultural and historical context, it's important to note that the popularity of

14 BEAUTIFUL

female impersonation in Julian Eltinge's day opened the North American door for several of Asia's best practitioners (and vice versa, in Julian Eltinge's case). Some Chinese impersonators enjoyed successful American tours, playing for both Asian-migrant and white audiences, respectively. The mainstream press predictably and clumsily compared many to Eltinge. Perhaps the best-known Asian artist was Mei Lan-Fang (variously called Me Lang Fan or Mei Lang Fang in the American media), who drove crowds "wild" depicting "the wiles of far-eastern [sic] women," in the words of an anglophone press. Mei was not only a brilliant impersonator but manager and producer too, "an impossible hybrid of [British actor-manager] Henry Irving and Julian Eltinge." Mei was earning $46,000 a month by the late 1920s, a paycheck that eventually rose to $63,000. American reporters called him "the John Gilbert, George Arliss, John Barrymore[,] and Julian Eltinge of the Chinese stage." In the 1930s, Sheu Lai Jeong, gifted with a "willowy figure" and "long, tapering fingers," was heralded "the epitome of delicate femininity" on a tour of Honolulu, New York, and San Francisco, of course receiving the clichéd moniker of "Chinese Julian Eltinge."[30] Cha Pih Yung, described as, yes, "the Chinese Julian Eltinge," earned $2,000 a month in his prime, around 1917—or over $43,000 in current terms.[31] The hugely talented Leong Luie Sang, but another "Chinese Julian Eltinge," beloved in San Francisco's Chinese American neighborhoods, won fame and wealth only to be shot dead by the boyfriend of a female fan with whom Leong had become amorously entwined.[32]

Other ethnicities had their Julian Eltinges too. Genoheba Garcia was the "Julian Eltinge of the Mexican people," though that didn't protect him from being arrested at the US border, which he crossed in-costume as "Gertrude Garcia."[33] On New York's Lower East Side, home to a rich Yiddish theatre scene, Russian-born Michal Michalesko was for many years vaunted as the "Yiddishe Julian Eltinge" until branching out into other kinds of roles. Yiddish theatre had its own tradition of men taking women's parts, notably the role of Bobe Yachne, title character in Avrom Goldfadn's The Witch (1878), often played by renowned actor Sigmund Mogulesko.[34]

Michel Matveieff, a Russian émigré who later took the stage name Michel Barroy, claimed he'd first donned female attire to flee the "Bolsheviki" during the Revolution. American, pro-business voices often linked homosexuality and transvestism to socialism, communism, and even trade unionism and women's suffrage. Julian Eltinge was quite clear never to associate himself with left-leaning causes, leading one jingoistic reporter to praise him in comparison to other drag artists who brought on "attack[s] of bolshevism." It was clear whom capital viewed as the real inverts.[35]

And a talented hockey player from Calgary, Eric Waite, traded in his hockey stick for a pair of "pantalettes" in a bid to become the "skating Julian Eltinge," which was not that strange when you consider that female impersonation was so popular it meant some artists had to subspecialize as crossdressed acrobats, wire-walkers, and circus performers. At the height of female impersonation in North America, around 1920, there was a "Julian Eltinge" of just about every kind.[36] Still, the question seemed to linger: who exactly was Julian Eltinge?

* * *

In addressing that question, many have found it essential to determine whether or not Julian Eltinge was gay. It is an understandable curiosity, particularly if we imagine that a man, a celebrity no less, had to keep that sort of thing deeply under wraps a century or more ago, though some have stated that the performer had numerous liaisons with men that he didn't conceal from his entertainment industry peers.[37] It is certainly true that in Julian Eltinge's day, same-sex erotic and romantic behaviors could not be freely and openly displayed in most settings, particularly those of greatest public scrutiny and status. People of course found other ways and places to express their desires and, conversely, may have had their horizon of wishes limited by what was both socially possible and tolerable. At the same time, it should not be supposed that people whose sexual and gender behaviors *fit* accepted norms did not themselves *also struggle to maintain appearances* and negotiate all kinds of feelings and frustrations regarding the outside, social world; Julian Eltinge's offstage performances of manhood make that quite clear.

Perhaps most crucially, in the late 1800s and early 1900s, sexual love was increasingly linked to what would come to be known as the nuclear family. Erotic activity, if it had to take place, was to occur between legally wed cisgender men and women in their economically quasi-independent households. Of course, *plenty* of erotic activity took place outside of that context. But that was deemed improper, frowned upon, and might come with serious consequences. In this way, sex officially served *procreation*, which served the growth of the family unit, which in turn served the larger social blueprint. The micro reflected and reinforced the macro, and vice versa. That was *how it should be*, believed those with the most influence and their allies.

16 BEAUTIFUL

Sex between men (or women) was therefore problematic not just because it resulted in ill-gotten pleasure, but because it couldn't lead to pregnancy and birth and thus went against the cultural grain. Similar prohibitions had long applied to sodomy, even between men and women, because it put "generative organs" purely in the service of pleasure. One might not be accused of homosexuality per se in the late 1800s, but one could be judged a "sapphist" or "sodomite" for implicitly undermining the basic unit of social consolidation, no matter how unstable that unit has turned out to be in actual practice. Earlier, in Great Britain during the mid-1700s, a man could be accused of sodomy without being considered somehow effeminate or unmanly; it would eventually take not just suspicion of certain sexual activities but also a flashy, foppish personal style to put one at risk of scandal in olde London towne. In other words, aspects of dress were an inherent part of the greater question authorities wanted to answer: what sexual behaviors were acceptable and which crossed a line that ought not be tolerated because it simply made things too confusing?[38]

It is also important to remember that even by the 1890s, the terms "heterosexual" and "homosexual" as we know them did not yet exist in common parlance. Therefore, using the word "gay" to describe somebody who lived then can have the effect of what is sometimes called a "flattening" of the past to fit our contemporary psyches. As we will see, from about 1900 to 1930, modern, recognizable notions of "straight," "gay," "heterosexual," "homosexual," and so forth were being born and coming into use as both language and concepts. Before these binaries calcified, aided by reactionary efforts in the wake of the Great Depression and World War II, many people, particularly men, enjoyed more freedom to relate to one another and dress in ways that would not automatically result in their being cast on the wrong side of a socially fatal line. Julian Eltinge thrived during a time when men enjoyed relative freedom in certain dress and group behaviors, until more binary notions of sex and gender blossomed to full flower during what historian George Chauncey terms the "heterosexual counterrevolution" of the 1940s and 1950s. Part of what makes Eltinge so interesting, and why observing his life and work may be fruitful, is that it sheds light on what one needed to do in the early 1900s to conform to changing gender norms, and what options remained as those norms altered in the face of a worldwide economic panic and subsequent war. Over many decades, Eltinge understood how to toe the line—masterfully—surviving both literally and professionally until the world he knew changed beyond his recognition. Because he did not leave much in the way of diaries, journals, letters, and other private communications that might shed light on his inner thoughts and feelings (though such sources are themselves complicated and must be interpreted accordingly), it is all the more important to interpret what we *do know* about his life and work in historical context, and make reasonable assumptions from there.[39]

* * *

Julian Eltinge's aforementioned failure to leave behind much, if anything, in the way of personal documents, diaries, and letters also speaks volumes about his personality. His steadfast and strenuous pursuit of privacy, even secrecy, suggests a man who felt his best strategy for being known was somehow *not-to-be-known*. Did he have "no love life," as has been written? Eltinge surely had friendships, some very close, intimate bonds with his mother and some of his professional peers, and other kinds of kinships that may or may not have had an erotic dimension. Like all of us, he obtained love where and how he was able to get it, according to his needs and the particulars of his environment. But much as he spent hours carefully applying his face before going onstage, Julian Eltinge was a man who minutely managed what he allowed to spill out beyond the mask and into the public psyche. Theatre historian Laurence Senelick laments that Eltinge "jealously guarded his privacy," while nostalgist poet Geoff Hilsabeck concludes the performer was "probably as illegible to himself as he is to us." Those who study history can hardly be faulted for wishing their subjects left behind the sort of raw materials that provide a look "inside" their minds, a wish that occasionally verges on reproach. When Roland Mitchell, the main character in A. S. Byatt's 1990 novel *Possession*, discovers love letters between Ash, a nineteenth-century poet he has long been researching, and a "reclusive lady," he becomes agitated. "He thought he knew Ash fairly well. . . ."[40]

But we can only wonder why Julian Eltinge ended up letting out so little of his private, truer self—if indeed there was a deeper, truer Julian Eltinge. It's possible that *he could not let himself become fully aware of aspects of his inner life*, rendering him in effect just as secretive as if he had consciously decided to do so. In assessing the artist's personality, very likely we have to arrive at some admixture of the two. But the actor's failure or refusal to tell us more about who he "really" was also underappreciates perhaps his most important trait: an intuitive, almost naïve understanding that surface and depth are inseparable in a marketplace culture like ours, and that trying to parse one from

18   BEAUTIFUL

the other—via scientific study, legal interrogation, exploratory writing, and so on—is a frustratingly circular, no-win scenario. Eltinge, (explicitly) apolitical for the most part, brilliantly laid bare the extent to which the surface *is* the depth and vice versa. As such, he fit well into an era shaped by the likes of showman P. T. Barnum, flashy impresario Florenz Ziegfeld, marketplace wizards Sears and Roebuck, shaper of human labor Henry Ford, and master self-mythologizer Teddy Roosevelt. Even those who sought to look below the surface and explain how depth ultimately makes itself known—Sigmund Freud, Max Weber, and others—could not help, ultimately, also revealing that *surface* and *depth* are not inseparable binaries, but rather concepts to which our limited, human thinking must resort.

Reading this story, and thinking about what was happening in and around this man, then, perhaps it is more useful to wonder what kind of "private life" the performer could have envisioned for himself given his context? What was *available* to him, psychologically and in the course of his subjective, lived experience? Also, what trade-offs were involved in the choices (he felt) he could make with regard to a domestic life? It should be noted that all of the same choices, forces, wishes, and restraints applied (and still apply) to *everyone* in Eltinge's world, whether their impulses were socially acceptable, satisfying to them, and so forth. Furthermore, to say that someone had no private life is loaded because it equates personal domesticity with sexual and/or procreative partnership—which again reflects specific cultural values that have changed over time. It would be helpful to keep all of that in mind when reading and thinking about an artist who was at his height over a hundred years ago. These might be more fruitful questions than trying to determine if we have, as one academic put in in the 1990s, "strong proof" that Julian Eltinge "was a homosexual" or not.[41]

* * *

In the West, the Christian Church had long influenced or determined rules concerning what people were supposed to wear. Queen Elizabeth I's "sumptuary" decree of 1597, which not only governed what clothing men and women could wear, respectively, in public but also how commoners and nobles ought to garb themselves, was based in part on the Book of Deuteronomy (22:5) from the Bible, which decreed: "A woman shall not wear anything that pertains to a man, nor shall a man put on a woman's garment; for whoever does these things is an abomination to the Lord your God"

(Deut. 22:5). Sumptuary statutes and codes like them were meant to limit social anxieties regarding high and low, "male" and "female," and so forth.[42]

But following the Enlightenment, the French Revolution, and the Napoleonic period, beginning the early 1800s, the Church's unquestioned authority began to slip. People still turned to religion for solace and community. But new authorities, scientists, stepped in to investigate and relieve human suffering. A lot changed in a short period of time. In 1828, for example, German scholar Gottlieb Paulus published a hugely popular book that argued that Jesus' walking on water was an optical illusion, while his peers argued for a "scientific" theology based on observation and reason. By 1883, Paulus's younger colleague, Friedrich Nietzsche, famously declared God to be "dead," meaning religion was no longer the supreme, guiding force in the West. That these writings flourished is remarkable; that their authors were not burned at the stake as they might have been a few hundred years earlier is no less astonishing.[43]

Scientific investigators replaced churchmen in determining the broad outlines of reality. A trickle that had started in the work of Copernicus (1473–1543), Bacon (1561–1626), Kepler (1571–1630), Galileo (1564–1642), and others was by now a torrent.[44] By the mid-to-late 1800s, men of science—and again, they were mostly men—trained their lenses on sexuality and gender, initiating a whole new field of study: *sexology*. Some were physicians or psychiatrists. Others fancied themselves bench researchers. Yet others were sociologists and anthropologists, treating human sexual behavior like all else in the animal kingdom: a phenomenon to be observed and remarked upon. Some behaviors—for example, men wearing skirts or women kissing women—were now no longer sinful. But they might be *pathological*, which is to say, implicitly harmful or deviant.[45] These new thinkers were not, for the most part, intentionally misleading or *trying* to oppress. Most really were trying to uncover the truth and move humanity past religious superstition. For the time being, though controversial, this new learning was heralded as a step forward.

Between 1864 and 1879, Karl Heinrich Ulrichs published a number of studies on what he called "Uranian"—that is, same-sex—love. People who engaged in "urning" were neither man nor woman, in Ulrichs's view, but a third sex. He counted himself among them and told his family so. Around the same time, physician Carl Westphal studied a small group of crossdressers and concluded that they suffered from a "contrary sexual feeling," thereby linking what people wore to their sexual desires.[46] Medical science now

20   BEAUTIFUL

started more broadly to associate people's sartorial choices with their erotic behaviors and thoughts.

But three men in particular were to have the greatest influence on discerning the aberrant from the healthy in human sexual life: German psychiatrist Richard von Krafft-Ebing, English doctor Havelock Ellis, and, perhaps most famously, Austrian neurologist and founder of psychoanalysis Sigmund Freud. All had influential things to say about sexual behavior and gender norms, and all were more or less contemporaries of Julian Eltinge. They propagated what French historian Michel Foucault would famously call a "discourse" surrounding sexuality and gender, which is to say, a scientifically (and, eventually, legally) focused cultural conversation about what was permissible and salutary and what was not.[47]

Richard von Krafft-Ebing's *Psychopathia Sexualis*, first published in 1887 (though it was to undergo many revisions and republications), argued for the idea that nonreproductive sex was, broadly speaking, "unnatural," or represented "perversions" of normal instinct, caused by hereditary "taints." Men who liked to put on dresses suffered from "dress fetishism," the result of a rerouting of normative sexual energy. Krafft-Ebing's work in effect relabeled the once-sinful as *sick*. But it also publicized the fact that people actually practiced and enjoyed quite a range of sexual and gender behaviors. Plus, in Krafft-Ebing's and his peers' view, the sick could be treated—perhaps *cured*—by modern medicine.[48]

Havelock Ellis's first installment in the multivolume *Studies in the Psychology* came out in 1897, taking up same-sex eroticism, crossdressing, and other apparent deviations. Looking at men who did things differently than the norm—made love to other men, wore dresses and skirts, and cared little for aggressive sports and business—Ellis concluded they were men somehow turned upside-down, *inverted*, and devised the term "sexoaesthetic inversion" to describe their condition. A British judge initially found Havelock Ellis's work not sufficiently "scientific" to be published. But the doctor pressed his case, and the study was eventually made available, in 1901. In *Studies in the Psychology of Sex: Sexual Inversion*, Ellis presented case studies of males who were in his view "decidedly feminine" because they preferred "effeminate" apparel and were "addicted to female occupations" (meaning pastimes or activities). One of his subjects was unable or unwilling to "whistle or play rough games" and exhibited an "inattention to business matters" and financial concerns. This was the *opposite* of what a man should be, implied Ellis. Julian Eltinge seemed already to understand this quite well.[49]

Ellis's terms, "invert" or "inversion," became popular in the early twentieth century to describe men who failed to conform to certain gender expectations or, worse yet, seemed uninterested in even trying. Not exactly a prude or a moral sanitizer, Ellis called for "prevention" and "treatment" of inversion, though not illegalization. He called crossdressing "eonism" after the real, historical individual known as the Chevalier d'Éon—properly, Charles-Geneviève-Louis-Auguste-André-Timothée d'Éon de Beaumont—swordsman, warrior, and spy in the court of King Louis XV of France who went about their life clad in the abundant noblewomen's finery of the age, arousing such curiosity that Parisians wagered thousands of francs on their "true" sex. But it was the more progressive thinker Magnus Hirschfeld who would coin the term "transvestism" in his 1910 book *The Transvestites: An Investigation of the Erotic Drive to Cross Dress*. Unlike Ellis, Hirschfeld disaggregated sexual from sartorial noncompliers. He actually found that men dressed in female garments for a variety of reasons, and most preferred sex with women. Hirschfeld even questioned whether men like Eltinge who crossdressed for a living were likely to be what we would call "gay," as some naturally assumed at the time (and now). Hirschfeld imagined a world where there were many types of gender and sexual behaviors.[50] (It should probably be pointed out that Havelock Ellis became more and more interested in eugenics, the pseudo-science of constructing racial hierarchies, whereas Hirschfeld—Jewish and gay—was persecuted by the Nazis and driven into exile.)[51]

Sigmund Freud also used the term "invert," notably in his "Three Contributions to the Theory of Sex" (originally published in 1905), and the fields of psychoanalysis and psychiatry long considered crossdressing and homosexuality, respectively, illnesses—as, for instance, the New York Academy of Medicine concluded in its 1964 report on homosexuality. Freud himself, who always believed in an "innate bisexuality" of humans, was not particularly focused on crossdressing, and when he spoke of inverts, he meant men who desired other men. But though Freud reinforced the idea that a gay man was one whose motive force traveled in the wrong direction, he considered men and women not so qualitatively separate as, ultimately, *separated*, "two halves" seeking to be "reunited" via sexual congress, rather than two species split by an "immutable gender divide."[52]

22   BEAUTIFUL

Significantly for our purposes, Freud was also interested in disguise and its ability to fool people's sense of reality. Taking off the mask could reveal that "This or that one who is admired like a demigod is only a human being like you and me after all," he wrote in 1905. (Exactly what Queen Elizabeth I had tried to prevent with her sumptuary laws!) At some level, Freud seems to have realized that the disguise, the costume, the uniform, *becomes* the status rather than merely reflecting it. He called disguising oneself "travesty." Travesty, a word closely linked to *transvestite*, was also close kin of *travesti*, a gender-fluid crossdresser in some cultures, or a drag venue, that is, a *travesti* cabaret.[53]

Julian Eltinge fit perfectly into an age when the smallest details of one's sexual and gender behaviors were scrutinized and analyzed. To look or act in a particular way was to pass as *normal*. Though, to do the very same things could also be to *fool*—and thus delight and impress onlookers. Context was all. In American cities at the time, a man with his hands on his hips, thumbs facing forward, might be taken for "a 'true' fairy." But when a Boston journalist observed Eltinge in 1907 with "his hands on the hips, thumbs forward, giving his waist a little downward push," she was in awe of his precision and professional expertise, both considered manly traits.[54]

In Eltinge's hands, perfectly resembling the opposite sex was praiseworthy. This was true for many other men in various theatrical settings. But it could also land you in a locked psych ward. Psychiatry, as we have seen, was coming to consider crossdressing and transvestism "perversions" or at least fetishes. In 1914, a St. Louis man who preferred dresses and claimed to be a "second Julian Eltinge" ended up in the hospital under medical "observation." In the 1940s, influential psychiatrist Otto Fenichel concluded that men who crossdressed were making a neurotic compromise, sidestepping castration anxiety by wearing a skirt while keeping a penis beneath it. (Fenichel considered this "more serious" than a woman in trousers, since she was only "pretending" to have the thing she purportedly envied between her legs.) It has taken a long time to consider that many people may simply prefer or naturally *feel more authentically comfortable*, more *themselves*, when exhibiting what some medical authorities still describe as "transvestic tendencies."[55]

Thus, the scientific thinkers of the last century may have separated sexual behaviors from considerations of Hell and Damnation. Still, they propagated a belief that it was only their subjects' so-called adjustment problems, rather than their own *discomfort*—and some researchers were clearly more uncomfortable than others—that warranted investigation and explanation. While the field of modern psychotherapy and psychoanalysis is finally getting wise to some of its own long-standing prejudices, including "complicity" in "antiqueer and misogynist" attitudes, it still has further to go in terms of properly psychoanalyzing and understanding itself.[56]

Beginning in the late 1920s but coming much more sharply into focus from the 1930s to the 1950s, the lines demarcating salutary from malfunctioning, natural versus perverted, and right-side-up versus inverted sharpened notably. Social upheavals and activism beginning in the 1960s changed things dramatically—arguably so much so that we now face an even more desperate neo-reactionary backlash against people whose subjective wishes and self-understandings seem to contradict a supposed natural order. Worse yet, it puts the "kids" in danger. "We're not trying to be anti-anybody, anti-trans, anti-anything, we're just trying to protect our kids," said the Republican sponsor of an Arkansas state law aimed at preventing children from seeing drag entertainments. Progressive as it may have been for the time, the medico-scientific framing of gender nonconformism nonetheless relied on two missteps of logic. First, it still drew a line between healthy and unhealthy, normative and deviant, thus instituting newfangled binaries. But two entities in binary relation to one another always need the other's existence. To erase one is to erase a pillar of the other, a quality French philosopher Jacques Derrida called "*difference*," because each member of a binary pair defers to and yet relies upon the other. Furthermore, classifying people and things based on their traits—for example, calling men who prefer skirts and dislike rough games "inverts" or "eonists"—blurs a line in which characteristics and causation are confused for one another. A man who stands a certain way is an invert. Why does he stand that way? Because he's an invert. This is a phenomenon known as "reification."[57]

* * *

In much of our current world, it is practically a given that quaint notions like "man" and "woman" are simply constructions, semi-pliable masks covering no intrinsic truth. Philosopher Judith Butler, in her 1990 book *Gender Trouble* and in other writings, has been hugely influential in this development, arguing that gender consists of patterned enactments akin to playing a role in the theatre, "a stylized repetition of acts," including how we speak, how we walk, what we wear, and how we position our thumbs when putting hands-on-hips. Gender is not waiting to be discovered or revealed, but rather

24 BEAUTIFUL

becomes via a "performative" process and a webwork of conversations. For Butler, "man" and "woman" are not so much nouns as verbs-in-progress. "If *Gender Trouble* was in the water in 2007," wrote a Millennial journalist in 2023, it's now "in the air we breathe."[58]

Given what we have come to accept about gender, or at least consider, how should we view the work of Julian Eltinge and other artists of his era? Were the mass of female impersonators slyly aware of the mutability and artificiality of gender, winking at audiences who essentially winked back in delight? Or does the entire enterprise suggest a huge, unconscious charade that simultaneously reinforced gender and yet revealed it for the acting job it is? Of course, there is no single answer, nor even a discrete set of answers. It would probably be more fruitful to think of the many questions raised by Eltinge's and his peers' artistry, and then consider how human minds with their many layers and parts, some in conflict, make sense of it all. Or don't.

What Eltinge's story *can* tell us, however, is that our ideas about gender change from period to period, and from social group to social group, sometimes dramatically. Eltinge's story is that of a man who tried very hard to meet and even anticipate mainstream social demands until it was no longer possible. And even then . . . he tried. As such, his performances didn't say, "This how women are" or "This is how a man is," but rather—and more important—"This is how a woman *should want to be*," and "This is how a man *should want to be*." Eltinge's story is therefore as much about the importance of trying to be better, to excel, to outdo—values reinforced by business and commerce—as about gender per se. He was simply doing a particular version of it, "a triumph of artistry over virile nature," but the mandate applied to all, especially women: if you are not meeting a certain standard, try harder. There are special products, processes, and services out there to help. Go get them. Eltinge succeeded not simply as an entertainer but as a technician, a specialist, like millions of other men who were learning to define themselves via their work. His office or factory happened to be a dressing room where he made himself look exactly like different women. In 1910, Chicago journalist Percy Hammond described Eltinge as "a pretty young man with a knack for counterfeiting, without the usual sickening consequences [such as] certain florid feminine airs and graces of a purely external sort."[59] Eltinge knew exactly how to play manhood such that it seemed inherent, nothing "purely external" about it. Whether he believed it, or what he believed, we may never know.

* * *

So if Julian Eltinge understood the ways of women in his day, he no less understood the ways of men, which contributed just as much to his phenomenal success. To be a man was to fight your way to the top of the professional food chain. The city, the skyscraper, the stage, and the factory had replaced the battlefields of yore. (Though, as it would turn out, not quite entirely.) In Theodore Dreiser's classic 1925 novel *An American Tragedy*, the protagonist Clyde murders his pregnant ex-girlfriend because she stands in the way of his ascent: he won't go back to "A small job!" with "Small pay!" (Spoiler alert: things do not work out well for Clyde in the end.) Everything became an opportunity to move up the scale, to spar for one's place, even "friendly" golf or tennis matches with one's business associates. Once "peripatetic" players like Eltinge were increasingly mere cogs in an entertainment "industry." A few decades earlier, Karl Marx wrote that work was now an "all engrossing system of specializing and sorting" human beings. The amusement industry was no exception. Julian Eltinge made himself "the one man . . . who impersonates feminine characters non-effeminately," according to an impressed fan.[60]

Men, Julian Eltinge among them, were thronging to North American cities to ply their trade as professional workers, leaving behind the farm and the artisan's bench. Between 1880 and 1900, US farmworkers increased their numbers 27 percent, to 10.9 million; over that same period, *non*-agricultural workers saw their numbers grow from 8.8 million to 18.2 million, a *106 percent* increase. New professions, specialties, and subspecialties were cropping up everywhere. Experts in "finance and real estate," for example, numbered 1.2 million in 1880; two decades later, that figure had risen 126 percent, to 2.8 million. From 1900 to 1910, men designated "Professional, technical, and kindred workers" grew from 800,000 to 1.03 million.[61] New fields and subspecialties including "[i]nspectors, gaugers, and samplers" and "agents" of all kinds mushroomed into existence. In 1910, the average nonfarm (and non-mining) worker made $630 a year, compared to $574 for their agricultural counterparts. More training, specialized schooling, and expertise meant more money and more opportunity.[62]

Some professions began flexing their muscles, limiting entry and sacralizing their knowledge. In 1910, the Carnegie Foundation issued its vaunted *Flexner Report*, which urged winnowing-out the "vast army of men . . . untrained in sciences" from those "rightly trained" and thus deserving of the title "doctor." (The *Report* considered "The Medical Education of Women" and "The Medical Education of the Negro" as separate issues for another

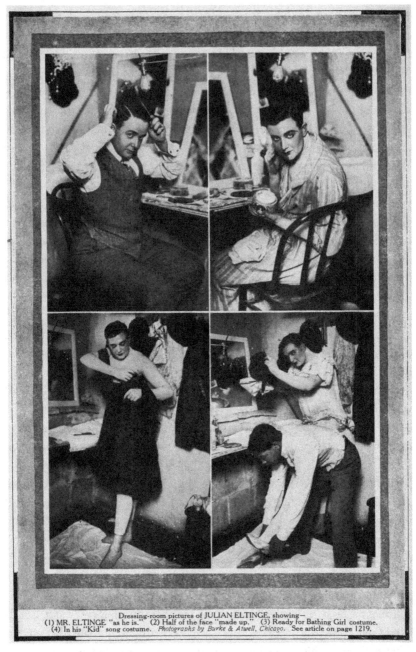

Figure I.3 Julian Eltinge's dressing-room transitions were no less a part of his overall spectacle than the women he portrayed onstage. By 1908, he was fortunate to have the assistance of Ko Shima, his valet/dresser. Shima worked with the impersonator for a decade. At the time, it was common for Japanese immigrants to work in personal services, in part because they faced structural discrimination in other industries.

Credit: *Billy Rose Theatre Division, The New York Public Library for the Performing Arts.*

time.)[63] Physicians felt this all the more essential in an age when medicine-show quacks and snake-oil barkers passed for legitimate healers. Indeed, in 1905, the Sears, Roebuck catalogue devoted an all-time high of eighteen pages to patent medicines and cure-alls for "catarrh, consumption, headaches, the tobacco habit, and 'female weaknesses,'" to name a few.[64] Soon, even advertising and public relations men would call for legal credentialing and "expert" titling, the former of which they didn't achieve but the latter very much fell to their favor, making billions for Madison Avenue in the years to come.[65] Hierarchies formed upon hierarchies. To reach the top, even as a female impersonator in the theatre, meant knowing how to navigate them one curious rung at a time.

Julian Eltinge presented himself as a craftsman par excellence, no sideshow oddity but an engineer. He happily welcomed the press into his office/laboratory—his dressing room—where they watched him methodically transform into the opposite sex. This was to become as much a part of his performance as the Gibson Girls and snake dancers. Newspapers loved it. In 1908, the *Chicago Tribune* devoted nearly a whole page to the feature, "How a Man Makes Himself a Beautiful Woman," with step-by-step photos of Eltinge arriving in his dressing room in a suit; applying cream and makeup to achieve "the pink complexion"; and finally, with protective coveralls over his costume and lipstick on his mouth, preparing to be wigged and accessorized. The article ensure readers that Eltinge, in *Directoire*-style gown, impersonated females only "by profession." In all other ways, he was "merely a man." The entertainer told an interviewer that he had to be "constantly on the alert" for new techniques and products to stay competitive, just like entrepreneurs in any other field. Beneath the makeup resided "muscles as smooth of those as a well conditioned wrestler." Whereas makeup had once been a sign of harlotry, it was now indispensable for middle-class women, consisting of "systems" and "treatment" regimens sold by experts. If you didn't believe it, you had only to look at how a husky young man, a dedicated expert in his field, managed to do it after night, sometimes twice a day, in playhouses across the land.[66]

# # #

1

A "Cute Little Beaute from Butte, Montana" (But actually, from Boston)

It's understandable that a celebrity might try to shave a few years off his age, especially one whose act also depended on shaving his arms, legs, and back. In many sources, Julian Eltinge's date of birth is given as May 14, 1883, though he's also reported to have been born, variously, from 1881 through 1884. The 1984 edition of the *Oxford Companion to American Theatre*, for example, which calls Eltinge "the most celebrated of American female impersonators," states that he was born in 1883, a detail likely taken from Eltinge's *New York Times* obituary. Because Julian Eltinge began disseminating what might be called creative details about his past from early in his career, we may forgive the fact that some of those details took on a life of their own. Eltinge, like many a public figure, had his own reasons for hiding parts of himself while embellishing or simply inventing others.[1]

In fact: William J. Dalton was born on May 14, 1881, just outside of Boston. Census and school-registration records from his boyhood make this clear, as does his birth certificate, though by 1910, he was old and famous enough to start lying to the government as well, inching his birth forward a few years like many showfolk in his day and ours.[2]

* * *

Julian Eltinge's father, Michael Joseph Dalton, who called himself Joe, was born in Boston in 1857.[3] Joe's father, Thomas H. Dalton, had been born in Tipperary County, Ireland, in 1816. Thomas migrated to Boston where he married Massachusetts-born Ann McAuliffe, fourteen years his junior, in 1851. "Joe" Dalton was one of their ten children. Devoutly Catholic and from an economically downtrodden family, Joe possessed drive, a modicum of cleverness, but little formal schooling or training. Julian Eltinge's mother, on the other hand, Juliana Edna Baker, soon called Julia, had been born in Pepperell, Massachusetts, in 1861, the daughter of a prosperous,

Beautiful. Andrew L. Erdman, Oxford University Press. © Oxford University Press 2024.
DOI: 10.1093/9780197696361.003.0002

A "CUTE LITTLE BEAUTE FROM BUTTE, MONTANA" 29

Presbyterian factory owner.[4] From the start, it seemed, the two were a poor match. But companionability was rarely why people married in New England in the 1800s.

Joe and Julia Dalton were living in the hamlet of Newtonville, Massachusetts, in 1881 when their only child, William, came into this world. Newtonville was one of a number of neighborhoods within Newton, a town just outside of Boston. It is possible that Joe worked as a policeman for a time, as a Sergeant Michael J. Dalton was on the force in nearby Cambridge. Of course, given the huge number of Irish immigrants at the time in Massachusetts—250,000 in 1900, second only to New York—there were likely other Michael Daltons lurking about. Indeed, when the family moved to Butte, Montana, a few years later, there was already a Michael Dalton in town, employed, like so many of his countrymen, in metals mining and refining.[5]

Today, Newton, Massachusetts is a well-kept, upscale town with pleasant streets, sizable homes, well-regarded schools, and an assortment of shopping and dining spots. A "a desirable community" of 89,000 souls "in which to live and work," according to the city's official website. Five miles west of downtown Boston, Newton occupies eighteen square miles along the Charles River where Harvard scullers have long famously rowed.[6] It is entirely possible that William Dalton wondered if he might someday count himself among the Ivy League oarsmen coursing down the Charles.

White Europeans first settled Newton in 1631, with instructions from the British Crown to buy up what land they could from the indigenous "salvages" who lived there. The area was annexed to the Massachusetts Bay Colony in the 1640s and given the indigenous name Nonantum—which meant *rejoicing*. Anglo-European laws and culture quickly took root.[7] There was a fine of three pence if your dog was "scraping up the fish" used to fertilize another's fields, penalties for using tobacco "publiquely" (eleven pence!), and an outright ban on "sell[ing] cakes and bunns" except at funerals and weddings.[8]

During the American War for Independence, the small number of Newtonians were more patriots than royalists. In 1800, there were but 1,491 residing there, a figure that rose to 19,759 by 1885 when the Daltons called Newton home. Less than 1 percent of the populace were regarded as "black" or "mulatto" according to historical records from the 1880s, though Newton's unsurprising whiteness didn't mean it was a quaint, sleepy, New England town obsessed only with the past or an idealized version of it. Commerce thrived. Railroads pulsed through town, connecting it to larger networks of

30   BEAUTIFUL

trade and communication. There was ferment, hunger, and a yearning for movement among the populace. Single persons outnumbered the married by a large factor. Sixteen percent of the residents were Irish-born, like Joe Dalton's father, no doubt wondering how they might ascend the socioeconomic rockface in America. Joe ran a barbershop on Washington Street, near Walnut, amid the bustling "emporiums of local commerce." Business was good enough that he could employ his brother at the salon, and provide his family a modest private home also on Washington Street. But Joe Dalton was "restless and unhappy." Householders might be told to value humility, thrift, and simplicity. But this was an age when robber barons and millionaires were grabbing gold by the handful and literally building their own castles. Where was *their* humility? In old Europe, acquiring nobility could take centuries if it could be earned at all. In this new land, though, it could be grabbed overnight, or so the fantasy went. A clarion call summoned men to become "self-made," rich, powerful, and admired—all the result, simply, of one's own will and toil. Again, that was the idea anyway. Whatever it meant to be a "self-made man," it surely did *not* mean patiently sticking around your New England barbershop while your brethren devoured their way up the mountain. Joe Dalton scanned the cultural, and literal, landscape for opportunities. After a new silver lode was struck in Calico, California, in 1885, he saw a big one. Like so many men of his era, it was time to go West and extract riches from the land. If the streets in America turned out not to be paved with gold, exactly, then maybe the wide-open spaces were. For Joe Dalton and so many of his countrymen—and indeed, they were pretty much all men—it was practically a spiritual calling, the dogma of the "self-made man."[9]

Meanwhile, Julia Dalton had ideas of her own. Her child, by now just "Billy," seemed anything but shy. She dressed him up as a little girl and entered him in popular Baby Shows of the day in Boston, where the little lad won blue ribbons. This youthful drag occurred in a day when there was little distinction between how little boys and little girls were dressed, respectively. In fact, if anything, boys were often attired in plush, loose-fitting, dress-like garments sometimes described as "girllike."[10]

To the delight of many and the concern of others, styles took a further turn after publication of Frances Hodgson Burnett's hugely popular *Little Lord Fauntleroy* stories beginning in 1885, which were quickly adapted to the stage. Fauntleroy, an American boy named Cedric, gets shipped off to England when it is discovered he is actually British nobility. (The *Fauntleroy* franchise of stories, books, and stage plays has been called the "Harry Potter

A "CUTE LITTLE BEAUTE FROM BUTTE, MONTANA" 31

Figure 1.1 Julian Eltinge when he was just a wee lad named Billy Dalton. His mother entered him in youth shows in Boston. At the time, there was little distinction between how boy and girl babies and toddlers were dressed. The smash hit *Little Lord Fauntleroy* book and play series (1885) led many boys to be groomed as longhaired, velvet-clad children, little fops and dandies, as it were, the very opposite of new notions of rugged masculinity.
Credit: *Anne Alison Barnet Collection.*

of its day.") In England, he is dressed in lace, stockings, and high-heeled shoes, and coiffed in long, silky tresses. Burnett cited her son, Vivian, as the model for Cedric/Fauntleroy, an image he tried to shake his whole life, enduring shouts of "Fauntleroy—Mama's boy" as he ran in track meets for

32   BEAUTIFUL

Harvard. Julian Eltinge, on the other hand, never complained about the ways his mother dressed him for competitions and performances, and he seems early on to have taken a natural liking to it. Nor did he mind becoming a stage kid, even if he wasn't doing it at the intense, professional level of some of his future peers like vaudevillian Eva Tanguay, Mae West, and actor-turned impresario E. F. Albee. Besides, the concept of adolescence as a lengthy stretch that separated childhood from adulthood was a relatively new concept at the turn of the end of the nineteenth century.[11]

* * *

Billy's father, Joe Dalton, had very different ideas about what it meant to succeed, particularly as a man. He didn't care for the stage and certainly couldn't countenance swathing oneself or one's son in silk and velvet finery. Like many American men of his time, Joe Dalton looked to the West with hope and longing. The American West of Joe Dalton's day has been described as a vast arena of "virile masculinity," a place where you could extract a new, rugged identity every bit as much as a fortune in precious metals. Many had been influenced by Teddy Roosevelt's popular book series, *The Winning of the West*, first published in 1889, in which he mythologized both the frontier and himself in epic fashion. *The Winning of the West* argued that the nation's founders had always envisioned domination of the entire continent, the "march of our people from the crests of the Alleghanies to the Pacific." In the process, white men would tap the land for riches and "strong young races" would triumph over "the unfit"; "civilization" would come "at the cost of savagery." This needed to happen by any means possible, which posed no problem for Teddy Roosevelt, a man never held back "by any taint of legality," in the words of his future attorney general, Philander Knox.[12]

Moving to the frontier allowed men to supplant socioeconomic *im*mobility with geographic *mobility*. For Teddy Roosevelt, the migration was the first act of a self-authored hero's journey. The asthmatic youngster from one of New York's ultrarich, founding families, "sickly" and cursed with "tiny feet and short legs," a Harvard grad and onetime member of its elite Hasty Pudding club (famous for drag shows), went to the Dakota Territory in what is today Montana and North and South Dakota. He came back a self-styled "Teddy, the straight shooter from the West," as John Dos Passos wrote in *U.S.A. 1919*. The West was an incubator that turned pallid boys into bronzed men. In 1907, a widower named Edward Slack offered $1,000 apiece to any men who would propose to his eight "ordinarily attractive" daughters, provided the suitor didn't hail from back East and presently lived in Montana or Idaho.[13] Many boys were sent to work on ranches or homesteads, given the so-called Western cure, like legendary *Follies* impresario Florenz Ziegfeld, whose folks sent him away "anemic, frail, [and] apathetic" in his teens, allegedly leading him to come back a seasoned, determined young man ready to compete in the world of business.[14]

Words like "frail," "sickly," and "anemic" were codewords at the time for feminine or female, housebound, and always somehow ailing. Before the Civil War, American women had played active roles in small towns, family farms, and local enterprises. Increasingly, though, by the time Joe Dalton shuttled his family out West, the proper place for a woman was in the quiet sanctity of the home, "behind closed doors." To deal with being a woman meant increasingly to rely on doctors, psychiatrists, ministers, healers, and other men expert at scrutinizing and repairing the inherently buggy female apparatus. Some women rebelled in creative fashion. Christian Science founder Mary Baker Eddy, for example, famously abjured medical interventions, promoting the "power of Mind over matter," not to mention fiddling doctors, in her Church's foundational text, *Science and Health*. Why couldn't a woman, after all, be a self-made man?[15]

* * *

By 1886, the Dalton family had embarked upon what would turn out to be a five-year gambol about the Americas. Father Joe led his brood around the West and Latin America leading "a sort of nomadic existence." Probably embellishing for effect, Eltinge would later claim to have been to every state in the nation, save Maine, while still a teen. The Daltons lived in San Francisco for a time, residing in a modest rooming hotel on Ellis Street, near the corner of Turk and Hyde. Billy was sent to the Mission Grammar School. Though dad didn't like his son's interest in the theatre and the lad's "parlor exhibitions," Billy would nonetheless sing for hotel guests as he had at other inns and hostelries along the way. He had a fine, alto voice and loved the applause. The West, it seemed, was turning into a frontier of self-discovery for Joe Dalton's son as well, though the results were rather different from what the father might have liked. Mrs. Moore, landlady of the San Francisco rooming house where the Dalton family lived, had an actor son who popped in for visits. Billy Dalton gazed upon the actor in awe. There was something

34 BEAUTIFUL

different about him. He had . . . *style.* He wore satiny vests and sparkling rings on his fingers. Actors got to be—*had to be?*—a little different, a little glamorous, even when not working, which seemed to be often and yet somehow never for many of them.[16]

Joe Dalton also tried Salt Lake City. The family lived on South Main near Walker Brothers Dry Goods in a house where Brigham Young's oldest son once lived. Father Joe scoured the Utah landscape, ever trying to ascertain where "nature had hidden her gold." But she yielded him no answer. Finally, in 1890, the Daltons pulled up stakes for the last time and headed north, to Montana, which had become a state just a year earlier. Perhaps he'd find his fortune, the place where Teddy Roosevelt transitioned from "jane-dandy" into future political wrangler. It had been a long, wearying road. Maybe here it would finally come to a satisfying end. As Joe Dalton and others would discover, Montana was a wild, often brutal corner of the world. Corruption, cruelty, and exploitation held sway. Politicians openly bribed influence-wielders and hired murderers to deal with troublemakers, especially those championing laborers. In Myron Brinig's 1931 novel *Wide Open Town*, set in a thinly disguised Butte, Montana, of the early 1900s, Phil Whipple, a character based on real-life labor organizer Frank Little, is at one moment making a courageous speech. The next, he is taken by antiunion thugs and hanged, his body swinging in the moonlight for all to see. Joe Dalton was going into a war among men, ill-equipped in terms of rank and weaponry, and somehow hoping to win.[17]

The mining industry in Montana in 1890 was largely contained in and around the city of Butte and its surrounding county of Silver Bow. Some folks back East might have considered Butte a minor outpost in the vast stretch between Chicago and San Francisco. But the area was booming thanks to huge copper deposits in what was dubbed "the Richest Hill on Earth." Copper wiring was crucial to the nation's (and the world's) growing telephone and telegraph infrastructure, literally the circuitry of capitalism. By 1890, the "copper metropolis" counted 23,000 souls, a figure that rose to 100,000 over the coming decade.[18] Helena, eighty miles north, might have technically been the capital. But Butte was the undisputed center of everything that mattered to ambitious businessmen of the day. By the late 1890s, Butte and its surroundings would be producing nearly all of Montana's copper, worth some $41 million annually. By comparison, the next-biggest copper state was Michigan, which produced $27 million yearly. In 1898, the United States supplied nearly two-thirds of the world's copper, over 40 percent of which came from Butte, which had truly earned its nickname, "Copperopolis."[19]

Joe Dalton dove into the fray. The time had long passed when individual speculators panning or digging for gold, known as "placers," could hope to strike it rich. Now a man like him had somehow to buy or rent a slice of earth and mine it for copper or silver. That required investment money, which men like Joe Dalton didn't have. He could have taken a job down in the mines. At the time, mining was briskly outpacing American industry overall in terms of job growth and salary. But it was risky and dangerous. Workers were "shot down in cages, into the mine shafts, down, down, five hundred, a thousand, three thousand feet, so fast that their stomachs were in their mouths," wrote Myron Brining who moved as a child to Butte with his family in 1900. Still, boosters of the day insisted that in Butte, all a man needed were "brain and brawn" to grab one's share of "present wealth" from a land with a "pregnant future," or so insisted *A Brief History of Butte, Montana: The World's Greatest Mining Camp, Including a Story of the Extraction and Treatment of Ores from its Gigantic Copper Properties*, published in 1900.[20]

Montana was indeed an open frontier, ready for the taking—at least, if you ignored or subdued the people who had been living there for quite some time. Lewis and Clark's famed 1805 expedition, which paved the way for westward expansion, would not have been possible without the aid of the Nez Percé—so-called because French trappers observed them wearing dentalium shells through piercings in their noses—in what eventually became Oregon, Idaho, and western Montana. In 1877, General Oliver Otis Howard was dispatched to confine the Nez Percé to small, inadequate reservations. Indigenous leader Toohoolhoolzote confronted Howard, asking him, "What person pretended to divide the land and put us on it?" An army with abundant modern weaponry, including early-model machine guns, would soon force the Nez Percé and other tribal peoples onto reservations. "We were like deer. They were like grizzly bears," said chief Heinmot Tooyalaket, also known as Young Joseph (and sometimes spelled "Tooyalakekt"). "We were contented to let things remain as the Great Spirit made them. They were not, and would change the rivers and the mountains if they did not suit them." In 1880, 21,650 tribal peoples lived on 45,876 square miles of Montana reservation land. Twenty years later, 10,076 remained on just 14,845 square miles. Meanwhile, the white population mushroomed from 38,813 to 241,806. Today, the Nez Percé reservation occupies 1,200 square miles, some 0.82 percent of the Montana's total land. It lies just east of the cities of Lewiston and Clarkston.[21]

* * *

36 BEAUTIFUL

The city of Butte might have been a hard place for a man like Joe Dalton to make a fortune. But it turned out to be a pretty good place for his son to cultivate his love of the theatre. For all its historical and behind-the-scenes brutalizing, the face of the city had become "richly cosmopolitan" by the 1890s, with fine retail stores, classy (and some not-so-classy) hotels and restaurants, and an array of venues offering "the best opera and drama that is known to the American stage," according to a local historian writing at the time. Butte folk could enjoy the hugely popular, frothy light operas that were all the rage at the time, such as *Amorita*, a "pretty representative of the Vienna school of operetta." In November 1893, no less a star than Lillian Russell, who would later loom large in Billy Dalton's life, passed through Butte with "a new opera comique" titled *Princess Nicotine*.[22] The Casino, Montana Concert Hall, and Columbia Gardens offered Butte residents the best in vaudeville and drama, while other establishments offered boozing, gambling, sex for sale, raucous entertainments, brawling, and more boozing. A fellow returning to Butte in 1914 for the first time in twenty years was surprised at how far the little mining town had come, with its theatres, hotels, elaborate department stores, streetcars, and "all else indicative of the so-called 'march of progress.'" Wide, paved streets arrayed in a grid had replaced "the cowpath irregularity" of yore.[23]

Rather than risk going down in the mines, Joe Dalton found employment in a barbershop. The haircutting establishment at 10 South Main was modest but was nestled right in the city's thumping, commercial heart. The eminent Casino theatre, with its spacious orchestra and overhanging gallery boxes, was just around the corner on East Galena. The neighborhood was home to pawnshops, cafes, gaming halls, groggeries, and the Empire Hotel designated for "female boarding."[24] One of Butte's less-flashy "concert" halls was also nearby, on East Park. This was the sort of place where waitresses led workingmen in singalongs called "free-and-easies" amid the haze of pipe and cigar smoke; where white comedians delivered monologues in blackface, sometimes employing supposedly authentic "Irish" or "Hebrew" accents, or even mixing them on occasion. The concert hall was a place where many a night ended, if not also began, with a flurry of fists. In 1895, a miner named Michael Tewey was walking past when he noticed two bruisers about to pounce on a buddy of his. Tewey rushed in to defend his mate only to be cracked on the skull with a revolver, leaving him with "a large sized head."[25]

The Daltons found a modest-sized, wood-frame house at 512 W. Park Street in Butte. Street names like Quartz and Granite make the city's neatly

A "CUTE LITTLE BEAUTE FROM BUTTE, MONTANA"   37

perpendicular grid map resemble children's rock-collecting kits from the past, with chunks of pyrite and mica glued into individual squares. According to some sources, papa Dalton also labored as a carpenter/handyman/house-painter, though his son, in a bit of retroactive up-classing, would later claim his dad had worked in a bank owned by mining industry tycoon William A. Clark.[26] "Michael J. Dalton" appears in the Butte city directory for the first time in 1890, cutting heads in a barbershop owned by C. M. Joyce. In 1893, Joe Dalton was still working as a barber, this time for E. M. Kunze, and residing with his wife and son at 208 W. Quartz in a pleasant, craftsman-style cottage perched atop a stone retaining wall.[27]

Across the street from the Daltons, at no. 211 West Quartz, in a brick-clad corner house a few doors down from the Methodist church, lived the family of Charles S. Eltinge. Mr. Eltinge ran a "real estate, insurance and foreign exchange" business at 205 North Main, a concern he advertised proudly on the back cover of Butte city directories. The businessman had a son, also named Charles, or possibly Willie, a "red headed freckle faced lad." Julian Eltinge would long hold the latter in his memory: "This youngster's name always impressed me as picturesque. 'Eltinge' had a fine sound to my youthful ears." Young Charles-or-possibly-Willie Eltinge soon became Billy Dalton's "best friend and chum." Like so much about Julian Eltinge's life, further details remain obscure. On tour many years later, the enter-tainer said he'd dined with "the real Will Eltinge" in Spokane. But the so-called real Will/Charles Eltinge was also reputed to have died in childhood, and that "[n]one mourned his death more than Willie Dalton," according to a Butte reporter. Whatever its provenance, the name would prove a good one: much more memorable than "Dalton" and echoing that of glamorous, midcentury actress Rose Eytinge, known for her "emotionalist" technique and also for having been one of a handful of famous Jewish performers in mainstream American theatre in the 1800s. In fact, George Fortescue, a female impersonator roughly of Julian Eltinge's day, became famous for his renditions of Rose Eytinge. Some have speculated that Eltinge's new moniker was also in part an homage to well-known actor, choreographer, and producer-director Julian Mitchell (1852–1926), who would go on to helm numerous *Ziegfeld Follies*. Mitchell, a renowned "master of detail" who gained repute for directing Charles Hoyt comedies in the 1880s, was regarded by 1905 "without a peer in America" for his masterful stagings of *The Wizard of Oz* and *Babes in Toyland*, helping rewrite, direct, choreo-graph, and design those huge hits and others.[28]

38   BEAUTIFUL

The Daltons enrolled Billy in the providentially named Broadway school. The boy, not terribly interested in book learning, was nonetheless sociable, popular, and resourceful, bonding with schoolmates John Corette, Will Kenyon, Harry Jack, Julius Jones, and Merle Davis, kids who were also into theatre. Davis, in fact, would later become manager of Butte's Broadway music hall.[29]

As he entered tweenhood, Billy Dalton ventured out to explore theatrical life in his adoptive hometown. One day, the lad came home and told his father he'd gotten an ushering job at Butte's Maguire Opera House. Dad was unimpressed and then some.

Joe Dalton took his soon out to the woodshed and beat him.

At the time, such a beating was sometimes called a "whaling expedition." It would not be the last such episode. Despite risking more thrashings at his father's hand, the lad continued to sneak out of the house at night to go to the theatre. One evening he slipped away, possibly to catch Lillian Russell at the Casino. Joe Dalton, a man "excessively fond of a drink," was awake to catch him. That night, Billy Dalton got "the whaling of his life" from his father, paying "dearly" for his love of the stage. Yet the older man's brutality would not deter the youngster. Other kids might want to grow up to become cops, firemen, or streetcar conductors. Not Billy Dalton. He longed to be an entertainer, to "apply burnt cork" in the manner of blackface minstrels so troublingly popular in the day, and to win ovations from those who appreciated his talent.[30] While the theatre gave women opportunities to escape social and economic confinement, men had to be careful. They might be lauded as great thespians. But they could also be considered somehow unmanly, playing in a world where they were supposed to work. In 1906, journalist and publicist Alan Dale, writing in *Cosmopolitan*, decried "sound, healthy, able-bodied men pretending to be someone else . . . cavorting around in musical comedy." Dale said he wanted to stand up and shout, "Go out into the world and do something, build things, invent things [instead of] posing as blossoming, silly make-believes'?" Ironically—well, maybe predictably—Dale would later become a huge Julian Eltinge fan and was credited with coining the catchphrase "The most beautiful woman on the American stage is a man."[31]

While Billy Dalton cultivated his future profession in Butte, he also learned the importance of competition and entrepreneurship, skills a freelance entertainer could ignore only at their own peril, particularly as huge, well-organized corporations increasingly controlled their livelihoods. Amid a mint julep craze, Billy found and "assumed possession" of a bed of mint plants on the city's outskirts. The summer heat and an "atmosphere sulphuric [*sic*]," thanks to all the smelting and refining, "inspired a thirst" among locals for the refreshing cocktail. It was an arduous, lengthy hike to the mint grove. That, combined with the profits he reaped, led Billy to regard this particular mint supply as "his'n," like a mining claim. Three hot summers in a row, young Billy repulsed "squatters" and "claim jumpers" doling out "bruises" and "closed optics" (i.e., black eyes). Even if he later embellished stories of his fisticuffs, it's clear that Billy Dalton knew the importance of defending one's turf. It's what a man did.[32]

* * *

If the West of Teddy Roosevelt's and Joe Dalton's day offered an overwhelming opportunity to play at manhood and fortune-chasing, it became all the more fabulous and overblown in popular culture during the twentieth century, a masquerade-ground for John Wayne and Clint Eastwood, "nothing but a show."[33] Billy Dalton must have noticed how much of being "a man, not to mention being a woman," involved dedicated performance as he tended the seedlings of his wizardry. But the West was of course more complicated, richer, and nuanced, as reality always turns out to be. It was a place one could escape to in order to avoid strictures on masculinity, as did an individual known to us as "M" who headed out to Nebraska in 1867 because he wanted to wear women's apparel and could not do so in the presence of his bitterly protesting preacher father. Surely there were others like M whose diaries and testimonies were never written down or did not survive. Indigenous peoples of the West, as has long been known, also included those who were neither strictly gender-binary nor forced to be. As early as 1825, white travelers encountered Cherokee men "who assumed the dress and performed all the duties of women and who lived their whole life in this manner." These "two-spirit" peoples came to be called "berdache" by white observers, apparently deriving from an archaic Arabic word, *bardaj*, a boy kept for sexual purposes, though this was plainly never the vocabulary of the Cherokee.[34]

The drag flourished in more presumptively macho settings as well. With his mother's encouragement—and presumably without his father's knowledge—a youthful Billy Dalton impersonated teenage girls and lasses for men in Butte's mining camps. Men and even some women in mining towns enjoyed crossdressing both within their own ranks and onstage. By the

40   BEAUTIFUL

1870s, a Colorado gold-mining district called Georgetown was well known for women who preferred to self-present as male, as well as for sundry "males in petticoats" wandering about. Eltinge competitor Bert Savoy debuted his drag character "Maude" in the saloons of Deadwood, South Dakota, and later brought his female-impersonation act to Montana, the Yukon, and Alaska, often passing for a woman in winerooms and bars. If Teddy Roosevelt could play at manhood out West, why couldn't others run their own gender experiments?[35]

From the end of the nineteenth century until at least the early 1930s, men all over America were skirting-up together to put on shows, perform club and fraternal-society rituals, raise money for schools and churches, and sometimes just because they seemed to like doing so. The Great Plains and Western frontier were no exception. In 1919, the St. John's Military School in Salina, Kansas, featured a "charming young lady" who was actually a Wyoming boy named Gardiner Hart, trying to "mak[e] her skirts behave long enough" in the wind so the photographer could snap a picture of Hart next to a proud cadet for the cover of *The Skirmisher*, the school's official newsletter for alumni.[36] Men's and boys' organizations of all kinds out West had resident experts at female impersonation. In 1924, the American Legion Club of Okmulgee, Oklahoma, celebrated Legionnaire Max Heyman for "doing the grass skirt dances or anything else that may be required along the line of female impersonation" at their functions. In Park City, Utah, the Score Club's resident impersonator, Lee Talbot, played women "very creditably" during the 1910s. Even Brigham Young, second president of the Church of Jesus Christ of Latter-day Saints, played the "diva" as Italian opera star Madam Pattirini, "swanning about in wig, makeup, gown and falsetto," earning no censure or stigma.[37]

Outside of certain all-male settings in which men were allowed to play at the drag and often get high praise for it, or within recognized theatrical confines, dressing against gender could bring trouble. In the 1890s, San Francisco began cracking down on public crossdressing, and at least one upset citizen, a cisgender male named "Jenny" who wanted to go outside in skirts, wrote to pioneering German sexologist Magnus Hirschfeld complaining about the arbitrary nature of enforcement. Twelve persons were arrested for crossdressing in San Francisco in 1898, a big jump over the prior year, suggesting that more folks were going out dressed against gender norms and getting more heat for doing so. A bit like the Elizabethan sumptuary codes, laws restricting what a person could wear were meant to maintain some kind of preferred social order. Minneapolis maintained ordinances barring public crossdressing from 1877 until the mid-1900s; sister city St. Paul's 1891 statute preventing civilians from donning "clothes not belonging to their sex" remained on the books until 2003. Ordinance 5022, passed in Los Angeles in 1898, not only cracked down on men and women in drag but also sought to rein in would-be rioters and rowdies during times of festival, a persistent fear of the powerful classes in American cities of the day. San Francisco statutes also aimed to prevent Japanese and Chinese arrivals from looking more "American" than they were supposed to. Meanwhile, Julian Eltinge enjoyed widespread acclaim in California. In 1908, the *San Francisco Dramatic Review* called him "a wonder," a professional who had "mastered all the arts and movements of femininity," exhibiting his "adaptability to wear handsome gowns."[38]

* * *

With his mining dreams yet unfulfilled, Joe Dalton became co-owner of Dalton & LaGue, a barbershop at 10 South Main in Butte. The family had moved to a modest brick home at 525 West Galena on the corner of Crystal Street. But mother and son had had enough of following the patriarch's unrealized and unrealizable dreams. They were headed back East to a different frontier altogether. Joe moved to 112 South Idaho, near Mercury Steet, determined to make a final stab at accruing "mining interests" in Butte. He and partner Owen Thornton paid $35 for a half-interest in a section of the Kerry Lode. The next year, Joe, Owen, and Norah Thornton sold a quarter-interest in the property to Thomas Bulger for $125, a modest profit but far from a jackpot. Dalton also partnered with John Casey to buy access to "the north lead of the Amy lode" for twelve months in order to "extract ore therefrom." But the cupboard turned out to be bare. The dream was over. It was time to follow his wife and son back East. Now the child would begin his own, significantly more fruitful adventure. In a few short years, the boy would even confer business success upon his dad, in name anyway, when the papers asked about papa Joe Dalton. But they would soon stop asking. As Julian Eltinge knew, unless you were a bona fide oligarch, where you came from didn't matter. What mattered was making yourself into the man you wished to be, seemingly all on your own. Voter registration records show Joe Dalton living with his family on Charles Street in Boston. Most likely, dad made a

42 BEAUTIFUL

few last trips out West to see if anything could be salvaged and, more to the point, close up shop.[39]

Increasingly, the bold and ambitious weren't going to the plains and prairies but streaming to America's urban centers. That was the *real* frontier, the place you could actually make a name and some money if you were clever and lucky. In 1890, the year the Daltons arrived in Butte, America's urban population was 22.1 million and the rural, 40.8 million. Over the next decade, the population growth of cities outpaced rural areas at a rate of three to one. In 1890, the US government ended effective resistance from indigenous persons at the tragic Battle of Wounded Knee. Oglala Lakota leader Red Cloud remarked that the American government had finally kept the only promise it had ever made to his people: "[T]hey promised to take our land, and they took it." By 1920, American city-dwellers would number 54.2 million, compared to 51.6 million in the countryside.[40]

With the frontier officially closed, as historian Frederick Jackson Turner famously argued in 1893, American business, government, and military leaders sought eagerly to "Americanize" foreign shores. Well-known evangelist Josiah Strong called for American "commerce, missionary work, and colonization" to span the globe. The Marine Corps and Navy expanded dramatically to secure markets and geopolitical interests in Haiti, the Philippines, South America, and elsewhere. Religious and social organizations like the Rotary International, founded in 1905, would spread American "goodwill" abroad. In 1909, the *Ziegfeld Follies* featured vaudevillian Lillian Lorraine singing "The Greatest Navy in the World" backed by chorus girls in battleship-shaped hats.[41]

Stateside, corporations and bureaucracies swelled unceasingly. Making it as a man meant scrabbling up the ladder, dodging or booting anyone who got in your way, or maybe forming a temporary, self-serving alliance. Men feared failure and, seemingly worse, anonymity. Woodrow Wilson, who earned his doctorate at Johns Hopkins University shortly before Frederick Jackson Turner would do likewise, saw "the little man on the make" surrendering what remained of his autonomy as they went to work for giant conglomerates with rigidly hierarchical structures. Small mining claims like the ones held by Joe Dalton would increasingly be gobbled up by huge conglomerates like ASARCO, the American Smelting and Refining Company. Entertainers like Julian Eltinge, no less than employees in other industries, had to respect big business and know their place. In 1908, Chicago mayor Fred Busse urged censorship of vaudevillians' "quips" poking fun at millionaires like Rockefeller and Carnegie, since comedy had "a tendency to stir up anarchy," which may indeed be its very point.[42]

To make his way up the ladder, Billy Dalton knew he had to navigate his professional life flawlessly, making the right connections, exploiting the right opportunities, and giving the proper impression of oneself. Everyone was looking at everyone, and everyone was being looked at. The new age, as Marx had observed, was one of "constant supervision," from factory floor to gala ballroom to the head office. Telegraphs, telephones, cash registers, new accounting and credit-rating practices, and railroads comprised the sinew and nerves of the new socioeconomic corpus.[43] How you *appeared* mattered more than ever in the world of commerce. How you dressed and spoke, what you did for leisure, what brands you preferred—those were all part of a winning formula. Businessmen were seeking new ways to armor-up against the competition; in 1908, Harvard would become one of the first universities to offer a new degree called an MBA. On the cusp of both adulthood and a new century, Billy Dalton returned to "the historical soil of the Hub," Boston, quite aware that things had changed a great deal since his dad took them all around the continent in search of an illusion.[44]

# # #

2

Mr. Simplicity, or a
Cadet-Turned-Chorus-Girl

Back in Boston, the Daltons moved to no. 18 Mechanic Street near what is today the city's main tourist district featuring the Faneuil Hall shopping concourse, historic Old North Church, the Paul Revere House, and the occasional colonial re-enactor in ruffled shirt and periwig.[1]

Billy Dalton, now in his mid-teens, tooled around, looking for a toehold. The city bristled with opportunities. He was smart and ambitious, looking for a way in. With little formal schooling and a father who was *not* in fact a mining magnate, Billy knew he'd have to make his way up from the bottom. But that was okay. Like much about his early life, Julian Eltinge would later provide mixed, confusing, or vague information. Opaqueness would come to suit him. Upon his return to Boston, it's possible he worked in a hardware store and then a dry-goods emporium before becoming a counter clerk at a department store. Department stores were good places to learn about what a newfangled generation of consumers wanted, especially if it was your job to smile and answer their questions. While such establishments may have become dinosaurs in an age of Internet-selling and big-box showrooms, at the time, department stores represented the cutting edge of the consumer economy, summoning desire and acquisitiveness. Dry goods shops of past eras, department stores' predecessors, had been little more than vaguely curated warehouses with piles and bolts of fabrics for customers who largely made their own apparel. The new department stores and retailers, however, used carefully designed lighting, huge display windows, and lifelike mannequins. Part museum, part theatre, part bazaar, the new stores relied on stagecraft as much as accounting and inventory management. Shoppers began to cultivate an "autonomous identity" as such, apart from their roles as, say, mother, laborer, or citizen. Like crowds in a theatre, they expected to be dazzled. In addition to working in retail, young Billy Dalton may have spent some time clerking in an architect's office. Architecture was a classy field, smart, sexy, and appealing to those with an eye for design. Being an

Beautiful. Andrew L. Erdman, Oxford University Press. © Oxford University Press 2024.
DOI: 10.1093/9780197696361.003.0003

architect, or pretending to be one, was a theme that would crop up through Julian Eltinge's career.[2]

But Billy Dalton's most important job by far before turning toward the stage was in a milliner's shop. Looking for "some sort of a career," he wandered into a woman's hat-making and -selling establishment and became entranced. Millinery shops offered women of the day a way to bring attention to the face and head while also coquettishly obscuring them. Sophisticated milliners knew quite well how much the right, or wrong, hat could say about one's place in the Great Chain of Being. A visitor to a fancy New York hat shop in 1900 said her interest in certain styles had been "extinguished" by a saleswoman who deemed them appropriate only for unschooled tourists from the South and West. "[T]he truth is," admitted the otherwise clever shopper, "that it is the milliner who owns the customer, body and soul."[3] When New York socialite Dorothy Arnold went missing in 1910, spurring a frenzy of speculation, descriptions and sketches paid so much attention to her lapis hatpin and velvet hat that, despite being of a fairly common style, it all seemed practically a part of her anatomy, its lining of "Alice Blue" a visual echo of Arnold's "Grayish-blue" eyes. In 1916, arguing that universities ought to limit male students' appearance in drag musicals for fear it would feminize them—Yale had just passed a rule capping participation at one year—NYU psychologist Dr. James E. Lough warned of a young man whose work in a hat shop had "eliminate[d] much of his normal masculinity and endow[ed] him with many little effeminate mannerisms." (Dr. Lough also wrote of a female college student whose "predisposition" to male behaviors led her to become a successful "man-actor" at school. Upon graduation, the erstwhile student thespian went to work for her father in his machine shop where she "dons a pair of overalls and runs the factory with the precision and efficiency of a highly trained executive.") What is clear about Billy Dalton's tenure in the millinery trade is that he looked, listened, and learned, cultivating "a taste for the beautiful in design and harmony of color." It was work that suited him and would come to serve him well.[4]

But Billy Dalton was intrinsically a creature of the theatre, not of quotidian commerce. That much he had long known. Some might accept their lot by laboring from the lowly, unglamorous bottom to the slightly-less-unglamorous, if respectable, middle. Not Billy Dalton. He'd find a way to succeed without perspiring over ledgers in a basement "counting-room" like Ragged Dick, the culturally admirable protagonist in Horatio Alger's 1868 novel of the same name.[5] Billy Dalton was an unlettered, lower-class scion

46 BEAUTIFUL

of a cultural group (on his father's side, anyway) that many in society's upper reaches found suspect. Julian Eltinge, however, was a talented young man determined to make his mark and fortune. Presently, he noticed a way in.

* * *

When society folk in Boston felt like a bit of fun in the early 1900s, they sometimes brought the theatre to *them*, like Mohammad summoning the mountain. Holding private piano recitals, musicales, dances, and other cultural interludes was a nice way for many a doyenne to pass an afternoon, circulate among friends and rivals, and showcase the fruits of her husband's success.[6]

The swell set enjoyed festivities that featured *cakewalking*. The cakewalk was a dance supposedly derived from the authentic practices of enslaved persons on Southern plantations of yore. Allowing a peek into the lives and folkways of enslaved Black persons, cakewalking, like its close cousin blackface "minstrel" shows, allowed white audiences of various social strata to glimpse a seemingly raw, unrestrained energy denied or delimited in so much of the white world. At the same time, cakewalking and blackface shows reinforced notions of racial and caste superiority. When middle- and upper-class white audiences watched a cakewalk dancer, they were amused at an exotic culture that, though lively, would never become mainstream or associated with power—or such was the desperate hope. Black Americans and their folkways were depicted as cartoonish and strange, amusing but not fully human in the scheme of things. To play them meant merging the grotesque and the comical in the form of eccentric dance stylings or a clownlike visage slathered in greasepaint and burnt cork. Of course, what was presumed inherently *different*, even if somehow lower, was also rather *compelling*, unrestricted, and scenting of freedom. The cakewalk's flexibility and athleticism gave it an unmatched immediacy. It allowed the body to do what it could not do elsewhere. Cakewalking conveyed a spontaneity that belied the training and practice behind it—unlike, say, formal dancing and ballet, which fairly shouted strata of authority and lineage. Ada Overton, one of the few Black performers to achieve mass popularity in mainstream vaudeville and musicals, synergized cakewalking with emerging modern dance practices, bringing the art form to a new height in the early 1900s.[7]

So, many a guest welcomed a cakewalk show at a private gala, even if an opera singer or harpsichordist was supposedly classier. The cakewalker offered a bit of fun and abandon, a respite to onlookers encased in silk and tweed, seated politely in an oaken parlor or among manicured gardens. Cakewalkers, drag artists, and other creative types let the swells dip a toe in the demimonde. This was an essential aspect of bourgeois life: the purchase and curation of vital experience. After some entertainment, followed by cucumber sandwiches and tea, the men could retire among themselves, as men were wont to do, with their cigars, talk of investments, and reminiscences of having rowed for "New Haven" or "Cambridge," since the anointed rarely said Yale or Harvard out loud, as Billy Dalton was learning. Nick Carraway, the aspirational narrator of *The Great Gatsby*, knows very well to call Tom Buchanan "one of the most powerful ends that ever played football at New Haven," and leave it at that.[8] Learning to cakewalk would be a good way for Billy Dalton to work his way into society, perhaps even make a little money on the side in vaudeville shows, though he would keep his professional aspirations to himself for now.

The best place in town to learn the cakewalk was Lilla Viles Wyman's dance studio. Wyman not only had a knack for teaching and an eye for talent but was also keenly aware of how the Boston 400 liked to party and what amused them. Wyman, born in 1854, was a Boston-area native like Julian Eltinge. The daughter of a noted violinist, she began teaching dance in the 1880s, eventually earning the nickname the "Grand Duchess of Dance" and training many an amateur and future professional. Despite instructing "the children of the Back Bay" in ballroom technique, Wyman was an avid learner who read voraciously and traveled widely to keep up with developments and innovations in the terpsichorean art.[9] Billy Dalton signed up to study with her.

One day in 1898, he showed up a little early for his lesson. Wyman was finishing up with an octet of chorus girls who were getting ready for a big show. When they left, Billy lampooned the work of one "large, awkward" young woman whose skills he found lacking. Wyman and her student collapsed in laughter. Even amid the giggles, though, the mentor saw something in the novice. Yes, he was funny, charming, and witty. But also, he moved with style, precision, and fluidity, down to the slight rustling of his fingers, which "flowed and darted in soft, graceful curves and butterfly-like flutters." This seventeen-year-old boy could not satirize a woman without also betraying a deeper, more empathic understanding of his subject's physics and emotions. Wyman, "impressed with his peculiar grace," advised Dalton also to study "fancy dancing" with her, something more balletic than just the cakewalk. Billy agreed. He was dedicated and it showed. He spent hours a day on ballet,

Figure 2.1 With little formal schooling and no family pedigree, a youthful Billy Dalton wasted no time matching his talent, intelligence, and ambition to a bustling world of opportunity in Boston.
Credit: *Anne Alison Barnet Collection.*

modern dance, and the minute, yet all-encompassing "laws of expression" developed by Frenchman François Delsarte in the 1860s and 1870s. In an age when naturalists, scientists, and physicists were attempting to uncover life's minutiae, Delsarte offered a way to externally convey a person's inner life. While the Delsarte method might seem a bit simplistic or mechanistic to us today, it provided a structured approach to communicating intention and emotion via precise gesture. It would inform Billy Dalton's female-impersonating skills as he became Julian Eltinge, allowing him to execute "the illusion of womanhood" beyond the use of elaborate makeup and gowning, without stylized, overblown cliché or resorting to the grotesque. Lilla Wyman was teaching the youth what it meant to be an *artist*. Indeed, young Eltinge would soon be lauded for giving "microscopic care to every typically feminine action." To those who saw him, he not only sat and rose in a womanly way, but spoke in "the graceful manner of a lady of refinement," flirting as a genteel woman might do, and stepping into "the most bewitching poses." Just like separating copper ore from rocks or performing a surgery, there was a science, a métier, to all of this. From the start, Julian Eltinge would build his career on putting this science into action and, just as important, constantly reminding his public that he was doing so. His was a learned, technical skill set, a trade mastered like that of a financier, attorney, or architect. Of course, he also had a deeply embodied *feel* for this craft, its nuance and humanity. It would soon set him above the pack. It didn't hurt that he also managed to become a good overall dancer, mastering the waltz as well as the cakewalk. On one occasion when he could neither speak nor sing due to throat trouble, Eltinge merely danced and showed off his dresses to a delighted crowd. Flexibility like that was essential for a touring vaudevillian. By 1917, an upscale Los Angeles hotel, cashing in on the dance fad inspired by famed dancefloor duo Irene and Vernon Castle, awarded the "Julian Eltinge Trophy" to the couple who won its rooftop dance contest. Because his naturally lower voice didn't quite fit with delicate female impersonations, Billy Dalton decided that Julian Eltinge, rather than faking a soprano, would master a sonorous, velvety contralto.[10]

* * *

At the time, Lilla Viles Wyman's dance academy was located upstairs from one of Boston's respectable, if not exactly state-of-the-art, venues, the Tremont Theatre. Perched on the edge of Boston Common, the Tremont was typical of its time: part storefront, part office building, part auditorium for light opera, melodrama, and vaudeville. Designed by architects J. B. McElfatrick & Son, it had gone up in 1889 and would give Bostonians many reliable decades of plays, spectacles, and extravaganzas.[11]

It so happened that in the winter of 1899/1900 the Tremont Theatre hosted one of Boston's most celebrated events, one in which men of all ages put on skirts, hosiery, and makeup, and sang and danced without fear of social

50   BEAUTIFUL

rebuke. In fact, if anything, participating could win a man kudos and lively applause from cheering crowds. For it was here that an organization properly known as the First Corps of Cadets of the Massachusetts Volunteer Militia was doing what confraternal and paramilitary groups of the era had grown quite fond of: putting on lush drag shows allegedly for fundraising purposes. Fate, talent, and dedication now put Billy Dalton within striking distance of a way in, and *up*. That year, amid the blustery cold and bone-chilling winds coming off the Bay and sweeping across the Common, the First Corps of Cadets was rehearsing its big musical, *Miladi & The Musketeer*. It was their tenth such production, with book and lyrics by Robert A. Barnet and music by Harry Lawson Heartz. The show required the manpower of over a hundred Cadets to populate the chorus, play the leads, choreograph and costume the production, design and build the sets, get the publicity out, sell tickets and count receipts, and generally support one another's morale.[12] The Tremont Theatre was abuzz with creative energy.

As the Cadets were rehearsing one day, Billy Dalton wandered in and approached a member of the group's entertainment committee, likely Robert Barnet himself. The lad inquired whether they might find a place for him in the chorus. He was a decent singer, he said, downplaying his true abilities, particularly if nestled amid vocalists who could hit high and low notes beyond his range. The polite young man also allowed that he could dance "well enough to compensate for any shortcomings," again soft-selling his talent. Barnet looked the youngster over and liked what he saw: pleasant face and a "modest and gentlemanly bearing." He instructed Dalton to meet him later at the Cadets' headquarters, the vaunted Armory. Part clubhouse, part inner sanctum, part fortress, the Armory was an imposing building, at least from the outside. It suggested a castle with granite battlements, Romanesque arches, and a huge clock tower above an angled, stone façade. Despite having been built less than ten years earlier, the Armory was in constant need of repairs and upgrades, which provided endless, happy excuses for the Cadets to put on shows. "The Cadets' theatricals are now an institution," reported the *Boston Home Journal* in 1894, wishfully adding, "and will remain so indefinitely."[13]

Billy Dalton and Robert Barnet met behind the Armory's fortress-like façade in a room with a piano so the lad could audition properly. Here, the youth showed off not only his singing and dancing, but also threw in a taste of his woman-impersonating magic. Barnet, "veteran" of many Cadet seasons, was treated to "the poetry of motion such as he had never before seen in the grim and gloomy Armory." Although *Miladi & The Musketeer* was, technically speaking, fully cast, Barnet knew a good thing when he saw it. He assigned the teenager to the last row of the ballet corps. Maybe nobody would mind a late-joiner back there.[14]

Billy Dalton, eighteen tender years of age, had to tread carefully. He was not a pedigreed Bostonian. While many of those around him had gone to Harvard and summered in Saratoga Springs or on Nantucket, his dad was a barber and failed mining speculator. Not only were a lot of his fellow thespians "older by many years," they had also racked up prior tours of duty in Cadet theatricals. The veterans understandably longed for promotion to bigger, juicier roles. For Dalton, the key was to stand out without standing out, as much a skill for the acting-troupe newcomer as remembering your lines and blocking. During a break at his first rehearsal, Billy repaired to one side of the stage, just far enough from the mingling and meandering performers, but within sight of Robert Barnet. There, he began innocently "practicing his dance steps." Barnet again witnessed the newcomer's prowess. Maybe it was a frustrating day, when the veterans just weren't getting it—Barnet, after all, was reputed something of a martinet. Maybe the director wanted something fresh in his show. Whatever the causes, Barnet ordered Dalton up to the front lines of the ballet dancers. The next day, the kid was given an even better position in the fore of the chorus, since his voice was also clearly superior. By the end of the week, much to the astonishment, and no doubt envy, of over a hundred fellow players who had been rehearsing for the last six weeks, Billy Dalton, the boy from Butte or maybe Boston depending on how you looked at it, was given the supporting role of Mignonette, attendant to Richelieu. He not only got to show off his contralto voice and skill at comic patois, but was also featured in a "a skirt dance" with Arthur G. Briggs, formerly a supernumerary in the Cadets' 1894 hit production, *Tabasco*, but now given the meatier role of an "eccentric captain."[15]

Billy Dalton's political skills and amiable personality assuaged egos bruised by his rapid ascent. He was charming, sociable, and disciplined, dispelling "a great deal of ill feeling among the old stagers," including, presumably, the trouper he'd replaced as Mignonette. If the world was now imagining itself a meritocracy, this young man was evidence of its viability. It didn't hurt that the newcomer made *Miladi* an even better show, allowing the First Corps of Cadets of the Massachusetts Volunteer Militia to repair their beloved, castle-like clubhouse.[16]

* * *

Figure 2.2 Julian Eltinge got his start with the First Corps of Cadets of the Massachusetts Volunteer Militia, which was supposed to guard against anarchists but also devoted a lot of time and effort to producing original musicals in which men played women and girls. Robert A. Barnet was the creative mastermind behind the Cadets' theatricals, many of which, like *Tabasco* (1894), packed houses in Boston.
Credit: *Billy Rose Theatre Division, The New York Public Library for the Performing Arts.*

Like other First Corps of Cadets shows, *Miladi & The Musketeer* was a "burlesque," a term applied to many other productions of the era meaning different things in different settings. "Burlesque" had not yet come to mean sleazy leg-shows in grimy theatres as it would by, say, the 1920s and 1930s, though some of the seeds were present, including plenty of "rumbustious" double-entendres. Rather, *burlesque* referred to musical productions, often British in origin, that took classical or well-known source material—poems, fables, dramas—and turned them into glittery extravaganzas with ornate sets, long chorus lines, satirical songs, and abundant, often painful, punning and wordplay. The most famous burlesque performer of the age, the one who helped the art form migrate across the Atlantic, was Lydia Thompson, a gifted actress and dancer who got her start in UK productions like *Magic Toys* (1856) and *Cupid's Ladder* (1859). Burlesque also commonly employed women in male roles, though not to fool audiences as Julian Eltinge would later do or to consciously create a "third sex." Rather, in burlesques, women were usually *thinly* disguised as men, clad in tights and short skirts to show off their legs and arms. This brand of genderbending appealed to men who liked to cast an erotic gaze on the female form while simultaneously enjoying a dose of topnotch dancing and singing. Burlesques and melodramas were often cannibalized or pared down for presentation in other settings. Legendary vaudeville impresario Tony Pastor turned Lydia Thompson's title *Ixion, or the Man at the Wheel* (1868) into *Ixion on the Bowery* to give it a local flavor.[17]

About the same time that British burlesque was invading American shores, so too was a more decidedly sexualized, if no less extravagant, kind of entertainment. *The Black Crook*, which debuted in New York in 1866 almost by accident when two unlikely productions were forced to collaborate, was reckoned a "musical extravaganza, part melodrama, part ballet" by the *New York Clipper*, which also called it "an undress piece" due to its numerous "symmetrical legs and alabaster bosoms." *The Black Crook*, (very) loosely based on *Faust*, ran for a then-unheard-of 474 performances. Knockoffs and derivatives abounded. One strand of lineage became the "cooch" shows famously marketed to working-class men by the Minsky organization beginning in the 1910s. Florenz Ziegfeld, meanwhile, objectified the female body in more elegant wrapping—if scantily—for his popular, upscale *Follies*, beginning in 1907. By the end of the 1800s, consumers of American popular musical theatre were learning to expect sensual bodies onstage, usually female, but in the case of all-male shows, simulated. In fact, some of the

54   BEAUTIFUL

simulators were so good there seemed little need of cisgender women. Billy Dalton took careful note.[18]

* * *

Miladi & The Musketeer went up at the Tremont Theatre on February 5, 1900. The winter was a cold one. The day of the premiere, winds up to forty miles an hour punished the Hub city. Icy gusts "filled all the cracks and crevices and moved small articles from one point to another with wonderful velocity [and] flirted gayly with umbrellas." Schooners were dragged ashore and a coal barge was blown into a frozen mudbank.[19]

None of it, however, prevented the First Corps of Cadets and their rising star from taking the stage. As might be guessed from its title, *Miladi & The Musketeer* was a sendup of the 1844 novel *The Three Musketeers*, by Alexandre Dumas, *père* (father of *Camille* playwright, Alexandre Dumas, *fils*). The plot, commonplace in burlesque musicals, centered on a search for some long-lost person or item. Characters' names like "Ah-Those," "Pork-House," and "Arrah-Miss" were themselves *Mad*-magazine-like precursors. In *Miladi*, the Queen gives her love, Buckingham, a pawn ticket for the securement of twelve diamonds. When the diamonds go missing, Richelieu, D'Artagnan, and the rest, go off to Calais to find them, though the gems eventually wind up in the Paris Louvre. Burlesque audiences loved being taken on journeys far afield. Americans were getting used to glimpsing international news thanks to telegraphy, shopping for imported fashions thanks to steamships and railroads, and admiring "exotic" décor as the Occident trained a fascinated gaze on its sister, the Orient. *Miladi's* music was "light, tuneful, spirited," in the words of the *New York Dramatic Mirror*, which reviewed the show when a revised version titled *My Lady* landed on the professional stage in 1901. Barnet's original libretto contained some saucy humor, which was subsequently cut for general audiences, plus more than a few dumb one-liners and moments of awkward slapstick. But *Miladi & The Musketeer* was a hit for the Cadets, bringing in the cash needed to repair their Armory and praise for the men who put on skirts and danced and sang their blue-blooded hearts out.[20]

Even by the demanding standards of the age, a time when hundreds if not thousands of men's groups put on shows "*en travesty*," the First Corp of Cadets' commitment to impersonating women was impressive. Whether dancing *en pointe* or delivering an aria, the so-called Men of the Dancing

First took their avocation seriously, achieving an exceptional "lightness and airy grace." They were not professionals, but definitely more than amateurs. Despite the name "burlesque," they often conveyed verisimilitude rather than sheer parody. Ironically, it seemed, the more a man submerged himself in a female portrayal, rather than camping it up, the less he might be thought a "fairy" by onlookers. That was important for the Cadets' ablest newcomer.[21]

Cadet extravaganzas took well-known content and polished it to appear highbrow. The wordplay and often canonical or culturally admired source material was rendered even more valuable issuing from the mouths of many Harvard and Harvard-adjacent fellows in the cast. With increasing class separation in American cities, in part fueled by immigration and industrialization, the respectable had to stake out their turf. Culture was being sorted into high-, middle-, and lowbrow, so people knew where to go and where to be seen. As French sociologist Pierre Bourdieu would later put it, "Taste classifies, and it classifies the classifier." Things were in flux. It was confusing. Was a "museum" a place of oddball curios and second-rate vaudeville, or was it a temple for civilization's most prized artifacts? How could you stay in your lane when there were so many new and tantalizing spaces to explore? Esteemed actress Ethel Barrymore, scion of theatrical nobility, famous for appearing in prestige productions, declared her surprise at finding "you have to be awfully good" to succeed in vaudeville, as she discovered during a sojourn there in 1912. The First Corps of Cadets made the middle ground safe for the upper classes and their aspirational allies. Their confabulations involved all sorts of playful inversions and satire but somehow managed to land on the right side of respectability. After all, could a Harvard graduate beginning a career in law or banking risk having it otherwise?[22]

With the premiere of *Miladi & The Musketeer*, the secret of Billy Dalton and his remarkable female-impersonation skills was out of the bag. Many in Boston society saw the lad depict a "lovely and refined girl" as few others could. "Never for a moment was there the suggestion of burlesque in gesture or action," wrote one of his admirers, a "perfect impersonation of a beautiful, graceful, well bred, self-possessed and charmingly gowned young woman," just like a professional actress in a "legitimate production." As we have already seen, words had flexible, almost contradictory applications. Reviewers, twisting and upending verbiage in their breathless praise, described how Billy Dalton displayed "none of the color of burlesque" but rather, remained "real," "healthy," and "buxom . . . without swagger or smirk." His simulations

56   BEAUTIFUL

somehow brought a non-burlesque reality to the burlesque genre, a tasteful accomplishment indeed.[23]

* * *

Created in 1726 as a bodyguard unit for the royal governor of the Massachusetts Bay Colony, the First Corps of Cadets of the Massachusetts Volunteer Militia had become something of a finishing club for "young aristocrats" by the 1870s. They soon needed a fortress to protect against anarchist uprisings and, more usefully it would turn out, hold gatherings and produce musicals. "Cadet Theatricals" were thus inaugurated in 1884 to build, renovate, and fix their "preposterous little structure." Most of the early productions were minstrel shows with names like *Isaacs, Cohen, and Cuniffs Elephantine, Eleemosynary, Inaccessible, and Incapacitated Senegambian Serenaders*, until 1890 when they decided to produce a proper musical comedy, or what passed for one at the time. To the Cadets' great fortune, Robert Ayres Barnet, originally a New Yorker and eventually the man to discover Julian Eltinge, stepped in to take charge.[24]

Barnet was born in New York City in 1853 to an aged father who had migrated from England to the United States in 1833. His great-granddaughter and biographer, Alison Barnet, believes it's possible the family had Jewish ancestry, though there is no hard evidence. Robert Barnet's father, James Colby Barnet, eventually worked as a law journal editor and also as manager of William E. Burton's Chambers Street Theatre in lower Manhattan. When Robert's father died in 1862, an uncle named Robert Ayres "gained Mother's consent" for the boy to live with him and his wife up in Boston. It was not a happy situation for young Robert. "I never felt or knew hardly a mother's love or care," he later wrote. Like many a forlorn youth, Barnet discovered the theatre to be his true home. He eventually started managing a local minstrel troupe, while working in the sugar and molasses trade to pay the bills. Barnet was good at churning the risible wordplay minstrel audiences loved, such as, "Did Bacon write Shakespeare? I have spent much time and money on this question and find that Bacon did not write Shakespeare. Bacon did not write Shakespeare, he telegraphed him." A different gloss on William Shakespeare from what might be heard in the lecture halls of Cambridge and New Haven.[25] Barnet's first original musical for the Cadets, which he cowrote with composer Carl Pflueger, was *Injured Innocents*, a "merciless lampoon" of the sixteenth-century English folktale *Babes in the Woods*. The shows, in which

Harvard alums and successful businessmen portrayed "very gentlemanly ladies," soon become the stuff of legend. Between 1891 and 1902, Cadet musicals raised $186,055 from nine productions, permitting "erection of the Head-house," repair of "battlements," and other critical undertakings.[26]

During this era, while women sometimes appeared as entr'acte entertainers, none would appear in a Cadet musical proper. The organization embraced genderbending not only onstage but backstage and all around the clubhouse. The Cadets' talented "Premier Danseuse Assoluta," Malcolm D'Wolfe Greene, envisioned an interview he might have with a reporter visiting his dressing room: "Wish I were one of you ballet girls with nothing on," he'd say, "I've got a poker down my back, I reckon, at least it feels so," inviting the journalist to "see me disrobe" after the show, but only "if you won't publish all I say and do then."[27]

The Cadets had a huge hit with *1492*, which in 1892, capitalized on the 400th anniversary of Columbus's expedition and the World's Columbian Exposition in Chicago, formally dedicated in 1892 and officially opened in 1893, which celebrated the supposed "onward march of civilization." Loosely based on *The Black Crook*, *1492* featured Barnet himself as Queen Isabella, played like a "daisy" or a "pansy," according Barnet's biographer. By this time, flowery terms like "daisy," "pansy," and "buttercup" were in-group argot for younger gay men, aka "horticultural lads." (Alison Barnet believes Robert Barnet to have been attracted to women and "happily married" to his wife, Sarah Jessie Swasey, whom he wed in 1881.) Arthur Boylston Nichols, Harvard '91, played Infanta Joanna, "in love with Columbus." *1492* netted an impressive $20,005.[28]

The Boston Armory wasn't the only "homoaffectionate" locale where men retreated behind walls to dress up and dance. As early as the 1850s, "Song and Supper" clubs in London, such as the well-known Lambeth, gave military officers, athletes, university professors, and others a place to skirt-up and put on a show.[29] In a time of rapid industrialization and bureaucratization, clubs and clubhouses gave men a way to *belong*. In Nebraska, a fraternal order known as the Knights of Ak-Sar-Ben ("Nebraska," inverted) was so invested in its performances *en travesti* that members grew "jealous" of women replacing some of them in their 1912 extravaganza, *The Jolly Musketeers*. From Butte to Boston, men let it be known that they would play the ladies' parts in shows: no girls allowed.[30]

In Boston, the First Corps of Cadets faced competition from only one other organization, the enthusiastic, talented Bank Officers' Association. In

58   BEAUTIFUL

truth, the Bank Officers, who loved to "strut and fret upon the stage in tights and frilly skirts," shared many a cast member with the Cadets and hired Lilla Viles Wyman as a dance coach. Moreover, they sometimes relied on Robert Barnet to write and direct. Burlesque operettas such as *Pinafore on the Half Shell* (1897) and *Coreopsis* (1898) made them Hub city favorites. Eminent Boston scions Richard Sanborn and John F. Tufts appeared in the "Girls' chorus" of *Coreopsis*, which starred an otherwise mustachioed W. F. Beale in a title role denoting a "flower that grows in Egypt and elsewhere."[31]

* * *

Barnet wrote the Bank Officers' 1901 show, *Miss Simplicity*, with "Billy Eltinge," as the youthful Billy Dalton presently decided to call himself, specifically in mind. Eltinge played Claire de Loinville, clad in "one breathtaking costume after another" and "intoxicatingly beautiful" in each. His contralto was so "velvety" and his demeanor so "delusively feminine" that a few folks in the audience found Eltinge's performance "unsettling." With the Bankers, the young impersonation artist took careful note of how modeling one sumptuous outfit after another appealed to a large section of the audience, like a fashion show stuffed into a play. Department store mannequins might have been the latest thing, but none was as lifelike as Billy Eltinge. This would also be his first paying gig; the Bankers gave him $2.50 a week. Not a bad start.[32]

Claire de Loinville, Eltinge's part in *Miss Simplicity*, was a "soubrette" role, a common character type in comedies of the day. Soubrettes were usually clever, resourceful, and charismatic. They could be rebellious young women who refused to do what was expected of them. Sometimes, the soubrette was a wily servant critical of the romantic leads' bewildering love-blindness and determined to do something about it. In *Miss Simplicity*, noble-blooded Claire rejects marriage and flees to the French countryside where she encounters her former suitor, now in disguise, who just happens to be traveling to the same village. Eltinge was able to "sink his individuality" into his role, aided by a costume budget that put a sumptuous gown of turquoise-blue velvet and other modiste creations on his person. The more he sank into the women he played onstage, the more Eltinge reinforced his inherently manly nature off of it, a strenuous rendition of the "separate spheres" ideology, which dictated that men and women could never engage as true equals in the same activities. He took as careful note of how to play a man as he did a woman. He was no less successful in this new endeavor. Soon, observers described him as a "manly, whole-souled young fellow" with "an aptitude for business" when not in skirts. Emerging from the stage door in suit and tie, Billy Eltinge might ask "pointed questions about stocks." He was repeatedly said to look like a stockbroker or a lawyer, admirable jobs for men in this new economic climate, not unlike Horatio Alger's Ragged Dick who finally "felt himself a capitalist" after triumphantly opening his first bank account. Wall Street was becoming American manhood's new frontier.[33]

Miss Simplicity proved a hit thanks to Billy Eltinge's performance, plus some helpful script edits like the removal of an anarchist character after an alleged real-life anarchist, disgruntled steelworker Leon Czolgosz, assassinated President William McKinley. This brave new world of opportunity was also marked with danger. Would genteel values win out, or would the anarchists and agitators have their way? "Politeness, let me tell you is a very gentle art / It softens all asperities and heals the wounded heart," sang our protagonist soothingly in *Miss Simplicity*.[34]

* * *

With *Miss Simplicity*, Julian Eltinge became the popular pet of Boston society, welcomed into its topmost reaches. Some months earlier, he had performed at an elegant children's carnival, demonstrating "high kicking," an important dance metric of the day made famous by Mlle. Proto (who would later take over the Eltinge-originated role in *My Lady*). The carnival guests requested half a dozen encores, one of them insisting, "But it isn't possible that this is a young man."[35] Another fraternity for grown-up men, the Megatherians of Malden, Massachusetts, tapped the impersonator to star in *The Omero*, a "mythological burletta," opposite Bank Officers veteran F. W. Bailey. The increasing work opportunities from Boston's "swell circle" put Eltinge perilously close to becoming a full-time, professional female impersonator, about which he had mixed feelings. He had aspirations to do more than play women, good as he was at it. Talking about banking was highly preferable to working in it. But if he kept showing up in dresses, never singing or acting as a man, some people might suspect he enjoyed it. The performer redoubled the story that, yes, he was talented at playing the opposite sex. But it was simply the result of circumstance, an unplanned but lucrative opportunity that he'd have been foolish not to take. The story he concocted was that he got that part of the lead in the Megatherians' *Omero* because the fellow who was supposed to play the part backed out at the last moment.[36]

60   BEAUTIFUL

He couldn't offer up the same excuse when, come Christmastime, the Megatherians of Malden hired "J. D. Eltinge" to skirt-up in a pantomime "enchantment" called *Fairyland* and then, later, star in their own production of *Coreopsis* in 1901.[37] The young actor was soon playing galas, fêtes, and private theatricals, singing and dancing in dresses and delighting scores of Bostonians. He accompanied Miss Florence Linnell, daughter of a prominent Somerville family, in her piano recital, and starred in vaudeville-style sketches such as in *Mamselle of the Varieties* and *Serious Situations in Burleigh's Room* at private shows for invited audiences. Eltinge even impersonated a prima ballerina and somehow managed a "fore-and-aft" split, though he ultimately found it impossible to repeat the move in future shows.[38] The "belles of Back Bay" asked J. D./Billy/Julian Eltinge to star in their "Society Circus" in January 1902. Mrs. Stuyvesant Fish, once Harry Lehr's patron, asked the impersonator to help her introduce a new strain of violets she'd bred in her hothouse, about as big a deal as there was for a Back Bay belle at the time. In May 1902, he was even invited as a proper guest in civilian togs to the elite Commonwealth Club to meet and socialize with important folks "fresh from their victories at the whist table." This was a one-off. Otherwise, it was the ballgown or velvet dress and not the tuxedo that gained Julian Dalton Eltinge entry to high society. It might have been a deal with the devil, but when the devil wore silken gloves and offered you a glass of champagne—and a paycheck—almost as though you were one of them, it was hard to say no. His father's goldmine had proven a bust. There was no way to turn down this motherlode.[39]

* * *

With his brand in the ascendant, Billy Dalton realized it was time to settle on a stage name. From here on, and for the rest of his professional life, Billy Dalton would be *Julian Eltinge*, even if he sometimes asked intimates to call him "Bill" or wished others to think of him as "Bill Dalton," a normal-sounding guy. For all intents and purposes, though, Billy Dalton was gone and Julian Eltinge was here to stay. A reporter wondered if the moniker might tempt "saucy" detractors to drop the "n" and call him "Julia." Eltinge said it had never occurred to him.[40] He did insist, though, that "Eltinge" ended in a hard "g," rhyming with "swing" rather than "twinge," or "belting and not fringe." It's "Elting" not "Eltinj," he would tell the *Boston Globe* in 1911. The hard "g" chimed like a bell or a wine glass tapped by a silver butter knife.

It hinted of nobility and storybook tales. Plus, his reputed childhood friend of the same name had often been taunted as "Eltingy" and "Eltinjy," making the soft "g" sound seem somehow weak or puny. Many continued to mispronounce his name, and over time it seems the actor let people use the soft "g" or "j" version, sometimes even caving in and saying it himself.[41] But that would be later. The more his future blossomed, the more he edited his past. When silent legend Mary Pickford asked him where he got the name "Julian Eltinge" from, the actor said he'd borrowed it from a "college chum," hoping Pickford (née Gladys Mary Smith) wouldn't find out he'd never gone to college or, more accurately, happily collude in the story as a fellow thespian.[42]

Around the same time he finalized his *nom de guerre*, Julian Eltinge also became a Harvard graduate. There was no better place to say he'd studied, even if it were eminently deniable by any number of castmates and audiences around town. Still, if all those less-talented fellows had attended Cambridge or New Haven, why couldn't he? They had had to do so much less—little more than be born into the right family, it seemed—to enter the world's upper echelon and enjoy all that came with it. Harvard men were still quite free to play women's parts in their dramatic societies in college and even well after commencement. A cranky journalist writing in 1898 found female impersonation an "abominable and disgusting practice" in general but applauded the "scholarly effort" of the fellow portraying Jocasta in a Harvard production of *Oedipus Rex*. Like the Cadets' ersatz battlements, Ivy walls could sanitize or occlude what happened within. The female impersonators of the University of Pennsylvania's legendary Mask & Wig troupe were reckoned "just a lot of rollicking lads" having fun, and nothing more.[43] As he watched the Harvard Glee Club belt out "Johnny Harvard" and the "Champagne Song" at Jordan Hall in 1904, while bluebloods with their own weighty surnames—Livermore, Mayo, Rockwell—applauded, Julian Eltinge knew he had the right idea. He'd keep mentioning to anyone who asked, and even many who didn't, that he'd gone to Harvard. After all, wasn't that what actual Harvard grads did?[44]

In the nether region between part-time, semi-amateur and full-time, professional entertainer, Eltinge began working with manager J. C. Trowbridge, who helped his young charge take the Harvard thing to the next level. The impersonation artist said he had "coached dancing" at the famed nearby university for several years. But he was soon just calling himself "a Harvard man," or at least, not bothering to correct anyone who assumed he was. He would presently sign his name "Julian Dalton Eltinge, Harvard 1902," an

62   BEAUTIFUL

architecture major. Sometimes Eltinge waxed nostalgic about his nonexistent days with Harvard's Hasty Pudding Club, famed for its crossdressed theatricals. The press loved it, printing headlines like, "Womanly Photographs of a Manly, Athletic Harvard Grad, Who, When He Dons Skirts, Fools Even His Own Manager."[45]

Being a Harvard alum elevated Julian Eltinge from passable guy to downright-admirable specimen of manhood. The 1893 World's Columbian Exposition, which put aboriginal and indigenous peoples on display to reinforce fantasies of racial order, also featured statues of a Harvard and a Radcliffe student, respectively, to represent humanity's "ideal types." Harvard was elite, but elite was not yet equal to *effete*, particularly when the individual in question was an athletic young man. When the Harvard Club of St. Louis put on the musical comedy *The Perpetual Student* in 1913, starring William C. Stribling as Priscilla, the theatre was mobbed; "everybody who was anybody" showed up. "It is difficult to conceive of anything prettier or daintier" than Stribling's Priscilla, wrote a society columnist.[46] If you learned dragging-up at Harvard and continued it with your former college chums, it was more than okay.

It would have been easy enough to check Julian Eltinge's claims of having been a Harvard student or a member of Hasty Pudding. At the time, much journalism, particularly society and theatrical reporting, however, was not thought to be concretely fact-based as is supposedly the case in our era (at least until recently). Journalists were often more like diarists, allowed and even encouraged to be subjective their reporting, practically characters themselves in the narratives they composed. Later, in the 1920s, movie-star scandals would drive reporters to ferret out the alleged truth-beneath-the-mask. So Eltinge could pass as a Harvard grad in part because those around him wanted him to. Newsmen and -women were "overly helpful" in co-creating Eltinge's myth. They loved telling readers that Boston's, soon the country's, favorite female impersonator was a manly, erstwhile Ivy League boxer and footballer. It would soon become common lore, however untrue, that professional female impersonators had nearly all started out in college, baptizing the art form in the supposedly innocent waters of campus tomfoolery. Plus, having gone to an elite university made it easier for actual elites to feel comfortable inviting the young man into their circles. Agnes Booth Schoeffel, ex-wife of legendary stage actor Junius Brutus Booth, was happy to invite Julian Eltinge to a sanitarium fundraiser in wealthy Sharon, Massachusetts, to appear with the likes of Ethel Barrymore and John

Drew. Would she have been as comfortable inviting an unlettered barber's son named Billy Dalton?[47] The stakes were high for all parties concerned, higher than for a crowd at a dime museum or curio exhibit. No comprehensive listing of Harvard alumni or history of Hasty Pudding bears the name Julian Eltinge or William Dalton (though there was a "Byron Elting," class of 1932, in Hasty Pudding). Finally, an email inquiry to the university's official archives in October 2021 resulted in the following reply: "Alas, we could not find a listing for Willian Dalton or Julian Eltinge in the Harvard Alumni Directories." Perhaps if they had instead read the newspapers 120 years ago.[48]

* * *

Organizations like the Megatherians and the Knights of Ak-Sar-Ben gave men a place to *belong*. Skirting-up in musicals and sketches was a *central part* of that belonging. In Boston, the Cadets, Bank Officers, and the Tavern Club gave Hasty Pudding alums and others an opportunity to keep playing women.[49] College had ended but college life could live on. Plus, with more and more women entering higher education and the workforce, men desperately needed places to be among their own kind. If women insisted on playing themselves in the real world, it was all the more important that men play them in specialized settings. In 1900, women made up less than 20 percent of the United States' 5.1 million white-collar workers. By 1920, they comprised almost a third. Also telling, the ratio of women working in "domestic and personal service" compared to those in professional jobs dropped by half from 1900 to 1920: women were no longer just maids or housekeepers, but clerks, salespeople, and skilled laborers. In 1870, women made up a fifth of all college students; by 1920, they were nearly half.[50]

Clubs like Hasty Pudding, originally founded as a drinking and debating society in 1795 but which turned to all-male stage productions beginning in 1844—with notable ferocity, it should be said—popped up at many other schools. In time, the University of Wisconsin's Haresfoot Club, the University of Michigan's Union Opera (aka the "Michigan Mimes"), Princeton's Triangle, and the University of Chicago's Blackfriars were creating and producing original musicals employing highly illusionistic female impressionism. Over the years, these troupes and others would incubate the careers of Jimmy Stewart, Oscar Hammerstein II, Cole Porter, and Stephen Sondheim. By the 1920s, there were enough college musical clubs to form the College Musical Comedy League. Their all-male musicals were often

64 BEAUTIFUL

about life on campus or in that other realm of compelling make-believe, Broadway.[51] Conventional fraternities also boomed during the period. In 1900, amid what one contemporary dubbed "the golden age of fraternity," there were some 150,000 Greeks on campuses around the nation. At the same time, five million adult men belonged to secret societies and confraternities like the Knights of Pythias. Onboard a train, the youthful narrator of Willa Cather's 1918 novel *My Ántonia* observes the conductor's many "rings and pins and badges of different fraternal orders to which he belonged."[52]

Teddy Roosevelt himself, later apoplectic about the alleged "tide of feminization" scuttling American manhood, had once helped run Hasty Pudding. Deciding one drag group wasn't enough at Harvard, the rival Pi Eta dramatic society moved toward increasingly naturalistic female impersonation. Clubs like these often used the flimsy claim that, because they were at single-sex schools, they had no choice but to perfect their drag. The excuse fooled few. Gender illusionism and drag-play were compelling arts in their own right. As early as 1851, Hasty Pudding trouper Stanford Chaillé demanded the club risk near-bankruptcy by renting a pricey, historic gown from the Boston Museum or he'd refuse to play the female lead. During the Eltinge era, Pi Eta star Mal Dill would show off "the prettiest pair of eyes" to be seen anywhere.[53]

Naturally, there was reactionary pushback, those who believed that too much make-believe could trigger the real thing, turning otherwise healthy men "effeminate." Dean Frederick S. Jones of Yale and others feared "the effeminizing influence of women's roles upon college men" and tried to limit the practice, though with little lasting effect. For now and for the foreseeable future, female-impersonating was a growth industry. Academics were often among the most suspicious, fancying themselves experts looking out for disease immanent within the greater corpus. George Herbert Mead, for example, argued that it was crucial to identify "the criminal and defective classes" within the "social body," in an influential 1899 essay in the *American Journal of Sociology* (though to be fair, Mead wondered if their defectiveness might be a symptom of their lowly cultural and economic status in society). Many had feared that the drag tradition at elite British universities would tear the nation's social fabric asunder, which alas it did not. Undergrads in the UK were actually granted "a large meed of license" like their stateside brethren.[54] In France in 1883, administrators at the venerable *École polytechnique* shut down the popular "Point Gamma" festival in which men had played ballerinas, wet nurses, and other female types since the 1860s. But Point Gamma was later revived and lives on today. Columbia

University banned drag in 1894, a decision so unpopular the administration had to rescind it two years later. University of Michigan faculty strenuously protested the Mimes' 1913 show, *Contrarie Mary*, for its gender "deceiving." The production was briefly halted until the 1,500-strong Chicago chapter of the school's alumni association protested harder yet, citing *Mary* as the best

Figure 2.3 Organized athletics were an emergent signifier of manhood in the early 1900s, though women were increasingly asking for a chance to compete as well. Soon, crossdressing in college musicals would become practically a varsity sport in its own right.
Credit: *Laurence Senelick Collection.*

66   BEAUTIFUL

Michigan Mimes show so far and helping it secure a run at a professional the-atre. The best Yale could do was to limit students to a one-year tenure in these specific, highly distinctive all-male musical troupes—Harvard followed suit in 1917—while the University of Pennsylvania's provost insisted that the university's "best girls" were "just as much men as ever" once they stepped out of their hoop skirts and petticoats. From the standpoint of professors, scientists, and psychologists, the newly sanctioned experts on matters of sex-uality, transvestism was a potential scourge. From the view of participants and fans, though, it was something quite happily else.[55]

So popular were all-male college musicals and so committed were its practitioners that some began likening them to a proper sport. Drag shows were dubbed "varsity" events, like football games or track meets, often held to raise money for new athletic facilities, such as with the Indiana Hoosiers' 1909 "Julian Eltinge Show." "To select a crew of oarsmen is easy," wrote the *Buffalo Inquirer* in 1911, "and the applicants for places on a football team are numerous. But where is the man who, proud of his muscles and manly brow, is still willing or anxious to be arrayed in the despised garments of fem-inine creatures?" Actually, that "man" could be found on many a campus. That women were also denied the chance to play sports in college—a gym instructor at single-sex Vassar had tried to organize a baseball team until the administration shut it down—only reinforced the manliness of all-male musicals. Blurring the line between college sports and drag productions fur-ther lubricated Julian Eltinge's loose, confidant banter about his days as an oarsmen, wrestler, and gridiron star. Dartmouth's Halsey Mills, after all, was reckoned a "college hero" equally for his drag-show skills as for his quarter-backing, the implication being that the two endeavors had much in common. (All-male Dartmouth's serious attention to transvestic dramatics had been pioneered by Walter Wanger, class of 1915, who would go on to produce numerous classic Hollywood movies such as *Stagecoach* [1939, dir. John Ford, 1939] and *Cleopatra* [1963, dir. Joseph L. Mankiewicz].) Officials at Brown University in Rhode Island tried to assuage anxieties by arguing that when men spent time with other men, it led all parties to become manlier yet, even if they were busy impersonating women.[56]

* * *

Though he publicly still denied wanting anything beyond a high-profile, amateur career, it seemed inevitable that Julian Eltinge would have to wade further into professional waters, especially if he also wanted to make real money. The year 1903 would see the actor's biggest—and final—triumph on the quasi-amateur stage. Robert Barnet wrote *Baron Humbug* for the Boston Bank Officers, once again with Julian Eltinge specifically in mind. The impersonator would star as Countess Sylvia opposite Henry D. Gardner as Princess Natali Dazikoff, Charles Dasey as Lurline Crabbe, and other "financier-actors" in gowns. Other men filled out the chorus of "Roumanian Gypsies" and "Magyar Girls" in settings ranging from the "Munkacs castle on the Danube" to Chicago and Yokohama.[57]

Baron Humbug had plenty of topical jokes, soon to be a central feature of Florenz Ziegfeld's *Follies*. "Pretty Phrosia of the Sparkling Spa," a song in *Baron Humbug*, for instance, referred to the new trend of men flirting with lunch-counter waitresses as the guys ordered soft drinks from a soda fountain. Even the name "Phrosia" was the same as that of a popular female detective character played by iconoclastic rising star Eva Tanguay in the hit musical *The Chaperones*. (Tanguay had also appeared in *Miladi & The Musketeer* when it migrated from the Cadets to the professional stage as *My Lady*.) Social life seemed to have a new, transactional nature to it. You might flirt with a waitress but you still had to pay the bill and leave a tip. Going to work meant "making profits" rather than "making goods." It was all so dizzying and new, exciting and overwhelming.[58]

Baron Humbug was definitely not Robert Barnet's best work. But it might have been Julian Eltinge's. One paper called Eltinge "a revelation," the "bright particular star" of the show. His Countess Sylvia betrayed "not . . . a single false movement" or misstep. "One almost wondered if the bank officers had not secured a remarkably attractive woman to the play the role," wrote an attendee. In a sense, they had. With *Baron Humbug*, the press began its long-time routine of not merely praising Julian Eltinge but simultaneously criticizing womankind for falling short of the artist's portrayals. One theatrical reviewer concluded that there were "few actresses behind the footlights that combine as much that is attractive" into one package as Julian Eltinge in *Baron Humbug*. The counterfeiter of females was too good to stay local, part-time, and semipro. He needed to head squarely to the next level. "I have often stray'd in a garden fair, Idly passing the hour away, With a 'good day' here and a 'good bye' there, All among the flowers gay," sang Eltinge's Countess Sylvia. Soon, there would be little idleness in Julian Eltinge's life.[59]

# # #

3

Mr. Wix of . . . Vaudeville

Edward E. Rice was a New York–based producer who had long been in the habit of swinging up to Boston to see if any of those original musicals, the ones where men played women, might be developed for Broadway. Others sometimes ventured to the Hub city to see what the Cadets, Banker Officers, and others were up to. But Rice was the most persistent, a true believer that these local extravaganzas held untapped value. He further understood that, for general audiences in New York and around the country, it would mean making changes in the script, the songs, and most significantly, recasting women in women's parts—some of them, anyway. He knew how to balance the popularity of male drag with the crowd's expectation, honed by shows like *The Black Crook* and its offshoots, for chorus lines of attractive, cisgender females.

Early in his career, Rice had taken a lumbering musical based on Longfellow's *Evangeline*, lightened up its dialogue, cast a plus-sized George Fortescue in drag, and created scenes in Africa, Arizona, and other distant realms. The resulting *Evangeline*, which debuted in 1874, has sometimes been called the first "musical comedy" as we know it. The show enjoyed a long run at Niblo's Garden in New York and toured in various forms for over thirty years. When he decided to adapt the Cadets' 1892 extravaganza, *1492*, for broader audiences, Rice approached it the same way. He gave some of the female roles to women, though the lead, Isabella, went to popular female impersonator Richard Harlow. A reworked *1492* toured successfully before landing at New York's Madison Square Garden for an impressive 411 performances. He would also adapt the Cadets' *Cinderella & the Prince* (1904) into a children's show, featuring an older, plumper George Fortescue in drag. Rice eventually urged Robert Barnet, king of Boston's transvestic extravaganzas, to go completely professional and mounted a New York State tour of Barnet's *Show Girl*. Unfortunately, it wasn't a hit, despite compositions from a young songwriter named Irving Berlin. When the Boston musical scene faded, so did Robert Barnet's composing career. Some of Barnet's alumni, though, would fare considerably better.[1]

Beautiful. Andrew L. Erdman, Oxford University Press. © Oxford University Press 2024.
DOI: 10.1093/9780197696361.003.0004

In 1904, Rice convinced a talented actor from Barnet's shows, a lad who had recently started calling himself Julian Eltinge, to appear in a new play he was producing in New York that would also make a regional tour. If it were a big enough hit, it could end up back on Broadway or maybe even London for extended runs. The show was a new comedy from England titled *Mr. Wix of Wickham*. The young actor agreed. He needed to break out of being Boston society's best-kept secret. It was time to swim with the big fish.[2]

Mr. Wix of Wickham, starring comedian Harry Corson Clarke as the titular Mr. Wix, previewed in New Haven and opened at New York's Bijou on September 19, 1904. The plot involved a young heiress, played by Thelma Fair, who, unhappy with her arranged marriage to a cousin, flees to Australia. There, she finds work in a store that sells men's fashion accessories. A number of intrigues, mix-ups, and subplots involving the military fighting "a native chieftain," a forged letter, and sundry mistaken identities completed what passed for a storyline, along with two dozen songs. Naturally, the heiress ends up happily married to Wix. Though some speculated that Eltinge might appear "disguised as a man or a woman," and the actor himself no doubt wished he'd been considered for a non-drag part, it was obvious that hiring him meant exploiting his singular talent. Advance publicity, in fact, noted that Eltinge regularly visited Paris to bring back the latest styles for his audiences, which was not exactly true, though it planted the seeds for a key part of his brand appeal: knowing what women should—and shouldn't—wear.[3]

Mr. Wix of Wickham had a rocky go of it from the start. When the show played Hartford, the *Courant* found its music "catchy in spots, very frothy all the time" but the plot thin even by the threadbare standards of the genre. Eltinge showed up *en travesti*, but only after a deluge of female bodies in skimpy, sparkly outfits, and at least one thespian garbed as a kangaroo, alit and disappeared. For some critics, all they could see were so many "pretty girls" showing off their bodies. There seemed to be a hint of desperation, of appealing to the crowd's lowest instincts. A local editorialist who saw the show remarked that "even a chorus girl is entitled to at least a modicum of clothes." At the game for many years, E. E. Rice may have been losing his touch, leaning too heavily on skin and gown rather than other aspects of the drama, like plot and music. For his part, Julian Eltinge got a hundred dollars a week, a forty-fold raise over the Cadets and Bankers.[4]

Perhaps realizing he had a dud on his hands but determined to press on, Rice can hardly be blamed for leaning even more heavily on what had become a pillar of American popular culture, bigger even than its place in plays

Figure 3.1 Julian Eltinge's first professional production, a comedy initially titled *Mr. Wix of Wickham*, produced in 1904, was a resounding failure that stalled the young performer's career. He was cited as one of the show's few bright spots, though, facilitating a successful move to big-time vaudeville.

Credit: *Photo by White Studio, © The New York Public Library for the Performing Arts.*

and musicals: the chorus girl. Since the days of *The Black Crook*, theatrical producers increasingly found it essential somehow to include an abundance of apparently cisgendered female bodies onstage. High-kicking or gyrating in unison, the chorines functioned en masse rather than as an assemblage of individuals. By the time of *Mr. Wix of Wickham*, "it was the chorus girl who fascinated the American public . . . more than any other figure on the American stage," writes historian Lois Banner. After gazing upon choristers, many a stage-door Johnnie, from businessman to college boy, eagerly sought their affections, often plying them with flowers and asking them to dinner. For many fellows, landing a chorus girl was the ultimate trophy.[5] The 1900 musical *Florodora* featured six actresses swooshing about the stage as suitors inquired, "Tell me, pretty maiden, are there any more at home like you?" Like *Mr. Wix of Wickham*, *Florodora*'s script was no great literary achievement. But a claque of enthusiastic Yale boys rushed down to New York to boost the show and its fabled six. (Ivy Leaguers, Yalies in particular, had a long history of inserting themselves into actresses' and showgirls' careers, often championing those they found most desirable. Because many productions previewed in New Haven, Yale undergrads thus played an outsize role in their success or failure.) Flooded with gifts, jewelry, mash notes, and dinner invites, all six *Florodora* women eventually married millionaires, a narrative reinforcing the link between feminine beauty and upward mobility. In 1908, the men of an Elks Chapter in Minnesota impersonated the *Florodora* six with impressive fidelity and elegance.[6]

* * *

Alas, the chorus girls in their scanty attire couldn't save *Mr. Wix*. Wrote the *New York Globe*:

> After three hours of agony fearful to behold, Mr. Wix of Wickham died last night at the Bijou theater in the presence of assembled friends and relatives, many of whom had anticipated the funeral and brought flowers. A number of specialists attended the deceased in his last moments, but their efforts were unvailing [*sic*] in preventing the inevitable denouement. Rigor mortis set in at 11:15, with the fall of the curtain in the second act. The corpse will in all probability be removed next Saturday. The cause of death was a complication of malignant diseases, chief among which were anemia and acute insanity. The patient became violent with the rise of the curtain at

72 BEAUTIFUL

8:15, and save for a brief respite between the first and second acts[,] was delirious until the end. The death of Mr. Wix was so painful that the majority of the bereaved left the theater, unable to endure its sight, yet so hardened and unfeeling were the ushers that they strove with one another in giving evidences of enjoyment and glee at the spectacle.[7]

Mr. Wix of Wickham somehow maundered on for forty-one performances. But E. E. Rice was not yet ready to cremate the body. Reworking it yet again, the show was now called *Jolly Mr. Wix of Wickham and the Merry Shopgirls,* underscoring the presence of the chorus. Rice even took out ads quoting awkwardly manufactured compliments from generic-sounding, in all likelihood nonexistent publications: "An agreeable surprise to even the most surfeited appetites," declared the "*Record,*" while the "*Press*" raved about the "large chorus of pretty and effectively costumed girls who sang effectively and danced attractively." All the while, Julian Eltinge noted the potential appeal of building a chorus line out of good-looking retail-counter maids. "If I could go through your large department stores here and make my choice, I could recruit a beautiful chorus from the girls behind the counters in a few minutes," he would later tell a Boston newspaper. In an environment that constantly stoked desire and grabbing-at what one wanted, female sexuality became part of the retail economy in a way it never quite had before. Some gazed at shopgirls like expensive furs or watches in a store window, while others beheld them onstage thanks to the entertainment industry. A fortunate few who chased hard enough and spent sufficient money might land a date or even a wife. When the titular Sister Carrie in Theodore Dreiser's classic novel from 1900 trades up from "little shop girl" to actress, she realizes several men are now obsessed with her. Because of her beauty, sexuality, and, most important, public visibility, she has power. "She was realizing now what it was to be petted. For once she was the admired, the sought-for." Of course, she is valuable only as a suitor's object, her "independence" really a temporary state of affairs as she is fought over and bartered for.[8]

The show's producers injected "new and catchy" songs to give *Jolly Mr. Wix of Wickham and the Merry Shopgirls* a new lease on life, though Rice must have been aware that any odds of success were long and getting longer. A bit like contemporary movie producers who hope that shoveling in more popular comic book heroes will blind audiences to what's missing in the plot, Rice bet on the rebooted show's appealing to theatergoers who were learning to love browsing and buying. Maybe crowds would see *Jolly*

Mr. Wix of Wickham and the Merry Shopgirls as a sort of elaborate window-shopping expedition. If anything, in recent years the overlap between theatre and retailing had only increased. Both were supposed to make you feel energized and special. The playwright and author of *The Wonderful Wizard of Oz*, Frank Baum, founded the National Association of Window Trimmers in 1898 to help bring the magic of stagecraft to department stores. Joseph Urban, the well-known architect who helped design Gimbel's department store and the famed Reisenweber's restaurant, would design for the *Ziegfeld Follies* in the mid-1910s. Even the owners of Hennessy's, a fancy retail store back in Butte, wished to make their establishment feel like a stage on which shoppers were the star, with huge, "French" plate-glass windows, bronze balustrades, and a "Moorish Room" where weary shoppers could relax amid teakwood furnishings and decorative battleaxes. Correspondingly, theatre entrepreneurs were building nationwide chains along the retail model, often putting vaudeville venues and music halls in or near upscale shopping districts.[9]

If Rice's ploy to make his show look like a department store with music failed to salvage *Mr. Wix*, it nonetheless helped Julian Eltinge. Crowds and the papers loved his display of stylish, sumptuous outfits, even as the rest of the show continued to leave them cold. One reviewer lauded the actor for exhibiting "marvelous confections of the dressmakers' art" and giving women ideas for classy outfits. In due time, that would mean taking steamer taking steamer trunks packed with thousands of dollars' worth of gowns, dresses, and outfits with him wherever he toured.[10]

Unsurprisingly, the reboot of *Jolly Mr. Wix of Wickham and the Merry Shopgirls* faltered almost immediately. There were empty seats at many performances and the songs inspired few to sing along, despite new tunes by a then-unknown "score doctor" named Jerome Kern. And the script: "devoid of plot and action." Alas, there was just so much a lot of attractive chorus girls and retail trimmings could do. Still, J. D. Eltinge stood out. In his bounteous skirts and wide-brimmed sunhat, the young impersonator made up the only "bright spot" in the show, according to one who suffered through it. In effect, *Jolly Mr. Wix* needed the young actor more than he needed it. When the production wound down its tour in the wintry, early months of 1905, however, Eltinge found himself in a tight spot. He'd acquitted himself admirably, it was true, but in a show that carried the stench of failure. He couldn't quite make the leap to Broadway as he hoped, much less shake the label of female-impersonation specialist. Going back to Boston's silver-spoon circuit was

74 BEAUTIFUL

out of the question. *Jolly Mr. Wix of Wickham and the Merry Shopgirls* closed with Edward E. Rice owing the impersonation artist seventy-seven dollars, a debt Rice would take with him to his grave in 1924.[11]

Even if he'd wanted to go back to First Corps of Cadets of the Massachusetts Volunteer Militia and ask for his old job, it would have been impossible. As if nudging the former Billy Dalton toward his inevitable future, the Cadets would stage their last extravaganza, *Miss Po-Ko-Hon-Tas*, in early 1906. Renovations were nearly done at the Armory, though it still carried a hefty, $145,000 mortgage. Without its spectacular musicals, the Cadets would have to appeal to the community for funds to keep their headquarters up "as a museum." Robert Barnet and his Cadet theatricals would eventually be remembered as much for having launched Julian Eltinge's career as for their own beloved productions in which thousands of men advanced the art of female impersonation, to their fans' delight and their own, over seventeen extraordinary seasons.[12]

* * *

There is of course no single, simple reason why men have dressed as women onstage over the centuries. Settings, historical factors, and social values all change, influencing the art of female-impersonating this way and that. Theories that, for example, drag acts as a "safety valve," allowing men to engage in otherwise socially unacceptable impulses, are pat and "simply too neat" in the wise words of one scholar. What motivates men to dress as women, onstage and off—and reaction against it—in one place and time is different from what does so in another.[13] The sumptuary laws of Elizabethan days, for example, were meant not only to ensure that men dressed like men on the streets but also to discourage what we might call conspicuous consumption, meaning that only the rich ought to be allowed to dress like the rich. By Julian Eltinge's day, however, people were eagerly encouraged to buy to their heart's content and make a public identity of it. What you bought, wore, and drove was a form of "freedom" or "self-expression," of taste and status in a supposedly nobility-free society. A 1915 newspaper ad for Cadillac compared the car brand to Wagner and Whistler, the "Master-poet" and "master-painter," respectively. To acquire and display was to be happy in America, as sociologist Max Weber famously observed in his 1902 opus *The Protestant Ethic and the Spirit of Capitalism*.[14]

As far as the theatre goes, the plays of ancient Greece famously used men in all women's roles. This was so in part because the plays were not meant for entertainment but rather as part of larger civic festivals that celebrated the harvest, social unity, and the viability of the city-state. Thus, those who acted in the dramas with which we are familiar, mostly from Athens' "Golden Age" beginning in the 490s BCE and lasting about a century, were executing a public, even quasi-governmental, task, which meant women were perforce "totally excluded."[15]

Cisgender men played such famous female characters as Clytemnestra in Aeschylus' *Oresteia* cycle (458 BCE); Jocasta in Sophocles' *Oedipus Rex* (ca. 430 BCE); and all the titular Trojan Women in Euripides' work of the same name (415 BCE). To play women, actors wore large masks, high-waisted gowns, and ornamental jewelry, and they used conventionalized gestures that symbolized "woman." The Athenian playmakers used *emblems* to signify the female rather than somehow trying to recreate the appearance of women one might encounter in day-to-day life. The latter, a style known as naturalism, would not emerge until the 1800s in Europe and North America. By Julian Eltinge's day, naturalism, influenced by the rise of empirical science, meant "present[ing] a reasonably faithful imitation of what may be called the visible and the audible surfaces of life," according to a drama textbook from 1923. The female impersonators of Golden Age Athens operated under a very different set of artistic principles, though it's important to realize that both the ancient Greeks and Julian Eltinge were using the most powerful tools at their disposal to imitate women, according to their respective cultures' beliefs and wishes.[16]

The Romans, famously emulative of their Greek forerunners, still assigned men to women's roles, while adding creative embellishments of their own like a curly, red wig and stilts for the man who played the tragic heroine Phaedra. In classical Rome, however, so-called private life, a space apart from state, society, and the political arena, grew, as did a corresponding entertainment-for-entertainment's sake, something closer to a commercial theatre that had nothing to do with civic rituals and festivals. Citizens of Rome enjoyed the presentations of traveling mime troupes. These itinerant players, whose wandering craft connected them more to one another than to the nation-state at large, were among theatre's first outsiders—or insiders, depending on how you look at it. As such, they felt freer to experiment and began employing women artists, some of whom eventually became popular and famous. In the sixth century BCE, a mime actress named Theodora married Justinian,

76 BEAUTIFUL

emperor of the eastern Roman Empire in Constantinople, a kind of pre-modern "power couple" mixing glamour and politics.[17]

But as a church controlled by men took over from the collapsed Roman Empire in early medieval Europe, women were again forced to exit the stage, making room for an embedded, centuries-long tradition of female impersonation. In ancient Athens, a practice of reciting epic poems at ritual performances turned into drama as we know it when some orators began delivering passages of dialogue in the first person, *becoming*, in effect, the speakers in these stories. Something similar happened with Christian liturgy in the Middle Ages: call-and-response passages morphed into an early version of dialogue between distinct parties. By the tenth century, for example, (male) priests using the barest hint of costume represented the three Marys approaching Christ's sepulcher. "Whom seek ye?" asked a priest in the role of an angel. "Jesus of Nazareth, who was crucified," reply the Marys. Alas, responds the angel/priest, "He is not here; he is risen." It has been pointed out that even when not engaged is such proto-theatrical endeavors, priests wore vestments that more resembled ordinary female dress than male. Clerical authorities were devising effective new ways to reach parishioners, not just for the sake of the parishioners' souls but for the stability of the Church itself. Dramatic performance turned out to be a compelling tool in those efforts, much as it had been for their Athenian precursors.[18]

In fact, turning biblical material into skits and short plays proved so effective, especially with a largely illiterate population, that churchmen engineered platforms and small stages in and around houses of worship to depict "miracle plays" about God's wonders, and "mysteries" about the lives of saints. Men and teenage boys dressed as women in many of these shows. A document from the early Middle Ages referred to boys "arrayed [i.e., dressed] like . . . Vyrgyns," while a 1445 production in England featured priests "danc[ing] in the choir as women." On important holidays and feast days, rolling stages on wheels known as "pageants" brought Bible-themed, though increasingly "despiritualized," fare to the masses. Guilds often sponsored these pageant shows, usually in accordance with their respective expertise. Thus, the goldsmiths produced a Magi play, while the boatwrights sponsored a sketch about Noah's Ark. Despite some plays' increasing distance from, and embellishment upon, sacred source material, men, mostly connected with the church, played all the parts, including women. Aside from traveling mime troupes, there was not yet something understood to be a freestanding, commercial, fully secular theatre apart from the church at this time, which meant that men filled all the positions and controlled its production. Whatever passed for public life in this era, women had little agency or prominence within it. Men would thus portray Eve and Mary, not to mention the Wife character in *The Second Shepherd's Play*, a hilarious, original allegory thought to have been performed in Wakefield around 1450. Men also dragged-up in "Morality Plays" like *Everyman* and *The Pride of Life*. These more serious and poetic works continued well into the 1500s and may have influenced a young spectator named William Shakespeare.[19]

* * *

When a professional, commercial theatre apart from the church emerged in Britain in the 1500s, though, women continued to be barred. According to authorities, most of them male, women needed "protection" from the playhouse and its drama. Even going to a play, much less appearing in one, could sully a respectable woman in name or fact. That gave men yet another opportunity to refine the art of female-impersonation, which they did to great acclaim. As they did so, dramatists created more nuanced and challenging female roles. As had been true in ancient Athens, costuming remained more emblematic than detailed and realistic, at least to modern eyes. The actors wore simple, white satin skirts and used broad gestures to convey gender to an often-noisy crowd, some of whose members might be seated forty feet away, distracted by wandering orange-, nut-, and tobacco-sellers all barking their goods like beer-hawkers at baseball games. A number of actors enthusiastically rose to the challenge and began to specialize in women's roles. The popular thespian Nathaniel Field played Ophelia in the very first *Hamlet*, and the highly regarded Alexander Cooke rendered the original Lady Macbeth.[20] By "protecting" women, authorities were unwittingly allowing greater leeway for the art of gender impersonation. Just as important, they were implicitly helping demonstrate that many "male" and "female" behaviors were but easily read conventions that worked in social life, if in subtler form, much as they did in *Hamlet* and *Macbeth*.

Not unlike in our day, all the pieces were in place for a moral panic, which took the form of a "pamphlet war," the sixteenth-century equivalent of a social media or news outlet imbroglio and counter-imbroglio. Stephen Gossen's 1583 monograph *The School of Abuse* claimed that crossdressing would muddy and "adulterate" otherwise self-evident gender lines. In the 1590s, Puritan scholar John Rainolds argued that Deuteronomy prohibited

78 BEAUTIFUL

crossdressing *onstage* just as much as in civilian life, while Oxford academician William Gager agreed that men must not put on female attire "unless they [do] so to save their lives or benefit their country." Under Elizabeth I, the theatre was permitted to flourish with less intervention. But in the years leading up to James I's accession in 1603, things began to change. Cultural authorities increasingly worried that the theatre not only let commoners play monarchs and men play women but was capable of seducing even good Christian women to sin. In 1600, a "gentlewoman" named Alice Pinder was tried for "coming from a play" with her moral fiber so frayed that a "gentleman" named Robert Welch could easily bid her "come to him" in a dwelling where "he had a cooche [couch or bed] redy and took her into the cooche with him" and "thuse had carnall knowledge of her bodye."[21] And all that because she had gone to the theatre.

In Renaissance England, then, the theatre became "[no] place for a woman in moral terms," onstage and even in the house, in the eyes of the powerful. Though women attended as fans, doing so could tarnish their reputation. Men, on the other hand, risked little censure in perfecting the drag in their cordoned-off companies. To the contrary, they were applauded for their skill and suffered "no sly remarks or lecherous sneers" until social conditions shifted, much as would come to pass in the career of Julian Eltinge 300 years thence. Some historians have argued for a powerful if unspoken erotic dimension as spectators were made to behold that "underneath the velvet and lace were the sturdy limbs of growing boys" decanting their lines in "clear, choirboy tones." Others have argued that Elizabethan actors and dramatists consciously used the fact that boys and men impersonated women to undermine ideas about the fixity of gender. Indeed, more than a few dramas of the era used "transvestite heroines"—boy actors playing female characters who disguise themselves as men—including Lyly's *Gallathea* (ca. 1587), Jonson's *Epicoene* (1609), and Shakespeare's *As You Like It* (ca. 1600).[22]

The ferment over crossdressing on the stage came to a head in 1620, four years after Shakespeare's death, with the publication of two influential pamphlets: *Hic mulier: or, The Man-Woman; Being a Medecine to cure the Coltish Disease of the Staggers in the Masculine-Feminines of our Times* and a retort titled *Haec-Vir; or The Womanish Man: Being an Answere to a late Book intituled Hic-Mulier*. To make matters worse, crossdressing was starting to spill into civilian life, notably in social clubs and taverns. King James turned to the church for guidance on what to do about these "sexually 'unnatural' " behaviors. Various factions engaged in the fray, but things would decisively change when the Puritans deposed Charles I, James's successor, in the English Civil War and banned the theatre altogether.[23]

From 1642 to 1660 there was no public theatre to speak of in England, and therefore no need of female impersonation and its partisans, pro or con. But with the Restoration of the monarchy, in the person of Charles II, playmaking was permitted to come out of hiding. So too were women, who could finally appear onstage. (In France, women had been permitted to appear in non-liturgical theatre since at least the 1200s, and were also key members of *commedia dell'arte* troupes that roved Europe.) Sir William Davenant received a patent—that is, official approval to run a theatre—stating that, "whereas the women's parts have hitherto been made by men, at which some have taken offence, we do give leave that for the time to come all women's parts be acted by women." In the English-speaking theatre, the age of the actress had dawned, along with new suspicions about men in drag. The advent of women onstage did not mean the end of men playing female parts, however, leading to a time of strenuous competition between the former and the latter. This would end up having profound implications for the future of female impressionism.[24]

Thanks to powerhouse talents such as Nell Gwynn (1650–1687), Elizabeth Barry (1658–1713), and Ann Bracegirdle (ca. 1663–1748), actresses came to the fore of British theatrical life with astonishing speed. They shared the stage with several equally talented impersonators, notably actor and playwright Colley Cibber (1671–1757) and so-called boy player Edward Kynaston (1643–1712), a legend in his own time and beyond. In 1661, famed diarist Samuel Pepys saw *The Beggar's Bush*, which featured women in women's roles, then several days later saw Kynaston play the title role in Ben Jonson's *The Silent Woman*, whereupon he was struck by "the loveliest legs that I ever saw in my life" (similar to compliments paid Julian Eltinge 250 years later). John Downes, who also saw Kynaston at Drury Lane, wondered whether "any woman" might "so sensibly touch . . . the audience as he."[25]

By the 1700s, though, actresses had so established their primacy that fewer men tried to impersonate women with subtlety and nuance. Instead, impersonators moved toward the clownish, the carnivalesque, or what might have been called campy or "burlesque" in Julian Eltinge's era. While Kynaston had "ravished his audiences," his successors sought to make playgoers laugh using parodies that relied on presumed essential differences between male and female, a transition from "*real* disguise" to "*false* disguise," in one historian's phraseology. While those labels are simplistic, they underscore the fact that Kynaston's eroticism and psychological nuance were gone,

80   BEAUTIFUL

and that such an approach would continue to diminish until the period that brought Eltinge to the fore, at least in the Anglo-European West.[26]

Meanwhile, men who enjoyed aspects of the drag in private or civilian life fell under increasing scrutiny and reproach. They were no longer colorful, urban denizens but outcasts, often thought guilty of that most "unnatural" act, sodomy—at least, if such an act were undertaken between men. The art of drag and skirting-up receded further underground, as did same-sex erotic behavior. Onstage, men who played women did so for "comic diversion," as in John Gay's 1781 *Beggar's Opera*, giving rise to an over-the-top "dame" character who flourished from the mid-1800s onward. Popular dames included George Robey, Wilkie Bard, and Dan Leno, known for his "squeaking voice and sweeping gestures." Leno died in 1904, the year that Julian Eltinge depicted women in a very different way in *Mr. Wix of Wickham*.[27]

* * *

By the time Julian Eltinge started his career, enough time, mystification, and cultural sedimentation had accrued that artists like Kynaston and Cibber could be resuscitated as icons to be admired, even emulated. They were linked to Shakespeare—not William Shakespeare the canny playwright, actor, and producer of the quasi-grimy London theatre scene in 1500s and early 1600s, but rather, the pillar of high culture whose dramas had become revered "literature" in Ivy League classrooms, a brand name in the Western canon. Throughout the 1700s and 1800s, Shakespeare plays were parodied, sampled, riffed on, and reassembled for popular audiences. But that time was drawing to a close. Julian Eltinge, despite knowing next to nothing about the actual lives and times of performers like Edward Kynaston and Colley Cibber, nonetheless linked his brand to their names, positioning himself as an heir to their vaunted artistry. The newspapers were happy to assist in this imagined lineage, none knowing, nor caring to know, that in Restoration days, for example, dressing too stylishly or floridly—being regarded a *fop*, that is—could raise suspicions of being thought a sodomite. (Kynaston himself was widely considered the Duke of Buckingham's "catamite," and the dandyish Cibber was both applauded and suspected for the curious "effeminacy" he displayed.[28]) In 1912, the *Detroit Free Press* ran a lengthy essay on the "Eltinges of Queen Elizabeth's Time as Shakespeare's Heroines." The article, which featured a headshot of Julian Eltinge in curls piled high above bare, milky neck and shoulders, described how Kynaston and his brethren "must have been accomplished impersonators of women," or how else could they have pulled off renditions of Shakespeare's "beautiful heroines . . . Viola, Rosalind, Juliet and the rest?" In other words, after many years in shadowy abeyance, precise, artful female impersonating could be an esteemed male profession once again.[29]

Julian Eltinge wondered what it might have been like to have worked with Kynaston, playing opposite his heroines one night, then swapping parts the next. In his understanding, Kynaston had been the toast of society, invited for public carriage rides with Lady This and Lord That. Perhaps he himself might also be regarded as an artist *nonpareil*, revered and held aloft by society. He'd already had a taste of it. The actor seemed to know little of the sodomy rumors that followed Kynaston, nor those that dogged Kynaston's talented, crossdressing peer, James "Bugger" Nokes (or Noakes).[30]

* * *

It didn't take the impersonator long to find well-paying, professional gigs. He was about to discover that the amusement-going public at large, not just Boston high society, was eager for his talents. It would take a while to land a role in a scripted musical comedy. But for now, vaudeville supplied the perfect platform: ten or twelve minutes to give an array of female types, accompanied by song and dance. It was tiring, involving travel, lots of fast-paced costume changes, and multiple shows a day. But playing the Keith vaudeville circuit, the biggest name in the business, meant lots of work, decent salary, and prestige. He wouldn't be headlining yet, but that was okay. If he succeeded, the well-oiled Keith machine would see his value and recognize him accordingly.[31]

Keith's Boston, where Eltinge landed in February 1905, reflected the aspirations of a new generation of executives who sought to take popular entertainments and repackage them in ways that could appeal to a rising middle class with leisure-time income. The Boston theatre had cost between $600,000 and 700,000 to build, even though originally budgeted at an already-high $100,000. E. F. Albee, B. F. Keith's righthand man and chief architect of the company's organizational structure, later claimed that their "ideal" was "so high" as to make corner-cutting anathema. Albee, hardly an elite or a Harvard man, nonetheless understood how to cast his enterprises in the proper light. On the one hand, he knew mainstream American crowds liked an assortment of diversions, from standup comics

82 BEAUTIFUL

to trained animals. On the other, though, he and his partner Keith had somehow to dissociate such popular fare from its quotidian, unglamorous origins: the concert saloon, burlesque shows, dime museums, carnivals, traveling circuses, and so on. These time-tested favorites had to be simultaneously reproduced and "lifted . . . from the mire" for mainstream consumers who might never think of visiting a smoke-filled tavern or sideshow. He even had some good examples of how to pull that off: Sears, Roebuck managed to hawk patent medicines to a vast swath of Americans, and Ford Motor was learning to appeal to "the people who counted," which is to say, white, middle-class, family men and women. Even if the banjo players and strongmen would do pretty much the same thing they used to in groggeries and at the carnival, Messrs. Albee and Keith would package it, physically and rhetorically, to make it all appear quite palatable and even classy. When patrons read the menu of talent at Keith's Boston, they gazed at elegant fonts imprinted on fine, heavy paper stock, "the most elaborate, artistic, tasteful, expensive [playbills] ever gotten out for free distribution." Albee and Keith cast themselves as visionaries who saw the future and acted on it, turning lowly variety amusements into "vaudeville . . . the proud queen of the stage." They forged order from chaos, turning countless artists and venues into "the monster vaudeville machine," which *Billboard* called "the most efficient and powerful organization known in the amusement field." The public was happy to see Albee and Keith as visionaries endowed with superhuman foresight and capability. How else should they trust that the new world of large-scale commercial entertainment was safe, much less worth the money? "Things ran as systematically and efficiently as in a large business concern," observed Ethel Barrymore during her stint in vaudeville. Vaudeville offered consumers the chance to enjoy their longtime favorites while steering clear of disrepute or perceived danger. It also offered businessmen like Albee and Keith a chance to ascend the class ladder and claim the laurels of self-made men.[32]

Eltinge played down-the-bill at Keith's Boston on a program headlined by Prevost & Rice, popular comedians who produced "an absolute scream throughout," according to house manager M. J. Keating. Esteemed thespians Sidney Drew, a Barrymore relative, and Gladys Rankin brought a more serious note to the program with their one-act play *The Yellow Dragon*.[33] At the Keith-run Temple in Detroit in May, 1905, "Harvard man" Eltinge shared the bill with lion-tamer Adgie who cradled the adorable cub "Teddy Roosevelt" in her arms. As a female impersonator, Eltinge had "no superior," felt one observer. The performer started writing some of his own songs, including the lyrics to a tune titled "Widows." He also referenced the popular culture of the day by portraying Hebe Damm, a character recently made famous by actress Diamond Donner in Klaw & Erlanger's production of John J. McNally's "musical travesty," *Lifting the Lid*.[34] Though new to vaudeville, Eltinge already had a following, drawing notable applause simply by coming onstage—perhaps some were impressed at his stylish outfits—before giving a thirteen-minute routine. One Keith employee reckoned the young actor "a great artist . . . better than [blackface female impersonator] Stuart or any of the rest of that class." Perhaps most important, the performer's aesthetic was seen to be "absolutely without suggestion," an illusion so perfect it passed the credibility test essential for big-time vaudevillians. Hervey Jolin, a retired decorator in his nineties who was asked about Julian Eltinge in 1998, recalled the artist, whom he'd seen in vaudeville, as "a knockout. There was no satire in his performance." It was another crucial turning point, a door opened, in the young artist's burgeoning career.[35]

Even though he wasn't yet a top star, it wasn't uncommon for Julian Eltinge to get more applause than anyone else on the bill, save perhaps the headliner herself. A future that so recently had looked bleak now bloomed like a hothouse flower. The Keith brass believed this actor who "makes a handsome girl" could "make good in any vaudeville house in the country." They were right: vaudeville fans in Boston, Buffalo, Detroit, and New York were getting a whole new look at the art of impersonating a woman, and they liked what they saw.[36]

* * *

Julian Eltinge's talents fit perfectly into a mainstream amusement for audiences accustomed to variety. Popular fare, from vaudeville to carnival to minstrel shows, was marked by its eclectic variability. As historian Robert Lewis puts it, for most of the nineteenth century, "every program in the theater was a variety show," no matter what label it gave itself.[37] Vaudeville, where Julian Eltinge would spend the first, crucial part of his career, famously promised "something for everybody." Woodrow Wilson loved vaudeville in part because, if you were watching "a bad act . . . you can rest reasonably secure that the next one may not be so bad." The American consumer had practically a God-given right to satisfaction; anyone seeking access to their wallets understood that or perished.[38]

84 BEAUTIFUL

The vaudeville theatre of Julian Eltinge's day evolved from saloons, variety halls, so-called opera houses, and other places where patrons enjoyed diverse, quotidian amusements and usually bounteous alcohol and carousing.[39] As the American populace coalesced into potentially larger markets, some began to wonder if there might be a way to take the best of variety and cleanse it of its rough, proletarian setting and associations. In 1860, Frank Rivers had experimented with a "strictly high class" show for women and kids, a "Grand Matinee" where there would be no drinking or smoking. The time wasn't quite right for such a venture, but soon enough, it would be. On October 24, 1881, legendary entertainer-producer Tony Pastor produced a program at his New 14th Street Theatre in New York that was free of suggestive material. More important, booze and tobacco, two symbols strongly linked to rowdy masculinity, were prohibited. Entertainment was now after what might be called the family trade. Others followed Pastor's lead. Proctor's Pleasure Palace, a sort of all-in-one spot for entertainment, gambling, and drinking, inaugurated abstemious afternoon shows where patrons could no longer "sip the insidious absinthe or swallow the foaming beer," and Koster & Bial's, a music hall notorious for mixing burlesque with vaudeville, announced "strictly high class" Wednesday and Sunday matinées with no smoking, no drinking. It should be pointed out that many lowly variety saloons, which welcomed smoke and drink, were also tolerant of gender and erotic nonconformers, making space for "fairies" who might or might not want to hook up with other men, and might or might not dress and act in women's clothes. A crucial rift had opened in the world of diversions: more than ever, sexual outliers were lumped in with gender outliers, the whole lot seen as especially deviant and, more to the point, avoided at all costs by the makers of big-time, mainstream entertainment, men like E. F. Albee and B. F. Keith. Julian Eltinge, however, fit right in, a near-perfect symbiosis of artist and industry, each in its thrilling ascent.[40]

* * *

New Englanders Benjamin Franklin Keith and his protégé Edward Franklin Albee built their vaudeville empire in part by posing themselves as self-made men "destined for greatness" and linked to the cultural authority of a white, Anglo-European heritage. Albee trumpeted the fact that he was a direct descendent of one of the American Revolution's Minute Men, while Keith, of Scottish and French ancestry, closely forged alliances—and secured investment capital from—the Catholic Church to grow and pass the moral sniff test.[41] By contrast, Southern European immigrants Sylvester Poli and Alexander Pantages were harder-pressed to secure financing and, as many newcomers must, initially marketed their product to poorer, lower-status populations. While the largely Jewish immigrants who later built the Hollywood studios were censored and surveilled by Catholic authorities and cultural conservatives, Keith and Albee were constantly admired for the "good taste" and "absolute cleanliness" of their product. They had, in the words of *Everybody's Magazine* in 1905, transformed the "v'riety" hall of old, a place "frequented by men of the lowest order and intelligence," into "an institution, respected and respectable."[42]

Hardly a man of refined tastes, B. F. Keith had opened a dime museum on Washington Street in Boston in 1882, where he displayed Baby Alice, an infant who supposedly weighed one-and-a-half pounds; Amelia Hall, "a jolly fat Brooklyn Miss" tipping the scale at 516 lbs.; another woman "invisible below her head and shoulders"; and "the biggest frog in the world." Audiences liked illusion, spectacle, and the "wow" factor. Keith, like Eltinge, was aspirational and thus sought the bourgeois-leaning demographic. He located his establishment near the Jordan Marsh department store to attract respectable ladies—perhaps the ultimate sign of cultural safety—and eventually called it "Gaiety Hall," a name reminiscent of Paris's legendary pantomime and satire venue, the Théâtre de la Gaîté. There he inaugurated "continuous" shows, which meant six, two-hour bills effectively playing back-to-back from 10:30 A.M. until 10:30 P.M., the entertainment equivalent of a factory that rarely quit.[43] E. F. Albee, a generation younger than Keith, had gotten his schooling in the circus, working as a "tent boy" for Great London, Burr Robbins, and others, which meant he did everything from caring for animals to brewing lemonade.[44] "In my opinion," Albee later said, "the advantages gained which fit a man for later years in business cannot be found in any other calling; the diverse experiences which one encounters in traveling with a circus—the novelty, the contact with all classes, the knowledge of the condition of the country, its industries and its farming." He was right.[45]

Teaming up with Keith made good sense, not only because the men had a lot of experience in attracting mainstream audiences but also because Albee knew that even so-called polite crowds wanted a little racy fun sometimes, while the devoutly Catholic Keith secured the imprimatur and appearance of moral hygiene. Together, from small productions like a knockoff of Gilbert & Sullivan's *The Mikado*, the two men built a vast theatre and booking chain,

86 BEAUTIFUL

leading a journalist of the day to declare that Keith and Albee were "to vaude-ville what Frick and Carnegie were to steel."[46] This was an age when capitalists aimed for size, consolidation, monopolization, and the vanquishing of labor, at all costs. It was how business was done.

* * *

B. F. Keith and E. F. Albee consciously chose the toney, French-sounding term "vaudeville," as opposed to "variety" or "burlesque," to create their brand. Vaudeville had various etymological roots, but to Keith and Albee, it sounded like something that would impress prospective customers, sim-ilar to the words "gourmet" or "organic" in our day.[47] By 1914, the Keith-Albee circuit owned forty-eight venues outright and controlled many more through a booking syndicate, enforcing an alleged "purification" code, admonishing performers that their acts had to be "free from all vulgarity and suggestiveness, in words, action, and costume," and that utterances such as "Liar, Slob, Son-of-A-gun, Devil, Sucker, Damn" could subject a player to a fine or "instant discharge." Crowds were also trained not to laugh or stamp their feet too loudly, and to dress appropriately.[48] Perhaps most important, the Keith-Albee organization had created a massive booking organiza-tion in 1907 called the United Booking Offices of America, or "UBO" as it was known in the trade, whereby it dominated a huge part of the American vaudeville industry, from playhouses to routes to audiences to performers, like Julian Eltinge.[49]

Just as Julian Eltinge was groping for professional success after the dis-astrous *Mr. Wix*, he found the perfect setting for his singular talent. Symbiotically, Keith and Albee, forging a mass-market product aimed at middle-class families and allegedly cleansed of earthy carnivalism, hired an artist who knew what both a woman and a man, respectively, ought to look like and how they ought to comport themselves. Eltinge soon became a cen-terpiece in the expanding Keith "two-a-day" vaudeville empire, so called be-cause it offered two purportedly high-quality shows each day, as opposed to small-time operators who put up three or more bills a day. (Keith actually ended its once-signature "continuous" vaudeville in 1907. What had been a mark of distinction had become a symbol of the discount trade, quantity over alleged quality.[50])

As the vaudeville industry calved-off submarkets, Julian Eltinge hitched his star to the rising, higher-class, mothership. Small-time vaudeville might be cheaper and feature plenty of talented players. But this was the dawn of the American Century, when life's journey increasingly focused on trading-up. Keith and Albee threatened that talent might not be rehired, or their wages downgraded, should they stray into small-time—which was often the only option for those finding without a current UBO contract.[51] When it turned out that many Americans liked getting more entertainment for less—they didn't all need marble-floored lobbies or Persian rugs, just funny comics and awe-inspiring jugglers—Keith and Albee quietly acquired interests in some 350 small-time houses across the country.[52]

The changeability and, at the same time, clockwork precision of Julian Eltinge's impersonation act made him a perfect fit for an entertainment in which each part had to "harmonize" with one another, and with the bill as a whole.[53] Performers had to be able to start or finish "in one" if possible, so others could assemble mid-stage, "in two," behind a curtain or fly-away sets, ready to go on without missing a beat. Audiences loved the admixture of variety and seamless fluidity, the more of each the better. Performers who had problems with this process could be labeled "disagreeable" by management, nearly as bad an epithet as "untalented." With rare exception, Eltinge was as agreeable as they come, regarded by one Detroit theatre manager "best ever . . . female impersonator" and usually happy to start in one and finish in two.[54]

* * *

When Julian Eltinge first mounted the vaudeville stage, the industry was well into its heyday, lasting from about 1895 to 1915. It was a good time to be a vaudevillian if you could do what you were told. There was a lot of work, relatively speaking. According to various sources (which don't always agree), there were some 2,000 vaudeville houses in the United States and Canada in 1900. By 1912, the United States had 1,000 big-time and 4,000 small-time venues. Others have estimated 4,000 theatres in the United States between 1875 and 1925, providing work for 25,000 artists. A tally of vaudeville houses from 1923, by which time the genre's popularity had fallen off, found sixty-two big-time Keith and/or Orpheum houses in the United States, supplemented by 705 small-time theatres. (Excluded of course was the vast ecosystem of the "Negro Circuits," about which more will said.) Bigger venues could seat 2,000 patrons, while smaller houses might accommodate no more than 500. Ticket prices usually ranged anywhere from five cents to a dollar-fifty, though more prestigious venues could charge upwards of two dollars.

88   BEAUTIFUL

In 1912, a million people a year were said to regularly attend vaudeville, with the industry taking $100 million in revenues. Given that most of the companies involved were privately held, and that many figures that appear in books and news articles are estimates from potentially biased parties, these numbers should serve as rough guidelines rather than precise economic history.[55]

* * *

Some alleged that women patrons formed the bulk Julian Eltinge's fan base in vaudeville. W. C. Fields once joked that when the famed impersonator went onstage, "Women went into ecstasies . . . [and] Men went into the smoking room." While the artist clearly had many female followers, many of whom loved his fashion sense, Fields's jab nonetheless seems a remnant of the "separate spheres" ideology. Nothing suggests a male exodus during Eltinge's act. Indeed, there is ample evidence of men rather liking his performances. In 1902, the *Buffalo Courier* reported that the "male half of the audience heaves a sigh of regret when it is remembered that the stunning beauty is one of them." Internal Keith documents also do not describe men (or women for that matter) getting up and walking out. In their reports to the Keith head office, in which they were highly motivated to be honest, manager after manager praised Eltinge and noted his popularity with the "majority" of the crowd. Some even argued he merited a longer slot and/or more space to move about the stage. On the other hand, when customers left the auditorium during an act—as happened, for example, when "people left in droves" during comedian George Wilson's turn at Keith's Philadelphia in 1905—it was clearly documented by the facility manager and conveyed to the brass forthwith, a calamity in need of quick intervention! The manager of Keith and Proctor's 125th Street theatre in New York likewise reported that "the best part of the house left" midway through the troublingly-named McMahon's Minstrel Maids and Watermelon Girls. Nothing of the sort was said about Julian Eltinge's act.[56]

It's also hard to imagine Julian Eltinge succeeding in vaudeville if men disliked him since, despite so many efforts to attract women and children, males seem to have made up the majority of customers. While women and children may have made up about half the crowd at earlier shows, evening and nighttime audiences were up to three-quarters male. In fact, for all of Tony Pastor's and B. F. Keith's efforts, vaudeville venues often had to cut ticket prices to get women into the theatre. They also used animal acts—everything

MR. WIX OF . . . VAUDEVILLE   89

from elephants to cats to donkeys—to entice moms with kids, but, alas, the "sterner sex" seems to have enjoyed these menageries just as much. An oft-cited 1911 survey of a New York City vaudeville audience found 36 percent of the audience to be female, a proportion that appears stable over time, though there is limited hard data.[57]

Because vaudeville managers found he could "please all classes of theatergoers," Julian Eltinge shifted his sights from popular-but-ghettoized specialty act to mainstreamer, possibly even headliner. The sumptuous gowns, pleasant voice, and skillful dancing allowed the artist to combine multiple appeals into a unified package: song-and-dance artist, visual illusionist, and department-store mannequin. By the fall of 1905, he was called "the male Vesta Tilley"—a reference to perhaps the world's best-known *male impersonator* of the era—after fooling Orpheum crowds into thinking he was a "buxom" gal, before yanking off his curly, black wig. Eltinge soon moved to the ninth slot in many shows, a good place to be, usually right before or after the headliner.[58]

As his popularity grew, so too did the impersonator's pay. From $250–$300 when Eltinge started out in vaudeville, he was taking in $350–$450 a week by 1907. Although stars like Eva Tanguay, Nora Bayes, and Elsie Janis could command several thousand dollars, the average vaudevillian at the time made about $40 a week. According to E. F. Albee himself, any player earning over $160 a week was unusual, and even many a solid, popular artist got only $125–$150 weekly. In terms of monetary value, Eltinge was outpacing his peers.[59]

But Julian Eltinge, enterprising, eager, and entrepreneurial, found other ways to fill his coffers. Working closely with promotion manager Jake Rosenthal, a businessman known for being at once creative and "voracious," Eltinge formed alliances with merchants to promote their products, some of which bore his name. In time, he would start hawking his own product lines like today's "lifestyle" gurus. Being his era's version of a "cross-merchandiser" was the first step. "Wearing women's togs is no picnic. . . . These things nearly kill me, as you would realize if you tried to get a No. 7 foot into a No. 4 shoe," Eltinge grumbled to reporters in his dressing room, where he simultaneously struggled to squeeze his thirty-inch waist into a twenty-two-inch corset. But, if he had to endure it all for the sake of his work, the artist reckoned he preferred R&G brand corsets. At $1.50 apiece, and containing no uncomfortable "steel armor reinforcements," R&G got the job done. Washington, DC's upscale Palais Royal department store trumpeted the "Corset Worn by Mr.

90 BEAUTIFUL

Julian Eltinge." The impersonator spoke so frequently of his love for R&G that *Variety*'s Sime Silverman wished "Mr. Eltinge could with propriety dispense with the free advertisement of a certain make of corset." Others figured that if Eltinge wouldn't quit, maybe they should get on the bandwagon as well. Theatrical magnate J. J. Shubert urged Chicago advance-promoter P. S. Mattox to get "ahead" for female impersonator Bothwell Browne, just as Rosenthal had done in convincing stores to carry "the 'Eltinge Corset' and 'Eltinge Dresses' and things of that kind," and to promote them all heavily when Julian Eltinge himself came to town.[60]

* * *

With vaudeville success happening more quickly and robustly than even he had counted on, the entertainer decided to take his next big step sooner rather than later: playing in Europe and Great Britain. Vaudeville customers in America were becoming more and more interested in both imported talent and domestic artists who conquered abroad, the latter returning home with a glossy coating of Continental glamour. Playing in Europe would almost surely increase a performer's value and asking price and add to their brand appeal. In 1907, the *New York Times* noted how common it had become for vaudeville stars to mention their nationality—or at least refer to "some interesting nationality"—in playbills and on posters, making the former "strongly resemble hotel registers." Remarked Sophie Tucker on a UK tour during the 1920s, "The prestige I was rolling up in London should be good box office for me when I played vaudeville houses in the United States again."[61]

Julian Eltinge embarked on his first international tour in the spring of 1906. After coheadlining London's Palace (theatre) with Rosalie Stahl for $250 a week, he headed to Paris. A British producer offered the impersonator a twenty-eight-week tour of the Isles, but Eltinge declined. In Paris, the crowds cheered "*Eltang*," as he impersonated American women at the Théâtre des Folies-Marigny. *Eltang* was popular enough that the artist Armand Jean-Baptiste Ségaud created a poster of the performer's face, which was soon pasted all over the City of Lights. Eltinge's former mentor, Robert Barnet, reached out to see if the lad would be interested in a Klaw & Erlanger production of *Miss Pocahontas*, but the young artist turned him down. In Switzerland, Eltinge appeared with Loie Fuller, popular for her controversial mix of burlesque and avant-garde dancing. The entertainer managed to sneak away for a few weeks of mountain air in the Swiss Alps, enjoying the "simple, razorless life close to nature," before tour dates in Vienna prompted him to shave—face, arms, and legs—once again. He enjoyed a successful run in the Austrian capital in January 1907. The entertainer liked Europe. He lingered overseas. Dates at Hurtig & Seamon's Music Hall in New York as well as popular roof garden theatres were canceled or postponed. Some even speculated that Eltinge might remain in Europe for a few years. But it was not to be. By February 1907, he was again in the United States, touted "Just Back from Europe," filling Keith time at $400 a week.[62]

In England, Eltinge forged an important friendship with Aaron Burlingshaw, founder of the Burlingshaw Cutlery concern in Sheffield. Little is known about the precise nature of their relationship. Some say the actor and his future benefactor "became very close" in a short period of time, while a source from the 1940s describes Burlingshaw as a "relative." Furthermore, in 1907, upon Burlingshaw's passing, it was reported that the cutlery-maker gave Julian Eltinge and his mother, Julia, the entirety of his £200,000 estate. By this time, Eltinge was well into constructing a glamorous, larger-than-life— well, larger than *his* actual life—persona, garlanded with tales of Harvard heroism and a mining-magnate father. It's hard to say as well whether this bequest was true on its face, partly fabricated, or just another delectable fiction in the artist's increasingly creative biographical rendering. After all, it was also reported that Eltinge had gobsmacked a stagehand who called him "Lucky Lucy" upon hearing news of the inheritance.[63]

Europe and Britain had certainly endowed him with an air of value and refinement. Back in the States, he showed off gowns by Felix of Paris, hats from Viennese milliners, and a German-made "frilled sunshade" to "prettily adorn" the "perfect lady" he often imitated. American women loved gazing at Parisian creations in store windows. It was like beholding a "jewel gleaming in a velvet case," as a novelist writing in the 1930s recalled of the decade before World War I. Paris symbolized intoxicating excess, its gowns and finery a delicious "death to reasonableness." In addition to showing off his latest fashion finds, Eltinge also displayed his new companion, a "very ugly English bulldog" that he had supposedly received as a "souvenir" from King Edward VII after a command performance at Windsor Castle. Eltinge said the animal, named "Smith," was not just a gift from the King but in fact, an offspring of one His Majesty's own dogs. This meant Julian Eltinge was, in effect, now related to the Royal Family if only by a pet. Smith, who liked to nap on a chair in the actor's dressing room while his owner visaged-up, "rightfully" had a "regal air of indifference," joked the artist. The performer's royal pet

92 BEAUTIFUL

became almost as important a prop as his Harvard pedigree or penchant for fist fighting. But just like those other things, the Smith story may not have been what its teller claimed. Sarah Mitchell of the Royal Archives at Windsor Castle "closely" examined records and documents from the period May/June 1906, when Eltinge was in England, including the King and Queen's engagement diaries, Court Circulars, press clippings, and "files relating to private Royal Family functions and visits," and reports that none mention Julian Eltinge. But like much about Julian Eltinge, the myth of his dog's royal lineage persists.[64]

# # #

4

"George M." Is for Minstrel

Back home, the entertainer was indeed welcomed as a returning hero, "one of the brightest and most artistic features ever imported from America," headliner at all "the famous continental amusement palaces." Julian Eltinge, America's latest cultural export, unveiled new characters: as a young woman "garbed for the ball" in a drop-shoulder, embroidered dress; and as actress Maxine Elliot who would later have an affair with Winston Churchill and also befriend none other than King Edward VII of England whose grand-dog supposedly ended up in Eltinge's care. To an even greater extent than before he'd gone to Europe, Julian Eltinge became known as an artist who submerged himself into womanhood more completely than any of his peers and rivals, "a genius" who was "unexcelled anywhere." Yet, his presumably truthful, normative masculinity lay just below the thinnest of membranes, waiting to burst forth in an instant. His "remarkably women-like arm[s]" made the very picture of a "a dainty, piquante girl." But when he "laughingly tears off his curly wig," the actor immediately "discloses a manly physiognomy." Julian Eltinge's nascent brand was thus predicated not only upon his creative mastery but on the notion that masculinity was a natural or baseline state, while femininity necessitated—demanded—unceasing *effort*. A few unplucked hairs or unperfumed bodily regions could tear the wig off a woman in everyday life, and that would be no laughing matter.[1]

The magical duality of the actor's gender led many a journalist into verbal contortionism. "He is the one man," wrote the *Boston Evening Transcript* in 1907, "who impersonates female characters non-effeminately." Eltinge permitted theatergoers to enjoy gender's illusional dimension while keeping *man* and *woman* in distinct containers, a compromise that would serve him well for decades. The actor apprehended acceptable, mainstream womanhood for what it was: a moving target. He had to keep up with changing tastes, demands, and expectations without crossing into dangerous, censurable territory. As many Americans grew more curious and desirous, so too would his artistry. For now, critics liked that he was "[g]irlish enough in face and figure," yet "natural . . . [with a] grace which avoids offensive coquetry or

Beautiful. Andrew L. Erdman, Oxford University Press. © Oxford University Press 2024.
DOI: 10.1093/9780197696361.003.0005

94   BEAUTIFUL

excessive display of lingerie." His unarguable skill and ability to doff his female characterizations in a flash allowed Julian Eltinge to summon *femininity*
without coming across as *effeminate*. The challenge, of course, was keeping it
all up. As he would discover, playing the conventional man underneath the
makeup and corsets, while effortful, was nonetheless easier than keeping up
with ever-mutable womanliness. For the latter meant shifting one's attitude,
body shape, and size, as beauty archetypes moved from Victorian, to Gibson
Girl, to Bathing Beauty, to "hipless, waistless, boneless" Flapper.[2]

Being a vaudeville star allowed Julian Eltinge to present his dressing room
as a building workshop or engineering lab rather than a boudoir or wardrobe
closet. This was a man's space, and in it one would find a man going seriously
about his business, not a woman vainly primping to make herself look beautiful. Eltinge informed reporters that to create a character with "phenomenal
fidelity to life" required "deep study and research." Broadly speaking, that put
him in the same arena as scientific sexologists like Ellis and Krafft-Ebing who
closely observed and categorized what made up a man, a woman, and/or an
invert. Playing women onstage was hardly "easy money," remarked the actor
during an hours-long process of delicately layering rouge, blush, cold cream,
and a special "bluish black greasepaint" onto his face and neck.[3]

For Julian Eltinge, makeup was all but an industrial chemical, at least on *his*
face. Yes, it had to be applied artfully like tempera or oil paint on a canvas. But it
was a technical substance that required the right handling. Similarly, while his
costumes might be luscious, stylish gowns, they were really his *uniforms*, specialized workwear, like a fireman's jumpsuit or a surgeon's apron, but with more
sparkles and less blood. Eltinge allowed that women might look forward to
putting on a special wig or "high slippers [and] dresses." Not him. Even when
tip-to-toe in silken gown, pearls, and satin pumps, Eltinge remarked he would
just as soon attend a "boxing or wresting match" as give his song-and-dance
routine. His face and form were female, but his mind and essence were male. It
would be different for women, of course. The right makeup and clothing were
essential in order for them to be thought "real" or authentic. Such comments
were also meant to dissuade anyone who might think Julian Eltinge enjoyed
wearing women's attire for its own sake when nobody was looking.[4]

* * *

A little more than two years into his vaudeville career, Julian Eltinge was now
regarded "the world's greatest impersonator," according to *Variety*, the trade's

bible. He introduced a dead-on imitation of famed actress and beauty icon Valeska Suratt. Fans were impressed at both his general ensemble and his detailed "mannerisms," all those "little tricks" that looked impossibly "ladylike." He drew enthusiastic crowds at Keith's Cleveland, the Boston Orpheum, and elsewhere on the big-time circuit.[5]

Julian Eltinge was the toast of Keith/UBO vaudeville. For most players, it didn't get better than that. But there was just so far he could go in vaudeville, even in the glitzy two-a-day. To earn thousands a week and to become the master of your artistic destiny in the big time, you had to be a dancing, singing, joke-telling, bantering comedian who radiated charisma. The few artists who fit such a bill were almost all women. Indeed, "single woman" stars were the backbone of the industry. Without an Eva Tanguay, Irene Franklin, or Fanny Brice, a vaudeville show would be like "a jet plane that doesn't jet!" in the opinion of former vaudevillian and 1950s memoirist Joe Laurie Jr. In any case, how long could he tolerate trotting out new characters swagged in the latest fashions? As his technical side flourished, his creative side yearned for greater freedom. The vaudeville star began to speak openly about transitioning to "the legitimate," starring in a real play or full-length drama. He wondered, mostly to himself but with increasing constancy, what it might be like to be a more conventional *actor*, a man who played a variety of roles in a variety of dramas. Every time his career shifted forward, this desire burst forth with greater fervor. Eltinge told the papers that a musical play was being written especially for him. In it, he said, he would "essay a dual role; one that of a girl; the other that of a man." The project was titled *A School for Girls*, developed in collaboration with his new manager, J. H. Harras. The performer seemed to want it both ways. He declared he would soon be "positively" stepping out of tranvestic roles, but for now would play a young man "masquerading as a girl in the seminary." It would not be the last time the actor's wishes collided with reality and tumbled out of his mouth unedited. For someone who had learned to lean into the lie, it may be that Eltinge eventually barely noticed when he was doing it. But what options did he have? The main employment for crossdressing actors in legitimate theatre came in the form of plays like *Charley's Aunt*, a farce written by Brandon Thomas in 1892. *Charley's Aunt*, which would be revived, repackaged, and spun off countless times over the years, involved a man forced to impersonate a woman but in the "knockabout" style of a highly parodic "dame," exactly the sort of performer Eltinge had chosen *not* to become. Nothing, or nothing right, materialized; the actor would have to wait patiently for a shot at the "legitimate."[6]

96   BEAUTIFUL

Other offers trickled in, but none was a good fit. Producers in far-off St. Petersburg, Russia, offered the impersonator a cabaret show but on the condition that he change his name and "not disclose his sex either on or off the stage." Pass. Despite its being a decided step backward, Eltinge passed some time in Boston making society-gala appearances and collecting a fine paycheck, no doubt relieved to remove the corset and the plastered-on smile after such jobs. *Variety* reported he still did more private shows than any other major vaudevillian—something of a precursor to today's celebs showing up virtually or in-person at corporate gigs and toney parties for a hefty paycheck. If so, it was a mere holding pattern, a little side money and social coquetry as he reckoned his next move.[7] In early 1908, the Order of the Eastern Star, one of many quasi-secret societies in America, hired the artist to appear at a charity bazaar and gala at Horticultural Hall in Boston. The group, which had been founded in 1850 by Rob Morris, a Freemason, and his wife, Charlotte Mendenhall Morris, claimed affiliation to an eighteenth-century sect of French Masons that had tried to confer "Androgynous Degrees"—that is, admit women. Members of the Order, which was indeed unusual for being mixed-sex, claimed to be bound by an oath to act according to "Biblical examples of heroic conduct." Mostly, they held charity events with refreshments and entertainment.[8]

There were many attendees at Horticultural Hall despite the stormy weather. Men and women in the Order of the Eastern Star milled about, making polite conversation and awaiting the start of *The Gentle Jury*, a one-act play directed by Mrs. Effie King, recent chair of the Order's Massachusetts chapter. Suddenly, all heads turned toward a "striking blonde" in a "velvet gown, en train, and a large picture hat" being escorted from her sedan into the Hall by two ladies from the event committee. Who was this striking "stranger," murmured the attendees? The play began and, of course, the striking lady was now onstage, singing in a velvety contralto and dancing splendidly. The confraternity's members and their guests loved *The Gentle Jury*. As the play ended, its featured player stepped forward and removed both her fashionable hat and a bounteous wig of red and gold hair. Before the audience stood a fellow with short, dark hair, parted to the side. They roared. "O, it's a man!" shouted one woman; "I thought his voice was pretty heavy for a woman," said someone trying not to appear fooled; "I told you so," protested a third. It was hard to tell what made the men and women of the Order of the Eastern Star giddier: being fooled or insisting they hadn't been![9]

* * *

"GEORGE M." IS FOR MINSTREL 97

Figure 4.1 The impersonator and his producers spared little expense to make sure he appeared in sumptuous gowns appealing to an American public increasingly persuaded that shopping and entertainment were two closely related, retail pleasures.
Credit: *Laurence Senelick Collection.*

With more money than he'd ever had and a brief hiatus in his work schedule, Julian Eltinge decided to focus on something he'd never been able to before: making a home for himself. Though he'd be traveling, of course, the actor figured he'd soon become a Broadway regular. He needed a sanctuary within reach, a nest, somewhere that would not only demonstrate that he'd *made it* but also let him replenish body, mind, and soul. It would of course

98 BEAUTIFUL

also have to be a place where he could live the life of a "regular" guy pretty easily.

Perhaps there was a way to create a thin sliver of the Western frontier back East, but cushier and with less sulphureous air. Men were increasingly looking for places to temporarily ditch the urban grind and stultifying office or factory. They had clubhouses and fraternities, of course. But the outdoors and the sporting life became appealing destinations as well. Hunting, fishing, canoeing, and even golf allowed men not only leisure but a chance to feel some mastery, some power, and resharpen their competitive edge.[10] A new space, head- and actual, started to be born as never before. It was called "the outdoors," a sort of catchall that connected mountains, rivers, and lakes to the ball field. It was a place of exploration and sublimation. Like many of his showbiz kin, Eltinge found himself drawn to a glacially deposited palette of flatland commonly known as Long Island. It was close enough to New York City to attract many entrepreneurs, writers, actors, and artists—but also, somehow, very far from the metropolis.

Eltinge bought a comfortable, farm-like property for himself and his mother. It was not exactly primitive but did nonetheless scent of "untamed land and the rough outdoors." It was just a few acres, not a real farm, but it had the appearance of one. The impersonation artist, clad in straw hat and overalls, showed reporters around the place as he fed chickens, watered crops, rode a horse, and generally played the rancher/settler in a manner that "would have made [Teddy] Roosevelt proud." On his Long Island farm, the actor had only "farming and his mother" on his mind. Being near the Long Island Sound allowed him to indulge his love of fishing when not "up to my knees in rough, *outdoor* work." He could also manage a bit of hunting. All things considered, the long-wandering Billy Dalton/Julian Eltinge had found a lovely spot to call home.[11]

The Eltinge farmstead was in Fort Salonga, a village partly in the township of Huntington and partly in Smithtown, forty miles east of midtown Manhattan. Fort Salonga abuts the Long Island Sound whose waters, gentler than those of the Atlantic-facing coast on the island's south side, allow for leisurely sailing and boating and provide small beaches and coves for swimmers, sun tanners, and clammers. The actor relished his Fort Salonga estate. He was finally able to give his mother, Julia, the succor she had long sought but was ever denied following her alcoholic husband on his fruitless wanderings. The actor could sit on his porch and read the paper or just stare at the grassy fields before getting "busy among the string beans and

"GEORGE M." IS FOR MINSTREL 99

Julian Eltinge and His Mother.

Figure 4.2 With his success in vaudeville and with Cohan & Harris's minstrels, Eltinge could afford a peaceful farm property on Long Island. There, he could escape the demands of his work, play the gentleman-farmer-outdoorsman, and give his mother, Julia, a comfortable home.
Credit: *Billy Rose Theatre Division, The New York Public Library for the Performing Arts.*

100 BEAUTIFUL

cucumbers." He could finally sense what it meant to put down roots, literally and figuratively. Entertainers were by definition an itinerant lot. But Eltinge was starting to wonder if he might have a little of both: a domestic life of some sort *and* a show business career—that rare, enviable overlap of bourgeois' prize and artist's dream. In tall work boots and a slender wheat stalk in his mouth, he waxed on "ecstatically about raising chickens and keeping a cow." *Variety* only partially jested in commenting that Eltinge could "impersonate an amateur farmer" or a "hayseed" in his dungarees, or when riding Fanny X, one of favorite horses.[12]

Harris Henschel, a local real estate investor and businessman (sometimes misnamed "John Henshal"), sold Eltinge the property, though the actor put his mom's name on the deed. There had only been a two-room cottage and small outbuilding when the land was first developed back in the 1840s. Its eventual owner, Ebenezar [*sic*] Hudson Ketcham, committed suicide in 1903 and was buried on the lot. (Ketcham's tombstone was eventually removed to a local cemetery.) Eltinge undertook extensive improvements and renovations, erecting a spacious but in no way disproportionate Dutch-style farmhouse in a style that would become common on Long Island, Cape Cod, and elsewhere in the American Northeast. Peter Sullivan, who owned the Eltinge property with his wife, Kathy, as of 2023 believes the rustic image was indeed part of an effort by Eltinge and his handlers to suggest the performer "was not gay, but a gentleman farmer." ("Apparently, in 1908 gay men did not milk cows," says Sullivan.) A frieze of women dancing hand-in-hand adorned an outside wall, complemented by another classical touch: a long, elegant arbor of the Doric order extending northward from the residence. Eltinge's four-acre plot lay along the abundantly named Bread and Cheese Hollow Road, at no. 368. It was not as large as some nearby estates, like the Gerner family's fifty-two acres or Mr. Rowley's thirty-six. But, it would do just fine and then some.[13]

Over the years to come, Fort Salonga and its environs would give respite to Jack Kerouac, Marlene Dietrich, Jackie Gleason, and others. "For some reason, it was their map," says Terry Reid of the Northport Historical Society. In addition to the Eltinge/Dalton plot and larger ones, there were also modest districts nearby, places where aspiring working-class or immigrant families could rent a bungalow for a few weeks in summer. Thus, even though Fort Salonga was home to some famous actors and artists, it was still somehow distinct from the Long Island where the "fast set" of showbiz and finance went to mingle. Less glitzy and farther from Manhattan than the North Shore homes of the fictional Jay Gatsby and the very real Groucho Marx, Fort

"GEORGE M." IS FOR MINSTREL   101

Figure 4.3 Julian Eltinge made fast friends with the family of John Henschel, for whom this publicity photo is autographed, a Long Island businessman who sold Eltinge the farm at Fort Salonga.
Credit: *Copyright reserved, Northport Historical Society (Long Island, NY).*

Salonga was a place where Julian Eltinge could consider "positively" quitting the skirts and instead raising "high class French bulls."[14]

For all the talk of farming and animal husbandry, of course, the farm at Fort Salonga was still an actor's abode. The impersonator built a small theatre in the barn, claiming it was there solely "for rehearsal purposes." He threw a housewarming in the "miniature theatre" and invited showbiz folk including composer Percy Wenrich, librettist Otto Hauerbach, vaudevillian Kathryn

102   BEAUTIFUL

Osterman, and the acting brothers Dustin and William Farnum. Also present was a man who would soon have a seismic effect on Julian Eltinge's life, theatrical producer A. H. Woods.[15]

Even more than working the land or entertaining industry chums, Julian Eltinge loved just lolling lazily around his new homestead. He liked to read on the veranda with his dogs—his "boon companions"—at his feet, or stretch out with them beneath a large, shady apple tree. He sailed and swam in the nearby Long Island Sound. He drove his car into the village for groceries or just to motor about. "I'm a man's man," said Eltinge almost reflexively by now, "and I like to do the things a man likes," like hunting on horseback with rifle in hand. Still, he conceded, "I never get tired of the theater," despite sometimes working himself to a "frazzle" and "perspiring myself to death in women's togs." Sooner or later, the overalls and straw hat would have to be traded in for a velvet gown and tiara.[16]

Although Julian Eltinge's father, Joe Dalton, was listed as "Head" of the household on census records, it seems dad spent little time there. (Joe Dalton's presence at the farm is reflected in no other articles or records encountered in researching this book. Quite likely, he was living mostly at 240 West 75th Street in Manhattan in a property paid for by his son.[17]). Eltinge and his mother lived at 368 Bread and Cheese Hollow Rd. with a servant named Pence Weber. Everyone knew that, as much as Julian Eltinge might enjoy the farm at Fort Salonga, it was his "home" mostly in the sense that "[my] mother is there and where she lives is always home to me." He'd made some friends in the area, it was true, growing close to Harris Henschel and his wife Maude, a noted suffragist. The actor also befriended the Henschel's children, daughters Elsie and Mildred, to whom he wrote personalized notes on promotional photo-cards of himself in drag. Julian Eltinge also developed a friendship with the Henschels' son, Howard, who would later appear in transvestic, all-male "Womanless Wedding" shows, a phenomenon that would sweep the country in the 1920s.[18]

Not surprisingly, Julian Eltinge's real life, the one in which he impersonated women onstage, soon beckoned. Even before he'd been able to put all the final touches on the farmhouse, he was again headed abroad, this time to lucrative shows at the Marigny in Paris and the Ronacher in Vienna.[19]

* * *

Upon his return from the Continent, the UBO offered the now-celebrated impersonator $350 a week for a forty-week tour. Many a vaudevillian would jump at a contract like that. But Julian Eltinge understood that, for him, the two-a-day was but a way station, a well-paying steppingstone to greater artistic and professional goals.[20]

In part thanks to his own success, it was getting harder to stand out as a female impersonator in vaudeville. Rivals abounded. At Keith's Cleveland, female impersonator Max Waldon was "the most talked of feature" on the bill, the "most interesting of the entire program," in the opinion of manager H. A. Daniels. In Detroit, manager J. H. Finn felt Waldon's seventeen-minute turn was simply "superb." Julian Eltinge kept up, employing new characters and costumes that Carl Lothrop, manager of Keith's Boston, thought were "great," and the actor himself, still "the best of all female impersonators." But the entertainer was showing signs of fraying at the seams. He was becoming irritable and overstretched, leading to an uncharacteristic row with Charles Lovenberg, manager of Keith's Providence, regarding stage-positioning. Eltinge played a few fancy Manhattan "roof gardens," like the New Amsterdam and the Aerial, trendy perches that offered a summer-time alternative to stuffy theatres in the days before modern ventilation and air-conditioning.[21]

In 1908, during the hottest summer in a decade, the artist was invited to play perhaps the most prestigious of all roof gardens, the one atop Hammerstein's Victoria. Oscar Hammerstein I had opened the massive Olympia theatre and pleasure resort in 1895, between West 44th and West 45th Streets by what was then known as Longacre Square. (It was rechristened Times Square in 1904.) For fifty cents, Olympia patrons got access to stage shows, bowling alleys, billiard rooms, smoking salons, rathskellers, and a Turkish bath, all amid gilt-edged furnishings and statuary in the style of Louis XIV—an early prototype of Las Vegas's candy castles. Unsurprisingly, the Olympia failed to turn a profit. But Oscar I, never one to think small, opened the Victoria in 1899 at West 42nd Street and Seventh Avenue. Willie Hammerstein, Oscar's son and manager of the Victoria, coaxed patrons up to the roof garden by hiring big-name entertainers and also by heating up the elevators, which then opened into suspiciously refreshing rooftop air. (Hammerstein was also reputed to have hidden a chunk of ice underneath a large thermometer, further convincing customers they were in a cool aerie above the hot city streets.) Perhaps in part because his audience was so perspiration-free and comfortable, or at least believed themselves to be, Eltinge scored big at the Victoria, delighting the crowd in particular when de-wigging. At the nearby American rooftop, theatergoers craned their necks to see Eltinge's new red bathing suit, a perfect summertime theme.[22]

As he entertained on New York's fanciest roofs, however, the wheels of Julian Eltinge's next big opportunity were already turning. The job would involve a name as big and legendary as that of the Hammerstein or Keith & Albee: George M. Cohan. Cohan, considered by many one of a handful of

Figure 4.4 As beaches became popular for urbanites, women's bathing outfits also became more stylish, permitting women public, bodily freedom unknown to prior generations. Julian Eltinge's Bathing Beauties always sported the latest seaside fashions.
Credit: *Laurence Senelick Collection.*

"GEORGE M." IS FOR MINSTREL   105

true pioneers in the musical comedy genre as we know it, was in the process of putting together a major minstrel show with that genre's usually assortment of comedy, variety acts, and musical numbers. It would tour the country, visiting dozens of cities and towns. Cohan's barnstorming extravaganza, which he would produce and direct, was to star famed minstrel man George Evans, aka the "Honey Boy." Cohan needed a big complement of talent, from backup singers and supernumeraries to featured stars and specialty acts. He wanted America's favorite female-impersonation star on the bill. It was a high-profile engagement, a kind of merry, hugely racist Lollapalooza of its day. Julian Eltinge, looking for a way out of, and up from, another year of vaudeville, agreed to do it for a modest $175 a week, reasoning quite logically that hitching one's wagon to George M. Cohan's star was a no-brainer.[23]

* * *

The minstrel show, of course, presents a richly harrowing vein of American cultural history, one that can hardly be examined without in effect scrutinizing the very underpinnings of US nationhood. That is an ongoing project, as is scrutiny of the reactionary agitation such projects inevitably unleash. Even theatre historians and scholars must continue to tell us more—and grapple with what exactly to say and how best to say it—when exploring an entertainment genre that was so popular, influential, and reverberant as to be almost without equal during its lengthy tenure and beyond. For our purposes, it is crucial to point out the obvious: that blackface minstrel performers worked and lived in environs where to be "respectable"—that is, of the highest human social value—you had at least to be, if nothing else, white. At the same time, somehow reinforcing this dualistic hierarchy, white performers and fans became obsessively interested in Black culture, or in harvesting and reimagining aspects of it (as if there were, or is, a single thing called "Black culture"). To complicate matters further, it must be understood that Black performers had long developed their own artistic traditions, some in adaptation to white needs and demands, some in contradistinction to them, many sui generis. While the flow of creative energy was two-way, circular, even Escher-like, between (broadly speaking) white and Black artists, it was always predicated upon an enforced arrangement that inherently prized white skin, a dominant white culture, and mainstream white politics above their Black counterparts, *while yet needing the latter for their own legitimacy.*

106 BEAUTIFUL

After all, how could whiteness reign supreme without there being something else, something different, that most whites insisted they were *not*?[24]

In the 1830s, white men in America began blacking-up their faces and playing the part of enslaved persons, supposedly reflecting the latter's humor, sensibilities, mannerisms, and musical stylings. Minstrels' cartoonish, overblown, yet somehow purportedly authentic depictions at once conveyed a rich Black *subculture* while rendering Black *individuality* largely valueless. It might be instructive to remember that at about this time, white Europeans were in the process of colonizing nonwhite peoples, a venture made possible by the former viewing the latter as "human beings who lacked the specifically human character," as Hannah Arendt would later put it. The folk culture of enslaved Black Americans was therefore seen as raw material to be extracted, reconfigured according to the needs of power-holding groups, and turned into a lucrative commodity—a kind of *colonization* process some might say. It was a one-way transaction, on the conscious surface, anyway. It well-served a nation in its Jacksonian adolescence experimenting with a new self-identity, something approaching a religion: "American." What did it mean to be *American*, and who could be considered the most "American," and who . . . well, *not so much*? These were crucial questions of the day and would come to be linked to other inquiries such as, What did it mean to be a *man*, or an *invert*? The answer to, What does it mean to be "American"? increasingly meant prioritizing Anglo-European whiteness in general and ethnicity in particular as a means of organizing the social landscape—rather than, say, linking people to economic class or their place in the huge pyramid of labor. By the time Julian Eltinge joined George M. Cohan's minstrel troupe, the enemies of "progress" in the eyes of the controlling classes were those who proposed different allocations of power and resources, not those who believed in a racial hierarchy. The ethno-racial hierarchy was normal, natural, as it were.[25]

Thomas D. "T. D." Rice (no relation to E. E. Rice) was one of the first "Ethiopian delineators," an early term for minstrel players. Rice, a white man, claimed to have seen a Black stable hand do a "catchy little song and dance," which Rice supposedly copied and began performing while singing a tune about "jump[ing] Jim Crow," thus birthing a catchphrase that would live in infamy. Meanwhile, a New York performance troupe claiming to interpolate the songs and dances of enslaved Black persons renamed itself the Virginia Minstrels. Virginia was the symbolic heart of slaveholding culture, home to what would later become the capital of the Confederacy, Richmond. At the time, a popular act known as the Tyrolese Minstrel Family was yodeling its way across America with the result that calling yourself a "minstrel" was a good promotional tactic. Prior to the US Civil War in the early 1860s, blackface minstrel shows were mostly popular in the North, which had less direct access to plantation life but no shortage of racialized fascination with it. When Dan Emmett, one of the original Virginia Minstrels, entertained in New York and Boston saloons, he was met with enthusiastic crowds who clapped and stomped and sang along.[26]

By the 1850s, the typical minstrel show had developed a recognizable, three-part structure. At the start, the cast came onstage singing songs like "Camptown Races" or "Old Folks at Home" (aka "Swannee River"), which became enormously popular and made composers like Stephen Foster famous. "Mr. Interlocutor," sometimes called "the original straight man," engaged in comical patter with the characters on the ends, "Mr. Tambo" and "Mr. Bones," respectively, who usually delivered punchlines as well as playing the percussion instruments their names implied.[27]

Minstrel humor often derived from an increasingly frustrated Mr. Interlocutor trying to get a straight answer out of Tambo or Bones and repeatedly failing. For example, Interlocutor might say, "I presume he was a pretty good physician?," to which one of the End Men would reply, "No, wasn't fishin', he was home." Minstrel comics also delivered monologues in consciously absurd pidgin to shed humorous light on aspects of uptight, white culture while making the supposedly Black speaker seem innocent and unaware of what he was saying. A well-known minstrel monologue, for example, satirized lecture-circuit moralizing, making fun of people "so religious dat they eat pies at tea, so dat dey may hab pie-ous dreams," and others "so perfect dat dey reject all sincerity because it begins wid sin."[28] Next came a variety show known as an "olio" because it took place in front of an oilcloth curtain behind which the cast set up a sketch or one-act play to round out the proceedings. Many a vaudevillian honed their trade appearing in the olio portion of minstrel shows.[29]

Minstrel shows were also early incubators of female impersonation. Famed minstrel George Christy played a character named Miss Lucy Long, while others developed a "wench" caricature dubbed the "Funny Old Gal." Playing the so-called wench was a rite of passage for many entertainers, including Francis Wilson, who would go on to become the first president of Actors' Equity, and George "Honey Boy" Evans, star of troupe that hired Julian Eltinge.[30]

108   BEAUTIFUL

A bit like the Elizabethans, the more minstrel men impersonated women, the more seriously they took it, and the better they got at cultivating nuanced impressions. A characterization with a lighter complexion, known as a "yellow"—or "yaller"—"girl" became a standard subvariant. Playing a *yaller* could earn a man some of the best pay minstrelsy had to offer. The "Funny Old Gal" caricature often performed a "rubber-legged" dance, paving the way for "eccentric dancers" in vaudeville, such as Roscoe Ails. Minstrel men also developed a drag "balladist" and an "elegant mulatto" who satirized operatic divas.[31]

By the time minstrelsy reached its fever peak in the 1870s and 1880s, in part by further appealing to disgruntled white audiences in the South, it was increasingly clear that the darker a female character's skin, the less beautiful she was considered, which of course echoed and reinforced standard-issue white supremacism. If he didn't understand this already, working in minstrelsy led Julian Eltinge to make his most intentionally beautiful women not simply white but "hyper-white." In fact, whiteness and beauty were so closely allied in the dominant mind that a darker-skinned person might be thought not fully female *or*, respectively, male, sexed but not *sensual*. That is why the less-cartoonish, "High Yaller girls" conveyed a romantic eros that other minstrel impersonations did not. Amid the zany humor and anarchic slapstick of the minstrel show, the *yaller* could render a heartbreaking sentimental ballad or a tragic love song. White women *not* wearing blackface would later appropriate minstrelsy's "coon songs," which were often racy or pugnacious. Artists like Ziegfeld star Anna Held thus became, in effect, "whiteface" artists, combining the supposed vivacity of nonwhite culture without surrendering conventional beauty norms. Although Anna Held, Sophie Tucker, and others could hide or downplay their Jewish heritage, something that set them apart from the dominant Anglo-American culture, a Black artist could never hide their ethnicity. While the press and public often cooperated with the former, wanting to see Held and Tucker as "American," much as they wanted to see Eltinge as a "normal young man," they expressed disgust when Black performers tried the same. A balladist and woman of color named Margaret Scott who used facial powder to "look white" at Keith's Boston in 1904 was deemed "ghastly" by house manager M. J. Keating. Nonwhites, such as comedians Brown & Navarro, could at times play *other* nonwhites, like Chinese or then-somehow-less-than-fully-white Italians. The latter would evolve into Hollywood's Italian-American cliché of gangster or streetwise ruffian, while the former would long be used to express "the mysterious East"

"GEORGE M." IS FOR MINSTREL   109

and its allure. In time, of course, the Italian could Americanize while the Asian would always scent of the exotic, if somehow sinister, "Orient."[32]

* * *

By the time Julian Eltinge joined George M. Cohan's Honey Boy troupe, the formal minstrel show, though far from defunction, was declining in popularity. But its offspring and cousins, including cakewalkers, "coon" singers and dancers, and white performers in blackface or employing a minstrel dialect, were still immensely popular in vaudeville. In fact, many white comedians performed in blackface, a composite of greasepaint and burnt cork, not because they understood themselves to be giving a minstrel show, per se, but simply because it had become a convention, a vestigial reminder of American racial dynamics that had all but sunk into the collective white unconscious. Al Jolson and Eddie Cantor often blacked their faces, sometimes singing a minstrel song, but many times, not. The Nichol Sisters, aka the Kentucky Belles, were reckoned by some insiders as the "best black face women in vaudeville." Former minstrel artist Lew Dockstader stopped using burnt cork because he felt he no longer needed it and instead "worked in white face," while comedian George W. Day suddenly started "doing his work now in black face" in 1905. When Julian Eltinge recalled that as a youth, "It had always been my ambition to be a black-face comedian," he didn't necessarily mean that he intended to become a minstrel man but rather, a run of the mill, comical, song-and-dance artist.[33]

Blackface star George Evans had earned his nickname from singing "Honey Boy" by Jack Norworth, who also wrote the lyrics to "Take Me Out to the Ball Game." ("Honey" could signify Blackness to white audiences, as could "molasses" and, as we have seen, "yaller." The popularity of Norworth's songs suggests he knew at least two things—baseball and racism—would typically play well with mainstream American fans.) Evans was hugely popular on Keith time, taking his blackface act around the country. "Worth all the money we pay him," in the opinion of the manager at Keith's Boston. He was dedicated, known to soldier on even when ill or hungover or both. Evans was popular in vaudeville because, like others such as Eva Tanguay, he took seemingly awkward or hackneyed material and interpreted it in magnetic fashion. "The same stuff in other hands would fall flat," averred a Keith manager. To work under the banner of George M. Cohan was major feather in

110   BEAUTIFUL

Julian Eltinge's cap; but at the time, working alongside George Evans was a pretty decent score in its own right.[34]

Still: it is difficult to overstate George M. Cohan's cultural influence at the time he recruited George Evans and Julian Eltinge and beyond. Born July 3, 1878—ever the jingoist, he famously claimed to have been "born of the fourth of July"—into a theatrical family, Cohan was onstage from his earliest youth. He and his siblings formed "The Four Cohans" vaudeville act with young George as its chief writer and composer. He adapted sketch material into full-length musicals, such as 1904's *Little Johnny Jones*, which contained the hit numbers "Give My Regards to Broadway" and "Yankee Doodle Boy." He followed up in 1906 with *Forty-Five Minutes from Broadway* and *George Washington, Jr.*, the latter featuring "You're a Grand Old Flag."[35]

Like other artists of his era, Cohan was not a composer-librettist who labored in writerly seclusion and then conferred his masterpiece upon a herd of actors. Instead, he gathered talented players and drew on their well-known skills to create a concept that Cohan would then shape to perfection. The age of the auteur and their canonical script had not fully arrived in American theatre. Cohan's contemporary Frank Perley, for example, collaborated with his Comedians, a "munificently equipped musical organization," to develop hit shows like *The Chaperons* (1902), which consisted of well-known stars supplying their signature talents while traversing a "thread of a plot."[36]

Artistically innovative as he was, Cohan was also deeply conservative, committed to unfettered capitalism and a thoroughly whitewashed view of American history, all of which was not unusual for the time but still sometimes made him an outlier in the theatre community. Cohan's white-idealizing, pro-business, expansionist outlook shaped and reflected an American "national identity" that had long been in development. His world-view was rather different from, for example, that of an immigrant in John Dos Passos's *U.S.A. Nineteen Nineteen* who declares, "I'm a good American" but has no interest in going to war for "Banker Morgan" and others who, in his view, exploit and divide. Cohan, on the other hand, strenuously opposed the creation of Actors' Equity and for a time refused to mount shows, in protest of the union's creation. Cohan's proto-libertarianism appealed to Julian Eltinge, publicly anyway; if he felt differently behind closed doors there is no evidence of it. To be overly sympathetic to socialism or even labor was to risk being seen as a "nance," an epithet that originally referred to eighteenth-century English prostitute and dancer Nancy Dawson but came to suggest a "finicky and effeminate young man," and had also been used derogatorily

"GEORGE M." IS FOR MINSTREL   111

when referring to female impersonators in minstrel shows. Eltinge would later join Actors' Equity but quickly "lowered himself out" out when a strike loomed in 1919. He once vowed to move abroad "unless America comes to itself and abolishes these prohibition and cigarette [restriction] laws," and maintained close relationships with business organizations. Like the fist fights and Harvard pedigree, airing these views may have been a proactive defense against suspicions of his manhood. Perhaps he didn't think much about what he saying or its longer-term consequences. He would, however, long maintain a friendship with the Yankee Doodle Boy, George M. Cohan.[37]

* * *

The Honey Boy Minstrels got off to a rocky start. From hundreds who auditioned, choreographer James Gorman initially found but one dancer worthy of hire, putting everything on a tightened timeline. Eventually, though, Cohan gathered enough of a crew and something approaching an outline, if not exactly a script. By the fall of 1908, the show was ready for previews in Atlantic City, after which point, if everything went well, it would spend a month in Manhattan, then move to Chicago and, after that, head "direct for the 'coast.'" There would also be dates down in Atlanta in December. Minstrel veterans George Thatcher, Eddie Leonard, the duo of Rice & Prevost, various "novelty" acts, seventeen musicians, twelve singers, another dozen "song and dance men," plus technicians, stage managers, and prop handlers—not to mention George Evans and Julian Eltinge—made up a rambling brigade of sixty-five souls. Eltinge forged a few enduring friendships with fellow troupers, including Jacques Pierre, who would later go on to manage shows in Los Angeles, and another with singer/composer Earl Benham, who would also become Broadway's tailor-to-the-stars. The motley, cumbersome enterprise would need $5,000 a week in ticket sales to break even. The producers added some stops in upstate New York where then-thriving industrial cities like Albany and Troy offered ready markets, and sprinkled in performances in Brighton Beach, Brooklyn, as well. Eltinge was reportedly under a two-year contract with the Cohan & Harris organization, though such a "contract" could simply mean a handshake, a wink, and bragging rights. There would also be a "novelty act" from Europe, "the identity of which is being carefully concealed." Promoters touted the show's sheer size, often seen as inherently appealing, particularly when it came to entertainment. Even by the 1870s, J. H. Haverly boasted the "FORTY—40—COUNT 'EM FORTY"

112   BEAUTIFUL

cast members of the "UNITED MASTODON MINSTRELS," to compete with "Leavitt's Gigantean Minstrels" and "Cleveland's Colossals." Railroads, telegraphs, telephones, and an improved mail system made it increasingly easier from a logistical standpoint to take large shows on the road for months at a time.[38]

Cohan & Harris promoted Julian Eltinge as a major fixture of their extravaganza, advertising him as the "World's Foremost Impersonator... A Glorious Triumph—Success Supreme—A Positive Furor." Eltinge delivered many of his usual favorites—Spanish Dancer, Gibson Girl, etc.—accompanied by the rapturous de-wigging, which inevitably triggered a "loud buzz of comment" and a flurry of sighs. For the first time in his career, he experimented with other-than-marble-white makeup. The impersonator donned burnt cork for "Oh, You Coon," a duet with Evans, and played a *yaller* Juliet opposite Evans as "Komeo" in a Shakespeare parody. His range of characters gave crowds different samplings of what they loved: Eltinge's classic, whiteface ladies conveyed "delicacy and refinement," while his dark-complexioned women could evoke tragic pathos or, conversely, low comedy. Knowledgeable observers agreed that Julian Eltinge had indeed surpassed the artistry of veteran impersonators Stuart and ?Lind?.[39]

The Honey Boy extravaganza gained traction as it trundled across the land, attracting crowds and giving Julian Eltinge the brightest spotlight he'd yet known. For his standard impersonations, the impersonator employed "a perfect dear of a complexion"—that is, the ivory whiteness that signaled feminine beauty to most mainstream theatergoers. But he also used tan or beige makeup in an iteration of the Gibson Girl he called the "Gibson Coon."[40] Minstrelsy had given Julian Eltinge and other white performers a trans-racial flexibility ever out of reach to actual artists of color.

* * *

A good vaudevillian knew how to combine time-tested amusements with current fads and trends. One season, a comic "monologist" might riff about Tin Lizzies and Teddy Roosevelt, while the next, it was all about Taft's corpulence and the latest dance crazes. In 1908, everyone in the entertainment world, from comedians to opera stars to female impersonators, simply *had to* take part in a massive fad the *New York Times* was describing as "The Call of Salome." Working the famed biblical temptress and her controversial dance into one's act, by any means necessary, was essential to keeping

"GEORGE M." IS FOR MINSTREL   113

in the spotlight. There was a plethora of interpretations and adaptations, all supposedly drawn from scriptural source material but in fact, leapfrogging off any number of recent works, including plays, paintings, operas, and even other vaudeville routines. It didn't hurt that at the same time the Salome craze hit American popular culture, consumers were becoming fascinated with the "exotic" East and the European avant-garde, ensuring that many a so-called Salome dancer fed aspects of both into their creative sausage-grinder to crank out some kind of strange-tasting Dance of the Seven Veils.[41]

Salome had been a subject of popular diversion since at least medieval days, when mimes interpreted her infamous dance for village audiences, sometimes weaving in dagger-balancing and swordplay. The biblical Salome had long been tarred as an "evil" seductress in Western culture because her sensual dance resulted in the beheading of John the Baptist, the responsibility for the Baptist's fate redounding to her alone, apparently. But by the late nineteenth century, she had been somewhat rehabilitated as a wily "femme fatale," not exactly virtuosic but at least complicated and compelling. Heinrich Heine, Nathaniel Hawthorne, Gustave Flaubert, Gustave Moreau, and Edvard Munch all used her as a subject in their respective art forms, as did Jules Massenet in his 1881 opera, *Hérodiade*, which played a big part in bringing Salome to mass-public attention.[42]

Oscar Wilde was probably her most famous modern champion, though. His 1891 play *Salome* was supposed to premiere in London with Sarah Bernhardt, but was banned by the Lord Chamberlain. Published in French the following year, though, the work gained traction. In 1894, an English print edition, accompanied by Aubrey Beardsley's erotic illustrations of the "dance of the seven veils," further popularized Wilde's creation. By 1896, future Julian Eltinge costar Loie Fuller was performing "La Dance des Nymphes," a Salome satire, at the Comédie-Parisienne, her bare feet and gauzy skirts raising eyebrows. Max Reinhardt's mixed-genre spectacle, *A Vision of Salome*, staged in Leipzig in 1904, and Richard Strauss's opera, *Salome* (Dresden, 1905), brought the biblical femme fatale into the twentieth century.[43]

Pretty soon, everyone in multiple amusement fields was whipping up a Salome of one kind or another, including dancer Pilar Morin, comedians Weber & Rush, and filmmaker Siegmund Lubin, whose twenty-one-minute movie *"Salome": "The Dance of the Seven Veils"* promised "vivid scenes." (Rental fee for exhibitors: $44.) Mlle. Dazie—stage name of Daisy Peterkin from St. Louis, Missouri—appeared as Salome in the *Ziegfeld Follies*

Figure 4.5 The quasi-biblical Salome was all the rage in 1908. No matter who you were, from vaudeville queen to prima donna, you had to work the Dance of the Seven Veils into your act. Somehow. By whatever means necessary. Cultural authorities panicked over the industry's supposedly loosened morals. As usual, nobody criticized Julian Eltinge, acknowledged as the most accurate depicter of women but never blamed like them. As Salome, his costume was called "more decent" than what top female vaudevillians wore, his act deemed "without any immodest suggestiveness".

Credit: *Photo by White Studio, © The New York Public Library for the Performing Arts.*

and gave classes for would-be Salome dancers.[44] But when the enterprising Willie Hammerstein sent Gertrude Hoffman to London in 1908 to cop Maud Allan's act, it didn't take long for every vaudevillian and musical comedy actress, and even a few female impersonators, to scurry aboard the Salome bandwagon. Probably the most famous were Eva Tanguay and Lotta Faust, members of what the papers called "The 'Salome' Club."[45]

The craze forced tightfisted impresarios to give meaty raises to many of their Salome-dancing stars, nearly all of whom were women. Vaudeville was fast becoming one place in the American economy where women consistently outearned men. Artists such as Tanguay, Elsie Janis, Irene Franklin, and Nora Bayes commanded up to $3,000 a week or more, while lesser-known players could make $750–$1,500. Subspecialists also triumphed with Salome, including Fanny Brice's "Sadie Salome Go Home," a hit with Yiddish audiences. According to *Variety*, the cry all around New York in the summer of 1908 was, "Take the automobile and let's go Saloming."[46]

* * *

Julian Eltinge pondered how to bring Salome into the Cohan & Harris show. Minstrel performers were already making Salome their own. He had to act quick. The vaudeville team of Hymer & Kent had already written a popular "coon" song called "De Sloamey Dance," which went: "Tho' 'way yo' clo'es—wear a smile, read hist'ry an' den take a chance; An' go do de Sloamey . . . Looks like old Hooch a-kooch to me." Carnivalesque impersonator Englishman Malcolm Scott parodied the Dance of the Seven Veils surrounded by whiskey bottles, and the enigmatic Lind? opted for an artistic, naturalistic rendition.[47]

Julian Eltinge's approach to Salome was not so much to impersonate or reinterpret the biblical figure herself as to cheekily comment upon the many Salomes populating stageland.[48] His version became a fast hit, "Heralded" for an artistry that eluded even many top female stars. "If all women dancers who delve into the realm of the Far East . . . kept within the same bounds of real art that Mr. Eltinge does, the stage to-day would be the richer therefor, [without] sensationalism and vulgarity," wrote the *New York Dramatic Mirror*. Eltinge's perfect drag was the ideal against which allegedly pandering women would be judged—no matter than many men in the audience delighted in Eva Tanguay's and Maud Allan's "vulgarity."[49]

116 BEAUTIFUL

Vaudevillians made a point of sparring with one another, usually the nastier the better. Eva Tanguay took out ads challenging her rivals to song-and-dance battles and boasting her superiority. "I rank only one 'act' above myself," she declared in a half-page ad in *Variety*, "It is Mme. Sarah Bernardt." On another occasion, she reprinted a critique of her own act that stated she had "not the slightest conception of 'Salome,' from either a Biblical or Oscar Wilde viewpoint," and came across as simply "ludicrous and grotesque." Next to it was a hand with extended index finger and the words, "This Criticism 'Doesn't Bother Me'" in boldface type. Trash-talking your competitors and taking it on the chin was but another grand, vaudevillian escapade, perhaps like professional wrestlers in our day. Julian Eltinge might have fibbed about his willingness to punch out a stranger. But when it came to PR turf wars, he was all in, favorably comparing himself not to other female impersonators but to the luminaries of "The 'Salome' Club." Before debuting his act at the New York Theatre in 1908 he declared, "No woman has adequately portrayed the dance of Salome." The impersonator even challenged his rivals to a "competitive Salome dance." A press that made many derogatory comments about female Salomes did nothing but champion Julian Eltinge; his Dance of the Seven Veils was felt to convey an authenticity and "poetry of motion" many others lacked. The *Chicago Tribune* declared Julian Eltinge—"Harvard graduate" and "enthusiastic sportsman"—the "only original male Salome." Whatever that meant.[50]

His Salome made Julian Eltinge the standout star of Cohan & Harris's Honey Boy Minstrels. From Buffalo to New Orleans, he was deemed more artful and modest in his "silver-spangled robe" than Maud Allan or Gertrude Hoffman who had actually pioneered the fad.[51] He also added a clever, topical twist. Most other Salomes danced around John the Baptist's disembodied head, which was usually perched atop a platform under a shroud that was eventually flung away. When Julian Eltinge plucked the draping off, however, audiences beheld a papier-mâché bust of Teddy Roosevelt, William Howard Taft, or sometimes William Jennings Bryan.[52]

The minstrel tour had its share of stresses too. Eltinge had long struggled with being able to eat as much as he liked, one of his pleasures, because it led to putting on weight which made it harder to corset-up or, worse yet, mimic an increasingly popular, skinny female form. If he edged much above 180 lbs. there would be trouble—and observers noticed he was beginning to plump up.[53]

* * *

The Salome craze marked a turning point in social mores. Audiences increasingly wanted more of the exotic, the sensual, even the iconoclastic. The creators of mass-market entertainment, who had built their brand on claims of careful oversight and purity, now found themselves having to walk a narrow line: give the public what it wanted (and enrich themselves in the process), or keep what had recruited those fans in the first place. Pretty much right on schedule, morally panicked voices started shrieking. The Salome and exotic-dancing trend was bound to corrupt American youth, traditional values, religion, and the family—all the usual suspects. In late summer 1908, New Jersey officials banned Salome dancing and arrested a performer in Newark, forcing her to replace the Dance of the Seven Veils with a routine that would not "offend even a deacon." Receiving complaints, New York City's police commissioner dispatched a bevy of officers to keep tabs on Salome shows, with particular attention to the players' "dresses, or lack of them."[54] Martin Beck, financially allied with the purportedly puritanical Keith circuit (presently making millions off the Salome craze), called the Dance of the Seven Veils "degrading" and in need of replacement by something "higher and loftier." Beck, a European-born child actor, was probably little bothered personally by Salome but understood that the American market was by turns prurient and puritanical. One might have to distract the public from seeing seductive dancing as base and sensual, instead persuading it to see it like any other refined art form. Take the sexual content out of its commercial context, present it as artistic, and then delicately replant it back into popular soil. That was the trick. "[O]ne of the commonplace insults thrown at the painter of the nude is that he is basely influenced by the commercial value of his product," observed *Scribner's Magazine* in 1892. Context would tell people what they were to find offensive and what, artful; there were good buttocks and bad ones, the framing being literally the only—and critical—difference. Businessmen were in a quandary: marketplace capitalism was meant by its very nature to foster desire, though many who supported the economic system could not somehow *abide* all that desire. Put another way, "the commercial" was intrinsically libidinal if one understood libido as a raw yearning that was not always specifically sexual, a "love in the broad sense," according to Freud's editor and translator Dr. A. A. Brill writing in the 1930s.[55]

Catholic and Protestant clergy, many from the Sabbatarian League, inveighed against Salome as well as Sunday shows—which were, after all, direct competition for their own spectacles—while a few performers, including Marie Cahill, joined the reactionary fray by calling for protection of, or perhaps *from*, the youth, particularly the "foreign youth" she said were breaching American shores. The "world is very far out of order," wrote a panicked pamphleteer back in 1620 as he surveyed crossdressing in London's theatres. To those troubled by Salome, the world indeed seemed out of order once again.[56]

But one Salome dancer served as a lightning rod for moral anxiety, partly by her own design, in line with her brand, and partly because she was a woman who was hard to classify: Eva Tanguay. As outspoken and brash as Julian Eltinge was circumspect and studied, Tanguay had risen to the top of her profession by defying many standard notions of womanhood, both onstage and off. If Eltinge concealed himself in the armor of proper femininity, Tanguay seemed uninterested in or unable to contain her vital, raw energy, which poured forth and lit up her performances. Fans adored her. Critics criticized her, as they are wont to do, but adored her just the same. Born in rural Quebec in 1878, Tanguay moved with her family to New England when just a child. Cutting her teeth in musical burlesques like *My Lady* and *The Chaperones*, she developed a quirky vaudeville act full of ludicrous comedy, energetic dancing (or something approaching it), and songs like "I Don't Care." A fan who saw her in 1914 characterized Tanguay as "A Song and Dance artist who does not dance, cannot sing, is not beautiful, witty or graceful, but who dominates her audience more entirely than anyone on the Vaudeville stage."[57]

Although many, predominantly male writers who described Tanguay lauded her for her brazen sexuality and smutty humor—famed British mystic and weirdo Aleister Crowley called her an "Avatar of 'sexinsomnia'"—the actress was more broadly libidinal than erotic, particularly compared to, say, Mae West who patterned herself on Tanguay.[58] Despite some racy lyrics and revealing costumes, Eva Tanguay scented more of "lunacy" than "lewdness."[59]

Still, while Julian Eltinge's Salome was praised for its propriety, Eva Tanguay's drew moral fire. Perhaps it was her frenzied energy, something considered unwomanly or uncivilized (but which her fans loved), or that her Salome employed a "Negro boy with big eyes" poking his head through a hole on a platter making for a Black John the Baptist.[60] Whatever landed her yet again in the moral crosshairs, controversy was nothing new to Tanguay. Which is why the press went into raptures at the news that she and Eltinge had gotten engaged. This was the performance event of 1908, brilliantly out-of-character for both artists yet somehow a perfect reflection of so many social contradictions and hypocrisies.

The two artists and their respective handlers surely salivated over what was in short order dubbed the "union of the Salomes." Eltinge and Tanguay said they'd marry on October 1, sidestepping whether they meant it in earnest or rather were faking it most enthusiastically. It was de-wigging and Barnumesque humbug on a whole new level. A reporter asked the "Honey Boy Salome" if vaudeville's wild woman would change her name following the wedding, but Eltinge "coyly" tucked his "bare feet" under his skirts and demurred. Soon, the theatre community chimed in. Vaudeville impresario Percy Williams insisted he had "Eva Tanguay" under contract to him for a year, and after that, she could call herself whatever she liked. It was the entertainment world's best inside joke of the year.[61]

The happy couple said there would be no Salome costumes or veil-dancing at the engagement ceremony, nor at the wedding itself. Rather, Eltinge would appear in a white gown and Tanguay would don a dapper tux. Why not? The press considered the Eltinge's Salome "just as much, if not more, the real thing" than Gertrude Hoffman's and Maud Allan's, so why not also as a bride? Partnering with Tanguay allowed the impersonator to be uncharacteristically cheeky and rebellious, poking fun at esteemed traditions and gender roles. Indeed, some saw Tanguay as an "impersonator" too since as a child and teen performer, she'd often played traditionally gender-fluid roles like Little Lord Fauntleroy and other girlish boys and boyish girls. In what has been called "the age of the bachelor," it was unclear who the real bachelor was: Eltinge, who avoided criticizing marriage but never married, or Tanguay, who openly loathed marriage but nonetheless wed at least twice—much to her immediate regret on both occasions. In this curious betrothal, Eva Tanguay was cast as the outlier, not her white-gowned fiancé/fiancée. *Her* promise to marry, not Eltinge's, "excited stageland" in way not seen "for a long time." The developing storyline was: *Will-the-wild-woman-go-through-with-it?* and not, *Will-the-suspected-homosexual-marry-a-woman?*[62]

Interest in the engagement grew to a fever pitch in what social critic Daniel Boorstin might have described as a marvelous "pseudo-event," if a cheeky and self-aware one, had he been around to witness it. "When Girl-Boy Weds Boy-Girl, Who'll Be the Boss?" wondered the *St. Louis Post-Dispatch* in a headline that itself sounded like a vaudeville skit. The "astonishing matrimonial" was now supposed to take place on or about October 14. It was rumored that Eltinge might be a Gibson Girl–type bride while Tanguay would appear as Little Tommy Tucker or Jack Horner, juvenile roles often filled by girls or young women. "Tanguay Looks Better than Eltinge in Boy's Clothes,

120   BEAUTIFUL

and Vice-Versa," wrote one journalist. The betrothal took on a life of its own, spurring participant-observers to join in the story like modern-day fan fiction scribblers. Eltinge and Tanguay, it was rumored, had hired a clergyman who was "sufficiently seasoned in the marrying business not to get mixed up as to the sex of the contracting principals and pronounce a reversed 'man and wife' sentence." Eva Tanguay would supposedly say "I Don't Care" rather than "I do" when the big moment arrived. Marriage had long been a target of vaudeville humor, a social shackle one could not avoid and thus complained about for the rest of one's earthly days. There were literally thousands of one-liners like, "Love is a ski ride down a hill; marriage is the climb back" and "She calls him her time-clock. Every time he comes home, she punches him."[63]

The Eltinge/Tanguay nuptial affair pushed each to the top of the Salome frenzy. Eva Tanguay was starting to become as famous for playing "the wicked wriggler"—that is, Salome—as for her trademark song, "I Don't Care." Meanwhile the "good looking Harvard grad," Julian Eltinge, would be "Saloming a few himself" after his tour with Cohan & Harris ended.[64]

Realizing they'd milked the joke for all it was worth—a good vaudevillian's crucial, sixth sense—they wound it down in the late fall of 1908. Tanguay introduced a new song titled, "Do You Wonder, Girls, [Why] I Never Married Him?" She wasn't going to marry America's number one female impersonator or anyone else for that matter. The actress was "nonmatrimonial," telling the public, "I have decided that it would be folly for me to sacrifice my independence by marrying any one [sic]." She played a new kind of woman who was skeptical of, rather than socially brainwashed by, the notion of wedlock, much like Carlotta Dashington, the character Tanguay played in her 1904 musical hit, *The Sambo Girl*. Carlotta was a cakewalk instructor who raced a motorcar "on account of trying to get away from a man." The year after she pretended to become Julian Eltinge's fiancée, the actress quashed rumors that she was to wed entertainment executive Eddie Darling, quipping that "wedding bells don't sound like music to me." She was permitted to employ an excuse long socially available to men but relatively new for a woman: "She Loves Her Work Too Well to Become Mrs. Julian Eltinge or Mrs. Anybody Else."[65] As for Julian Eltinge, he did what any respectable bride would have done when left at the altar: disappeared discreetly to dodge further gossip.

* * *

The Salome craze burned on but never with the intensity of late summer/early fall 1908. Some artists pandered with exoticist, Salome-adjacent routines like Adeline Boyer's "Princess of Israel" and Cleopatra en Masque's "Oriental Snake Dance of Mystery."[66] Eva Tanguay had other fish to fry. Salome was yesterday's fad, receding in the rearview as quickly as it had burst upon the scene. She was among vaudeville's top earners and that meant keeping things fresh. Every once in a while, she gave a nostalgic taste of Salome, but for the most part, her Dance of the Seven Veils was literally mothballed, its sets and costumes sometimes borrowed by small-time imitators such as Mimi Aguglia.[67]

Julian Eltinge concocted some "Eastern dances," including one involving a cobra that he claimed to have developed with Ruth St. Denis "when were in the same company"—which of course they never were. His newfound success allowed the female impersonator to lie a bit more fluently, though this hardly set him apart from a new breed of celebrities who fancied their lives as mutable as any minstrel extravaganza or vaudeville sketch. Arthur Alexander replaced him in Cohan & Harris's Honey Boy Minstrels, while Julian Eltinge strategized, as ever, how to get to the next level, professionally, financially, and artistically. He would soon discover that not everyone in the business was so comfortable with inversion after all.[68]

# # #

5

Fascinating Stardom

Julian Eltinge had promoters and PR folks. He'd had fellow cast members on tour with *Mr. Wix of Wickham* and Cohan & Harris's Honey Boy Minstrels. He had his mom, Julia (and father, Joe, for what that was worth), although she was back at home in Fort Salonga. But the star impersonator was, in so many ways, on his own. Without a spouse, companion, or even a creative costar, life on the road was challenging. Sophie Tucker often cried herself to sleep because she felt so "lonesome" touring the vaudeville circuits. Maybe Julian Eltinge was fine with it. Maybe he *had to be* fine with it, or come across that way. Unlike Tucker and many other entertainers, he left no memoir of his feelings. Still, it couldn't have been easy. Riding the rails to strange cities, checking into hostelries that tolerated theatre people, and getting to the stage door early enough to pass "two whole hours before the glass" making-up, day in, day out—it was a lot for one person's shoulders. Other performers could get to the theatre mere minutes before their turn on the bill if they wanted. Not Julian Eltinge. Playing the two-a-day sometimes meant up to four hours of prep time for what amounted to two fifteen-minute performances. Plus, it wasn't as if all he had to carry with him was a fiddle or a notebook with joke scribblings. "I envy some of those other artists who are able to prepare for the stage in fifteen minutes," Eltinge groaned as he recalled fellow vaudevillian Ethel Levy rushing into her dressing room, slapping on some rouge, and going out under the lights. Increasingly, the entertainer needed an armada of trunks to carry the tools of his trade. Though his promoters blithely publicized the fact that he toted $900 in apparel and accouterments—close to $30,000 in today's money—it added up to an exhausting ordeal. To tour as Julian Eltinge was to tour as an entire cast of women, some playing Salome, some a Bathing or Gibson Girl, all rendered by a guy trying to keep ahead of the competition. And the competition, it should be noted, was gaining ground. If Eltinge was touring with a thousand dollars' worth of custom dresses, his rivals made a point of traveling with more, or at least claiming to. Keeping up with his own act was hard enough. Making sure he was bigger

Beautiful. Andrew L. Erdman, Oxford University Press. © Oxford University Press 2024.
DOI: 10.1093/9780197696361.003.0006

and better and fancier than other female impersonators was all but unsustainable. He needed a helper, a brother-in-arms. He needed a friend.[1]

In 1908, Eltinge placed an ad for a dresser.[2] Dressers were essential for many stage artists, especially those who changed costumes multiple times during a show. They could be supporters, confidants, and cocreators too. Taking off and putting on another's raiment cannot but build a certain intimacy. At the time, hiring such a person in the United States often meant hiring an immigrant from Japan, much as today securing a home health aide or nurse often means hiring somebody from the Caribbean or West Africa. Japanese persons had started moving to the United States in greater numbers, often via Hawai'i, starting in the late 1800s. Violent white-supremacist groups such as the Industrial Army drove many of these newcomers from agricultural and industrial jobs, forcing Japanese men and women to look for employment elsewhere. In 1905, labor unions, fraternal orders, and political groups—many of whom were likely staging crossdressed musicals—formed the Japanese-Korean Exclusion League. To be American was to be white and of Anglo-European ethnicity, and vice versa, even if more than a few of the "Americans" who led the movement had come from Norway, Ireland, and Germany, or their parents had. California passed a law in 1879 limiting land ownership by Asian migrants, and in the first decade of the 1900s, papers like the *San Francisco Chronicle* stirred up an early iteration of Fox News–style animosity among readers with headlines such as, "Japanese a Menace to American Woman" and "Brown [meaning, in this case, Japanese and Chinese] Men Are Made Citizens Illegally." Still, Japanese people continued to take their chances in this new land. Immigration from Japan peaked in 1907, a tide that would be halted abruptly with the Immigration Act of 1924.[3]

For a number of interrelated reasons, some Japanese newcomers were able to secure employment in the domestic sphere, labor associated more with women than men. They worked as personal secretaries, assistants, valets, and in some cases as actors' dressers and attendants. Having a Japanese assistant was so common that in 1909, vaudevillian singer, dancer, and comic Carter DeHaven began his act in a set resembling his dressing room, where he began "'making up' with the assistance of his little Japanese valets, in full sight of the audience."[4]

The first person to show up for Julian Eltinge's want-ad was, unsurprisingly, a Japanese man. His name was Ko Shima. "Do you speak English?" Eltinge asked. No, shrugged Shima, though he could presumably write his name. Fifteen interviews with fifteen other Japanese job applicants followed,

124 BEAUTIFUL

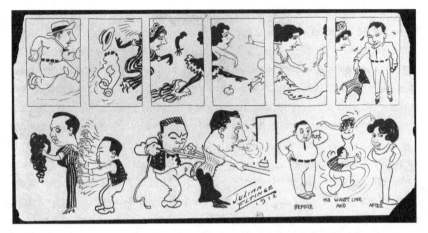

Figure 5.1 The Eltinge machine didn't run without the labor of his assistant/confidant, Ko Shima. Shima is depicted as shorter but also determined and energetic. This cartoon conveys a complicated partnership, with aspects of servility intertwined with warmth and intimacy.
Credit: *Billy Rose Theatre Division, The New York Public Library for the Performing Arts.*

with none of the individuals communicating quite well enough to qualify or otherwise lacking in some important skill. The story goes that the persistent Mr. Shima came back and somehow pleaded for the job, whereupon Eltinge relented. "It was hard work making signs," admitted the impersonator. But the new hire nonetheless turned out to be more than capable, "a wonder," so "I put up with it." Thus began a long, professional relationship that was essential to help the actor meet the mounting burdens of his trade. Several months after hiring Shima, supposedly, Eltinge walked past his assistant, who was crouched in a corner of the stage near a prop closet. "Come, you babies, make the six," shouted Shima at a pair of dice. "Five and one; four and two; three and three. Come on you babies. Shima needs a new pair of shoes." Eltinge looked at him and queried, "Do you know what you are saying?" *Yes, absolutely*, responded Shima. Apparently, he had known English for a while but continued to make his employer formulate crude signs. "Me learn English," said Ko Shima, satirizing himself like a white vaudevillian doing an Asian caricature. Eltinge appreciated the irony, later saying, "I'm sorry I was bareheaded [because] I wanted to take my hat off to him."[5] Like many other immigrants, it was hard for Japanese folks in America. They had to conform to certain demands—language, customs, deportment—while not challenging their place on the cultural chessboard. In some places, Japanese people could be persecuted for "crossdressing as 'American' " in public. That meant walking the ever-impossible line: fitting in while remembering to be an outsider.[6]

Despite such treatment, Japanese migrants were regarded above other nonwhite arrivals. They were praised for filial piety and, as *Popular Science Monthly* wrote in 1893, "fraternal fondness." The Japanese were also compared favorably with the Chinese, an important distinction as the United States gazed across the Pacific. "Th- Japs ar-re Chinymen well-done," remarks a character in a short story from 1901. These "little brown people" from Japan were not so much threatening and uncivilized as "Quaint" and retiring in nature.[7]

In part due to Japan's startling victory over Tsarist forces in the Russo-Japanese War of 1904–1905, they were also considered competent and well organized if not actually a serious military threat to America. (The Russians had considered the Japanese backward and incapable of prosecuting a modern war.) By seeming to subordinate their personal egos for the greater good, a notion anathema to many Americans, the Japanese were thought capable of remarkable feats—if one cared to pay the price of surrendering one's alleged individuality. The Sugimoto Japs, a popular gymnastics and balancing troupe, impressed both the fans and manager Charles Lovenberg at Keith's Providence in January 1905. That it was just after the devastating Russian surrender at Port Arthur only added to the crowd's enthusiasm. Other acts, like the Imperial Japanese Guard, showed off how they scaled walls and executed other martial tasks. Also popular were short movies and/or recreations of the Port Arthur siege. White vaudevillians like Valerie Bergere even developed Japanese minstrel routines.[8]

Impressive as they were—indeed perhaps because they were so impressive—many white Americans worried the United States would soon be "blighted" with Japanese arrivals and their kin. In the 1890s, Washington State governor John H. McGraw admitted he admired the Japanese but could not "for a moment approve of their becoming citizens of the republic."[9]

Much like Julian Eltinge, Ko Shima understood how to navigate appearances and propriety, meeting cultural expectations while exploiting blind spots and contradictions. In a certain sense, that made him a good match for the nation's top female impersonator. To fans and the press, Shima was the "polite" gatekeeper who informed them, for instance, "Mr. Eltinge is not down yet. Will you please come in and wait please?" while helping keep his employer's life running as smoothly as possible. If Eltinge wore long skirts,

126 BEAUTIFUL

Shima carried the train or cleared a path so nothing got snagged. Shima also helped his boss manage onerous travel logistics, making sure that all those wardrobes and makeup kits were onboard, then sitting next to Eltinge as two bounced along on train carriages across the land. It might have looked as if neither man a had family, but in a very real sense, they had each other.[10]

Backstage, Ko Shima was a critical part of the Eltinge machine, a "faithful servitor that combines valet and ladies maid [*sic*]," according to an observer in 1910. The press often delighted in pointing out that Shima's most important job was to help the impersonation artist fit into unforgiving corsets. "Shima pulls me into them—O my," confessed Eltinge.[11] The public loved images of Ko Shima subduing his employer into corsets. A popular cartoon showed the valet with his shoe on Eltinge's rear, yanking corset strings as the actor gripped a shelf, sweating and heaving, eyes bulging in disbelief—Shima, smaller yet dominant, Eltinge bigger yet submissive.[12] The performer admitted he felt "sympathy" for women each time Shima strapped him into "old ironsides." The dresser's "patient and artistic" efforts made him a key player in the backstage drama that was ever part of the Eltinge show, a "sort of star in his own right." Corseting was likened to boxing or wrestling, with actor and dresser fighting "a few preliminary bouts" before subduing the foe.[13] Eltinge was soon said to be "entirely dressed by his man." Shima seemed something like a spouse, best friend, manager, and creative collaborator in one, a category for which many did not have words.[14]

Not that Shima was ever accorded totally equal status, even were it understood that the artist could not properly function without him. The valet was rumored to wield a kitchen knife should he need to cut his boss out of a nasty corset. Cartoon depictions of Shima make him smaller and shorter than Eltinge, fulling a cultural need to see Asians as "little" and quasi-feminine.[15]

Black men might be thought aggressive and libidinally appetitive. More often than not, though, Japanese men were imagined somehow more effeminate, which meant less combative and less overtly sexual. Whites imagined and depicted Japanese men as fine-featured, smooth-skinned, and more fragile than Caucasian males. For a white man to drag-up in Japanese draping was, therefore, to double the feminizing effect. To that end, kimonos were powerful symbols—not just of Japanese womanhood but of a diffuse, Asian femininity. When a U.C. Berkeley football rally devolved into a Bacchic, campuswide "pajamarino party" in the early 1920s, one male undergrad grabbed a kimono and put on a drag satire of the college president gazing cerebrally into a telescope. Berkeley men wearing the "flimsiest of feminine lingerie," supposedly "pilfered" from female students without the latter's knowledge, cavorted about the campus in carnivalesque chaos.[16] More insidiously, in 1914 powerful publisher C. V. McClatchy assigned a reporter to infiltrate a "society of queers" who held private parties and balls in and around Long Beach in Southern California. The reporter was almost as horrified that participants were "given a silk kimono, wig and pair of slippers" as at other "unnatural practices" he observed.[17]

* * *

Ko Shima's expertise and support would prove especially helpful on Julian Eltinge's next, trying, assignment: touring with hugely popular Scottish raconteur and singer Harry Lauder. Lauder was one of the few vaudevillians popular and fortunate enough to commit his talents to recorded sound, a relatively new technology at the time, giving him an even bigger following. He recalled in his 1919 memoir, *Between You and Me*:

> I never work harder than when I'm makin' a record for the phonograph. It's a queer feelin'. I mind weel indeed the first time ever I made a record. I was no takin' the gramophone sae seriously as I micht ha' done, perhaps—I'd no thocht, as I ha' since. Then, d'ye ken, I'd not heard phonographs singin' in ma ain voice in America, and Australia, and Honolulu, and dear knows where beside. It was a new idea tae me, and I'd no notion 'twad be a gude thing for both the company and me tae ha'me makin' records. Sae it was wi'a laugh on ma lips that I went into the recording room o one o' the big companies for the first time.[18]

In January 1910, producer and talent agent William Morris struck a blow against Keith/UBO hegemony by signing Harry Lauder to a coast-to-coast tour of North American cities. "The world's foremost vaudevillian" was reportedly paid somewhere between $3,000–$5,000 a week to sing Scottish ditties and wax on in deep brogue about life back home, his travels, and his observations about a rapidly modernizing world. Lauder communicated his parochial suspicions in warm, folksy tones. Forty-seven supporting players, accompanists, technicians, handlers, plus his wife and son, traveled with Lauder in a luxe, "handsome Pullman." On this particular tour, though, Harry Lauder would have to share the billing with America's most popular

128   BEAUTIFUL

female impersonator, which, it seems, the conservative-minded Scotsman di'nae like very micht.[19]

In contrast to the stiff, uncharismatic B. F. Keith and the sly, finagling E. F. Albee, William Morris was amiable and encouraging, a friend to the artist. "A finer man and a more lovable character never lived," recounted Sophie Tucker, Morris's client for nearly three decades.[20] Morris had been a booker for the Klaw & Erlanger organization when it briefly branched out from legitimate theatre to vaudeville and challenged Keith's dominance. When Keith eventually vanquished Klaw & Erlanger, in part by buying them out, an ambitious William Morris launched his own vaudeville chain. In March 1908, Morris announced plans to open a chain of thirty or so vaudeville houses and eventually "circle the globe." (Remember, this was an age when bigger intrinsically meant better.[21]) Morris promised longer shows with higher budgets. He raised $1,000,000—$30 million in today's terms—to buy talent for William Morris's Independent Vaudeville circuit.[22] Keith and Albee hated Morris, despite pretending publicly to respect him. If anyone could pierce the Keith/UBO juggernaut, it was Morris. But the industry's heady growth at the time assuaged fears on all sides. It was said that working for Morris could land performers on an "alleged [Keith] black list" though the list, if it had ever existed, was supposedly decommissioned by 1911. For now, there would be enough demand and work for everyone, and then some.[23]

Morris coaxed Lauder by promising vast riches and huge crowds, tactics oft-used to get artists to cross the Pond. The Scotsman claimed to be reluctant at first, riven with "doots" about partnering with "this black-haired handsome Jew with the little nose." William Morris not only offered a hefty salary but literally brought Lauder bags of gold coin. "Rustle a bag of money anywhere and the Scot will beat the Jew to it every time," wrote Lauder. However he'd managed to pull it off, this was a major coup for the handsome Jew with the little nose.[24]

Harry Lauder had grown up poor, making ten shillings a week as a journeyman coal miner. The jingle of gold was new to him. "Proud I was the morn when I went doon into the blackness for the first time," he recalled. Early on, the Scotsman recognized that he had a magnetic "temperament"—that is, charisma—and could hold others' attention when he sang or told stories. By 1907, he had left the coal shafts for the stage.[25] But going to America was a different matter altogether. Would his folksy references and regional brogue even work in the United States? It turned out that, even when some American audiences missed Lauder's "manifest inflexions," they delighted in him nonetheless, getting the gist of his tales, enjoying the musicality of his voice, and grinning at the funny way he stood and walked.[26]

Like Julian Eltinge, Harry Lauder understood that if you were going to play a character, even one based on your supposed self, you had to *commit*. You had to go deep. Lauder variously depicted a "laddie" from the Highlands, a kilted "ruddy and regal clansman," an "old tar" whose pipe refused to stay lit, and other Scottish character-types. It's not hard to see why audiences who appreciated his art might also like Eltinge's. Just exactly "wherein rests Lauder's excellence is not easy to say," wrote San Francisco journalist Walter Anthony, who reported the Scotsman made "good every promise" trumpeted by his publicity machine. Patrons loved to hear Harry Lauder sing "She's Ma Daisy," "A Sprig o' White Heather," and "I Love a Lassie," which is what convinced Victor Gramophone to pay him £5 a song to put them on wax. Technology that could easily reproduce creative work at high volume introduced entertainers to an entirely new, sometimes flabbergasting pay scale. "Why five pounds for singing a few songs was as much as a miner could earn by hard work in a fortnight!" marveled Lauder. More important, it meant an artist could play for many people, millions even, in different places all at the same time, altering the amusement economy forever. If recorded sound hadn't yet made this clear, the new moving pictures definitely would.[27]

* * *

Harry Lauder might not have known just what he was signing up for when he agreed to a fourteen-week tour with Julian Eltinge. He knew *he* was the star, the headliner, and Eltinge the opener. He was certainly making more than the female impersonator—by one report $5,000 a week to Eltinge's $3,500— though the actual figures were probably closer to $3,000 and $1,000, respectively. As for billing, it would also clarify that Eltinge played "clean-up" to the main attraction, Harry Lauder. The Scotsman's name appeared in larger, fancier fonts on marquees and newspaper ads. He traveled with his family in a "handsome Pullman" with a brass bed "just as saft and comfortable as ever I could ha' known in ma own wee hoose at hame." (Later in his career, Lauder would again travel on a cushy train, with its own bar, originally designed for none other than Teddy Roosevelt.) The impersonation artist, meanwhile, often had to make do with "primitive little dressing rooms[s]" with damp floors and creaky chairs. Poorly heated backstage facilities sometimes forced Eltinge to cut his prep time in half. Thankfully, he had Ko Shima.[28]

130 BEAUTIFUL

To William Morris's delight, the "Lauder-Eltinge combination" tour, which some called a "double treat," got off to a good start. Americans packed theatres to see the famous Scotsman and "the equally famous impersonator." Julian Eltinge indeed seemed the perfect opener. As the receipts poured in, Morris's smile grew "broader and broader." Lauder recalled peeking over Morris's "shouther" for a glimpse at the ledgers. There was plenty to smile about.[29]

But trouble started to brew as Lauder realized playing in North America meant covering many more miles, playing many more shows, and appearing in much larger venues than what he'd been used to. His voice grew "manifestly troubled" before a packed crowd in Los Angeles in the first week of 1910, with the Scotsman barely making it through the performance. Playing a "huge pavilion" at San Francisco's Dreamland Rink proved overwhelming for the famously bow-legged, "short and wide" entertainer who preferred to chat with audiences as if they were gathered in his living room or at a local pub. Folks in the way-back strained to hear the broguing raconteur.[30] Lauder was out of his element, recalling that "for the first time, I had to combine long travelling wi' constant singing." US cities, he felt, were full of "turmoil and frenzy," conveying a "sense of oppression." America was big. That's why there was so much money to be made and so much to be spent. Even mining, a trade Harry Lauder knew well, was different here. In Julian Eltinge's quasi-hometown of Butte, Montana, Lauder gaped at a mine "far deeper than ever we [had] at Hamilton" in Scotland. If he had been proud to descend into the earth's maw as a youth, he was terrified at the size of seemingly bottomless mineshafts he presently beheld. They appeared to swallow thousands of men whole. "I went doon three thousand feet—more than half a mile, mind ye!" Lauder also grew suspicious, (even more) tightfisted, "carfu' wi' ma siller [silver]," as he put it. He hated the "audacity" of American merchants who "tried tae sell me things I didna want." Shopping with his wife in San Francisco one day, his costar, also along, spotted a beautiful, inlaid Chinese screen of ebony and mahogany. Julian Eltinge's delight sparked enthusiasm in Mrs. Lauder, which in turn led her husband to ask the shopkeeper, how much? Thirty-five hundred dollars (about $100,000 in today's money), said the storeowner. Lauder, trying to appear "liberal," peeled off thirty-five one-hundred-dollar bills and forked them over. Eltinge said Harry Lauder didn't mind the transaction, but it could not have been easy for the famously thrifty Scotsman who made a living at least *pretending* to prefer the simple life. Now a stylish female impersonator who liked the finer things was influencing his wife's tastes.[31]

FASCINATING STARDOM 131

More important, Harry Lauder had also failed to realize just how popular his "clean-up" act would be. Female impersonation was surging and Julian Eltinge was its frontrunner. In addition to his popular Salome and Society Girl characters, he unveiled new impersonations to match the changing times. Eltinge conjured a Brinkley Girl based on Hearst newspapers' illustrator Nell Brinkley. In contrast to the semi-constrained Gibson Girl, the Brinkley character, whom the actor named "Ella Riley," was a curly haired denizen of everyday life, enduring its joys and challenges with a touch of modern neurosis that made her all the more lively and relatable. Lauder couldn't believe how audiences let themselves imagine that Eltinge's renderings were *illusions*. When someone pointed out there was a man under those curls and makeup, a person in the next seat replied, "Nonsense. That's a woman alright and a very fine one too." Eltinge updated his Bathing Girl and did a post-Salome Cobra Dance. Holding a snake in her hands, she gyrates and shimmies to mimic the reptile's "sinuous coils and writhings." Eltinge claimed it was a realistic portrayal of an authentic ritual from India, which of course it wasn't. It was just good marketing. At a time many observed the rise of the "wild woman," a new breed of female who discarded "venerable law[s] hallowed by . . . custom [and] consecrated by experience," according to an article in *Nineteenth Century* magazine, Eltinge's women seemed increasingly to grow a bit wilder, at least up to a point. When actual women, like Eva Tanguay, danced energetically or told saucy jokes, they were often criticized, called a bad example (in part because they were clearly adored by millions). But no one ever suggested Eltinge's women were bad examples.[32]

Fissures between the Scottish raconteur and the country's favorite female impressionist widened amid "persistent rumors of jealousy," with Eltinge feeling sidelined and Lauder feeling Eltinge wasn't sidelined *enough*. In Omaha, Nebraska, Lauder was preparing to go on when he heard a "riot" of applause and cheering. The Scotsman summoned his manager brother-in-law, Tom Vallens, and asked what was going on. Vallens explained it was just the audience anxious to see him, working itself into a lather. Lauder grinned. But when the same thing kept happening in other cities, the Scotsman decided to investigate for himself. To his dismay, he discovered all the "tumult" was over Julian Eltinge. Crowds were loving Eltinge's act and demanding encores, curtain calls, and generally letting him know how much they admired his artistry. The Scotsman grew more agitated when, in his view, the press began apportioning the "lion's share" of its praise to his opener. When Eltinge appeared to earn a bigger ovation than him in Denver, Lauder went

132 BEAUTIFUL

ballistic. From now on, in Lauder's mind, the two were no longer peers but rivals—*nae*, enemies.[33]

Which was okay with Julian Eltinge. The impersonation artist neither wanted nor needed to take the matter lying down. In Kansas City, Missouri, Eltinge threatened to quit unless his name was made bigger and "louder" on publicity materials, approaching Lauder's font size. Soaking up the crowd's delight night after night, he never deferred excessively to Lauder nor apologized for anything. After all, he hadn't done anything wrong. For his part, Lauder began playing the homophobia/inversion card. After Eltinge had been especially well received at a show in the Midwest, he bade goodnight to Lauder and exited the theatre. Harry Lauder sat quietly for a moment and then groaned to Tom Vallens, "If Eltinge ever plays in Glasgow, I hope the printer sets his name 'Julia Neltinge.' Then we'll see if he can get by." The impersonator was getting by just fine in New York, Los Angeles, Vancouver, and Chicago, not to mention London, Paris, and Vienna. And if someone ever called him "Julia," Eltinge pointed out, he'd knock them squarely on the jaw. When *Vanity Fair* later ran a praiseworthy spread, declaring, "(O) Julia," no one got hit—and no one ever did. The threats were part of his offstage masculine drag.[34]

Harry Lauder and Julian Eltinge finished their tour and mercifully went their separate ways. Afterward, Eltinge tried to downplay the bitter rivalry between himself and Lauder, calling many of the rumors "unfounded." Yes, he sometimes got bigger ovations, and sometimes the crowds seemed to prefer him over the Scotsman. But Eltinge, more politic than Lauder, suggested a budding friendship existed between them. On one occasion, Eltinge recalled how Lauder walked into his dressing room, calling him "my laddie," then doing "me the honor of buttoning me up the back." (Ko Shima was out sick that day, explained Eltinge.) The anecdote paints Lauder as something of an erotically curious husband stand-in. Meanwhile, the famously loquacious, yarn-spinning Harry Lauder decided that silence would be the best revenge.[35] In *Between You and Me* (1919) and *Roamin' in the Gloamin'* (1928), the memoirs that describe his American tours, Harry Lauder nowhere mentions the name Julian Eltinge—or Julia Neltinge, for that matter.

* * *

Even if he'd been touring with a more amicable headliner, it was increasingly apparent that Julian Eltinge needed to star in his own show. His second-fiddle days were over, even with promises of higher pay. In July 1910, he signed a contract with producers Rogers, Leonhardt & Curtis for an upcoming "transcontinental tour of the first-class theatres." He was developing a Revolutionary-era lady appealing to America's nostalgic past and a Spanish-American character reflecting the nation's developing interest in Latin America. There had to be "something for everybody" in vaudeville, after all. He'd also perfected a honeymooning "maiden," a "stately minuet" dancer, and a lady from "days long ago" in brocade with a fan flitting over her face. The performer also kept current by working a newly popular musical genre called "ragtime" into his shows.[36]

His new tour kicked off August 1 at the Cora in Chicago. It was scheduled to go four or five months, focusing on the middle of country, which often had less access to top-flight stars. Eltinge led a bill that included La Marilynn, a woman who herself impersonated vaudeville's famous ladies, and her Five Columbians; the "Yama Yama Girl" Bessie McCoy; Riccobona's trained horses; and a one-act play titled *A Texas Wooing*. Tickets cost two dollars, on the high side but not unreasonable for a show chock full of diverse talent and headlined by the biggest female impersonator in the business.[37]

Eltinge got the usual plaudits for his "optical illusion[s] of the female in form and deportment," which he kept "free from any objectionable features," unlike other drag artists, at least in the eyes of many a critic. In Duluth, Omaha, Cheyenne, Denver, Salt Lake, Vancouver, San Francisco, and Los Angeles, he sang new numbers like "Days Long Ago" and "The Spanish-American Rag." In an era when most people still consumed popular music via sheet music, having a big performer's name linked to a song could mean tidy profits for publisher and performer alike. John Kemble and Lester W. Smith had composed the waltz "Come Over on My Veranda," a hit promoted as: "sung by Julian Eltinge America's Leading Sex Simulator." When the impersonator came to town, as with other big-name artists, local music stores often raised prices on his popular tunes, like an Indianapolis merchant who charged twenty-three cents for Eltinge's hits compared to a dime for most other stars'. William H. Penn and Raymond Brown were his main songwriters at the time, though other tunesmiths contributed to his songbook as well.[38]

Barely a month into the new tour, though, fate intervened. A bona fide New York producer wanted to know if Julian Eltinge would be interested in starring in a genuine, full-length, musical comedy. Plus, this wasn't just any producer. The impresario after Julian Eltinge's artistic heart was the legendary

Figure 5.2 Before the advent of widely available recordings, popular music was consumed in the form of sheet music to play on one's home piano. Music publishers put the faces of stars associated with popular numbers on their score sheets, like Julian Eltinge and his rival Karyl Norman (aka The Creole Fashion Plate), respectively, to help move product.

Credit: *Laurence Senelick Collection*.

A. H. Woods. Scrappy, fatherly, and (for the most part) quietly determined, he was the champion the impersonation artist desperately needed. Woods, who'd been stalking Eltinge for some time, convinced the young actor to back out of his contract with Rogers, Leonhardt & Curtis. In the short term things might get ugly with lawyers wreaking their usual havoc. But the upside, potentially becoming a Broadway star, was more than worth it. Further sweetening the pot was the fact that Woods had a script in which Eltinge would not be impersonating women, per se, but rather, playing the part of *a man forced by circumstance to impersonate women*. He'd be *acting*—a step closer to his artistic dreams and a step further away from being a high-class oddity and suspected invert. Sure, he'd have to put on skirts. But now there would be two degrees of separation between the man and his women. "I have played the girl 'stunt' six years now," he remarked. Now he'd play a presumably regular fellow, in fact a college guy (as he so often would in roles to come) who needed to *play a woman* to advance his aims. In a sense, the role was a meta-comment on some version of his actual life narrative. It was a giant leap forward, which is precisely how it felt to Eltinge, leading him to talk about soon playing Shakespeare's great characters, particularly Shylock in *The Merchant of Venice*, curiously, a character whose Jewishness and scheming mark him as unmanly and passive in anti-Semitic discourse. "I hate a sissy," said Eltinge to a reporter backstage in Omaha as he mulled his future.[39]

Rogers, Leonhardt & Curtis sued the actor for $25,000 for backing out of his contract, but a settlement was reached allowing Eltinge to take up Woods's offer, which had been temporarily put on hold. By late July 1910 it was full-steam ahead. The producer was ready to help the country's favorite female impressionist step up to "the field of high-class productions." Woods even promised Eltinge a Broadway theatre of his very own, a sign of having arrived if ever there were one. With Ko Shima at his side and A. H. Woods in charge, the next phase of Julian Eltinge's career was taking fine shape.[40]

* * *

Aladore Herman Woods was born in Hungary on January 3, 1870, but migrated with his family to the Lower East Side of Manhattan when just an infant. Like many others in show business, he was an unschooled, ethnic (in this case, Jewish) outsider with plenty of grit, street smarts, and will to succeed. Like other Jews, he'd have to feint at Americanization or at least try to blend in. So Aladore became "Albert," taken from an actor he admired.

136 BEAUTIFUL

Lewis Maurice Shanfield, after all, had become Lew Fields, and Sonya Kalish, Sophie Tucker. If men like P. T. Barnum and B. F. Keith could fashion themselves "self-made," Woods could become American.[41]

Albert Woods started out as a billposter. Like being a newsboy or a bootblack, it was a job that could teach the right kind of kid a lot about city life, particularly folks' spending habits. The youth developed an interest in the theatre, and when playwright Theodore Kremer invited him to write a play based on a lithograph, Woods (likely with the help of playwright John Oliver) concocted *The Bowery after Dark*, which eventually became a hit. The young Woods was not exactly a solitary *artiste*, so much as a schmoozer, idea man, and encourager of others. Much like George M. Cohan, Frank Perley, and others, he was a collaborationist: part dramatist, part director, part producer, part dreamer, and networker extraordinaire who cocreated with others in an age when that was the norm. Novels might come from a singular pen, but plays and musicals were closer to a group mural or graffiti wall, though that would soon start to change. As an anonymous editorialist explained in an article titled "Why Authors Go Crazy" in the *New York Times* in 1930, getting a "contract" didn't mean a producer wanted your artistically precious script. "I'm not buying a play. I'm only buying an idea," was more like it, much to the chagrin of many serious-minded, greenhorn writers.[42]

The Bowery after Dark was in fact a mashup of the Dion Boucicault's famous melodrama *After Dark* and Steve Brodie's "gory" play, *The Bowery*. Plays and musicals, even supposedly "classic" works, were often cut apart, reworked, borrowed from, and sampled without the protection and pretenses of "intellectual property" as it is now enforced. In fact, although the United States had first enacted copyright laws in 1790, authors and creative artists didn't make much use of them until Mark Twain began making noises over the matter in the 1870s, and even he often failed to see his works protected. It wasn't until 1910 that authors were given full rights over derivatives, translations, and adaptations of their works, though of course what appears in solemn lawbooks can take a while to worm its way into gritty reality. Woods entered the "ten, twent', thirt'" business, playhouses that charged a dime to thirty cents and featured so-called blood-and-thunder melodramas with clichéd plots, unvarnished villainy and heroism, and jaw-dropping visual effects. He sometimes teamed up with another Jewish impresario, Sam Harris—the "Harris" in Cohan & Harris's Minstrels. If Julian Eltinge played the cool, contained Harvard man who hit the marks of mainstream American manhood, A. H. Woods was an altogether different character: eccentric,

FASCINATING STARDOM   137

affectionate, lively, and not terribly concerned with how he might come off to others. He famously greeted people, male or female, "Hello, sweetheart!" He signed his correspondences, "With love and kisses," no matter who it was meant for. The impresario had special nicknames and bespoke greetings for his intimates: "How's Lulu?" when greeting actress Lulu Glaser; "How you feeling, Dusty," for actor Dustin Farnum; and "Guten Morgen fraulein," for German-born opera singer Lina Abarbanell. A. H. Woods sometimes called his new protégé "Julian" but preferred "Hello, Bill." If Eltinge dressed the part of a young stockbroker or serious outdoorsman (when not in skirts), Woods curated an appearance meant to satisfy some strange, inner audience with its own unique tastes. In warmer months, he liked to sit in shirtsleeves on a stool, tipped back on two legs against a wall outside his offices, cigar in mouth, watching customers go in and out his theatre, peering from beneath the brim of a Panama hat that shielded his sensitive eyeballs from all those bright lights on Broadway.[43]

Also at times given to "very profane language without meaning it," A. H. Woods favored hunches and intuition. Keith and Albee engineered show business into a rationalistic machine for which Woods had little use. His laboratory was his scrambling, scampering mind, ever bubbling with ideas, some more promising than others. Never a fan of high-flown experts, his favorite drama critic was "a poor guy who can't write but knows what he likes." When unemployed actors came to see his shows, Woods strove to find them work.[44]

Yet it would be mistaken to think Al Woods rudderless or a dilettante. He'd gotten where he was, creator/cocreator of a long string of hits with even more on the way, by possessing one of the keenest minds in show business. He read scripts voraciously, sometimes plowing through six a day, downing cup after cup of coffee and chewing on cigar after Havana cigar. Sometimes he became so engrossed in reading he'd unwittingly let a cigar burn down to an ash—which to him was usually a sign that he had something good in his hands. Lunch was typically soup, milk, and pie from the nearby Automat rather than long, time-wasting meals at trendy restaurants. A. H. Woods was friendly with eminent dramatist George Bernard Shaw—Woods called him "Buddy"—but couldn't quite abide the famed Irishman's nuanced, artistic writing style, turning down Shaw's *Back to Methuselah* because it made him "nervous." "I've got to know the next day if I've got a hit," said the producer. He disliked overly cerebral material or anything that stretched freshness too far into the realm of experimentation. Nervous by nature, he slept with the lights

Figure 5.3 Around 1900, the actor began experimenting with the stage name "Julian Eltinge." Only to some of his closest friends or the occasional person who'd known him since childhood was he still Billy Dalton. Otherwise, his past—including the origins of the name "Eltinge"—remained a mix of fact and fabrication.
Credit: *Billy Rose Theatre Division, The New York Public Library for the Performing Arts.*

on and seemed to be in a state of near-constant rumination. On Broadway and on the road, he'd enjoy many hits over the course of his career, popular but forgettable affairs like *Madame Sherry, Getting Gertie's Garter, Potash and Perlmutter, The Shanghai Gesture*, and some two hundred others. His favorite playwrights were Owen Davis and Samuel Shipman, reliable if not memorable craftsmen. He had boundless energy and made quick decisions. Woods supposedly turned down both Charlie Chaplin and Douglas Fairbanks before they were big stars because they wanted more money than he thought they were worth—thirty dollars a week when he refused to go above twenty-five. At the same time, Al Woods gave a start—or claimed to, another trope for male impresarios of the day—to Claudette Colbert and Joan Blondell. He did, however, recognize a uniquely talented child actor named Gladys Mary Smith who would later call herself Mary Pickford.[45]

Sifting through as much raw material in as little time as he did, Al Woods was destined to miss a few diamonds in the rough. But he could never be accused of passivity. Acting as his own publicity advance-man for *The Bowery after Dark*, he ambled into a Kansas City jewelry shop and asked if he could post a photo of the star, Terry McGovern. He saw a woman browsing and offered her free tickets. Afterwards, he inquired how she had liked it. "You've got a nerve sending me to that rotten show," she answered. Albert Herman Woods and Louise Beaton were soon married. Whatever the eccentricities and quirks of his mental gadgetry, Woods knew how to operate it. Sometimes a doorman or desk clerk would ask him if he wanted a cold beer as he sat on the sidewalk, perched upon a tilted chair in the muggy, summer night, watching patrons enter the theatre. "When the house gets in, sweetheart," he'd say, "When the house gets in."[46]

Al Woods would stop at little to gather new projects and top talent. He was known to finish a day's work, rise from his desk, and leave for Europe with "all the thought and preparation you give to going to a movie." Later in his career, he sailed across the Atlantic to entice celebrated French actor Sacha Guitry, appearing in London at the time, to come to America. As the two dined in Guitry's suite at London's Savoy hotel, the Frenchman repeatedly made it clear he had no interest in traveling that far to ply his trade. "Sweetheart, you'll have New York at your feet," implored Woods, who then turned to the actor's interpreter and said, "Tell him, sweetheart." Sacha Guitry asked for $12,000 a week. A. H. Woods gave him $13,000.[47]

* * *

In 1908, producer Woods was in Hammerstein's Victoria watching a show when he spotted "a pretty girl on the stage," one with real talent at that, not an everyday occurrence in his book. That girl, of course, turned out to be Julian Eltinge. The producer kept his eye on the impersonation artist and eventually approached him about collaborating. Woods said he could pay Eltinge several thousand a week for the right venture, on par with the top vaudeville and musical-comedy performers. Eltinge was excited by those prospects but said he needed the right vehicle. No more twelve-minute vaudeville turns or tagging onto another star's coattails. Yes, Julian Eltinge wanted out of variety shows. But another bomb like *Mr. Wix of Wickham* could ruin his Broadway, not to mention his Shakespearean, aspirations for good. On the other hand, a bona fide hit would open many, many doors.[48]

140   BEAUTIFUL

Woods offered Eltinge *Barberiza*, a French import to costar Blanche Walsh. The impersonator passed. He wanted something written specifically *for him*. Woods, it turned out, felt similarly.[49] A few months later, the energetic producer asked composer Karl Hoschna and librettist Otto Hauerbach—Hauerbach would later massage his surname to "Harbach" and cowrite "Smoke Gets in Your Eyes" with Jerome Kern—to come up with a vehicle for his newest talent. Hoschna and Hauerbach did not disappoint. In August 1910, Eltinge formally announced he would not be returning to the Leonhardt organization and would instead star in a new musical called *The Fascinating Widow*. A coordinated ad campaign ensured it would be "A Real Novelty" with "An-All-Star-Cast."[50]

The Fascinating Widow, a "comedy, with music, in three acts," was like other fluffy, rollicking confections of the day. Given that, however, *Widow* was skillful, well-crafted, and absorbing. Its plot consisted of absurd twists and convolutions centered on Eltinge's transvestic turns. In one reviewer's opinion, it left the audience with "keen regret that the fun is at an end" when the final curtain fell. In addition to an "adroitly developed plot," already an accomplishment compared to much of the competition, *The Fascinating Widow*'s popularity was "amplified by the tuneful score."[51]

In *The Fascinating Widow*, Julian Eltinge played Hal Blake, a college junior who has fallen for fellow student Margaret Leffingwell, and vice versa. Blake is a roguish character, at least by college standards. He smokes, drinks, and wantonly "uses slang." His campus pals think him a decent chap, but Margaret's mother naturally feels otherwise. In addition to being Margaret's mom, Mrs. Leffingwell is also the house chaperone at her daughter's dorm. As such, she believes she has "good reasons" for believing Hal was the "scamp who sneaked all those bottles of intoxicants into the Girls' dormitory last fall." (Hal was indeed the scamp who sent the "gargle that made Milwaukee famous" to the coeds' quarters.) Mother Leffingwell wants Margaret to couple up with Oswald Wentworth, a bookish, nerdy sophomore, a "perfectly dear mollycoddle" with a rich dad. Bespectacled Wentworth, his nose buried in Schopenhauer, is "a gentleman" in mother's eyes, while Hal "spill[s] slang all over the place and smoke[s]" like a fungus run rampant. Hal ends up smacking Wentworth, and after learning that it's "a most serious offense" to hit someone with glasses decides to make himself scarce. Hal is the regular guy doing what regular guys were supposed to do: smoke, drink, and punch the book-reading, four-eyed sissy square in the mug—a castration on so many levels. In America, the fist beat the book, and real men were self-made,

Figure 5.4 *The Fascinating Widow* (1910) was the first of several musicals starring Julian Eltinge and produced by A. H. Woods. These popular, if formulaic, comedies-with-songs situated the impersonator as a heteronormative young man forced by circumstances to don skirts, thereby removing him a degree from what he truly was: an artist uniquely gifted at embodying the opposite sex.
Credit: *Laurence Senelick Collection.*

not passive trust-funders. (Of course, one also had to be from a "good family," and it was better if your dad had been a "mining entrepreneur" rather than, say, a barber who never struck it rich. But these were details better left unexamined.) Rather than flee, though, Hal makes perhaps the manliest choice of the era: he drags himself up as a lady, a fetching one at that, emerging as the alluring widow, Mrs. Monte. In seductive guise, Hal insinuates *shimself* back into the action to vindicate his reputation and win Margaret's hand, which we know he will eventually do.[52]

As we have glimpsed, the US college campus was becoming a crucial new bridge connecting middle-class boyhood to respectable manhood. It was a place between worlds that conferred a moratorium on activities like openly overindulging in drink and tobacco, and carousing until dawn. (After graduation, middle-class men would have to find discreet places behind closed doors to carry on their predilections.) College offered men an identity and bonding experience that would prove psychologically useful and

142 BEAUTIFUL

economically essential. On campus, excessive drink, once associated with low-class degeneracy, became a "badge of manhood" in the right situation. Clever pranks and verbal jabs replaced boyhood rituals of beating up weaker kids in the schoolyard.[53]

As *The Fascinating Widow* also made clear, college could be a place of unwitting homoerotic, or at least homo-*curious*, wanderings. Inversions that might rankle psychiatrists and youth reformers in the outside world were given wider berth within campus walls. Hal's ability to confuse his college chums about his sex paralleled his portrayer's ability to do the same with his audiences. Men could not openly court other men in college. But they could steal silken camisoles from female classmates then dress up as women and call it a "varsity" event. In *The Fascinating Widow*, Hal jokes that he may have to marry Oswald himself if that's what it takes to solve a number of problems, while Oswald ends up proposing to the alluring Mrs. Monte—that is, Hal Blake, that is, Julian Eltinge. Mrs. Monte, it should be pointed out, is more overtly seductive than are the female college students in the story, or Mrs. Leffingwell for that matter. It may be surprising to discover that, throughout much of the late nineteenth and early twentieth centuries, widows were seen as cheeky, flirty, and fun-loving. Widows of Julian Eltinge's day could easily be depicted as relatively youthful, lively, and even hedonistic, rather than superannuated and secluded, in endless mourning after losing their man, sipping tepid cups of tea and gazing blankly out picture windows into the mist. At the time, it appears there were a lot of widows, statistically speaking. In first decade of the twentieth century, women started to outlive men by greater intervals, from two years in 1900 to 3.4 years in 1910. In the 1877 true-crime memoir *The Detective and the Somnambulist*, famed sleuth Allan Pinkerton describes an unlikely scheme in which he had a confederate infiltrate a small, southern community by playing the part of a "fascinating widow" who got men to spill their secrets. Widows were partiers. Whiskey was sometimes called "the widow's beverage," and widows could be known for winning "boozing matches" that went late into the night, according to one diarist. "The charms of widows for mankind cannot be denied," Eltinge told the press. They were shrewd and tactful, but in a "womanly" way. They knew how to get what they wanted and suffered fewer constraints.[54] As the show's title song put it, "The widow seems, through experience, to gain love's confidence," she's good at "stealing" every "beau." The widow was a recurring character type in dramas of the day, featured in such huge hits as *The Widow Bedott* (adapted for the stage in 1887) and the comedy *The College Widow* by

FASCINATING STARDOM   143

humorist George Ade, which ran for a substantial 278 performances after its 1904 New York debut and would go on to see many revivals over the years.[55]

* * *

A. H. Woods's production of *The Fascinating Widow* starring Julian Eltinge premiered at the Columbia Theatre on F Street in Washington, DC, in November 1910. The venue was in dire need of a hit and with the *Widow*, it got one. *Washington Post* critic Amy Leslie raved about Eltinge and the entire ensemble, including Ruth Maycliffe as Margaret, Gilbert Douglas as Oswald, and Carrie E. Perkins as Mrs. Leffingwell. Instead of can-can dancers or Florodora beauties, the "show girls" of *The Fascinating Widow* were female college students, not exactly a proto-feminist's dream but a step in the right direction. The play made clear that men were simply going to have to accept women, maybe a lot of them, in class and strolling around campus. Songs like "Everybody Likes a College Girl" encouraged college boys to make the best of it. Character actor Neil McNeil played buffoonish detective Nick Bulger, a "low-comedy" archetype with a "Dutch" dialect straight out of vaudeville. ("Dutch" often referred to the Yiddish accent used in anti-Semitic, Jewish stage stereotypes, though it could also mean an exaggerated Germanic caricature.) Critics appreciated *The Fascinating Widow* on its own modest but successful terms, "fun from first to last . . . a 'bully performance,'" in words Teddy Roosevelt himself could have used. The show's lightheartedness, clichéd character types, mix of music and dialogue, and clever crossdressing gave fans much of what they loved in one convenient, vaudeville-adjacent package.[56]

For all those various elements, though, *The Fascinating Widow* was ultimately a hit because of its star, without whom all else would have been futile. An artist who'd labored in the two-a-day, minstrelsy, and as an opening act was finally under the limelight. The "handsomest and most graceful woman of them all is the man," declared the *Washington Post*. Artistically and culturally, Julian Eltinge arguably represented—and helped create— female impersonation's highest peak since the days of Edward Kynaston. The *Washington Times*, the *Post*'s crosstown rival, felt Eltinge had perfected "impersonating—not imitating merely—the beauteous feminine."[57]

After its debut at the Columbia, *The Fascinating Widow* moved to Ford's, the very venue where, six years earlier, *Mr. Wix of Wickham* had nearly scuttled Julian Eltinge's career. The audiences at Ford's "delighted" in the *Widow*

144   BEAUTIFUL

just like those at the Columbia. It looked as if A. H. Woods had not just a hit on his hands but the kind of hit he liked: immediate and unambiguous. In Buffalo and Boston, the production packed houses and earned "phenomenal" receipts. Weekly box office never fell below $10,000 during a multiweek run in Chicago. (For an average size theatre with conventional pricing, earning less than $5,000 was troubling, while anything over $12,000 indicated an exceptionally big hit.)[58] In Boston, Julian Eltinge was given a hero's homecoming when *The Fascinating Widow* rolled into town. Fans, friends, and well-wishers flooded the Boston Theatre lobby with floral arrangements and other "tributes to a prima donna and not to a mere man artist." The crowd went nuts when Eltinge made his first appearance—which, as Hal, marked perhaps the first time he was applauded in a male role. Harvard's most famous nongraduate of the era had truly arrived. For his part, the actor praised Boston, particularly its womenfolk, who in his view were superior to the "fluffy ruffle girls" he saw elsewhere, notably Baltimore.[59]

A few cranks still held their noses at this whole business of men dressing up as women. But they were, indeed, few and getting fewer. A Pittsburgh reviewer considered *The Fascinating Widow*'s plot "rough as coke," rife with "suggestive lines and situations," which his fine publication had "too much self-respect to print." Impersonating women was, in his view, simply "uninviting." Much as in our current moment, female impersonating and drag served as a lightning rod for reactionary anxiety over social and demographic upheaval. Whereas restraint and virtue once signaled manliness, men had now to be aggressive, competitive, even feckless at times. Men could differentiate themselves from women on campus by roughhousing and indulging in tobacco and drink. If a fellow were abstemious or excessively moralistic, he risked betraying "the woman within." The temperance crusade, after all, long had a female face. Women allegedly couldn't handle the edgy stuff: sex, booze, fighting, and so forth. When the Cadets' *Miladi & The Musketeer* moved to Broadway as the mixed-gender *My Lady*, a critic for the *New York Dramatic Mirror* groaned that "probably some Mrs. Nation has taken an axe to it," meaning removed all the racy humor, which is to say, all the fun.[60] As Hal-turned-Mrs.-Monte, Eltinge refined the art of playing the woman *without*. It also gave him another opportunity to advertise a major factor in his success: R&G corsets style B-94, size 23, which Ko Shima strapped on to him with great determination and agility.[61]

* * *

Figure 5.5 The impersonator was both bride and groom in this publicity shot for *The Fascinating Widow*, pointing to the highly performative nature of weddings and marriage—echoing his engagement stunt with Eva Tanguay several years earlier.
Credit: *Laurence Senelick Collection.*

The smoothness of Eltinge's artistry in *The Fascinating Widow*, of course, belied the sweat and effort that went into it, and not just his own. Because the actor had bulked up to 174 lbs. before going on tour, Ko Shima now had to help Eltinge "mould [his] goodly girth" of thirty-eight inches into a twenty-three-inch waistline.[62] What's more, Shima had to help the performer execute rapid costume changes and never miss an entrance in a show that relied

146 BEAUTIFUL

on fast-paced mix-ups. When Eltinge had to make his first big change, from Hal to Mrs. Monte, he dashed to his changing room, where Shima had all the necessary props and accessories arrayed on a table. Shima yanked off his boss's shoes, while the actor removed his own trousers and gauzy undershirt, leaving him in long stockings held up by garters. Eltinge smoothed his undershirt to make way for the corset, which Shima foisted on to his employer's trunk, grunting all the while. "Here's where the Japanese navy gets in its work," said the dresser as he wrangled the corset. Once the device was cinched, Shima took a black velvet dress off its appointed hanger and carefully spread it in a circle on the floor for Eltinge to step into while fitting a wig and rouging his own cheeks. Shima now held up pointy shoes into which his employer slipped his feet. Julian Eltinge's women often look flat-chested, a reflection of his sometime refusal to use padding, which he worried might make him look hyper-female or, worse yet, campy. (On other occasions, this seems not to have bothered him, particularly when impersonating a Victorian or Lillian Russell type.) Makeup and a corseted waist gave him an idealized, hourglass figure. The actor's next transformation was into bathing wear. For logistical reasons, this had to occur in a jury-rigged changing station behind the set rather than in the dressing room proper. All through the play's three acts, Ko Shima helped the actor slip in and out of gowns, footwear, swimsuits, and jewelry. Sometimes, the women's choral dresser stepped in to lend a hand. Both Eltinge and Shima knew the star could never miss a change or skip a beat, night after night, matinée after matinée, encore performance after encore performance, which they never did—including the "prize change" at the *Widow*'s climax in which Eltinge assumed full bridal attire in under a minute. While other actors had understudies in case of "contingencies," Julian Eltinge had no such cushion. He was irreplaceable; increasingly, so too was Ko Shima.[63]

Meanwhile, A. H. Woods took care of his newest charge like a general looking after his troops in the trenches. The producer lavished not only praise and encouragement on the actor but a hefty salary and some delightful gifts. "Sweetheart, you're a big money maker for me," he'd regularly remind the impersonation artist. Figures vary as to how much Eltinge was paid, but they all point to: *handsomely*. Some say he got $46,000 for twenty-six weeks' work, about $1,770 a week, while other put it was a bit lower, though nothing under $1,500, making him the highest-paid male performer in 1911, according to a tally by the *San Francisco Examiner*. That put him below the female megastars—Gertrude Hoffman, Eva Tanguay, and so forth—but way

FASCINATING STARDOM 147

above male artists like Harry Von Tilzer and Fred Niblo. Woods made sure Eltinge had the best *materiel* too. The actor's five outfits cost $10,000 (about $63,000 per outfit in 2023 dollars), ensuring that "the handsomest woman on the stage is a man," in the words of a Kentucky paper. Al Woods bought his star a new Pierce Arrow for his twenty-eighth—which is to say, his thirtieth—birthday in 1911. The artist could now cruise around town in fine style.[64]

But Al Woods offered Julian Eltinge more than money and gifts. He provided his new star with a kind of sanctuary he'd never known, and which he'd definitely need as his fame blossomed. The two developed a bond that not only paralleled more traditional connections—parent-child, mentor-mentee, business partners—but also connected them as outsiders, both culturally and as creatures of the theatre. Sometimes Eltinge would wander into Woods's office in New York's theatre district. The producer sat behind an imported walnut desk, his feet clad in expensive shoes resting clumsily on the desk's lacquered surface. Blue, silk damask wall-coverings matched the blue satin garters that held the producer's shirtsleeves. A. H. Woods was an amusing collision of opposites: classy, expensive accouterments colliding in a frisson of nervous energy, like fine plates and teacups in midair just after the bull has charged into the China shop. Whatever his idiosyncrasies, Woods somehow held it all together, even if it sometimes meant boarding an ocean liner with only a toothbrush, which he was known to do. His shoes were top-quality but deposited bits of Manhattan sidewalk filth onto a fancy desk. His hair was tousled and unkempt. His chair was plaited in gold, often tilted back as he stared blankly at a Florentine ceiling, figuring out his next move. This kind of overblown, even garish aesthetic was becoming par for the course in emerging impresario culture. One had to pay heed to the twin gods of fame and wealth, even if it turned out the gods were mere papier-mâché idols. Keith and Albee had patterned themselves after conventional business titans, their offices stately and efficient, with desks "ranged in close formation" to accommodate "huge ledgers" and the contents of what the *New York Clipper* felt were "wonderful card indexes." A reporter for *The Standard and Vanity Fair* visiting Keith/UBO headquarters in 1912 was so impressed with its "magnificent" skyscraper location he believed he could just as easily be near Wall Street "going to interview Mr. Pierpont Morgan or Mr. John D. Rockefeller." But Al Woods was a different kind of creature. He'd never be allowed near Rockefellers, nor did he really aspire to their company. The theatre district had a culture of its own. Keith and Albee might have tried to make themselves in the image of corporate titans, but many an impresario didn't bother with

148   BEAUTIFUL

such pretenses. Old money spoke in hushed tones, while theatrical money shouted. The key figure in this world of wheeler-dealer showmen, of course, was Florenz Ziegfeld. Ziegfeld had three gold telephones on his desk despite usually being in arrears thanks to overspending on the *Follies* and anything else in sight. This was a different kind of business, one rooted in the carnival rather than the counting-house. A. H. Woods liked two-dollar Havanas. But when ashes fell on his shirt, he'd distractedly brush them onto a crimson-carpeted floor. He kept a loosely curated array of pictures, tchotchkes, and objets d'art, each of which meant something personal. They included a small clay statue of a boy, said to bring luck; a bronze desk clock gifted by actress Hazel Dawn; and lots of snapshots and cast photos. Surrounding them all were towers of scripts, notes, and contracts.[65]

The whole look and feel, it should be said, while very *much* A. H. Woods was very much *not* Julian Eltinge. The artist preferred clean, distinctive, bold décor on himself and in his surroundings. Nothing muddled or confusing. Everything to a "T," refined and defined, like the women he brought forth on the stage. His aesthetic sense was classical or neoclassical, rooted in a search for archetypal beauty and splendor. Al Woods never judged him. The impersonation artist was always free to share his deepest thoughts and wishes with this man who was a decade his senior. Their outsides might not have matched, but their interiors were somehow in sync. Woods paid loving attention to the artist he was turning into a star, a star who would in turn permit the onetime producer of twenty-cent melodramas to climb up a notch or two on the scale of cultural regard.[66]

"Why so dejected, Julian?" asked Woods. *The Fascinating Widow* was a smash, the critics loved him—most of them, anyway—and after a summer break at Eltinge's Long Island farmhouse, there'd be more lucrative tours. "Do you know, Al," replied the actor, "that it is torture for me to see ugly things or ugly persons?" Eltinge was bothered by the cheap, mass-market commodities that increasingly flooded the sublunary world. What seemed expensive or classy was often counterfeit or pretentious. Would he become coopted, his artistry turned into yet another assembly-line product? "The best wine annoys me in a badly turned glass," allowed Eltinge. He'd rather have pork and beans on the finest, authentic ceramic than "delicate game on an earthenware plate" of factory origin. Woods knew how to comfort and humor the lad who had had to invent and reinvent himself since practically infancy. "I can perfectly understand your enthusiasm for beauty," Woods responded. Indeed, the producer pointed out that in ancient Greece, judicial hearings were held in the dark because the "good looks and gracefulness" of the lawyers might sway the judges—or that was his understanding anyway. If I were a painter, dreamed Eltinge, I'd depict only "goddesses, nymphs, madonnas, cherubs, and cupids," his portraits only "those of beautiful people."[67] Woods understood. Of course, you would, sweetheart, of course you would. For now, though, we must descend into the belly of commerce. Maybe with the money I'm paying, you'll be able to build a beautiful life for yourself. Woods knew a thing or two about beautiful imagery, after all. A visitor to his office once pointed at a large, framed panel displaying a dozen women's headshots and said, "And those . . . are the great loves of your life, I suppose."

"No dearie," said Woods, "Them's all Julian Eltinge." Perhaps the visitor wasn't so terribly wrong.[68]

* * *

As the summer of 1911 approached, Julian Eltinge prepared for a much-needed break. All the costume-changing, travel, making-up, and making-down took its toll. Being a bigger star than ever required a geometric expenditure of time and energy. Hovering in stardom's highest reaches could be dizzying and disorienting. Then, once the wig and stage makeup came off, another kind of performance began. When *The Fascinating Widow* played the Colonial in Chicago in May 1911, at the close of its first season, its star gestured for the crowd to quiet down so he could say something. "Ladies and Gentlemen—I crave a moiety of indulgence at your hands," he said in fluent quasi-Shakespearean, "and, if I get away from the book, pray condone the offense, because it is committed in deference to the grandest, brightest and most ennobling figure on the American or any other man's stage. I am speaking of and to the 'queen,'" whereupon he pointed up to a spot several boxes back, perhaps the best seat in the house. There sat Lillian Russell. "It was she whose regal beauty first inspired me with the nerve sufficient to essay this counterfeit presentment of my husky self." The impersonator had long linked himself to Russell, for decades one of the country's most famous celebrities. He claimed to have "learned his makeup" from her, which turned out to mean, according to Russell, that the young artist had simply "watched me night after night" as she performed. She hadn't actually known him *personally*, though the actress never felt the need to contradict Eltinge's claims. She was, though, impressed by his illusionism and figured that in his "private life it is probable that Mr. Eltinge is a virile looking chap."[69]

150   BEAUTIFUL

Born Helen Louise Leonard in Clinton, Iowa, in 1861, Lillian Russell knew a lot about reinventing oneself, morphing your image as situations required. Brought to New York in 1877 by an ambitious stage mother, she appeared in a few light operas. But after Tony Pastor cast the twenty-one-year-old actress in his Gilbert & Sullivan spoof, *The Pie-Rats of Pen-Yan*, she became a rising star. (Pastor and other male producers such as Florenz Ziegfeld often claimed to have "created" or "made the career" of this or that actress, a trope and trophy of the trade.[70])

Lillian Russell, buxom, voluptuous, and wide-hipped (and brutally corseted), helped transition America's beauty ideal from "frail, pale, willowy" figures of the mid-1800s to a more full-featured, vital, and robust female body. Eltinge had done well to study Russell night after night. Women had increasingly to strike a balance between litheness and corpulence, a nearly impossible goal the actor both apprehended and preached in turn to female kind. In an "Eltingegram," one of the style-and-beauty advisories that let him extend his brand into the pages of major publications, he would write, for example, "Always wear a bracelet. It makes the arm look plump," but also, "Powder and rouge the fingers to make them look tapering."[71]

It's possible he saw Russell when she came to Butte in *Princess Nicotine* or some other theatrical novelty. He claimed he'd first met her in person during his time with the Boston Cadets. He had just graduated from Harvard, he explained, where his experience with Hasty Pudding gave him the idea of doing some comical drag in the "nature of burlesque," nothing more. The Cadets, he elaborated, had hired Lillian Russell as their acting coach. She helped him to look like an "ideal heroine," like her, and talked him out of a campy, dame approach. When the "American Beauty," as she was known, lent him a piece of her wardrobe, he looked so good that "quite by accident" his discovered his career path. "I never dreamed of going on the stage as a professional, much less of wearing women's clothes," he fibbed. The details sometimes shifted. In another version, Eltinge described having been in Harvard's "Dramatic Society" when Russell—again, "coaching" the cast—urged him to take the female lead in an upcoming production. The "boys all gave me a laugh," Eltinge faux-reminisced, but with Russell's encouragement he took it on and the rest was history.[72] If Julian Eltinge wisely chose Harvard as the school he'd never attended, he just as wisely chose Lillian Russell as the female mentor and role model he'd never had. Both conferred legitimacy and class in the popular mind. Besides, even if they never met, they *got* one another. The American public made impossible demands of them as women and as celebrities. The American Beauty praised the Most Beautiful Woman on the Stage for his "slimness," even as she, in her autumn years, let go of many of the burdensome expectations heaped on her over her life. Like Eltinge, she enjoyed sumptuous meals and smoked fat cigars in public. She married men and disposed of them at will. During his act, noted one journalist, Julian Eltinge changed outfits "oftener than Lillian Russell changes her husband." The outsiders would never understand.[73]

The Fascinating Widow enjoyed a successful, multi-season run. Al Woods was not one to fiddle with a winning formula. In any case, the fascinating widow industry was booming. Florenz Ziegfield debuted *A Winsome Widow* in 1912 with Harry Kelly as Ben Gay, president of the otherwise all-female "Purity League." Merchandisers jumped onboard, with one Washington, DC, haberdashery taking out ads declaring, "We'll provide the Clothes, gentlemen, that'll win the winsomest of widows." In 1913, a farce titled *Mrs. Leffingwell's Boots*, "effervescing with humor and incident," debuted at the Columbia in DC. A few years later, an ambitious high school troupe in El Paso, Texas, put on a show called *The College Co-Ed*. Its star, Dave Hughes, played Tad Cheseldine, "the college cut-up." The local society columnist found Hughes's female-impersonating "decidedly clever," but felt the lad was "no Julian Eltinge."[74]

# # #

6

From Crinoline to Celluloid

After wrapping-up *The Fascinating Widow*'s first season, Julian Eltinge dashed back to his beloved farm at Fort Salonga for two weeks, even making time for a rare visit from his father. The actor loved his hard-won retreat, a place where he refueled body and mind amid the trees, tall grass, and animal companions. Alas, the respite wouldn't endure. Al Woods arranged for his new star to go to Europe on June 1 aboard the not-yet-ill-fated *Lusitania* following a lavish dinner in Eltinge's honor at the St. Regis hotel in Manhattan on May 30.[1]

The nearly 800-foot-long *Lusitania* took six days to steam across the choppy Atlantic, making port at Fishgaurd, England. Eltinge was to play the biggest cultural hotspots of Europe: London, Paris, Vienna, and Budapest. Continental crowds were eager for Eltinge after the performer's four-year hiatus in the States. After his shows, which netted him $2,500 a week, he'd attend festivities for the coronation of King George V and his queen, Mary.[2] As putative owner of the previous monarch's dog, Julian Eltinge was practically family. Back in America, the actor would enjoy a few more precious weeks at Fort Salonga before starting rehearsals for *The Fascinating Widow*'s second season.

A. H. Woods had been to Europe as well, in May, to round up scripts and ideas for Eltinge and other prized creatures in his stable of talent. He also commissioned French and German translations of *The Fascinating Widow* thinking it might make a hit in Europe if Eltinge could collaborate with local stock troupes abroad (although nowhere is there evidence of the actor having proficiency in any language other than English). The producer also announced plans for British and Australian tours of *Widow*, respectively, earning its lead player $3,000–$5,000 a week. Julian Eltinge was becoming a global star.[3]

Making over $3,000 a week in 1911 put you in the topmost tier of the industry. It was a ceiling many longed to shatter, though few actually did. The $1,750 rate Eltinge received during the forty-week-long 1911–1912 *Fascinating Widow* touring season was handsome, for sure. He and his

Beautiful. Andrew L. Erdman, Oxford University Press. © Oxford University Press 2024.
DOI: 10.1093/9780197696361.003.0007

FROM CRINOLINE TO CELLULOID   153

promoters were quick to point out that the nation's and possibly the world's most popular female impersonator made more than President William Howard Taft, who earned $75,000 for (presumably) fifty-two weeks of work. "More Profitable to Be Eltinge than President," explained the *Butte Miner* in a headline suggesting just how much things had changed since Joe Dalton beat his son for sneaking out to the theatre.[4]

Woods promised Eltinge the very best backing company, "society ladies who can sing and with wholesome pedigrees."[5] But A. H. Woods was about to bestow the biggest gift of all on his young associate. He was going to build a Broadway theatre named for Julian Eltinge—a theatre in whose profits the actor would share.

Al Woods had initially considered building a $100,000 playhouse in Albany, upstate New York. But now that hardly seemed appropriate for one of the topmost performers in the land.[6] In late summer 1911, the impresario announced the construction of the Julian Eltinge Theatre at 236 West 42nd Street. It would occupy an 80'×100' plot next to the popular Liberty Theatre, which had been erected in 1904. Woods leased the land for twenty-one years in a deal brokered by producer, songwriter, and, later, politician and coauthor of the UN Charter, Sol Bloom. Bloom, also an equity partner in the Eltinge playhouse, had first risen to prominence when he was in charge of creating the Midway Plaisance at the legendary Chicago World's Fair of 1893. The Midway was famous, or perhaps infamous, for its presentation of indigenous peoples from around the globe as if they were sideshow oddities in order to preach the "material advantages" of "civilization." Construction on the thousand-seat Eltinge playhouse was to begin as soon as possible so that Woods could start filling it with product and recoup his investment. He said it would open by mid-1912, ambitious even by the impresario's own, workaholic standards.[7]

By the end of summer 1912, the Julian Eltinge Theatre was open for business, only a few months after Woods had promised. Its inaugural production, *Within the Law* by Bayard Veiller, had been a hit in Chicago. In New York, it netted $150,000, of which Eltinge would be entitled to "a comfortable share," the rest going to Woods and Bloom. *Within the Law* would turn out to be the most successful stage production the Eltinge theatre would know during its several decades as a legitimate playhouse. But other than his name being on the front of the building, the impersonation artist had nothing to do with the production, kicking off a lifelong pattern of Julian Eltinge never appearing in his own playhouse. A entertainment journalist later dismissed Woods's

154   BEAUTIFUL

christening the venue after Eltinge as mere "diplomacy," even though it had been among the first instances of a Broadway theatre being named for a specific artist—a ritual that would become more common in the years to come. But Al Woods had a another connection to his new playhouse. The producer moved his offices to the Eltinge, draping the walls around him in blue silk and spending hours there amid piles of playscripts, coffee cups, and cigar ends. Furthermore, the Eltinge Theatre was squarely in the epicenter of New York's theatrical hotbed, eventually flanked by eleven other playhouses, the vaunted "Street of Hits," on its block between Broadway and Eighth Avenue.[8]

The Eltinge Theatre wanted for little. Designed by eminent architect Thomas Lamb, who would design many big-time vaudeville houses and, later, movie palaces, it featured a sprawling, terracotta façade; a huge atrium; and bountiful nods to classical design. Overall, it was thought to convey a "new level of composed, urban grandeur," which is to say, formidable but not grandiose or gaudy. (The "stripped down," modernist approach to playhouse and cinema design would not arrive until the late 1920s and 1930s; during the Depression, a simplified, cleaner look seemed more fitting.) A. H. Woods was never one to skimp, and in an age when B. F. Keith was spending millions on his vaudeville palaces, it made sense to keep up some appearances. The Eltinge's exterior alone cost $200,000; the roof was covered in red tiling; "Egyptian paintings" frescoed the interior; and a golden, plush curtain echoed golden-brown interior walls. The seats were blue, one of the producer's favorite colors. Perhaps most important, huge murals depicted three women—or rather, Julian Eltinge impersonating them in various roles (all supposedly rendered from publicity stills)—gazing down from the ceiling, reminding theatergoers they were entering a sanctum of imposture and disguise. The images were later called Eltinge's "muses."[9]

But the Julian Eltinge Theatre was to have one more feature that set it apart from the rest: a retail counter where women could get makeovers and buy the performer's branded beauty products. As far as anyone could tell, a major theatre had never been named for a female impersonator. So, why not another novelty? A "beauty parlor for the demonstration of complexion creams, rouges and other fairylike beautifiers," which fans could buy after seeing the artist's breathtaking dissimulations under the limelight. According to one journalist, no female impersonator had ever "given his name to a cold cream" meant "for the embellishment of feminine loveliness."[10] Eltinge had previously endorsed Melrose facial products. But like many a lifestyle celebrity in our day, he soon figured out it was better to sell his own brand than pitch

Figure 6.1 The actor developed a line of skin care and makeup products sold in connection with his stage productions, making Eltinge a forerunner of today's "lifestyle" brand entrepreneurs and goop-hawkers. If "Julian Eltinge Cold Cream makes me look like these [attractive women]," the implication to female consumers was that they too could look better—and indeed, ought to work harder at it. Buying his products was a step in that direction.
Credit: *Billy Rose Theatre Division, The New York Public Library for the Performing Arts.*

another's. Though it is impossible not to see the irony and contradictions in the Eltinge beauty parlor, in many ways it made perfect sense. Like department stores and retail shops, theatres had focused their efforts on securing a large, middle-class, white clientele whose chief exemplar, and possibly top spenders, were women. The anecdotal buzz that Julian Eltinge knew more about beauty than women, that he was indeed *more beautiful* than them, came together in a clever marketing scheme. It wasn't just that the impersonator *might* know what a woman could do to improve her looks, but rather that he *must intimately* know such things and provide the service of sharing them. In a time when women were increasingly directed to worry about their figures and keep up with changing beauty ideals, Eltinge spoke openly about his struggles with weight and waistline as no other man could do. From disclosing his own challenges and secrets, he progressed to dispensing dieting regimens. Eltinge's "Advice to the Fat" columns preached a combination of "gentle exercise" and five meals a day to "reduce" even "the stoutest person."[11]

156 BEAUTIFUL

Whereas earlier he aimed his wisdom at men, women, and anyone unhappy with their body size, he was now speaking clearly and squarely to women alone. In 1912, the *Washington Herald*'s Julia Chandler Manz wanted the actor to tell the readers of her "Page for Every Woman" who were "inclined to stoutness" what to do when nothing else worked. In response, the actor described his "off-again on-again flesh method," though he also conceded that corseting played a major part. In an opinion piece titled "Ladies, Get Thin," Eltinge, who constantly struggled with losing weight and allowing himself to eat what he wished, admonished female readers, "obesity is a disease."[12]

If he could change his body shape and size apparently at will, the logic went, so too could women—and if they could, they *should*. Eltinge informed "every over-plump maid or matron" that a combination of binge-dieting and exercise had helped him lose up to eight pounds a week, which he needed to do as touring season loomed. His reduction menu consisted of dry toast and fruit at breakfast and a dinner of mutton or fish and vegetables. In between those meals, he ingested only "quarts of buttermilk." The actor also suggested staying awake as much as possible because, as he understood it, "one surely puts on the flesh during sleep." (Recent scientific studies suggest the opposite, incidentally.)[13] Putting on weight in his leisure time then dieting for work suggested Julian Eltinge the *man* was free to look as he pleased, while Julian Eltinge the *woman* was not. Men were the weight they were meant to be; women were inherently too heavy or too skinny. A joke from 1915 asked if prizewinning racehorse Luke McLuke could refer to any of his "plump male friends" as "corn feds"—that is, *fattened cows*. The punchline: "There ain't no such animal as a plump male friend [except] Julian Eltinge."[14]

Weight loss and fitness were starting points. But Julian Eltinge echoed the culture at large by making it clear that being a woman was, in effect, a *technique*, a specialty. It required work. Why should civilian women be exempt from what he had to go through? "Study color effects in dress. Get plenty of fresh air and avoid anything which tends to make you angular," he advised, broadening his scope. Another "Eltingegram": "Never show the breadth across the back of the hand if you want people to think it is small." American women, he believed, "lack[ed] the knowledge of when to wear their clothes," or worse, donned attire of the wrong "personality."[15] Being a woman meant being not only attractive and properly dressed, but simultaneously, thrifty and not too ambitious. Women, it seemed, faced the challenge of needing to act deceptively, and be thought deceptive, in order to be judged authentic and

Figure 6.2 The entertainer boosted women's shoes and corsets, sometimes in obvious and annoying ways, similar to blatant product placements in modern-day TV shows and movies. But Eltinge launched a line of beauty products based on his own "system," which was exactly what mass-market merchandisers were doing as well: selling women *processes* they needed to master if they wished to do beauty correctly and precisely—like a master female impersonator.
Credit: *Billy Rose Theatre Division, The New York Public Library for the Performing Arts.*

158   BEAUTIFUL

real. The impersonator said he knew "every trick in the category of feminine artifice" and was wise to it all. He understood "more about women's foibles than any other man in the world," which was not entirely untrue. Nobody, he insisted, was "fooled" by abundant powder and rouge (except, of course, his audiences). American women, he believed, needed to master a lighter touch, just something "to take the shine off." It also bugged him that US females wore shoes that were usually too small, making their feet look swollen and ungainly.[16]

Julian Eltinge's lifestyle brand, however, found its greatest expression in *Julian Eltinge Magazine and Beauty Hints*, which he and A. H. Woods published for several years in the early 1910s. A cleverly designed booklet full of intriguing photographs—some of Eltinge in his civvies, some of him in drag—plus advice columns, humor, sundry "Eltingegrams," and commentary that aimed at wryness, the *Magazine* was made widely available to fans and admirers for a mere ten cents an issue.[17] It contained articles such as "Julian Eltinge Advises Ladies to Learn Gentle Art of Boxing." The study of boxing could make a woman both be "strong" and "fashionable," and also teach her "to take defeat in a manly fashion." The *Magazine* strove to convey its namesake's unique empathy for women. Here was a man who got them. He was one of them and yet not, sharing observations such as "About the time a girl puts on her long dress, she begins to select her bridesmaids" and "The average man can make a fool of himself almost as easily as a woman can make a fool of him." Women were inherently misguided, prone to excess, and naive. Yet, according to a poem in *Julian Eltinge Magazine*, "With all her faults I love her still. / She was once young and slim and fair. / At present she can more than fill / An ordinary easy chair." She was gossipy, scolding, and lacked "a lot of charms," but despite "all her faults I love her still." Rather than suggesting the early roots of modern feminism, the magazine's rhetoric echoed the increasingly impossible task of womanhood at the dawn of the new century, and somehow made it just a tad *more* impossible.[18]

Julian Eltinge Magazine and Beauty Hints was of course also meant to push product. The performer created the Julian Eltinge Preparations Company to sell his cold cream, facial powder, and "liquid toilet powder," some based on stage makeup seen by "[t]housands of ladies throughout the country." Cold cream started at twenty-five cents, while Eltinge face powder and "liquid whiting" could be had for fifty cents each. Unlikely or humorous as it may seem to us, Julian Eltinge and A. H. Woods were very much on a cutting edge of consumerism, trying to exploit the emerging notion that women needed

Figure 6.3 *Julian Eltinge Magazine*, published by A. H. Woods for several years, was a sincere mixture of beauty tips, advice for women, ads for the actor's products, light humor, and the chance to further embellish Eltinge's "real" life when he wasn't working—that is, his *masculine drag*. The cover features the performer in his popular Bathing Beauty guise, popularized in *The Fascinating Widow*.
Credit: *Laurence Senelick Collection.*

sophisticated "systems" and "methods" to get their faces right. Who better to dictate such procedures than a man who spent hours each day painstakingly building the handsomest female face in America? In a few short years, the movie industry's most famous makeup artist, Max Factor, would introduce his "Society Makeup" line for civilian use, further suggesting that it was

160   BEAUTIFUL

possible and perhaps essential for ordinary women to look like celebrities, or at least try; the technology was now allegedly at their disposal.[19]

The third pillar of Julian Eltinge's brand, in addition to his impersonation skills and his instructions (and products) for women, of course, was an ongoing commitment to showcasing the "real man" he was "offstage." The delicate balancing act went on, all the more intriguing when it happened within the very pages of a publication titled *Julian Eltinge Magazine and Beauty Hints*. In addition to pictures of the entertainer as Dolly Dimples, Shakespeare's Juliet, and an Ingenue, *Julian Eltinge Magazine* had photos of the actor duking it out with boxing legend James J. Corbett and climbing trees in Fort Salonga. It also reaffirmed the centrality of heteronormativity's most important project: *marriage.* A husband was the "trimming on the tree of life," a "badge of merit more to be cherished than a Carnegie medal." *Eltinge Magazine* informed readers that "A manless woman is an abomination under the sun," while a womanless man, like Julian Eltinge, was but a carefree, cigar-puffing, tennis-playing, tree-climbing bachelor. Fans and observers naturally speculated about his unmarried state, as have others over the years. "Eltinge isn't married—he isn't even engaged" was typical of the gossip columns at the time. (More recent writers, as we will later see, have also scratched their heads over why the artist seemed to have "had no love life" and/or "never married.") The press rarely sniped at Julian Eltinge for his singleness as Eltinge sniped at women for theirs. In fact, the media was often happy to leak what they must have known were fabricated rumors of romances with actresses Pauline Frederick, Hazel Dawn, and others. By one estimate, the impersonator said he was engaged no fewer than ten times over the course of his career.[20]

Julian Eltinge Magazine was part of a rich publicity scheme that saw the performer make personal appearances to reinforce his brand's themes and goals, and vice versa. The night after Eltinge appeared in *The Fascinating Widow* in Cincinnati, A. H. Woods arranged for him to spar with retired "ex-champion of the fistic-art" James J. Corbett in a local gym where the two "handle[d] each other with the mitts" for an excited crowd. Woods arranged for copious publicity shots, which would be disseminated the world over. The actor would later buy the shoes allegedly worn by legendary fighter John L. Sullivan in Sullivan's final bout with Corbett. Eltinge's boxing persona allowed the impersonator to prove "himself a 'regular fellow,'" a manly chap with "a perfect right" and a "swift and efficacious left," which might slip past even Jim Corbett's "guard." Julian Eltinge's repeated protestations of his love of sports actually led to a homoerotic news item. The impersonator was

Figure 6.4 Boxing, fighting, and wrestling were among the most legible representations of manliness in the early 1900s. The actor took great pains to publicize his interest in the sports and his special relationships with members of the pugilism community, such as legendary fighter James J. Corbett.
Credit: *Billy Rose Theatre Division, The New York Public Library for the Performing Arts.*

friends with Joe Humphreys, "celebrated announcer, sporting authority and man about town." The story went that Humphreys's wife was going through her husband's pockets—because, it was implied, wives are naturally suspicious and snooping—when she happened upon a photo of a beautiful woman in revealing dress. Mrs. Humphreys demanded to know who it was, to which the sports announcer replied, it was his good friend, *Julian Eltinge*. "Forgive

162   BEAUTIFUL

me, Joe, I shall never mistrust you again," said this missus, though she might in fact have become more curious yet. Little more is known about Eltinge's relationship with Joe Humphreys, and others have suggested the performer may have had an affair with a sportswriter named Norman Cohen—though again, what evidence there is appears lost in an elusive past.[21]

* * *

As may be clear by now, if Julian Eltinge was undeniably intimate with anyone, it was his show business trenchmates. Performers from wandering mimes of old to modern-day vaudevillians had their own institutions, rituals, and bonds. Maybe even more than other subcultures, theirs was a breed apart, inherently inverted, with men playing women and teenagers playing lords and queens—as the powerful invariably kept a watchful, distrusting eye. Joining one of the trade's exclusive clubs, such as the Friars or the Lambs, meant sinking deeper roots into a de facto family and home. The impersonation artist was no doubt delighted upon being invited to join the Lambs and the Friars, respectively, among the theatre community's two most famous fraternal organizations. They had comfortable headquarters, special rules, privileges, and, like similar entities of the day, loved putting on talent shows. Of course, unlike other groups, their theatricals were by definition of professional quality—as if NASA were holding its own science fair or the New York Yankees started a softball team. Eltinge was a main feature of the Friars' 1911 *Frolic*. Produced by no less luminaries than Mark Klaw and Abraham Erlanger, the group's "gigantic all star entertainment" appeared at the New Amsterdam and costarred Fred Niblo, Raymond Hitchcock, Julian Eltinge's former teammate George "Honey Boy" Evans, Irving Berlin, and the duo Weber & Fields. Eltinge played Durabellam Dingle in "The Pullman Porters' Ball," a surely totally racist minstrel sketch penned by the country's favorite showbiz patriot, George M. Cohan. The Friars' crossdressing newcomer was "doubtless the hit of the evening." Eltinge also became a member of the even more prestigious Lambs, in whose *All-Star Gambol* he'd soon star.[22]

If America's many fraternal organizations created their own, respective, self-contained realities in the name of a sometimes-necessary developmental "regression" for joiners, the Lambs took matters to an entirely new level.[23] Perhaps inevitable for a club consisting of professional make-believers, the Lambs turned self-reference into the highest and strangest of arts. The club, which was founded in 1874 and, like Hasty Pudding, had long been a hotbed of crossdressing, loved making itself the focal point of its sketches and musicals. One of Eltinge's first big roles in the *All-Star Gambol* was as Mary the shepherdess in the sketch "Mary and Her Lambs." Like other clubs and societies, the Lambs took unity seriously, ratifying a constitution that might have impressed a political scientist. The president of the organization was "The Shepherd" and the vice president, "The Boy." There were numerous categories of membership, including Honorary, Life, Professional, Non-Professional, Non-Resident, and Armed Services. Abundant councils, proceedings, and adjudications ensured leadership would "have power to censure, suspend, expel or request the resignation of any member who shall be found guilty of any offense which . . . shall be deemed detrimental to the best interests of the Club." [24] Like many closed fraternities, the Lambs ultimately seemed to exist in order to affirm their ongoing existence, their very *club*-ness.

The Lambs, initially just a supper club, held their first *Gambol* in 1888. By 1904, the same year a subway line to the newly named Times Square had been completed, they had a clubhouse at 122 West 44th Street. The Lambs, which had about three hundred members at the time, appointed a "Collie," or artistic director for the *Gambol* and other extravaganzas. It might seem obvious, but the Lambs were also committed in a most impressive and dedicated way to getting smashed. Their regular "Washes" or "Washings" were little more than drunken parties designed to brighten moods and reinforce the bonds of Lamb-hood. At a Hollywood cocktail party in the 1920s, vaudevillian Florence Moore looked at the attendees, including Eltinge and George Jessel, and reckoned, "Looks like a Lambs' Wash around here." When a fellow partygoer asked what that was, Moore replied, "An alcohol rub!" Never one to abstain, Julian Eltinge fit right in, now part of a group that would never to close its doors nor admit "a stranger not entitled to privileges." The Lambs gave refuge to members of an unpredictable profession in an unpredictable world. Even Frank Fay, the vaudevillian who debuted the role of Elwood P. Dowd to great acclaim in Mary Chase's classic comedy *Harvey* in 1944, was admitted, despite a well-known reputation as a wife-abuser—especially when wed to Barbara Stanwyck—and ardent profascist. Even the fairly conservative Lambs disliked and disapproved of Frank Fay but nonetheless let the agitated comedian drink his coffee and read his paper in solitude. Miles Kreuger, Broadway habitué and, later, professor of musical comedy at New York University, was permitted to lunch at the Lambs' clubhouse after *Anything Goes* and *Life with Father* coauthor Howard Lindsay heard that Kreuger had

164   BEAUTIFUL

been settling for plates of spaghetti at quotidian cafés near Times Square. (Extra meatballs were five cents apiece.) Lindsay contacted his friend, Lambs' Shepherd Bill Gaxton, who in turn allowed the twentysomething lad to eat at the clubhouse. Yes, Gaxton told Kreuger, Frank Fay was a wife-beating, Nazi sympathizer. But he was a Lamb, and actors closed ranks, despite some moral compromises. "It was like being a member of a large family," Kreuger recalls, which is probably how it felt to Julian Eltinge too.[25]

* * *

On September 11, 1911, the impersonation artist embarked upon the second season of *The Fascinating Widow* with fifty-six performances at the Liberty Theatre, next door to what would soon be a playhouse bearing his name. On Broadway, the show drew mostly "lukewarm notices." But A. H. Woods knew by now that his crossdressing luminary was a star of the circuits, not the Great White Way—to that luminary's dawning disappointment. A substantial salary bump—Eltinge was accurately called "One of the Biggest Money Makers on [the] American Stage"—salved some of the hurt. With a few years, Woods would sign Eltinge to a five-year contract starting at $2,500 a week. Some estimated that he had become the world's second most popular stage performer, just behind French legend Sarah Bernhardt. That might have been overstating things a bit, plus Ms. Bernhardt was well past her prime by then. Still, it was a metric of his regard, how he might be thought of among the mighty. Over the next few seasons, both in *The Fascinating Widow* and in plays of a similar stripe, Julian Eltinge would surpass the $3,000-a-week mark, part salary, part profit-sharing. Woods and Eltinge had formed a fruitful partnership indeed.[26]

With the *Widow* winning "the highest approval" of press and public alike on the road, Julian Eltinge started to live more as celebrities of the day were increasingly expected to: as icons of consumption, liberated from various earthly restraints and freer to indulge. The actor's net worth was estimated around $600,000. In 1914, he spent $1,801.75 on a dinner that included oysters, flounder, steak, and other sumptuous courses—and which landed him in the hospital. In York, Pennsylvania, the actor reported that jewels and gems worth $1,500 had been stolen from his hotel room by a "sneak thief." At the time, diamonds and gemstones were almost more valuable to a celebrity when stolen. It made for spicy press and reinforced the image of being so rich and successful you couldn't keep track of all your riches. Actress Beatrice Brevaine,

Figure 6.5 After *The Fascinating Widow* made Julian Eltinge a superstar in the early 1910s, some argued he was the second most famous stage personality in the world after Sarah Bernhardt. That was probably an overstatement. Still, it suggests the regard in which he was held—even if the impersonator was not quite at the level of the legendary French actress whom he resembles in this publicity still.
Credit: *Copyright reserved, Northport Historical Society (Long Island, NY).*

known as "the fencing girl," accused a high-profile con artist of "abstracting" two diamond rings and a watch from her as she and the charming conman lunched at the Majestic Hotel in New York City in 1907, resulting in banner headlines. (Curiously, Eva Tanguay, also known to complain about stolen diamonds, rushed to the alleged perpetrator's defense, possibly because she

166 BEAUTIFUL

and the thief were having an affair.) As Al Manheim, the narrator of Budd Schulberg's 1941 Hollywood novel *What Makes Sammy Run?* observes, a "guy called Veblen said we make our reputations by how much money we can publicly throw away." After the federal income tax went into effect in 1913, Julian Eltinge paid the amount owed by his *entire troupe* that year, a sum of $2,000. (The actor claimed he'd lost a bet with A. H. Woods over whether the federal income tax amendment would pass.) Not only was Julian Eltinge the *man* worth a lot, Julian Eltinge the *property* was also enjoying a bull market. In 1913, he insured his teeth with Lloyds of London for $250,000, or "$8,000 per tooth." The artist was more than the sum of his parts, for sure, but those parts were plenty valuable on their own. Brides started carrying what became known as a "'Julian Eltinge' bouquet" at weddings.[27]

Keeping the Eltinge brand aloft meant modeling yet more sumptuous gowns, "absolutely the last word in the modiste's art," as Mrs. Monte in *The Fascinating Widow*. New jokes and songs, including ragtime numbers and a Salome bit, made the new season "fresher" and full of "vitality," crucial for a franchise.[28] Female-impersonating was out of the closet and out in public as never before. Julian Eltinge, dubbed "The queerest woman in the world" by one paper, led the pack, though competitor Bothwell Browne and his "Girl Types," which included Cleopatra and Browne's own version of a Bathing Beauty, were also flying high. Some police departments even created female-impersonation specialists to stop mashers and brutes from accosting presumably helpless women in theatres and other public places.[29]

Perhaps most important, *The Fascinating Widow* took Julian Eltinge a step away from impersonating women and a step toward being what he hoped would one day be proper acting. Rather than a young man who seemed born to slip into the very skin of a woman, Eltinge played Hal, a rollicking college lad who has no choice but to drag-up, echoing the actor's own self-fabling. With *The Fascinating Widow* and the productions that followed, Eltinge no longer played women but rather, "men playing women."[30] He would be marketed abroad using this rebrand. In May 1912, Eltinge and the cast of *The Fascinating Widow* embarked on an ambitious tour of Australia.[31] He was happy for the opportunity, though he still longed to work on Broadway, "in the metropolis," as the expression ran. But A. H. Woods had little intention of changing what seemed to be working so well, leaving his beloved, young performer "doomed to the provinces and the resulting dollars forever," as the *New York Times* would describe things a few years later.[32]

* * *

FROM CRINOLINE TO CELLULOID   167

The Eltinge production team had indeed hit upon a winning formula, one that would need only surface tinkering from season to season, even production to production: a breezy comedy with scattered musical numbers and an excuse for the main character to drag-up. *The Crinoline Girl* by Otto Hauerbach and Percy Wenrich, a "melodramatic mystery farce," would be Woods and Eltinge's second production. *Crinoline* amplified certain aspects of *The Fascinating Widow*, the new show making up in "speed" what it lacked in "class," according to the *New York Times*. *The Crinoline Girl* tried to cram some of the artist's vaudeville menagerie into the story, "from a Spanish dancer to a modern split-skirt heroine." It was good for the box office but, artistically speaking, a step in precisely the wrong direction for its star and his wishes to go legitimate. *The Crinoline Girl* also forced him to turn campy a few times, to "mince instead of swagger," which was definitely against the artist's grain and always had been. But with his pay, popularity, and success bursting like an uncorked magnum of champagne, Eltinge had to go along. Even he had to admit that for what it was, *The Crinoline Girl* was pretty good, having ten times as many laugh lines as *The Fascinating Widow*, by his reckoning. The new play would debut in February 1914.[33]

The Crinoline Girl told the story of Tom Hale, a young American "with a rich father and ample means of his own," who seeks to wed Dorothy Ainsley but is told by her stentorian, British father that he must somehow earn $10,000 on his own in order to qualify for his daughter's hand. It so happens that that family has had $200,000 worth of diamonds stolen from the hotel in Lausanne, Switzerland, where they live. Tom ends up donning crinoline-framed hoop skirts, a passé fashion item like the corset, to locate the missing gems, for which the reward is $25,000. It was the sort of comedy Eltinge's audiences would appreciate with absurd jokes, farcical plotting, mistaken identities, and a "hurry-scurry of characters." He had a good supporting cast, including Helen Luthrell and Herbert Corthell. When the former had to be replaced, Eltinge convinced Al Woods to hire up-and-coming talent Jeanne Eagels, despite the fact that the producer found her personally "impossible." Audiences ended up adoring her.[34]

Julian Eltinge's series of impersonations in *The Crinoline Girl* balanced moments of camp with his time-tested aesthetic, namely, conveying "the eternal feminine with such realism without crossing the line which would bring disgust rather than amusement." Possibly due to his age, now in his early thirties, and love of abundant food and drink, Eltinge wasn't quite the sprightly young beauty he had been when he started his career a decade and a half earlier. Women had to remain youthful to be beautiful; perforce,

Figure 6.6 *The Crinoline Girl* (1914) was Julian Eltinge's second musical comedy under A. H. Woods's stewardship. Eltinge played the formulaic-but-popular role of a young man forced to drag-up. His character, Tom, says, "Nowadays a woman is only 10 percent nature. The rest is art."
Credit: *Laurence Senelick Collection.*

so did he. But he could no more accept changes in his look and figure than could his audiences. What he perceived as ungainly or grotesque disgusted him. Like many of the women he counseled on dieting and beauty, he too was in the opening stages of an unwinnable war against time and social expectations. It was subtle as yet, even invisible to some. At least one observer felt he was still "a better-looking and more attractive girl than a good many

FROM CRINOLINE TO CELLULOID 169

Figure 6.7 Actors and producers handed out thousands of publicity cards in Julian Eltinge's day, a way of getting potential fans to remember you amid an increasingly cluttered consumer headspace.
Credit: *Laurence Senelick Collection.*

real ones." Interest in crossdressing had grown since Eltinge had taken up skirts with the Massachusetts Cadets and Boston Bank Officers. In 1910, pioneering German sexologist Magnus Hirschfeld, who was as openly gay as one could be at the time, argued that crossdressing usually began early in life—earlier than, say, in college—and coined the term *transvestism* to describe the phenomenon. Fellow traveler, English sexologist Havelock Ellis, agreed with many of Hirschfeld's findings but had come to believe that a man

170   BEAUTIFUL

who liked putting on dresses possessed a deeper, "feminine" identity. Ellis accordingly considered transvestism part of a larger condition he called *sexo-aesthetic inversion*. Julian Eltinge naturally raged against the idea that men who impersonated women were inverted or improper, insisting, "No man in woman's clothes, however skillfully disguised, could fascinate another man." His argument, however ironic given how he made a living, aligned with cultural beliefs that manliness was a kind of natural, resting state, while womanliness had inherently to be worked at, to be performed. As Eltinge's Tom Hale declares in *The Crinoline Girl*, "Any ordinary chap with a little skill in painting can make himself a good looking woman. . . . Nowadays a woman is only 10 percent nature. The rest is art."[35] Tom also strives to be Eltinge-when not in skirts, telling his sister, Alice, "I'll bet you a dozen pairs of gloves against a box of cigars" that he can "make up to look as well as you." Tom Hale also likes driving fast—well, sixty miles per hour, which was fast for the day—and gambling, increasingly thought of as a macho pastime thanks to betting legends like Arnold Rothstein, Dutch Schultz, and Owney Madden. Gambling, betting, and odds-fixing were becoming practically a sport in their own right, somewhere between boxing and varsity drag shows, an unlettered cousin of stock-picking and futures investing.[36]

* * *

Though Al Woods could have milked another season out of *The Crinoline Girl*, he chose instead to place Eltinge, recently called "one of the most certain moneymakers among all male stars," into a hopefully even more lucrative new project—new in name if not in concept, anyway. Like *The Fascinating Widow* and *The Crinoline Girl* before it, *Cousin Lucy* was a frothy excuse for gender confusion, homoerotic double-entendres, and Julian Eltinge in dresses—lots of them, one more fashionable than the last. It was looking as if it would be a while until he might enact Shylock or Iago; he'd aged-out of Romeo. *Cousin Lucy*, whose title vaguely echoed perhaps the most famous tranvestic farce of the era, *Charley's Aunt*, was "But Vehicle for Girl Impersonator," according to a headline that captured matters well. Despite the huge salary, cheering crowds, and expensive fashions, how much could a play like this take Julian Eltinge where he truly wished to be? Indeed, when *Cousin Lucy* playwright Charles Klein died tragically aboard the ocean liner *Lusitania*, many of his writings were deemed literally "valueless" by the court because they were so hyper-specialized, designed for one specific actor, such as David Warfield

Figure 6.8 Having one's name on too many cosmetic products could, of course, lead consumers to think one unmanly. Fortunately for Julian Eltinge, a line of cigars also bore his name. It was not uncommon for cigars to use the names of popular actors and entertainers. Here he appears a thoughtful young man in a business suit. Especially early in his career, the press loved to report on Julian Eltinge's cigar-smoking, a perfect manly—if not also Freudian—pastime.
Credit: *Laurence Senelick Collection.*

or Julian Eltinge. *Cousin Lucy* debuted at Cohan's Theatre in New York in August 1915 with music by Jerome Kern plus additional compositions by Percy Wenrich and August Kleinecke. (Kern was to have sailed on the *Lusitania* with his friend, producer Charles Frohman, but apparently overslept after a night of heavy drinking and missed the boat; Frohman, Klein, and nearly 1,200 other crew and passengers died after *Lusitania* was torpedoed by a German submarine on May 7, 1915.[37])

The "obvious and frequently inane" plot of *Cousin Lucy* involves Jerry Jackson, yet another freewheeling bachelor, "pestered alike by young women and creditors." To throw the latter off his trail, he arranges to make it seem as though he has been killed in a trainwreck out West. Jerry returns as his supposed cousin, Lucette, a claimant for his estate. Jerry/Lucette's scam is of

172 BEAUTIFUL

course complicated by an outside factor, in this case a woman named Queeny Belmont who claims she had been married to Jerry and is therefore also entitled to a piece of his estate. In what amounts to a homo-curious, Oedipal quagmire, an older man named Baldwin falls for Lucette (aka "Lucy") while Jerry in turn falls for Baldwin's daughter. Lucy also decides to open a dress shop. Whatever shortcomings these productions had, they managed to provide increasing stage time for strong female characters, like the role of Queeny, played to great acclaim by Jane Oaker and also by her equally talented understudy, Harriet Burt.[38]

Not only *Cousin Lucy*'s plot but its dialogue, "talky, and unnecessarily so" in one reviewer's opinion, proved wearying. Jokes were forced. At one point a character remarks, "I think I should look chic in that," to which another responds, "Yes, you'd look sick in that." In another scene, Baldwin's daughter asks Jerry if he likes psychology, to which he responds, "That depends on how it's cooked." Many felt sad that this was Charles Klein's final contribution to the world of letters.[39]

Critics were onto the Woods/Eltinge formula and tiring of it. They could sense that the impersonator's art had lost its vivacity and become a commodity. Eltinge's audiences wanted a predictable amusement and, well, "They got it," according to the *New York Times*. "For Julian Eltinge is Julian Eltinge, and an Eltinge show is an Eltinge show. And there you are." Influential *New York Tribune* critic Heywood Broun called *Cousin Lucy* "just another of those Eltinge plays." The star's $4,000-a-week paycheck offset the hurt, but not enough.[40]

Like a Hollywood comic-book or sci-fi franchise doubling down on flashy special effects, *Cousin Lucy* showered its star in the grandest fashions. Broun felt the play was all about costumes and outfits, "constituting as they did the plot of the piece, something precise and technical." As if putting on a one-man fashion show, the actor appeared in one ensemble after another, beginning "simply enough with a silk shirtwaist" but eventually displaying "a whole dressmaking establishment." Promotional materials advertised *Cousin Lucy*'s "Fashion Parade." As Jerry/Lucy, Julian Eltinge made no fewer than sixteen costume changes, only eased somewhat by the fact that Act 2 was conveniently set in a Manhattan dress shop. "The suspense lay in wondering what Mr. Eltinge would wear next," commented Broun.[41]

Cousin Lucy more or less rendered Julian Eltinge both a human mannequin and a cog in a well-oiled machine. The show did not serve its star, but

Figure 6.9 *Cousin Lucy* (1915) was the third Eltinge/Woods production. It used a veritable fashion show to thrill shopping-hungry audiences. "'Cousin Lucy' Displays Fashions and Julian Eltinge," read one sardonic headline. Rather than getting closer to playing traditional male roles or any kind of serious dramatic parts, the actor became even more of an object for audiences simply to gape at. He'd soon have enough of it and need to make a change.

Credit: *Laurence Senelick Collection.*

174   BEAUTIFUL

rather the reverse. "Take a plot concerning the fortunes of a rough-spoken, devil-may-care fellow and puzzle your brains till you have devised some situation wherein he must don feminine finery as a disguise," wrote the *New York Times*, add some other predictable ingredients, then "Stir briskly and serve in a hurry."[42]

In fact, if *Cousin Lucy* had a true star, it was fashionista Melville Ellis who designed the show's "creations." The production was said to consist of "now and then a song by Jerome Kern and now and then a gorgeous gown by" Ellis. Read one sardonic headline, "'Cousin Lucy' Displays Fashions and Julian Eltinge." Even the set seemed to outshine the actor. In Buffalo, crowds oohed and aahed at Lucette's store, white-paneled with sleek black borders, arrayed with "ravishing" sartorial creations, some fur-lined and classic, others "futuristic." Whatever Eltinge might have felt about being subordinated to the sets and costumes, the show's creators were not wrong in further bridging the already adjacent worlds of entertainment and shopping. Watching *Cousin Lucy* made men take "women's clothes seriously," half-joked a Buffalo journalist. In reality, many shrewd businessmen were already taking womenswear quite seriously. The problem was, how could Julian Eltinge maintain his singular image while exploiting what had become a mass-market commodity? He couldn't, it seemed. "The play itself is largely a matter of clothes," wrote columnist Charles Darnton, implying that it made little difference who wore them, which was good for ordinary women wanting to look special, but bad for an extraordinary entertainer whose career seemed to be plateauing.[43]

Trundling across the country, changing his costume sixteen times a show, could only have been exhausting for Julian Eltinge. In a sense, his complement of steamer trunks, perhaps fourteen in all, dragged him along rather than the reverse. He also had to keep his skin "velvety" and, like all women, "annex no wrinkles." The entertainer also had to maintain "masculine muscle" without becoming burly, a challenge for a man who so often turned to food and spirits for respite. "Sh!," wrote a Brooklyn paper, "Julian Eltinge has not the figure he used to, or ought to, have," not to mention a double-chin and girth beyond "a perfect thirty-six." Crowds trained their eyes not only on the actor's costumes but on his figure too: was it "slim" and "neat" as it ought to be?[44]

To keep up the usual offstage appearances, it was leaked that Eltinge had gotten engaged to actress Pauline Frederick. In Minneapolis, a meet-and-greet between the impersonator and local boxing promoter Billy Hoke

Figure 6.10 A "double shot" from *Cousin Lucy*. Note the actor's simplified, post-Victorian but not-quite-modern dress, an older aesthetic that nonetheless pointed to the future of style.
Credit: *Photo by White Studio, © The New York Public Library for the Performing Arts.*

resulted in apparently newsworthy sports banter. The impersonator's knowledge of Eddie Campi—"one of the greatest little fighting machines in the world"—played well in local papers. The boxing ring was one of the few solidly male redoubts in a world increasingly open to women and friendly to high-flown drag artists.[45] If hanging out with boxing coaches didn't make Julian Eltinge *the man* appear convincing enough, the performer made sure to keep putting space between him and Julian Eltinge, *enactor of woman*. Havelock Ellis and other scientific speculators were delving a little too deeply into the psyche of the invert, wondering what else a man might be doing if he practiced crossdressing. The artist told reporters he could "never stand one of those 'sissy' fellows" and reiterated that when not onstage, he hardly thought about skirts. "Just because a man earns $1.25 a day digging a ditch with a spade is no reason that he must talk about a spade all the time he is

176 BEAUTIFUL

not at work, does it? He does not eat with a spade, and walk up streets with a spade under each arm," argued Eltinge.[46]

* * *

A. H. Woods, meanwhile, was busy figuring how to squeeze another season out of *Cousin Lucy*. He promised the 1916–1917 tour would "eclipse" the past, with new song numbers and dance routines, and of course, updated fashions. Perhaps in part to keep its main player happy, the producer promised "none but stars" in the new supporting cast. For Julian Eltinge, it wouldn't be enough. He left *Cousin Lucy* in 1917. Classified ads for "clean-cut" performers "capable of making up for stunning woman of Julian Eltinge order" to star in an "A-1 musical comedy" production had already appeared in Los Angeles papers. Soon, talented, B-level impersonator Larry Richardson was recruited to carry on "Julian Eltinge's Success." Replacing Julian Eltinge in formulaic, crossdressed musicals was becoming something of a cottage industry, with well-known impersonator Hal Russell filling Eltinge's shoes in revivals and spin-offs of *The Fascinating Widow*.[47]

Eltinge had had enough of the now-rote musicals that brought him to the next level. To advance, he'd need to reinvent himself—somehow, at least in part. When he figured out how, the entertainer and his PR team devised an unusual, large-format newspaper that depicted Julian Eltinge the actor in conversation with his most recent stage persona, "Cousin Lucy." Photographs of each, respectively, flanked the page, with a column of dialogue running down the space in between. The layout played on a signature trope of the Eltinge brand: trick photography that depicted the artist's male and female characters engaging one another. In that vein, this playful quasi-advertisement invited fans and readers into the split, to sense what it was like to inhabit two—or more—differently sexed bodies, like a magician revealing just enough of their trick to let you feel included but hungry to know more. If photography provided superhuman powers of precision observation, it could just as easily be made to lie and turn reality into so much sculptor's clay. The promotional spread, "Julian Eltinge Has Interview with 'Cousin Lucy'," featured the character telling the artist who inhabited her, "For fourteen years we've been related. Aren't you getting sick of the acquaintanceship?" to which Eltinge replied, "While there's money in it and the public wants us? No!" "But Julian," replied Lucy, "I'd think you'd get so tired of it all"—tired of having to "reduce" and tour and, it was implied, put on the same show, or the same *kind* of show, ad infinitum. The artist had long insisted he was mostly in it for professional reasons, especially the money that came with it, once saying, "In what other line of business would such promotion be possible[?]" His career had advanced more rapidly than many men's, whether they were in banking, copper, retailing, or pretty much any sector of the economy. He had never faltered like his father. Lucy understood Julian. She listened patiently, before pointing out the obvious. "But it seems to me you're wasting an awful lot of time, Julian," maybe missing your shot at being "a Hamlet" or "a John Drew." But the female impersonator told his female impersonation not to fret. He had big news for both of them: "next year you and I are going into the movies." Lucy thought the plan "splendid," inquiring, "Guess I don't travel any more, eh, Julian?" No, you don't, Lucy. Eltinge told her that he— *they*—would make four pictures a year and receive $200,000. "But what'll we do with all the money?" wondered Cousin Lucy. "I don't know. How'd you like to buy Brooklyn a new court House?"[48] As it turned out, Julian Eltinge would find plenty of ways to spend his money.

# # #

7

Impersonating in the USA, 1919

By the time Julian Eltinge arrived at the Famous Players–Lasky movie studio on the Paramount lot in 1917 accompanied by a "small army of trunks," motion pictures had changed dramatically, blooming from experimental technology to popular entertainment.[1] Still-image photography was invented in the 1830s. But these were gauzy, often ghostlike, daguerreotype images. It would be several decades before a more precise, image-capturing technology—close to what we think of as photos—would emerge. The camera was indeed regarded as an empirical, observational tool, like a telescope or a thermometer. It could witness reality and record it with a "scientific accuracy" way beyond the capacity of the fallible human eye and memory. Few looked at it as a possible artistic medium. San Francisco–based photographer Eadweard Muybridge famously took a step from still-image to motion-picture photography—what we call *cinematography*—in 1872 when he set up camera to snap multiple shots, in succession, of a horse to see if all four hooves ever left the ground at the same time. (The answer: yes, they did.) So-called moving pictures were born.[2]

From the 1890s through the time Julian Eltinge started making pictures, the movies had grown from short tidbits of visually interesting or dazzling scenes—battles, the aftermath of natural disasters, newsworthy events, even trains and factories in motion—and comic gag films into longer "features," sometimes based on well-known plays and books, then garnished with serials, newsreels, and a few comical shorts in the theatre. Vaudeville shows were among the first to exhibit movies, beginning in the late 1890s, usually at the end of the bill; these flicks were sometimes derided as "chasers"—meant to empty the auditorium—though more recent research suggests this epithet was ill-deserved. Movies eventually found a home in cheap, storefront cinemas called "nickelodeons." But soon, especially following the forty-four-week run of D. W. Griffith's infamous *Birth of a Nation*, which premiered in New York on March 3, 1915, they were increasingly exhibited in larger, well-furnished movie theatres and cinema "palaces." Vaudeville, which had once given a home to the new entertainment form, now found itself increasingly

Beautiful. Andrew L. Erdman, Oxford University Press. © Oxford University Press 2024.
DOI: 10.1093/9780197696361.003.0008

overshadowed by movies' popularity, a situation that a recent graphic novel about Julian Eltinge and other vaudevillians likens to "matriphagy," which is when a swarm of baby spiders devour its own mother. For vaudeville, it was ugly and would only get uglier, declining and ceding ground to the film industry from the mid-1910s onward.[3]

Even before the rise of the feature and the picture palace, visual marvels like George Méliès's *A Trip to the Moon* (1902) and Edwin Porter's *The Great Train Robbery* (1903) provided stunning, action-packed and illusionistic "attractions" that vaudeville audiences loved. (The first commercial use of moving-pictures had actually come in 1894 when a collection of Edison's "Kinetograph" machines were installed in a New York City storefront. These gadgets allowed one person at a time view a series of shorts by staring through a metal-enclosed glass and cranking a handle. The Kinetograph parlor, which charged 5¢–25¢ per machine use, made a splash but soon went out of business for lack of interest, a novelty that came and went.) It would take others, notably the Lumière brothers, who debuted their ingenious camera-projector at Keith's Union Square in June 1896, to turn motion pictures into a collective, group-based amusement. Thomas Edison, relying heavily on his assistant William Kennedy Laurie Dickson and various third parties, had managed to scrape up naming rights to a pre-existing projection device that he renamed the "Vitascope." Thus, what came to be promoted as "Edison's Latest Marvel" brought projected movies to Koster & Bial's vaudeville and burlesque house in Manhattan around the same time. The age of projected motion pictures had begun.[4]

The more people who packed American movie houses—by 1910, 26 million Americans visited nickelodeons and similar "small-time vaudeville" venues each week—the bigger the business grew. That meant more consolidation of power and the need to ensure a steady output of product. Narrative films, which is to say fictional comedies and dramas, were easier to churn out since they could make use of the same actors, many of the same sets and props, and virtually the same slapstick or melodramatic storylines.[5]

Julian Eltinge began his film career in one of the industry's early and, it would turn out, long-lasting ventures. Movie mogul Adolph Zukor, whose Famous Players in Famous Plays unit featured James O'Neill in *The Count of Monte Cristo* and Minnie Maddern Fiske in *Tess of the D'Urbervilles*, was in the process of merging his interests with Jesse Lasky's Feature Play Company to form Famous Players–Lasky, the nucleus of what would become Paramount Pictures. Hollywood's first titans hoped that the public would

180 BEAUTIFUL

discern among movies as it did among, say, cars or cigarettes, becoming loyal to a specific brand. Why shouldn't they? The big film studios were becoming huge, "vertically integrated" concerns like many others, owning or controlling production, distribution, and exhibition. They shot the movies, shipped and routed them around the country, and owned many of the cinemas in which they were played. "The public is learning to buy its photoplay amusement by trademark," said Lasky, more wishfully than truthfully. It soon became clear, in fact, that filmgoers tended to select their movies based more on the actors than the studios. Julian Eltinge was not alone among vaudeville and Broadway stars to abandon the stage for the film set. Vaudeville star Nat Goodwin abruptly canceled a tour and disbanded his troupe in 1915 promising to work only in films from then on. *Variety* called it "the first time in the history of American theatricals" that so major an actor had traded stage for screen. The following year, Broadway impresario S. L. "Roxy" Rothafel demolished Hammerstein's Victoria, "the greatest of all vaudeville houses," to build the Rialto, which would play movies, and only movies. Julian Eltinge arrived in Hollywood just in time to mount the cresting wave.[6]

* * *

Well before he arrived on the Famous Players–Lasky lot in 1917, Eltinge, like many of his fellow performers, had been pondering working in pictures. In 1913, still starring in *The Fascinating Widow*, he signed with New York–based director Thomas Ince to shoot an adaptation of *Romeo and Juliet* in which he'd play not Juliet but Romeo opposite Anna Held as Juliet, "strange as it may seem," wrote one paper, echoing the sentiment of others. To keep things on-brand, however, the movie would be paired with a short featuring Eltinge in drag opposite Dustin Farnum as Romeo. It would have been the perfect opportunity for the impersonator, playing a classic, male role and entering film all at once. But it fell through. Two years later, he briefly played himself in *How Molly Made Good* (or *How Molly Malone Made Good*), the story of a newspaper reporter who sneaks around New York to get a look at the "home lives" of stars.[7]

Julian Eltinge's first starring movie role would come in 1917, in *The Countess Charming*. Originally titled *Mrs. Raffles's Career*, the five-reel comedy starred Eltinge as Stanley Jordan—or in some cuts, "Saunders Julian"—a well-off bachelor who falls in love with a young woman named Betty Lovering whom he meets at a Red Cross gala. Naturally, Stanley falls afoul of the gala's

Figure 7.1 Julian Eltinge had some success in movies like *Countess Charming* (seen here with an actress identified only as "Mrs. George Kuwa") and *The Clever Mrs. Carfax*. But like many of his vaudevillian peers, the vitality of his live shows was lost on a silent, black-and-white screen that could depict fantasies, monsters, and entities far more unusual than a man impersonating a woman.

Credit: *Billy Rose Theatre Division, The New York Public Library for the Performing Arts.*

doyenne, Mrs. Vandergraft, and finds himself shunned by high society. Just as naturally, he crossdresses his way back in, becoming Countess Raffelski, a Russian noblewoman welcomed into the very homes and country clubs from which Stanley was barred. Like Hal Blake in *The Fascinating Widow* or Eltinge himself, Stanley is said to have honed his transvestic skills in "amateur theatricals," which was not just a mechanically repeated cliché for Eltinge by this point but for many American men who earned laurels for their drag in local clubs and amateur troupes. They had gotten into it in college, or such was the readymade excuse. Stanley's Countess Raffelski subsequently steals from the rich and gives to the Red Cross until a stock-character detective gets wise to *shim*. Just when Stanley/Raffelski is about to be caught, however, Betty runs to the Countess's side, believing the latter to be mortally wounded. Raffelski's identity is revealed and the two are finally united.[8]

182   BEAUTIFUL

Released in September 1917, *The Countess Charming* was directed by Donald Crisp, later a popular character actor in such classics as *Mutiny on the Bounty* (1935) and *Jezebel* (1938). Humorist Gelett Burgess and novelist Carolyn Wells wrote the screenplay and Florence Vidor, recently married to influential silent (and later talkie) director King Vidor, played Betty. The movie, which debuted at Roxy's Rialto, was well received, the *New York Times* calling it "entertaining" and praising its star for his "aptitude for the screen," no doubt a relief for Julian Eltinge. Critics appreciated that *Countess* followed the Eltinge formula, which meant a storyline proffering "some reason or pretext for [Eltinge's character] donning of female attire." Audiences laughed. The artist's first picture was turning out to be a hit, even if the widely read *Evening World* mistakenly titled it "*The* Princess *Charming*."[9]

Paired with the usual complement of comical Keystone shorts, with titles like *A Pawnbroker's Heart* and *A Shanghaied Jonah*, plus Pathé newsreels, *The Countess Charming* did well across the country, not just in Los Angeles and New York. A Kansas paper praised *Countess*'s humor and pacing, rightly supposing that it would lead to more movie deals for Eltinge. While the actor was still hoping to break out of comical, crossdressing roles, he also understood the revolution that moving pictures heralded. For the first time in the history of entertainment, an actor could perform on both coasts, the heartland, and virtually anywhere else all at the same time. Some bemoaned what would be lost with non-live entertainment, but many others were delighted. Now people in rural areas who'd only been able to read about Julian Eltinge could see him just like their counterparts in bigger towns and cities. A newspaper in Bemidji, Minnesota, two hundred miles north of Minneapolis, applauded *The Countess Charming* for enabling the famed female impersonator to now "travel to the smallest and most remote villages." "The provincial towns are becoming accustomed to Julian Eltinge," wrote a Kansas paper the following year. From an economic standpoint, movies allowed a scaling-up not possible when a player and their entire show could be in only one place at a time. Logistical snags that could bleed a touring show to death were but paper cuts now, affecting a single cinema out of hundreds. Once a movie was shot, it was distributed by large, systematized commercial machines, while those who made it could remain where they were and start shooting the next one if demand looked good.[10]

* * *

The Clever Mrs. Carfax, Julian Eltinge's second picture, came out in November 1917, hot on the heels of *The Countess Charming*'s success. In *Carfax*, he played Temple Trask, a college fellow who falls in love-at-first-sight with Vassar undergrad Helen Scott, played by Daisy Robinson, as the two briefly lock eyes. Failing to secure a proper introduction, though, Temple tries to find out more about his mystery love. Helen, meanwhile, helps her tight-fisted grandmother recover after two of her servants, played by Noah Beery and Rosita Marstini, assault and rob her. Trask is eventually "forced by circumstances" to assume the personage of advice columnist Dorothy Carfax, who, a bit like Eltinge himself, instructs "blushing maidens how to deport themselves in matters of the heart." The usual set of complications and machinations advance what passes for a plot, until Dorothy Carfax's true identity is revealed, the wrongdoers are caught, and the lovers end up together. The formula worked, which was great from the studio's perspective but a mixed blessing for Eltinge, who still longed to play Romeo or at least the male lead in a garden-variety melodrama. Indeed *Carfax*, also directed by Donald Crisp (with screenplay by Hector Turnbull and Gardner Hunting), was even better received than *The Countess Charming*, in part because it seemed to perfect the formula, being skillfully "cut to fit" its star, in *Moving Picture World*'s opinion. With fast-paced humor and plenty of "pep," *The Clever Mrs. Carfax* was *The Countess Charming* on steroids or at least a half-dozen espressos.[11]

Shooting several *Carfax* sequences in Oregon's Columbia River valley gave its star the chance to play the rugged sportsman, a role he still welcomed even as it felt somewhat routinized and unnecessary. The Portland Chamber of Commerce, though, was delighted to have "big stars" like Eltinge filming in its "locality." (The Chamber was still recovering from a Douglas Fairbanks shoot that had fallen through at the last minute.) Preparing for one scene, director Crisp had reportedly sneaked a cactus needle beneath the saddle of a bronco to make it "sore" and give Eltinge a little more attitude. Like Teddy Roosevelt himself, the actor held on and never "pulled leather." The local business community grew fond of Julian Eltinge, and vice versa. A year after *The Clever Mrs. Carfax* debuted, the Oregon Chamber of Commerce invited the impersonation artist to headline its "High Jinks," a major networking event bringing business "greeters" from all along the West Coast together.[12]

The time in which Julian Eltinge transitioned from stage to screen, the final years of the 1910s, represented the very peak of female-impersonating in America, culturally and economically. Though the practice had been

184 BEAUTIFUL

widespread and would have good years to come, this was the height of the height. In fact, what Julian Eltinge was doing onscreen began to look almost quaint or de rigueur. Not only were the gender's separate "spheres" breaking down as women sought the vote and solidified their place in the labor force, but so-called normal men were freer to put on female garb—in certain settings, anyhow—than ever before. A leading metric was a rise in the popularity of often lavish "womanless weddings," elaborate shows, part-ceremony/part-performance, in which men shaved their body hair and assumed the role of bride, mother-of-the-bride, flower girls, and so forth. Some womanless weddings featured random entertainments, like hula dancers or ukulele strummers, as one might see in a minstrel production. In March 1918, while *The Clever Mrs. Carfax* was still in movie houses, the Austin, Texas, Lions' Club put on a massive womanless wedding as a Red Cross fundraiser starring well-regarded local merchant John Tobin as the bride. Clad in white and clutching a bouquet, Tobin stared tenderly from the pages of the *Austin America*, a male bride who "Out-Julians Julian Eltinge." Womanless weddings would continue to gain popularity in the early 1920s, even in smaller towns like Canandaigua, New York, whose "bewigged and muchly skirted" Knights of Columbus put on a ceremony, as did stolidly "Christian" men in Windsor, Missouri, for a church fundraiser.[13]

Between cultural developments and professional success, informed by a wisdom that comes with the years, Julian Eltinge began lightening the iron death-grip he'd long maintained over his masculine imagery. It was modest, but if you looked closely enough, it was discernible. Certainly, he did not discourage the press from depicting him as a fellow who loved "black cigars," poker, whiskey neat, and horseracing, a lad simply "picked too early" from the Montana wilds to have become a rough-and-ready miner. But in other ways, he was less worried about being thought eternally ready to box, spar, and take it on the chin. Living in comparatively freewheeling California among the Hollywood crowd made things easier. The actor finally came clean about not being "a Harvard man as many think." He also cut back significantly on having reporters visit his dressing room to show how he meticulously transformed from ordinary-guy-on-the-street to most-beautiful-woman-onstage. Indeed, as a film actor living in Los Angeles, Eltinge started to enjoy something approaching a private life. That didn't mean he could be invisible or anonymous off the studio lot. In recent years, in fact, the filmgoing public had become increasingly interested in movie stars' purported private lives. Whereas the media and the public (along with the studios) had been satisfied to see film actors as what historian Richard deCordova terms "picture personalities," a conflation of the performer and their roles, by the late 1910s, people wanted something else: *movie stars*. They wanted to know how these strange creatures of the silver screen dwelt in their natural habitats: How did they live and love? How did they manage their work and spend their money? Who were the people behind the spectral images, and were they ordinary enough to be relatable yet fabulous enough to be interesting? Knowing the "truth" about stars helped consumers enjoy movies even more thoroughly. It also helped those stars and their studios cultivate bigger, more lucrative brand names. Eltinge was stepping into a new role, taking pieces of his past identities while shedding others, for he was now a movie star with all its rights, privileges, and hazards.[14]

* * *

The impersonator chose a perfect stunt to help rebrand himself as a movie star: de-wigging. After a showing of *The Countess Charming* at Clune's Auditorium in Los Angeles in September 1917, he appeared "in his proper person" to chat with the crowd and answer questions, showing the "well-built, rather diffident young man" he supposedly was.[15] But Hollywood, he was finding, had a different, often more lenient, culture. Maybe the sharp cleft between manly-man and womanly-woman need not be hewn as strenuously out here. After initially requesting a screened-off path from his dressing room to his film set, the actor soon allowed himself to walk freely about the lot or location in drag if need be, his skirt swaying right along with his "masculine gait," pipe jutting from his mouth. He conveyed elements of camp without fully realizing it. To insiders and observers, this was a new Julian Eltinge, the Julian Eltinge of Hollywood, a man more comfortable in his and his characters' respective skins. While the public's desire to know more about stars' private lives would soon come with a downside, namely reactionary calls for censorship in the wake of star "scandals" (and implicit distrust of a putatively Jewish-run industry), for now, California felt liberating.[16]

An important facet of being a movie star meant spending money like one. The Hollywood crowd consumed on a whole different level than did ordinary civilians, which was part of what made them special. To practice Calvinist thrift and modesty might have been manly at some point in the past, and surely essential for a proper housewife. But being a star meant the opposite. This came more naturally to Julian Eltinge than did, say, dissimulating

186 BEAUTIFUL

the bruiser. He enjoyed the finer things in fashion and décor. His wardrobe budget with A. H. Woods had been an ample $10,000. Now he enjoyed an "extravagant" and even "a bit scandalous" $30,000 with which to choose the latest styles. Eltinge "could spare the money," so why not spend it on the best? Rather than business suits or dungaree overalls, the actor's clothing-and-accessory choices began causing a "flutter," with many onlookers wondering what he'd wear next. Would it be chunky rings, bejeweled cufflinks, elegant scarf pins, and if so, in what tantalizing combination? The impersonation artist grew so "enamored" of the fancy Los Angeles Country Club while filming scenes for *The Countess Charming* that he asked the director if they could find a way to shoot more footage there. Sometimes, when the workday was done, the newly minted movie star would hang around the Country Club, ostensibly to play tennis or golf but also to explore a locale that somehow spoke to him.[17]

Another key part of playing the movie star was being seen around town *as* one. Eltinge was spotted throwing open his arms and shouting, "Edna!" upon spotting frequent Charlie Chaplin costar Edna Purviance in the lobby of a hotel where the glitterati liked to mix and mingle. (Purviance blushed and shouted, "Julian!" Hugs, air-kisses, etc.) He attended parties hosted by Hollywood A-lister Raymond Hitchcock, where he hobnobbed with D. W. Griffith, Mack Sennett, Mabel Normand, and of course, Chaplin. He told stories about his past, some real, some fabricated, like having been "just plain Bill" until forced to impersonate the fairer sex in a college musical. He told Mary Pickford about a jealous wife whose husband had become enamored with him, prompting the wife to bang on Eltinge's dressing-room door—only to subsequently discover she was a *he*.[18]

Perhaps the most important thing for a movie star was owning a *movie star home*. For many Hollywood celebrities, then as now, your home had to be not just big and expensive but "immense, luxurious, and excessive." As a movie actor, Eltinge's lifestyle was changing. Playing vaudeville or live theatre involved working in the afternoons and evenings, usually on the road somewhere. By contrast, he now had 7:30 A.M. call times in part so that film shoots could take full advantage of Southern California's abundant natural light. "It certainly seemed queer at first," he reflected, "to be getting up at about the time I had been accustomed to going to bed." The net result was that he'd be spending more time at home, resting up and self-pampering.[19]

The actor chose a pink-walled, mission-style compound atop a hill in Los Angeles's Silver Lake neighborhood, then called Edendale, overlooking

Figure 7.2 Like any proper movie star, Julian Eltinge needed a mansion to call home. His Villa Capistrano, in which he played an active role as decorator and interior designer, was an early example of the now-ubiquitous Spanish Colonial style in America. The Villa gave him a place to rest and spend some time with his favorite author, Victor Hugo.
Credit: *Billy Rose Theatre Division, The New York Public Library for the Performing Arts.*

the treelined, now-decommissioned reservoir for which the area was later renamed. The property he bought was known as Villa Capistrano, and though the official address was 2327 Fargo Street, it was set back from the road and surrounded by out-buildings, gardens, topiary, and several spare plots should the owner wish to expand.[20] The Villa Capistrano looked like the kind of place where a Roman noble might have lived in the time of Caesar, surveying the area from on high "like a baron's manor." City records say the 5,000-square-foot main home was built with three bedrooms and two bathrooms—plus a gym, according to newspaper accounts at the time. Eltinge also apparently built a 711-square-foot guest house on the 21,818-square-foot lot, with one bedroom and one bath. The actor paid $75,000 for the 5,000-square-foot Villa, about $1.8 million in current dollars, though he'd invest heavily in its furnishings and landscaping, erecting a guesthouse on the half-acre lot.[21] Louella Parsons, perhaps the most influential West Coast showbiz columnist, dubbed it a "mansion," but a "beautiful" one and not some overblown monstrosity. Eltinge, unlike some of his professional peers, managed to retain his good taste even as his bank account mushroomed. He took special delight in furnishing his home, working closely with interior and landscape designers, transforming Villa Capistrano's rooms into a "wonderland of antiques and rare tapestries" fetched from the corners of the earth: Persian carpets, Sheffield silver and chinaware, a Steinway Duo-Art grand piano, ocelot and bearskin rugs, and more. The entertainer hired eminent landscape architect Charles Gibbs, who designed grounds at the Kellogg estate and also at Cecile B. De Mille's personal "paradiso," to beautify the Villa Capistrano with an "enchanting" array of shrubbery, plantings, and water features dubbed the "Seven Terraces." With the Villa Capistrano, as one journalist put it, Eltinge had embarked upon his "domestic regime." Fort Salonga had been but a modest rehearsal.[22]

Figure 7.3 The Villa Capistrano, considered architecturally important, is captured here on a sightseeing postcard. The majestic structure still stands atop a hill in what is today Silver Lake but was then called Edendale, a semi-secluded, early center of moviemaking and bohemian counterculture in Los Angeles.
Credit: *Author's own collection.*

While Eltinge's Long Island farmhouse harkened back to the simplicity of an earlier time, his California compound mixed colonial grandeur with arrivist real estate fetishism. Elegantly appointed at every turn and furnished with imported antiques, Villa Capistrano was a veritable private museum "of Norma Desmond proportions." In part thanks to the constant incubation of consumerism, Teddy's Roosevelt's version of manhood was morphing into Jay Gatsby's. In 1918, *Photoplay* ran a feature on the "wonder and the glory that is Eltinge's home." Not only women, but many "masculine appreciators" enjoyed pictures of the star's enormous canopy bed, supposedly the heirloom of an Iberian noble family. Wall sconces harkened to Ferdinand and Isabella's reign, complemented by supposedly authentic Spanish candlesticks. Eltinge's bedspread was woven in the "rarest ecclesiastical green and gold," once the possession, it was said, of monks who "helped Columbus on his quest of America." Villa Capistrano's Moorish-style bathroom was praised as the perfect counterpoint to its Castilian bedroom. Painted, Ionic columns and Romanesque arches added an Italianate feel to the "palazzo," though Levantine details, like a crescent moon with a star on pillars framing major windows, abounded. The Villa's soft eclecticism was not a misstep but in fact an example of the "conglomerate style" popular at the time in Hollywood, allowing celebrities to show off varied décor. There was a recessed balcony with deep orange walls "such as may be found in the wealthiest quarters of Algiers," and sunken, Roman gardens. The Villa's "unusual" stucco walls faded, ombre-like, from light-pink salmon on top to soft ivory below. In 1920, the American Institute of Architects cited the actor's palatial new home as one of fifteen "notable examples" of Southern California's best architecture.[23]

In fact, while Spanish Colonial–style buildings, from modest homes to business parks and universities, have exploded across the US South and Southwest, the look was new in Eltinge's day. Elements of Villa Capistrano were considered a pioneering example of an aesthetic that had taken off after causing a buzz at an influential design exposition in San Diego in 1915. Buildings with "old world" (i.e., early-colonialist) features such as "colonnades and graceful, softly-tinted walls" appealed to a nation embarking on its own emergent globalism. Somehow fittingly, the prime exemplar of Spanish Colonial architecture was the Los Angeles headquarters of the 72,000 member-strong Automobile Club of Southern California.[24]

When the Villa Capistrano was being built, the actor lived in a small but comfortable cottage a short trot downslope of the main structure. Here he could supervise and collaborate with the architects, designers, and builders,

190   BEAUTIFUL

appreciating each time the work-in-progress took an artful step toward becoming his new home. It may not be surprising that an individual with special ability to transform his face and body had also a craftsman-like skill at molding and shaping his domestic apparatus. Much as his bodily and facial artistry delighted theatergoers, his Villa would soon impress celebrity A-listers like operatic diva Geraldine Farrar. A paved driveway angling off a steeply graded side street would allow a select few through the Villa's gates and into a circular driveway area surrounded by fountains, gardens, and statuary. Dismounting their Duesenbergs and Stutz Bearcats, houseguests would pass through a main door to find themselves in a circular vestibule, a spiral staircase hugging stony walls under a canopy of colorful frescoes painted by the same artist who had rendered Eltinge's visages on his eponymous theatre in New York City. Visitors could ascend to an upper story and gaze out from an unparalleled aerie over palm treetops and gabled roofs. Passing through a living room hung with oil paintings and capacious enough to be the lobby of a modest inn, they might feel themselves a different kind of royalty, the sort that ruled nations and fiefdoms, when stepping out onto the pillared balcony. By some perspectives, the scantily windowed Villa Capistrano, perched atop a steep hill, was also an "impregnable fortress," in the words of *Architectural Record*, meant as much to protect and wall off its owner's private, domestic life as to cushion it.[25]

Villa Capistrano also had a boxing gym, though it's not clear if it existed for the actor to work out, for PR photo ops, or both. "If he had his way," said an Eltinge spokesperson, "he would develop arms like [heavyweight champ James Jackson 'Jim'] Jeffries and a chest—well, that is unthinkable." Instead of visiting sweat-stained boxing gyms for publicity events, sporting stars could now come to his upscale resort. When Australian boxing and swimming legend Reginald Leslie "Snowy" Baker—then in the process of launching his own Schwarzenegger-like, brawn-to-screen career—visited Villa Capistrano in 1918, he gave Eltinge a well-publicized training session. Eltinge sketched Kaiser Wilhelm II's face on a punching-dummy and shouted, "Come on, Snowy, let's give our peace answer to the Kaiser right here." The two grabbed wooden clubs and rained a flurry of blows upon the effigial "Berlin Beast."[26]

* * *

The boxing gym in the basement wasn't always enough to quell certain suspicions. Living alone in "palatial bachelor's quarters," no matter how impressive, left the actor open to speculation about his perpetually unmarried state. Without a woman present, something was seen as missing from his opulent nest. Ratcheting up the heat even more, the gossip press had grown increasingly interested in movie stars' family and domestic lives in general; the public was being trained to salivate like a Pavlov's dog for juicy details. *Photoplay*'s February 1915 series "Who's Married to Who in the Movies" both reflected and reinforced this hunger. It would "gladden my heart to hear that the mansion has a mistress," wrote a *New York Star* reporter who visited Villa Capistrano. Upon visiting the Villa, Louella Parsons described the actor as "heart whole and fancy free" but wondered when its owner would ever secure a "hostess" for it. Predictable questions asked of Hollywood's newest "most eligible bachelor" elicited equally predictable replies: he was too busy making movies, too busy traveling, and somehow all of sudden too thrifty. "Oh, but you see I know what women's clothes cost," he quipped. (Correspondingly, when successful actresses were asked about being single, they often defended themselves by insisting that no husband could provide them with what they desired. "I have never yet been able to find the man who could give me to spend what I earn myself," said Eva Tanguay when it was rumored she was affianced to vaudeville executive Eddie Darling. A husband who couldn't provide at least some luxuries for his wife was conceptually unnecessary, practically an abstraction.)[27]

To satisfy the marriage-mongers, especially those who pointed out that he wasn't "even engaged," Eltinge employed a clever diversionary tactic: he spoke of becoming a father. In the wake of the November 1918 armistice, Julian Eltinge announced plans to adopt a Belgian war orphan. Belgium, of course, had been widely praised for standing up to the Kaiser, proving fierce, if ultimately unsuccessful, resistors rather than mere "chocolate soldiers," as some had predicted. Tragically, many Belgian civilians were caught in the crossfire, losing homes, loved ones, and their lives. Adopting a little girl from the ruins of Belgium would help normalize Julian Eltinge's image while reinforcing the notion of America as the world's protector. An orphan known as "E. Galler" wrote Eltinge from her temporary home in Brighton, England, saying how much she loved his movies. The actor, now an international star, said he'd "long desired to spend some of his money on a Belgian child." He'd be "honor[ed] to look after your future in any way I possibly can, if it is proper and consistent for me to do so," he told the child Galler. But it soon became clear that the actor was talking more about sponsoring the girl, maybe paying for her schooling, than actually adopting her as a real parent. The

192 BEAUTIFUL

impersonator had long spoken of his love of animals, particularly dogs and horses. But he virtually never mentioned an affection for children. It's hard to imagine he wanted all that juvenile enthusiasm around the fragile vases and carefully curated china at his Villa Capistrano. The actor said he could be a parental figure to the girl "even if she is 3,000 miles away," which seems to be about as close as he cared to get. The impersonation artist finally resolved to become her "godfather" and pay for her to study in the United States "if the exigencies of her education required it." There is no mention of little E. Galler or any other child, war orphan or otherwise, in a will Julian Eltinge drew up in 1938.[28] Now that he was nearing forty, he was learning how to feint at a conventional domestic life every so often. A few years after he decided to not-really-adopt the little Belgian girl, he circulated snapshots of himself arm-in-arm with his purported "wife" aboard the SS *Siberia* in the port of Yokohama, Japan. Identified only as "Mrs. Julian Eltinge," the pleasant-faced woman, seemingly in her twenties or thirties, was never mentioned again by her "hubby" or the press.[29]

Eltinge's de facto domestic partner, of course, was his mother, Julia. She was the quiet, lifelong presence in his life, ahead even of A. H. Woods, Ko Shima, and his new Hollywood pals. Just as the Fort Salonga farm had been partly meant as a respite for her, so too was the Silver Lake mansion. In 1918, *Photoplay* not inaccurately called the Villa Capistrano "a sort of jewel box for his mother."[30]

* * *

Still, he was quietly forming other bonds. By the late 1910s, Julian Eltinge was cultivating what would turn out to be a lifelong friendship, or perhaps more, with a man named Fred FitzGerald (aka Fitz Gerald and/or Fitzgerald). Eltinge met FitzGerald in 1918 when the latter was stationed at the San Pedro US Naval Base in Long Beach, between Los Angeles and San Diego. During the summer of 1918, the base put on a minstrel show and invited Eltinge to participate, suggesting the actor already had ties there. By the early 1920s, Eltinge and FitzGerald were described as "old-time" friends, either to underscore their closeness, to deter the public from imagining them as more than friends, or maybe both. Though today San Diego is home to a major air and naval installation, during World War I, Long Beach, 110 miles to the north, had deeper harbors and was better suited for stationing submarines and other vessels. The Army Corps of Engineers had dredged San Pedro and constructed a 2.11-mile breakwater in 1898. By 1913, thousands of soldiers and sailors were posted there along with an armada of submarines and warships.[31] Fred FitzGerald was no ordinary seaman. He was the oldest son of noted Commodore J. J. FitzGerald and would go on to enjoy a long naval career. FitzGerald *fils* had circumnavigated the globe four times and visited distant lands and peoples at a time when many Americans passed their entire lives in the county of their birth. Fred FitzGerald would also work in the egg and poultry business in Northern California, helping run a cooperative that managed to greatly extend eggs' shelf lives using an innovative sterilization process. But his heart was in the navy, not agribusiness. He eventually took an inspector's post at the Mare Island Navy Yard forty miles north of San Francisco, having by that time married and started a family. When Julian Eltinge visited the area, which he did on several occasions, he stayed with the FitzGeralds.[32]

World War I changed American manhood in many ways, some better-known than others. Teddy Roosevelt famously believed that males in the United States needed war to toughen them up, to rouse them from "swollen, slothful and ignoble peace." Peace, slothful or otherwise, would come to an abrupt halt in 1917–1918 as millions of men were mobilized to fight in Europe. Never before had so many men, most of them young, been confined, connected, and organized in such large numbers. Barriers and behaviors that might have taken generations to shift changed with remarkable speed.[33] Men from rural America found themselves billeted in training camps and troop depots in or just outside major cities. In urban areas, individuals and groups could enjoy an anonymity not possible back home, permitting men to envision and explore same-sex erotic relations and otherwise "forbidden" endeavors. But the powerful and their allies worried that gathering millions of men together to make the world safe for democracy could also expose them to "evil influences." Entities like the Bureau of Social Hygiene, whose official mission was to keep the troops away from prostitutes and liquor, trained their anxious gaze on other things some doughboys were doing, like "waking arm in arm" near the Brooklyn Navy Yard and associated acts of "perversion." Still, enough soldiers and recruits were willing to take their chances that a new kind of community began to form, one reinforced from within by patterns of desire and from without by an emerging surveillance apparatus. This community formed one of the roots of a *gay subculture*, in which personal identity was linked to sexuality and masculinity. Whereas previously, men had freedom within certain spaces, usually away from the

194 BEAUTIFUL

glare of hierarchical probity, to enjoy loosened sexual and gender boundaries, they now implicitly rebelled against former limitations and in so doing found common cause—and encountered common demonization. The more they sought places and spaces to engage with one another in erotically and emotionally satisfying ways, the more it was assumed that there must be something inherently *different*—which is to say, *pathological*—about them. Aided by the new sexology discourse, observers and critics grew increasingly preoccupied with *who* these men were rather than simply *what* they were doing, a shift in focus "from the act to the person." A new lexicon facilitated this change in perspective. Whereas previously one might have acted like a "sissy" or partaken in "unmanly" and "unnatural" behaviors, it was now possible to be branded a "degenerate," a "pervert," an "invert," a "fairy," and, quite soon enough, a "homosexual."[34] Correspondingly, showing interest in allegedly unmasculine things could render you "queer," a "fag," or altogether "girlish" in others' eyes. Though it would be several decades before such views calcified into broader social truths, it would be increasingly hard to explain away one's behaviors, from drag to same-sex relations, as purely situational or opportunistic. While the Great War and the postwar era expanded the space for acts of alleged inversion, there was also a growing concern that what happened in or near the Brooklyn Navy Yard (or Boston Armory) might not stay there, and could thus end up on a medical file or police report.[35]

Much as the rise of fraternalism on college campuses had led to a renaissance for transvestic musicals, the organizing of men for war proved a boon for skirt shows. Canadian field-ambulance privates Ross Hamilton and Alan Murray became, respectively, Marjorie and Marie aka "The Dumbells" in 1917, shortly before the Battle of Vimy Ridge. Hamilton was said to "out-Eltinge Eltinge," in their revue *Biff, Biff, Bang*, a hit with the troops. Professional theatre critics, in fact, considered Privates Hamilton and Murray nearly as talented as Julian Eltinge and Bert Savoy.[36]

Brave and able though they were, the Canadians could not hold a candle to the American Expeditionary Forces when it came to crossdressing. In 1918, with war still ravaging Europe, hospital personnel at Mare Island, the very military base where Eltinge's friend Fred FitzGerald would later return to naval duty, produced a "benefit" drag show titled *The Rose of Queretaro*. With numerous crossdressed players, including A. C. Inness as "Miss Muffett" and J. L. Palmer "a la Julian Eltinge," plus a coterie of "chorus girls" in "camouflage," the production was such a hit that it later appeared at a professional playhouse in San Francisco. The navy, beefed up since the 1890s partly in the name of "race patriotism," was surging ahead in the transvestic arts.[37]

The army too was doing its fair share. Shortly after the end of hostilities, in December 1918, Carl Schroeder, a trucker from St. Louis, starred as "a remarkably pretty girl" alongside other beskirted AEF troops in *A Buck on Leave*, the "biggest and best show which the boys of the army have put on," according to a war correspondent, H. H. Niemeyer, who saw it. The "wonderful musical comedy splendidly played and splendidly staged" was such a hit at Tours, where it was created, that *Buck* was dispatched to conquer audiences at bases and garrisons elsewhere in war-torn France. Schroeder was one of eight leading "girls," backed up by a hundred other thespian-soldiers, plus "one real girl" named Orlo Lea Mayes who had to content herself with a small role since the bigger ones went to her doughboy "sisters." *A Buck on Leave* was not only entertaining but apparently salutary. During its run, soldiers at Tours needing medical attention dropped from several hundred a day to just over a dozen. Some fifteen thousand army personnel saw *A Buck on Leave* there, with many turned away at each performance. Though humorous to think about the show's success, it is also imperative to remember how powerful satire, comedy, and inversion can be to a populace subjected to constant trauma and lunatic orders to advance into machine-gunfire. Like the medieval Feast of Fools, in which peasants played royals and the unrelenting rigidity of everyday life went "topsy-turvy" for a few days, shows like *A Buck on Leave* could not but turn a funhouse mirror on the arbitrary nature of rank and the madness of an undertaking that seemed only to accomplish the murder of millions in the name of "peace." Before one performance of *A Buck on Leave*, an MP told a private seated in the first row that the front section was reserved for officers, to which the private replied, "I never heard them telling us that in the battle lines." During the play, the title character, a lowly buck private, kissed "the leading 'woman,'" causing the latter to sigh, "Just like an officer."[38]

A Buck on Leave's cast members became celebrities back home as well. Papers in Decatur, Illinois, boasted of hometown son and *Buck* costar Private Peter J. Doran, a "leading lady of the A. E. F. in France," while a St. Louis paper wrote virtually the same thing about soldier-thespian Carl Schroeder.[39] Like Julian Eltinge, the military men who crossdressed were portrayed as just-regular-guys, men's men, when not in drag. Newspapers reiterated that Schroeder was a dedicated, career truck driver, while Doran was "No Lady Off Stage." Even a few soldiers who crossdressed on active duty, a bit like

196   BEAUTIFUL

Corporal Max Klinger in the long-running TV sitcom adaption of Robert Altman's film, *M*A*S*H*, were both permitted to drag while also framed as ordinary fellows doing ordinary-fellow things. A Private Rodgers of the 354th Infantry division, for example, liked to wear women's clothing around his post sometimes, arousing little ire though "she" slept, unladlylike, with mouth open to accommodate a wad of chewing tobacco. The war's popularization of transvestic acting led even more youthful newcomers to enter the field and implicitly or explicitly vie for Julian Eltinge's crown. An urge to drag-up that may have long "lain dormant" sprang to life among "the students, the lawyers, the clerks, the merchants and the men of all the occupations which make up the great United States army," reported the *Buffalo Courier* in 1919. In the summer of that year, as the Paris peace talks were afoot, the Elysée theatre on Avenue Montaigne, in concert with the YMCA, was set aside strictly for "soldier productions," many developed by combat units formerly in the trenches, with nary "a female member in the cast."[40] Like college theatricals touted for improving school spirit and varsity pride, military shows were viewed as reinforcing the very qualities that made the army great. The 40th Infantry regiment's "breezy" musical *Days at Camp Custer*, produced at its Battle Creek, Michigan, base, featured soldiers "so faithfully interpet[ing]" their roles as draftees that it was hard to tell the "cringing pacifist and the mamma's boy" some of them portrayed from the "stalwart soldiers" they really were. It is worth recalling that, despite a cultural sea change during the interwar years, in 1942, Irving Berlin's fundraising, propagandizing musical *This Is the Army Now* was produced on Broadway with a cast of military personnel; two years later, a film version featuring future US President Ronald Reagan and future US Senator George Murphy in drag roles won an Oscar.[41]

When World War I ended, a mood of peace and victory allowed wider berth for men to come home changed by their experiences. Many leading ladies of the AEF continued their drag to acclaim stateside, including the 88th Division's troupe, the Runaways, which had packed houses at Toul, France, in 1918 before traveling the war-ravaged country, performing in barns amid the shell craters. The Runaways were so good that Brigadier General Merch Stuart arranged for them to become their own unit, the 175th Brigade, and take their play, *The Million Dollar Girl*, starring bugler Charles Le Valle as "Mother" and Private Lee Norris as her daughter, "Rose," to Washington, DC, for command performances.[42] When Major-General Charles G. Morton returned from the front lines in Europe in 1917, one of his main complaints was a "lack of entertainment" for troops. Morton appointed Captain Murray

A. Cobb "division entertainment officer," who in turn organized the "Twenty-ninth Division Vaudeville Troupe," which in turn developed perhaps the AEF's finest musical, *Snap It Up*. The show starred enlisted men B. C. Mortie as "Queenie Kiss, an American Soubrette," Earl V. Grimes as "Sadie, the Cashier," and Louis Samuels as "a lovely show girl." General John J. Pershing himself called *Snap It Up* "the best show in the American Expeditionary Forces in France," all the more remarkable considering most of the stars had to make or buy their own dresses and wigs.[43]

* * *

With the female-impersonation industry booming, Julian Eltinge's third movie, a comedy called *The Widow's Might*, rolled off the Paramount/Lasky production line in 1918. Widow characters continued to delight audiences. "Beware of widows," Eltinge warned, because they played by their own, sneaky rules. In *The Widow's Might*, Eltinge played Richard "Dick" Pfeiffer Tavish, a slick New Yorker who buys a Texas ranch where he has little to occupy himself since there are "a bunch of Mexicans to do the work," according to a cinema fan magazine of the day. Tavish fixates on a calendar model with "ultramarine eyes" and determines he must have her. He also decides to confront the villainous Horace Hammer, who has defrauded Dick and his neighbors in a real estate scam. It so happens that Hammer is vacationing at the same "fashionable resort" where that calendar model, Irene, and her aunt, Mrs. Pomeroy Pomfret, are on holiday. Dick is—wait for it—"obliged to disguise himself as a woman," in this case one Princess Martini, whereupon he goes about setting things right. An ensuing "series of amusing situations and side-splitting comic mix-ups" including the somehow hilarious "abandoning of a baby" bring Hammer to justice and Dick to Irene.[44]

Written specifically for Julian Eltinge by actress-turned-screenwriter Marion Fairfax and directed by William C. de Mille, Cecil B.'s brother, the five-reeler was shot mostly in and around Los Angeles and Pasadena. Like other filmmakers of the day, De Mille and cameraman Charles Rosher attempted to expand movies' artistic toolbox as the cinema stumbled out of childhood. In one sequence, they made a woman appear the size of a human palm, while in others, they experimented with nuanced lighting and cutaway-closeups of the star. Photographically and in other ways, *The Widow's Might* was reckoned a "definitive advancement."[45]

198   BEAUTIFUL

And yet, as the plot suggests, it was not much of an advancement for its star, leaving him ambivalent about what Hollywood held in store, much as he had felt after cranking out three clockwork musicals under A. H. Woods. He enjoyed the lifestyle, it was true. In Southern California, he could work without having to crisscross the country or the globe, toting trunks full of costumes, dragging-up and then down again a dozen times a week. From a sheer economic standpoint, movie work made more sense. There was also the fact that his natural "parlor voice," as Eltinge had discovered during his musical comedy tours, became strained when delivering page after page of dialogue, especially in an era when competing with fellow actors who employed a booming, declarative vocal style. Being in silent movies meant he hardly had to speak at all. Plus, his mother, comfortably ensconced in the Villa Capistrano, felt pictures were a better fit for her son. "Julian," said Julia Dalton, "go into the movies, where you can reach more people," no doubt also preferring to have her actor-son nearby rather than constantly on tour. Julia Dalton had given up much of her youth treading from mining camp to mining camp with nothing to show for it but a frustrated, alcoholic husband who beat their child. Now she had her literal place in the sun. In March 1918, Eltinge told a crowd in St. Louis, "This is my last week on the stage." Film work paid him an estimated $150,000 a year, about $3 million in today's value. Some also felt the aging actor had "freer play" in front of the camera than under the glare of spotlights and footlights. The December 1917 issue of *Photoplay* reported that Eltinge "could do you an ingenue that you would find yourself making eyes at" a few years earlier; now, however, the actor's weight and complexion made that increasingly difficult in-person. No impersonator, no matter how skilled, could play the fresh-faced ingenue while simultaneously waging "a masterly fight against the flesh" and sporting that supposedly most unladylike of features: a fledgling double chin.[46]

For now, Hollywood and the movies still seemed a good compromise. It was sunnier out there, generally more relaxed, and the impersonation artist was cultivating connections to friends and colleagues in the industry. Whatever they might have wondered about him, the public presently regarded Eltinge a "full blooded young nephew of Uncle Sam," like George M. Cohan, in part because he never so much as dabbled in socialism, a crucial line for a man, particularly one who wore skirts, never to cross in this period and after. Southern California, especially the corridor from Los Angeles south to San Diego, also seemed to be quietly offering space for men with less interest in conventional gender confines. Some liked to dress up as women.

IMPERSONATING IN THE USA   199

Many were gay or at least curious to explore wishes they'd elsewhere have to suppress. A "society of queers" held "drags" at quasi-private "96 clubs" in and around Los Angeles. A little further south, Long Beach, home to the San Pedro naval facility where Julian Eltinge met sailor Fred FitzGerald, was also home to an active gay, crossdressing community. In fact, when police led a crackdown they discovered "one of the finest wardrobes among the 'queer' people" they had ever seen. The police, it would seem, were impressed in spite of themselves. Transvestic arts flourished more openly elsewhere in Long Beach, including at the eminent Laughlin Theater, which featured top female impersonator Bobbie Lehman (promoted in local papers as "OH BOY! SOME VAMP!") in the early 1920s, and at a local Knights of Columbus chapter that invited celebrated female impersonator Lazelle the Vamp for a private show.[47]

* * *

And yet, something still tugged Julian Eltinge back to the stage. Yes, it was hard, and paid less if measured in sheer man-hours. No, he could not play the young beauties he had earlier in his career. But probably correctly divining that audiences would tire of more boilerplate, silent comedies with him in drag, the actor began talking about going back to vaudeville, despite his recent protestations about being done with the stage. Eltinge would engage in this very public flipflopping a lot in the next few years, more the echo of thinking-out-loud rather than of a well-orchestrated plan. This was a period when movies were experimenting with hybridized vaudeville, and vice-versa. The resulting "movie palace vaudeville" served Eltinge well, reportedly to the tune of up to $3,500 a week. He played New York's famous Palace in 1918, his twenty-minute turn containing many of his classic impersonations of yore. The patrons cheered at some and clapped politely at others. After a few more appearances, Eltinge announced he'd signed a deal with agent/producer William Morris to take a "vode" troupe of his own on tour. Managed by J. D. Barton, the performer debuted at Clune's theatre in Los Angeles in early 1919, before heading off to Omaha, Tacoma, and beyond. He served up some new tunes, plus several old favorites from *The Fascinating Widow* including "Mammy Jinny's Hall of Fame," "In the Land of Wedding Bells," and "Don't Go in the Water."[48]

Keith-Albee crowds liked the performer's timely songs, tuneful ballads, and "frequent changes of costume." Ko Shima, his longtime confidant and

Figure 7.4 Julian Eltinge swore off the stage when his movie career blossomed. But he soon changed his mind, perhaps sensing that his silent comedies, like his musical plays, would become repetitive and take him no closer to his long-sought objective of playing prestigious, non-drag roles. Fortunately, in the late 1910s and early 1920s, vaudeville still wanted him.
Credit: *Copyright reserved, Northport Historical Society (Long Island, NY).*

collaborator, had since gone his own way. Eltinge said he and his dresser/valet had split amicably so Shima could start his own business and get married—or that was the official story, anyway. With powerful California newspaper publisher C. V. McClatchy waging a war on "men who would have defiled Sodom and Gomorrah," it was best to avoid certain appearances.

Agnes Parker took Shima's place, overseeing Eltinge's gowning and wigging, her husband managing various logistical details. Though he hadn't really intended it, the impersonator's chronic mention of quitting—film for the stage, then the stage for film, then back again—earned him meaty publicity, as it has for other celebrities over the years. Any tour could be one's "last" and any subsequent reemergence billed as a triumphant "comeback." As early as the mid-nineteenth century, megastar actress Charlotte Cushman launched so many "farewell" tours from the 1850s to the 1870s, that fans welcomed her sundry "returns and retirements" as just another part of her show.[49]

Returning to the stage was also a way for Julian Eltinge to remind the world, as best he could, that he still longed to play un-dragged or at least more serious roles. If the cinema was even more reluctant than the stage to take artistic chances, Eltinge declared he had no problem with going legitimate. In 1917, just before heading to California, the artist had said that in movies, he'd appear solely as a "handsome juvenile man," wishful thinking that obviously hadn't panned out. In fact, if anything, Eltinge's age and bodily changes, combined with the slapstick aesthetic of silent comedies, forced him increasingly toward the "dame" and "burlesque" types he (and many early homophobes and drag-ophobes) loathed.[50]

But after three years and a handful of successful films, he was no closer to letting go the wig. While an amiable father figure like A. H. Woods might have at least listened sympathetically to the actor's wishes and longings, studio bosses like Adolph Zukor and Jesse Lasky couldn't be bothered. Even more so than vaudeville, the movies were a highly systematized, unforgiving industry, profit-driven to the core despite protestations of "art for art's sake," as the logo of Metro-Goldwyn-Mayer famously declares in Latin. To his Hollywood employers, Julian Eltinge was a specialty artist and mannequin, maybe even more so than when he'd starred in *Cousin Lucy* and other stage musicals. His movie characters were still just guys who got into funny hijinks requiring skirts, preferably of the fashionable variety. "More than one great Fifth Avenue modiste has sat down in the New York theaters copying the wonderful Parisian gowns worn by Julian Eltinge," read advertising copy for the film *The Widow's Might*. Whatever else they offered, the sunny frontiers of California had not permitted the impersonation artist to "make the jump" from gowns to trousers or from comic fluff to real drama. "His directors and managers [won't] stand for it," wrote one L.A. journalist.[51] Where else, then, might Julian Eltinge turn?

# # #

8

The Twenties

By the early 1920s, it would be increasingly difficult for an artist, even a singular one like Julian Eltinge, to keep a foot in both film and vaudeville, as he was trying to do. Unsure how or if to move forward, he found himself straddling a widening gulf. Although Hollywood titans like Adolph Zukor had once sought to link movies with the stage to earn prestige, the reverse began to happen as film matured into its own, distinct art form. Film acting had once meant something closer to "posing" or "modeling," an approach that suited Eltinge. But with the refinement of cinematography and more nuanced scenario-writing, new, cinema-specific skills were needed. Accordingly, film actors were becoming their own breed, aesthetically speaking. Eltinge was a deer in the headlights amid these changes, leading him quite sincerely to tell his public he was "loyal to the movies" in 1918 then, a year later, just as earnestly declare that he *wasn't* in fact "for the screen," before promptly heading overseas for a tour.[1] Most people in the entertainment field were quickly figuring out that today's stardom counted for little tomorrow. A simple twist of fate and the current faux "farewell tour" might actually *be* your farewell. "How fleeting a thing is fame," commented a journalist in 1919 who had just seen the impersonation artist's show in Oklahoma.[2]

Julian Eltinge still occupied a lofty spot in the entertainment world, although neither he nor those around him could appreciate just how precarious was his perch. He tied for sixth place in a "picture favorites" poll alongside Fatty Arbuckle and John Barrymore. (Much as in vaudeville, female stars like Gloria Swanson, Lillian Gish, and Norma Talmadge tended to be more popular than their male counterparts and many of their names are better known to us today, whereas male players like Thomas Meighan and Charles Ray, who also made the list, are all but forgotten.)[3] Eltinge's fans mailed him three hundred letters a week, to which his secretary replied, if at all possible, with a signed photograph. Most of the notes came from movie buffs rather those who knew him from vaudeville and musical comedy. The artist took this to mean that his film career was solid for now or tried to it interpret that way. But when he asked for $3,500, the studio gave him a hard

Beautiful. Andrew L. Erdman, Oxford University Press. © Oxford University Press 2024.
DOI: 10.1093/9780197696361.003.0009

no. In 1918, Eltinge and his team took out a large ad in *Theatre* magazine announcing "the successful consummation of his contract with the Lasky-Paramount Corporation," adding that he would "shortly announce" his next project.[4]

Julian Eltinge was discovering yet again just how fast things could change in Hollywood. Mounting, retooling, and reshaping live productions could take months and years, as critics, audiences, and artists gave them a measure of time to mature. Even the dreadful *Mr. Wix of Wickham* went through a number of convolutions and months on the road before its backers finally pulled the plug. When a show was a hit, as Eltinge's three A. H. Woods productions had been, they could roll on for a year or more with just a few tweaks. But bad reviews or poor audience reception of a movie debuting in many different locations all at once could have an equally rapid response. Frankly, the impersonator was lucky to have made it as far as he had in movies. Eva Tanguay, arguably vaudeville's most famous celebrity and certainly among its highest earners, had launched her own film career in 1917 with *The Wild Girl*, directed by Howard Estabrook and produced by Selznick Pictures. In it, Eva played Firefly, a "gypsy" youth raised as a boy. When her tribal chief discovers her "true sex," he forces her to marry but she flees, eventually coupling up with a newspaperman named Donald MacDonald. Despite high production values, the best technical and artistic talent, and intriguing, on-location settings, *The Wild Girl* flopped massively.[5] "Miss Tanguay's name alone is sufficient to carry any production to success," predicted the *Moving Picture World* before *The Wild Girl*'s release, only to recant a few weeks later with the dawning truism that what worked in vaudeville didn't necessarily translate into film. The "Eva of 'I don't care' fame is lost among the hundred other Evas who play the central character of 'The Wild Girl,'" eulogized *Moving Picture World*, correctly sensing that "Eva Tanguay of the music halls has disappeared." Like many a hopeful vaudevillian and stage thespian, Tanguay leapt across a chasm of cinematic hope but never landed on the other side.[6]

Despite some advanced lighting and photographic innovations, Julian Eltinge's movies were increasingly about the same thing: a slightly chubby man in his late thirties humorously impersonating a woman. The lightning-fast costume changes and living, breathing energy of his stage work were no more. In an art form able to simulate voyages to the moon and vampires stalking humankind, the artist's appeal seemed tepid. As for the storylines, they were made of the same formulaic stuff as his stage musicals: a

204   BEAUTIFUL

conventional if slightly impetuous young man is forced by circumstances to "play women." As we have seen, Hollywood audiences were coming to expect better, more involved storylines, even if they were interrupted by car chases, slapstick stunts, and other merry anarchy. Eltinge's stage performances had "vitality" by their very nature.[7] Onscreen, he was somehow less than the sum of his pieces, another actor waiting for the director to shout "action" for the hundredth time then waiting to hear "cut."

* * *

Ironically, then, vaudeville, despite being less popular than it had been a decade earlier, was emerging as the best format for Julian Eltinge to stay current and fresh. There was no avoiding the fact that he was aiming to be a big fish in an evaporating pond. Signing with Keith's "Supreme Vaudeville" program, he received what may have been the largest salary ever paid a "single" male act. The two-a-day was happy to have him again. Eltinge broke box office records at the Brooklyn Orpheum and, two weeks later, did the same at B. F. Keith's Bushwick Theatre. The entertainer wore bespoke creations by world famous designers Callot, Paquin, and Worth. Impersonating women *in person* still carried a charge lost on the silent, black-and-white screen. When the entertainer appeared at the Strand in Los Angeles, a man in the back said to his date, "There's a woman I could fall for," only quickly to reassure her, "if he only was a woman."[8] He also remained above suspicion, a hallmark of his brand. Conservative critic Leone Cass Baer praised Eltinge as above other impersonators, lesser players with names like—in Baer's homophobic if fertile imagination—"Query" or "Merry the Marvel," artists who provoked in her "a horror akin to that which a fellow convict must feel for the gallows." This horror feeling did not apply to Julian Eltinge, one of "the little band of correct imitators," in Baer's estimation. Eltinge was busy making himself "neater" and "trimmer" with his ongoing "reducing" regimens, and fans seemed to like it.[9] Accompanied by the Famous Footlight Favorites troupe, the impersonator sang "Siren Vampire," "He Was So Good to Me," and other tunes, interspersed with featured, standalone entertainers such as Eddy Duo—"Whirlwind Wizards—Dancing on a Silver Thread"—and the Radium Ballet.[10]

The artist called his new production the *Revue of Nineteen-Nineteen*, a kind of scaled-down *Ziegfeld Follies*. *Nineteen-Nineteen*'s centerpiece was "His Night at the Club," a sketch with sets by famed European designer

Erté and script by June Mathis, who would go on to become an influential screenwriter/producer, rare for a woman at the time. Fred Niblo, a "class" standup comic known for highbrow wit, directed. Despite the trappings of sophistication, "His Night at the Club" naturally featured the actor in his "usual dual role." (There was even a Japanese butler character played by S. Nakada.) Eltinge was adapting his core talents to the increasingly popular revue or cabaret-style format, something many talented live entertainers would have to do in the coming decades as big-time vaudeville faded. He even wore gowns by Ziegfeld costumer Cora McGeachy, though many of his impersonations such as the "seductive vamp" and "shapely beach maiden" were reboots of his older work or looked to the past, including a nostalgic song titled "Don't Trust Those Big Gray Eyes."[11]

With sufficient fan mail arriving from "the Orient," the impersonator and his team decided to take the *Revue of Nineteen-Nineteen* across the Pacific. He finished off what was now rechristened his "Farewell Tour Prior to Trip 'Round World" and set off for the high seas. Like many an entertainer before and since, he was probing the world for favorable, new markets. He had some interesting offers at home, including a possible role in new musical by Edgar Allen Woolf, future co-screenwriter of *The Wizard of Oz*.[12] But overseas markets had served him well earlier in his career, and now he wondered if they would again, though now he was pivoting toward Asia. Meanwhile, competitors and rivals continued to flood the American entertainment scene, including Herbert Clifton, whose ten-thousand-dollar wardrobe, "beautiful arms and shoulders," voice like opera star Amelita Galli-Curci, and Chaplinesque comedy led him to boast that he was "Better than Julian Eltinge" while promoting his extravaganza *Fads and Follies of Women*.[13]

By early 1920, the Eltinge flotilla was bound for points east. After a stint in Japan, the troupe played two weeks in Shanghai and entertained American troops garrisoned in Tianjin and Beijing. On March 2, though, Clara Littlejohn of the "Littlejohns," an act in the *Revue*, died unexpectedly in China of a postpartum infection. The cast eventually sailed to Manila for a few final appearances before heading to Australia and then back to America. As if the abortive overseas venture hadn't been cursed enough, another disturbing, peculiar event took place onboard their ship midocean. During the voyage, Katherine Balcom, Australian bride of the ship's radio operator, an American named Syndor Balcom, grew enamored of the ship's female-impersonating celebrity passenger. Mrs. Balcom invited herself to Julian Eltinge's "drinking parties" aboard the elegant, old liner SS *Sonoma* as it

206 BEAUTIFUL

plied the waters to her new home in California. The quasi-cuckolded radi-oman forbade his wife from associating with the impersonator, whereupon she tried to throw herself overboard. A judge later granted Syndor Balcom a divorce on the grounds of (his bride's) "extreme cruelty." Perhaps Julian Eltinge represented a freedom for which she longed but had been denied. The *Revue of Nineteen-Nineteen*'s international tour had been an abortive failure. Further plans for India, Africa, and Paris had to be shelved.[14]

* * *

Back in the United States, Julian Eltinge was confronted with another un-fortunate wrinkle, a further reminder of the movie industry's fickleness. In 1918, before going back into vaudeville, Eltinge had shot a picture called *Over the Rhine*. Anti-German sentiment ran high in the United States at the time, and the actor like many other entertainers sought to capitalize on it. As the war in Europe still raged in the fall of 1918, Eltinge told the press that he and his production team had telegraphed Kaiser Wilhelm II in Berlin to tell the German leader, "We hereby offer you 10,000 marks to play part of Kaiser in our propaganda picture, *Over the Rhine*. Answer at once. We will cable scenario so that scenes can be made in Berlin. We would offer you royalties on the picture, but after the war is over there will be no such thing as royalty, so it would not be of much use." Since the United States had pivoted from neutrality to interventionism, the impersonator had been tilting even fur-ther toward the patriotic. From praising Parisian and Continental style as the paragon of fashion, he began boosting American couture and style. A popu-lation he had recently considered dowdy and awkward was now, in his view, "more athletic and at the same time more graceful" than its European coun-terpart, able to "walk better than any women in the world if they follow their natural inclinations." American women possessed a "natural" quality that needed to be developed and brought out rather than covered in layers of stul-tifying finery. The Eltinge brand name was coming to signify an emergent American exceptionalism, somehow natural, spontaneous, and sui generis. In April 1918, the New Jersey Union League sponsored a "Patriotic Rally" featuring his picture *The Widow's Might*.[15]

Over the Rhine had been made in cooperation with the US military, part "propaganda story," part action flick. Eltinge flew for the first time in his life when a sergeant from the US Aviation Corps took him aloft to shoot some footage and generate publicity.[16] The military lent Eltinge's production team

102 aircraft for dogfighting sequences to be shot at sunrise. The actor called the resulting footage a "prophecy" of the United States' "ultimate conquest" of Germany and her co-conspirators thanks to brave American "birdmen" and their "monster" flying machines. The war gave many filmmakers new opportunities for high-tech action and thrilling visual effects often focused on aviation. Thomas Ince's *The Zeppelin's Last Raid*, for example, promised filmgoers the "newest and greatest spectacle" in aerial warfare simulation. Eltinge played both an aviator and the Statue of Liberty in another propaganda short, *The Call of Liberty*, meant to promote war bonds. The picture boasted the "distinct novelty" of men playing all roles, including women. Archetypal images of attractive, white women were becoming common in public messaging, including ads for naval enlistment and on the face of war-financing savings stamps. Female figures could convey moral messaging because women were thought more capable of sincere emotion than men, even though they were invariably blamed for hampering men's "natural" instincts. White, female spokes-symbols instructed young men to do their part for God and Country, suggesting other rewards might also be in the offing. Julian Eltinge's expertise at creating similarly white archetypes allowed him easily to collaborate with the Red Cross, appearing at its gala luncheons, and the Salvation Army, partaking in doughnut-eating fundraisers.[17]

Over the Rhine, directed by Fred J. Balshofer and written by Charles Taylor and Tom J. Geraghty, featured Julian Eltinge as an American college student living in Heidelberg, Germany, at the outbreak of the war. Naturally, he morphs into a "beautiful woman" to secure military secrets from the enemy. The picture was really just a timely, war-themed iteration of the impersonator's boilerplate product. Unfortunately, when it looked as if the war itself was going to end sooner than many had expected, Balshofer hedged his bets by shooting two different endings, one more conciliatory toward the Germans, another, less so. When the armistice finally came in November 1918, however, a new reality emerged: people seemed to want nothing to remind them of the bloody horror show that had been ravaging Europe for the past four years. War movies were suddenly out of fashion. Republic Pictures, the studio overseeing the production, put *Over the Rhine* on hold, maybe for good. Balshofer had spent endless hours making and retooling the film, and had invested $80,000 of his own money on the project, which he now stood to lose outright. Balshofer and Eltinge bided their time. Perhaps the winds would shift and people would again be open to war movies. There was reason to hope. In 1919, Mack Sennett released *Yankee Doodle in Berlin* starring

Figure 8.1 World War I provided the impersonator with opportunities to partner with the military in patriotic and propaganda films. He understood how images of white, female beauty were being used to promote nationalistic and moralistic entities like the Red Cross and the US Navy. Eltinge's nurse offers selfless devotion combined with a delicate sensuality.
Credit: *Laurence Senelick Collection*.

hugely talented impersonation rival Bothwell Browne as American aviator Bob White who transforms into a "femme fatale" and coaxes war secrets from the Kaiser himself.[18]

In the spring of 1920, Republic studios decided on a compromise. It would take *Over the Rhine* off the shelf and demilitarize it. Retitled *An Adventuress*, the movie now focused on comical characters in an European-ish country that overtly had nothing to do with the Kaiser or Germany. Eltinge now played Jack Perry, an "adventurer" who, along with a few fellow adventurers, becomes embroiled in a conflict between the government of the island nation of Alpania and evil, coup-seeking "monarchists." Perry becomes "Mam'selle Fedora" and infiltrates the royalists' ranks, while his comrade, Lyn Brook (played by Fred Covert), skirts-up as Thelma for a diversionary maneuver. The resulting, feature-length movie (five reels) used special, slow-motion photography to depict "beautiful" women in bathing suits diving from high cliffs into the "Balsatian [S]ea." Eltinge reframed it as his triumphant return to moviemaking.[19]

But *Over the Rhine*, aka *An Adventuress*, would rise yet again. A then-unknown actor named R. De Valentina had played a small part in *Over the Rhine*. By the early 1920s, though, he had become matinee idol Rudolph Valentino (often spelled "Rodolph" in those days). The footage was recut yet again, placing the heartthrob actor front and center. *Over the Rhine/An Adventuress* had boasted of Julian Eltinge, "A Genuine Novelty in Photoplay Entertainment," flying loop-the-loops in one scene and wearing "wonderful" couture in another. In the latest iteration, though, titled *The Isle of Love*, Rudolph Valentino was the star. You could hardly blame the studio. Thanks to the movies *The Four Horsemen* and *Blood and Sand*, Valentino now had a huge, bankable following. Still trying to recoup his losses, Balshofer had dug old footage "out of the vault," written some new dialogue titles, and edited in as many Valentino shots as possible. Thus, what had started life as an action/propaganda movie was now "a light comedy" focused on a handsome star who'd gotten twenty-five dollars a day when the picture was initially shot. (Balshofer put another $10,000 of his own money into the re-remake.) *The Isle of Love* was initially so successful that it triggered a wave of retrofits from other filmmakers anxious to re-edit Valentino back into stardom (no matter how woeful his acting), causing Balshofer's picture—and Eltinge's, to the extent that the movie was still his—to soon become lost in the deluge.[20]

In *The Isle of Love*, Eltinge plays Clifford Townsend, who has summoned his friend Jacques Rudanyi (Valentino) to become king of a "mythical" island nation. Townsend soon disguises himself as "a woman and a vamp" but is eventually forced to flee back to the United States, where he is reunited with an old flame. Rudanyi, meanwhile, hooks up with the main female character, Vanette. Townsend's companion in the movie is his mother (played by Lydia Knott), while "most of the love-making" fell to Rudanyi.[21]

* * *

210   BEAUTIFUL

What had been a promising movie career five years earlier now looked fragile. While a revival of *The Fascinating Widow* enjoyed a successful run in early 1921 with Charles Wilson doing the drag, a film adaptation starring Eltinge was "suddenly . . . dropped" by Fox studios. Fox executives apparently felt the movie industry's outlook had suddenly become "uncertain." The cast and crew were given a few weeks' pay and dismissed. American commercial moviemaking had entered what has been called its "monopsony" stage, meaning a few companies effectively controlled production, distribution, and exhibition. Fox, founded by former small-time vaudeville impresario William Fox, was one of a handful of companies, along with Paramount, Warner Bros., and others, which determined how the industry functioned. If one of them said the outlook was uncertain, then it was *uncertain*. Frustrated by being at the whim of autocratic, top-down-driven film studios, Eltinge teamed-up with actress Pauline Frederick to create the Pilgrim Picture Corp. Though the press sometimes playfully suggested a romantic link between the two—to the satisfaction of Eltinge's PR folks—they were simply trying to raise startup money together. Eltinge and Frederick traveled the country offering Pilgrim Picture stock as a "ground-floor investment." But the venture never took off, nor did a similar venture with actress Ann May that would have moved production operations up the coast from Los Angeles to Monterey.[22]

With his film career at a dead halt for the foreseeable future, Eltinge played some vaudeville dates under William Morris's management. (Though Morris had tried to launch his own circuit to compete with Keith-Albee and failed, he nonetheless remained a powerful agent/manager.) Florenz Ziegfeld offered the impersonation artist a role in the 1921 *Follies* but Eltinge declined, preferring not to spend so much time away from California. (Ziegfeld was desperate for "impersonations of the hairpin sex" in his big show and also tried to recruit impersonation artist Brooks Hunt, who also declined for unspecified reasons.[23])

Something else was also making it harder to go on tour: the actor's health began to go. Given the years of traveling the circuits, relentless corseting, and hours making-up in damp, poorly heated dressing rooms, not to mention the roller-coaster ride of gaining and losing weight plus a predilection for alcohol and tobacco, it's amazing that Julian Eltinge, staring at his forties, had made it this far without a serious collapse. His first big trouble came in 1918 when he caught a bad enough case of influenza, then a worldwide pandemic, that news outlets reported him deceased. In late October of that year, the impersonator got to read about himself succumbing to pneumonia triggered by the dreaded Spanish "Flu." He was likely more upset to see himself remembered as a "portrayer of female roles," rather than a serious dramatic actor, than for having died. In a few weeks, though, he'd recovered enough to will himself back to work, further enduring an ankle injury and a bout of ptomaine poisoning, neither of which put a dent in the *Revue of Nineteen-Nineteen*'s tour of the American Southwest. By this time, his work was attracting a kind of society attention in Texas and Oklahoma that he had known in Boston twenty years earlier. In Paris, Texas, he befriended the Clements, a prominent business and banking family, bonding in particular with R. M. "Mack" Clement and, later, Mack's widow. In Tulsa, Oklahoma, a gaggle of young society misses including Helen Delaney, Louella George, Margaret McKenzie, and Norma Miller organized a "theatre party" to see Eltinge's *Revue of Nineteen-Nineteen*'s in the city's Convention Hall. (Less than two years later, white supremacist terrorists would use Convention Hall as a "detention" center as part of their deadly attack on residents of Greenwood, Tulsa's "Black Wall Street."[24])

But a few years later, Eltinge faced a much more serious health crisis. In August 1921, complications from a botched appendectomy left the artist hovering near death. Lying in a Los Angeles hospital room, depleted and with uncharacteristically drawn features, the entertainer hoped against hope he'd pull through, as did his friends and supporters. But it didn't look good. Julian Eltinge, ever the fighter, would not admit defeat "until the last second"—which was, alas, "threateningly near," according to the *San Francisco Chronicle*.[25]

But the artist miraculously pulled through and, after several months' convalescence, was headlining at the Salt Lake City Orpheum albeit with an abbreviated act: four songs and accompanying impersonations with his now-classic "adornments of milady."[26] Playing big-time meant not only keeping his show up-to-date but differentiating himself from his now-numerous competitors, like Jean Barrios in "gorgeous gowns," and the trasvestic duo of Liddell & Gibson, one lanky and "robust as a hunk of baby macaroni" and the other able to sing so much like a woman the audience was utterly "fooled." One thing began to dawn on Julian Eltinge above all else, namely how much he loved the West Coast, how he preferred the "salubrious air of California." He breathed easier, felt himself healthier there, and even saw his complexion, battered by years of makeup and its removal, improve markedly. It was a compelling realization for a man who had recently read about his own death.[27]

212   BEAUTIFUL

Earning enough to keep up his California lifestyle, though, meant creating more cabaret-style confections like the *Revue of Nineteen-Nineteen*. Not only was that where the market was going, but productions like these tended to go on shorter, more manageable tours and featured a cast of other seasoned entertainers to shoulder some of the burden. With fewer Americans going to vaudeville, revues could be booked in restaurants and bars styled after popular New York nightspots like Rector's, Bustanoby's, and Reisenweber's. The crowds were more sophisticated as well, open to edgier fare.[28]

The 1920s saw the corresponding rise of an adjacent milieu, one of speakeasies and semiprivate nightclubs, a "*louche* world" that was both dodgy and seductive. Speakeasy culture informed the cabaret aesthetic and vice versa. Because of nightclubs' intentionally underground status, even if many knew of their existence, drag artists who performed there were increasingly assumed to be gay. Though the association of the two would not be complete until the later 1920s and 1930s, crossdressers onstage, once exempted from broader social censure, were becoming lumped in with perceived sexual and gender inverts of all kinds. Julian Eltinge could less and less identify as a regular guy with a special, technical talent, a lucrative skill he more or less had to put into effect, like the characters he played. The heat was notching up. Meanwhile, for those who cared less about leaning into the demands of mainstream culture, a new patois allowed clearer identification and self-identification of cabaret culture denizens. Comedian Lou Holtz said of popular drag artists Savoy & Brennan, who never feinted at normative masculinity like Eltinge: "I knew they were supposed to be fags." In the 1800s, "fagging" referred to older boys at English schools initiating younger ones, the latter having to perform humiliating chores and quite possibly administer sexual pleasures for their tormentors. By the early 1920s, though, fag could mean men who preferred sex with other men as well as effete individuals who enjoyed life's "finer" things, like art, literature, and design. The fag, in other words, could be a sexual invert or a gender invert, preferring womanly pursuits over presumptively masculine ones, with an increasing suspicion that the one kind of inversion necessarily denoted the other, and vice versa. The "fag" was also akin to another cultural subspecies that gestated within the 1920s piano bar and lounge world: "jaded cosmopolites." The "cosmopolite," an archaic term that meant something like our era's "yuppie," "metrosexual," or even top-knotted, urban "hipster," was someone who wouldn't be caught dead in a Keith vaudeville house or other middlebrow, retail amusement venue. Observers labeled Julian Eltinge a "thorough 'cosmopolite'," urbane, worldly, sophisticated, and

THE TWENTIES   213

no longer expected to spend hours boxing or hunting, or pretending he had. These modern, urban creatures, rather than being rough and tumble, and scenting of androgyny, were more concerned with "accuracy, precision, and perfect pitch and timing," in the words of historian Ann Douglas.[29]

If Prohibition, the "great national drouth" as one contemporary called it, which took effect in 1920, led to more bespoke platforms for female impersonation, it also got in the way of one of Julian Eltinge's favorite pastimes: drinking. Alcohol consumption surely didn't help the actor's health, and it also led to legal troubles. Shortly after the Eighteenth Amendment took effect, Eltinge and the *Nineteen-Nineteen* revue folks were playing a string of shows in the Southwest, including the border city of El Paso, Texas. Temptingly close to Juarez, Mexico, the star and his fellow troupers crossed the US-Mexico frontier and happily indulged. Who knew when another such opportunity might present itself? While the impersonator was able to discharge his duties onstage that night, suggesting something of a tolerance, other cast members teetered and fell. The show had to be called off midstream. Eltinge claimed to be "mortified" and darted home to Los Angeles.[30]

The next time the performer's thirst got him into trouble, it would be much more serious. Having appeared in Vancouver, Canada, in 1923, Julian Eltinge and four castmates were arrested upon crossing back into the United States with sixteen quarts of "assorted liquors." The actor and his entourage were summoned before US Marshal E. B. Benn in Seattle and asked to "explain" what they were doing with so much liquor in their possession. The matter was referred to a federal grand jury, who decided, perhaps because of Eltinge's celebrity status, not to pursue the charges further. The impersonator had to pay an eighty-dollar fine and, more painfully, surrender all the booze.[31]

But barely a year after his near-fatal bout with appendicitis, Eltinge had again to suspend work for medical reasons. Details are vague, but the performer needed further surgeries related to the appendicitis episode and its mishandled treatment. In any case, eager to return to work, he'd never properly recovered and was therefore more medically fragile than he cared to admit. He'd thus go under the knife in early summer and spend the next few months convalescing at the Villa Capistrano. Rather than Los Angeles, however, or New York City for that matter, Eltinge traveled to Buffalo where Dr. Thew Wright, an "old friend" and surgeon attached to the Buffalo General Hospital, would conduct the procedure. Eltinge had met Dr. Wright in Paris and they'd stayed close over the years. The actor had in fact formed a notable attachment to the Buffalo metro area since his vaudeville and minstrel days,

214   BEAUTIFUL

and vice versa. When he brought *The Fascinating Widow* there in 1911, the city's mayor begged him to add extra shows—which so alarmed at least one citizen that he insisted Buffalo outlaw female impersonation altogether. The actor had surgery on August 1, 1922, and emerged in stable condition. "Well, doc, you're dressing for the rehearsal this time instead of me," Eltinge said shortly before taking anesthesia. Dr. Wright would try to correct a number of thoracic issues in need of immediate attention including a serious abdominal hernia.[32] The operation was a success.

* * *

He rested for a few months. But he felt time slipping by, more quickly than in his younger days. The world, particularly the odd corners of it that employed artists like him, seemed to be moving faster still. Julian Eltinge took matters into his own hands. He'd become his own producer, an impresario for himself. Eltinge began previews for a new show in October. *The Vanishing Lady*, whose title had to be changed to *The Elusive Lady* because of copyright issues, was described as a "play with music." Julian Eltinge produced with assistance from Jacques Pierre, an actor-producer he'd known since they were both part of the Cohan & Harris "Honey Boy" minstrel show that tumbled across the country in 1908–1909. The impersonation artist wasn't the only big talent attached to *The Elusive Lady*. *Babes in Toyland* librettist Glen MacDonough wrote the book and lyrics, and *Ziegfeld Follies* contributor Raymond Hubbell composed the score. Though the actor continued to wax longingly about his "first love," by which he meant the "legitimate stage," *The Elusive Lady*, like so many other hopeful projects, didn't bring him any to closer to it. Rather, the script was recognizably Eltingesque, its plot a "tangled skein of consequences" involving, variously, an American woman married to the Grand Duke of the made-up nation of Zoolakia who flees a love-crazed admirer; a newsstand saleswoman from the made-up town of Gloomfield, Illinois; and Bert Blake, the ne'er-do-well son of millionaire parents who takes winnings from the horseraces at Longchamp and ventures to Monte Carlo to break the bank. Eltinge of course played Bert, a fellow with a scheme for the gaming tables who is forced to impersonate the Grand Duchess of Zoolakia. Now he found himself impersonating older ladies, dowagers, and dames. The ivory-skinned beauty dolls of his youth were mothballed.[33]

The Elusive Lady was well received. But it was no *Fascinating Widow* or *Crinoline Girl*. It played shorter stints in smaller, less prestigious venues including a one-night stand at the modest Stamford Theatre in Connecticut. In Baltimore, it shared the bill at Ford's with *The Blushing Bride*. Eltinge sang some of the show's tunes on WGR radio in Buffalo, his first time taking to the airwaves. But for any number of obvious reasons, including his increasingly strained voice, the new medium would not rescue Julian Eltinge's career.[34]

Almost as problematic was the fact that *The Elusive Lady* belonged to a genre of frothy, farcical musicals and operettas that increasingly sophisticated audiences no longer flocked to. Critics allowed that "admirers" of all things nostalgic would like the show well enough. But the 1920s marked a critical shift in tastes. In 1927, Jerome Kern and Oscar Hammerstein II would famously collaborate on *Show Boat*, the production perhaps most commonly cited as the "turning point" in American musical comedy. *Show Boat*, which some at the time believed merited its own genre designation, "popular opera," was lauded for its artistic substance and serious themes, despite that it may seem contrived and problematic to present-day audiences. Compared to *The Elusive Lady*, however, *Show Boat* seems not only from a different decade, but practically a different century. Eltinge's production featured *Crinoline Girl* veteran Herbert Corthell as the chief of the Grand Duke's secret police, his performance a découpage of broad, pantomimic facial gestures and "tricks suits" like those worn by vaudeville magicians. Oliver Smith played Ali Ben Al Kali, a clown for Orientalist fetishists, whose "sheiky" song-and-dance routine was among the play's most popular. These artists were skilled at caricature in an age when audiences wanted plays, novels, and even movies with psychologically compelling characters and at least the patina of verisimilitude. Vaudeville and scripted musical comedies, once coursing side-by-side from the same creative headwaters, were diverging into increasingly distinct phenomena.[35]

Julian Eltinge, of course, longed to jump forward, toward the land of serious art. But the very forces that had brought him to fame now pulled him backward or, at the very least, relegated him to a well-salaried holding pattern. Female impersonation was at its height. Thanks to all the "leading ladies" of the American Expeditionary Forces and a booming economy, the nation was socially and culturally at comparative ease. In 1923, *Variety* reported that there were more female impersonators than ever in vaudeville, sometimes even two on the same bill. In 1922, as Eltinge tried to revive his musical comedy career with *The Elusive Lady*, female impersonator Karyl Norman, aka "The Creole Fashion Plate," was packing houses and thought by some on the verge of succeeding Julian Eltinge as the art form's leading

216   BEAUTIFUL

delineator. Other ambitious rivals, like Karl Denton of Coburn's Minstrels and Boni Mack of the famed Al. G. Fields troupe, weren't far behind.[36]

Though barely in his forties, Julian Eltinge was becoming a legacy performer, inheritor of a tradition he'd pioneered and increasingly its *éminence gris*. He began mentoring college lads in the art of drag. In 1923, the impersonator paid a visit to Harvard's Hasty Pudding Club, instructing the Ivy League novitiates how to be "perfect ladies." No longer lying about having been an alum, the actor posed for snapshots with broadfaced, smiling youths draped in exotic gowns, capes, and shawls. He had finally become a Harvard man. Eltinge also shared his pearls of wisdom with the renowned Ram's Head troupe at Stanford.[37]

But the impersonation artist was drawn to one college-musical luminary above all the others: Lionel E. Ames of the University of Michigan Mimes. Ames was such a hit in the Mimes' 1923 production, *Cotton Stockings*, that it was booked for a tour of major theatres during Christmas break, including a date at New York's Metropolitan Opera House on December 18, 1923. The youthful, collegiate impersonator was serious about his craft, taking out a $25,000 insurance policy for his "pretty arms and legs." Though some considered Ames a "serious rival" to Eltinge, the two struck up a close, enduring relationship, the older man guiding and mentoring the younger. Julian Eltinge could spot someone who had that special gift, an ability to artfully and seamlessly become a woman. Ames indeed looked beautiful in broadbrimmed hat, tank top, and skirt splayed slightly open to reveal delicately crossed legs. "Bet a dollar you will say she is pretty," read a newspaper caption.[38]

The Michigan Mimes, properly known as the Michigan Union Opera, had been founded in 1906 and quickly became one the best-known collegiate crossdressing troupes in the Midwest, if not the entire nation. The University of Wisconsin's acclaimed Haresfoot Club had been formed in 1898 and its Big Ten rival in Ann Arbor was eager to get in the game. (Karyl "The Creole Fashion Plate" Norman would mentor the Haresfoot group. Not to be outdone, Eltinge later visited the Wisconsin troupe where he was photographed in a dragline with Haresfoot stars Porter Butts and Byron Rivers.) Universities earned kudos from their drag troupes. Like soldiers who became hometown heroes for their transvestic roles, talented college artists were brought to public attention. In 1923, the *Brooklyn Daily Eagle* boasted that Kenneth Ivers, a "leading lady" at Hobart College, was a "Boro Man" and actually supplied his address, 79 Lefferts Place, to prove it. (Publishing people's home addresses was not uncommon for newspapers back then.)

Figure 8.2 Julian Eltinge wasn't the only precise, naturalistic female impersonator of his time. Lionel E. "Iron Mike" Ames, who got his start with the University of Michigan Mimes, graduated to professional work with Eltinge's encouragement and sponsorship.
Credit: *Michigan Union Records (1884-1896), Bentley Historical Library, University of Michigan.*

Ambitious college groups would often appear at professional theatres playing for general audiences whose ticket purchases helped subsidize the troupes. Being in college also exempted impersonation artists from the "prejudice" sometimes aimed at drag professionals, especially those of speakeasy world. Indeed, many collegians took their musical impersonating quite seriously with clubs at even small schools, like Williams College's Cap and Bells,

218 BEAUTIFUL

touring New York City playhouses. For those in the female-impersonating business, it made good sense to cooperate, coordinate, and cobrand with the university trade.[39]

As far as Julian Eltinge was concerned, "Ames is the best female impersonator that I have seen in college dramatics," better than the "rafts of college boys coming on the stage in New York." While few college artists envisioned going professional, some, like Ames, definitely did, not incorrectly viewing their talent as a "business proposition with a chance of making good money." Though vague about the details, Eltinge announced he'd "sponsor" the gifted Michigan alum—who by 1925 had become "Iron Mike" Ames in the papers, probably because he could no longer claim collegiate normalization)—and offered the latter pointers, such as, "I never sing in a falsetto voice, and always try to think and act as a woman." As opportunities to make money in drag grew, so too did the seeds of new suspicions, aided by scientific and medical discourse like the emergent "hetero"/"homo" binary.[40]

By 1926, Lionel/"Iron Mike" was accruing a following in nightclubs and small theatres. Like his mentor, he sang in contralto. He portrayed an antebellum Southern belle, a "lissome" dancer, and a modern flapper. Some who criticized "[b]oyish-bobbed flappers" on the streets nonetheless praised Ames's non-satirical rendering. Eltinge designated Ames his official successor, whatever that meant exactly, earning both performers publicity. The younger impersonator presently explained that he'd put himself through the University of Michigan by driving a truck, which by this time was becoming a butch cliché. The Michigan lad further explained that "Mrs. Ames" made his costumes rather than he himself. Most important, he compared himself to men who "sit at important desks," graduating from college tomfoolery to a viable profession, as Julian Eltinge had repeatedly claimed to have done.[41]

* * *

Though he could not fully see it, the die had been cast for what remained of his career. Eltinge wasn't quite right for Hollywood or Broadway. He was, rather, an aging oddity and increasingly, denizen of a nightclub culture that would continue to fall under social scrutiny. In 1941, a reporter would reminisce that female impersonators had once been "a rage and mostly in good repute" at the turn of the century. But with drag artists retiring to recondite gin joints amid Prohibition, social and political forces "stressing Krafft-Ebing destroyed" public goodwill. It would not be the last time structural reactionism leveraged biomedical science to advance its agenda. While many people were fascinated with cabaret subculture, others could not but see it as a crucible of inversive, anti-masculine decay. Still others gazed through a sympathetic, if pathologizing, lens wondering why some who dwelt there enjoyed womanly attire and erotic relations with men. Aided by a now-regularized sexology discourse, many conventionally minded people strained to see the oddity of the other to avoid seeing their own arbitrary cultural conditioning. As sexual historian Jonathan Katz has written, "We do not usually name and speak of the strong desire to dress in the clothes of one's own sex."[42] Only recently has cultural critical mass reached a point of permitting (comparatively) widespread curiosity and de-normalizing, provoking the usual panic more or less right on schedule.

Collaborating with jazz trombonist Tom Brown, Eltinge created the *Black and White Revue*, a Ziegfeld-like soupçon of songs, dances, and sketches backed by a topflight orchestra. Its star once again promised—indeed, felt he *had to* promise—the "most elaborate costumes," some sixty-six separate outfits that, if arranged end-to-end, would stretch two-fifths of a mile. Replaying the heteronormative card, Eltinge said that some men declined marriage after "get[ting] wise to the cost of women's clothing." The sets and costumes had a modernist/deco aesthetic, but the content itself was tried and tired. The show's very conception seems not even to have been entirely original, echoing *John W. Vogel's Black and White Revue* (1920), which starred well-known impersonator Lester (aka "Lestra") LaMonte.[43] Eltinge and his ensemble played one-night stands in smaller California cities like Visalia and Fresno. He sang some new numbers such as "If You Want to Be in Fashion, Follow Me," and "Since I Fell in Love with Tabasco," both penned by rising tunesmith Norma Gregg. Critics, however, found the *Revue* an uneasy "mixture" of vaudevillian past and jazzy present. They reserved their praise for younger cast members like June and Jack Laughlin, a dance duo whose "hectic" energy better reflected current tastes. Stalwarts like vocalist Theresa Valerio and blackface comic Lew Dockstader, on the other hand, dragged the *Black and White Revue* backward, a cardinal sin in an age fascinated with speed and novelty, from technology to the very pace of life itself. As for Julian Eltinge, "one must regretfully admit" he was not what he used to be, according to a critic covering the show. The aging impersonator received one of his few unqualifiedly positive assessments from Rosetta and Vivian Duncan, a vaudeville sister act who penned a guest column for the *San Francisco Examiner*. They "enjoyed" Eltinge and his production "immensely"—though,

220 BEAUTIFUL

Figure 8.3 By the mid-1920s, Julian Eltinge found himself increasingly consigned to the world of cabarets and revues. He could still pull off ivory-skinned impersonations, but vaudevillian nostalgia was giving way to modernist sensibilities. It was unclear how—or if—he would survive.
Credit: *Photo by White Studio, © The New York Public Library for the Performing Arts.*

they confessed, it was the only show they'd seen in many months "excepting our own." *The Black and White Revue* soldiered on, a night here in Yuma, Arizona, a night there in Madison, Wisconsin.[44]

The impersonator's once-instructional, even sisterly public tone took a misogynistic turn. (It might not have helped that a newspaper poll found *Black and White Revue* trouper Agnes Sanford more beautiful than the man who, a few years earlier, was still being called "the stage's most beautiful woman.") Rather than offering useful makeup tips, Eltinge criticized American women as garish, verging on whorish. "I go along the street and see women with their faces smeared promiscuously with paint and he rouge," he said, "the powder slapped on any old way, and if they use a lipstick at all, usually the appearance is as though they considered it more to be used as a disguise rather than to enhance their charms." The performer's tone aligned with conservative and reformist voices of the age, respectively, both of whom argued that sex work was the result of dire, almost unconscious economic necessity and nothing else. It was threatening to consider female sexual agency and drive apart from a wish to procreate within a nuclear family. Much as older women were (and still are) finding it challenging to conform to social demands for slimness, so too did Julian Eltinge, though he directed his frustration at the wrong party. Fighting against his body's wish to return to its new, two-hundred-pound-plus base weight, he nonetheless rendered an "ultra-vampire of today" with knee-skirts and bobbed hair. Once masterfully poised, the artist grew clumsy, narrowly escaping death by immolation when his fringy, silver-tasseled gown got tangled in an electrical switchboard backstage and ignited a fire.[45] Both physically and professionally, Julian Eltinge had survived more than twenty years at the top. That time was drawing to a close. He still yearned, as he always had and would, to play a classic or serious role, to be regarded as a proper thespian. Until that opportunity appeared, if it ever did, he needed a new direction. He was still young enough and had credibility enough to make it happen. America still understood itself to be a land of abundant opportunity and second chances.

# # #

9

The Velvet Inquisition

It may seem unlikely that Julian Eltinge would ever look upon the American West, particularly its arid, open stretches, with entrepreneurial fantasies. And yet. . . .

In the fall of 1923, the actor bought a sprawling ranch property near San Diego. The 160-acre parcel occupied a high plateau at 3,500 feet near the town of Alpine, about thirty miles east of the city of San Diego. There, Julian Eltinge set about building what he would eventually call the Sierra Vista Rancho, a resort, spa, artists' retreat, and bungalow community with ranch homes and "a somewhat unusual hotel . . . for the convenience of the professional colony." He envisioned it as a place where he and his creative tribe could get away from the hustle and commune with their muses in the beauty of forested highlands. Eltinge said he already had handful of painters, musicians, and writers asking to rent cottages year-round when the place eventually opened. Sierra Vista Rancho would include an "art center" consisting of a dozen, adobe-walled studios resembling a Spanish village or what might pass for one in Hollywood movies. In addition, there would be eight to ten ranch-style homes, also in Spanish-colonial style, and forty cottages. There would be a small performance space—an "intimate theatre"—in the main hotel building, a nod to Strindberg's famed Intimate Theatre in Stockholm, as well as a wishful homage to the many "little theatres," like New York's Neighborhood Playhouse, which had recently started offering serious drama to theatergoers tired of melodrama and burlesque. Rather than waiting for an opportunity that might never come, the performer was creating his own artistic milieu "down San Diego way" in the shadow of the Viejas Mountains. There would also be an outdoor theatre harkening to classical Greece.[1]

And yet, the Rancho would be more than an artists' colony. It would offer guests and residents a taste of the rugged—or at least, rugged-adjacent—outdoors. There would be horseback-riding, golf, a hundred-foot swimming pool, and at some point, a thousand-acre hunting annex. The territory had a few lakes and ponds for swimming and fishing, plus "about a thousand trees."[2]

Beautiful. Andrew L. Erdman, Oxford University Press. © Oxford University Press 2024.
DOI: 10.1093/9780197696361.003.0010

Much as he had done at Villa Capistrano, the actor took charge of design and décor. The Rancho would exhibit his beloved Euro/Iberian aesthetic, part history, part poetry. Service staff would live in a low-slung, frontier-style ranch house fashioned after "Ramona's home" in the 1884 novel *Ramona* by Helen Hunt Jackson, a novel that reinforced the troublingly simplistic "Mission Myth" of indigenous persons happily intermarrying with and self-assimilating into the ranks of Anglo-European settlers. According to Eltinge, the central hotel and main building would be "practically a Spanish palace" with tapestries, French and Italian furniture, Asian and Middle Eastern rugs, and a selection of miniatures, cameos, and jewelry kept under glass as though at a museum. He worked with architect Martin Severtsen and a "Spanish" designer to create not only the edifices but also cactus groves, English gardens, and Italianate arbors. Echoing his old practice of going to Paris for the latest women's fashions, the performer-turned-hotelier traveled to Mexico City to handpick conquistador-era antiques, though like any good decorator, he kept a watchful eye on local estate sales for diamonds in the trash heap. Eltinge salvaged mahogany railings and circular windows from the Notre Dame convent outside Los Angeles when it was torn down in 1925 and also regularly popped into "wrecking houses" to see what orphaned architectural goodies might be lying around.[3]

Feeling that he'd finally found his next métier, happy and motivated as he hadn't been since first coming out West to make movies, Julian Eltinge announced he was done with female-impersonating, maybe even believing it this time. "I could probably keep going awhile longer," he reckoned, "But I don't fancy hearing people say 'Eltinge is getting heavy,' or 'he isn't the Julian I remember 10 years back.'"[4] He tried to sell it as best he could, though his retirements and farewells had become legend, with one journalist joking that the impersonator had "'retired for good' five separate and distinct times."[5]

But Julian Eltinge was quite dedicated to his new undertaking. He went about the property in trousers, digging, planting, pruning, and actually working the land rather than playing a farmer. He even asked employees at the Rancho to call him Bill Dalton. Julian Eltinge was no longer dissimulating. He had truly become a "horny-handed son of toil" and "shrewd, matter-of-fact business man" in one. He hefted rocks himself, cleared tenacious underbrush, knocked down hornets' nests, and plunged his hands into the local clay to see if it was right for adobe brick. The impersonator also gazed at his skin and saw something new, namely, "my brown face and hands, gained from being a farmer in the great open spaces." Nobody would

224   BEAUTIFUL

compare him to a "whitewashed statue" now. These days, a white man with sun-bronzed skin, presumably from toiling outdoors, was regarded genuinely "manly."[6]

* * *

The Sierra Vista Rancho was supposed to open for business by October 1, 1925, but that got pushed back to spring 1926. Things were going well but more renovations were needed. Some guest units were already "spoken for" by famous screen personalities, and two San Diego businessmen, Fred Rice and Roy Lichty, were trying to raise $25,000 to finance their own 255-acre "mountain resort" across the road from Eltinge's place. The Rancho eventually opened for bookings in the fall of 1926, a year behind schedule. Advertisements promised "A place built for artists, writers and people of distinction," with rates of $75–$250—fortnight and monthly rentals only. "I want to let the hair grow on my chest," said the proudly self-appointed innkeeper. He was tired of having to manage his "figger." He was now a builder, groundskeeper, and hospitality executive in one. "There will be enough about the building of that hotel and the improvement of those grounds to keep me busy for the rest of my life!" he confided to columnist Grace Kingsley as they sat in the downtown, Los Angeles offices of Grauman's Metropolitan theatre. Soon, ranch guests would be riding horses, painting paintings, and writing novels, or at least thinking about writing novels as they dragged on long cigarettes in the crisp California air. Meanwhile, the onetime female impersonator who ran the place would pick up a wheelbarrow and plant cacti in "manly manner." After the workday, he'd retire to a cottage whose coffee tables and countertops were strewn with women's magazines including his favorite, *Women's Home Companion*. Eltinge told his mother, Julia, who was spending more time at Sierra Vista Rancho—it would soon be her full-time home—that he was concerned about the upward creep of women's hemlines. His own legs, after all, were now hairier and rougher than they'd ever been. He was concerned he might have to go back on tour until the resort became financially viable, though hopefully that wouldn't be necessary. Mom suggested he could simply return to longer, older-style dresses to cover his semi-leathery extremities. But the son disagreed: "I always insist on wearing clothes in the height of fashion." Julia, who helped pick out the actor's costumes, understood. The performer/hotelier was relieved, however, to find out that "plumper figures" might soon be in vogue again. Still, all this talk was understood to be purely academic; Bill Dalton had a long track record of ambition, hard work, and shrewd moves. The Rancho was to be his crowning achievement, the final act. That was the plan. "I should expect this Bill Dalton person to succeed in anything he undertook," wrote Grace Kingsley.[7]

But it would take more than ambition and the displacement of cacti to put a venture like Sierra Vista Rancho in the black. Then as now, the hospitality business was costly and risky. In 1926, 928 hotels and restaurants failed in the United States. By 1928, well before the stock market crash of the following year, that figure would jump 20 percent, to 1,105. Few were surprised when Julian Eltinge admitted he'd have to go back to the skirts for a stint since he was in need of "beaucoup pennies." Like many an energetic entrepreneur rushing headlong toward their vision, the actor didn't look at the balance sheet until it was nearly too late. Buying and fixing up his desert retreat had, as he put it, "steadily emptied the pot." For now, off came the work trousers and back on went the evening gowns.[8]

* * *

More than just women's fashions were changing as the 1920s came to a close. In some ways, the cultural landscape barely resembled that of the turn of the century when he had gotten his start. Women could now vote, divorce more freely, and openly indulge in certain pleasures just like men. A 1920s PR campaign for Lucky Strike cigarettes encouraged women to light up "torches of freedom" in public and march proudly down New York's Fifth Avenue. When Julian Eltinge observed, in 1925, that "Girls are returning to the old-fashioned feminine types," it was wishful thinking and he knew it. His art had been predicated on an inherent separateness and distinctness of the sexes, which seemed less convincing all of a sudden.[9]

The Broadway theatre named for him still continued to provide the artist with revenue, but not enough to offset the bleed. Worse yet, while peers like Al Jolson, Nora Bayes, and George M. Cohan actually got to perform in or near their eponymous theatres, Julian Eltinge had never become a Broadway regular, not even at the playhouse that bore his name. He toyed with the idea of opening an Eltinge Theatre in Los Angeles that would seat 1,800 and produce high-quality drama. But another risky, expensive project was the last thing he needed right now.[10] He reached out to his former angel, A. H. Woods, who had not actively managed the entertainer's career since the end of *Cousin Lucy*'s 1917 tour. But Woods himself was chronically in and out of debt and

226   BEAUTIFUL

suggested only more stock-in-trade, *Charley's Aunt* derivatives or *Fascinating Widow* knockoffs. Instead, the impersonation artist dusted off *Miss Swift of New York*, a comedy he'd coauthored with newspaperman-turned-novelist Guy Steely back in 1913. Interestingly, Steely's first novel, *Wally* (1911), was "a clean, virile western" in which an "irresponsible and irrepressible" young chap falls in love with a "charming widow" at a Nevada mining camp. Nothing further came of *Miss Swift*, though, leaving Eltinge at a loss for income until the ever-unpredictable movie people came knocking.[11]

Originally titled *Madame Lucy*, the film *Madame Behave* virtually dropped into Julian Eltinge's lap. So unexpected was the offer that he had to pull himself away from the resort in Alpine to rehearse. *Madame Behave*, from Christie movie studios, was an "Americanized and modernized" adaptation of a French farce by Jean Arlette. Eltinge played Jack Mitchell, a down-on-his-luck architect who has sold a building design but won't be paid until and unless construction actually begins. In this picture, he was not the charming ne'er-do-well but rather, wingman to one, Dick Morgan (sometimes listed as "Dick Corwin") played by David James. Dick is the sort who "inherited a fortune in June but couldn't buy a firecracker in July." (F. McGrew Willis adapted the screenplay and wrote many of the clever intertitles.) Dick is in love with Gwen Townley, played by *Ziegfeld Follies* alumna Ann Pennington. Gwen is the ward of Dick's rich uncle, Seth, and her best friend is Laura Barnes (played by Evelyn Francisco). Jack naturally falls for Laura but, as with Dick and Gwen, complications ensue. Specifically, Henry is suing Seth who he claims wrecked his, Henry's, Rolls-Royce while drunk-driving on the wrong side of the street. (Seth is also Dick's landlord and is threatening to have him evicted.) There was but one witness to the accident, a mysterious woman whom Seth allegedly "spirited" out of town. (The plot is tangled but boils down to: two young guys are enamored of two young women, and vice versa, as two aged, squabbling jackasses get in the way.) The "crusty old fellows," Seth and Henry, compete to find the mystery woman first and marry her before the other can do so, because she won't be able to testify against Seth but could be made to testify against Henry, depending on which man she marries. Seth and Henry's mutual hatred makes for some good, vaudeville-style comedy, including a gag in which Henry launches himself at Seth only to be caught in midair by his attorney. Seth and Henry, "bitter enemies," hurl wonderfully outdated epithets at one another including, "you Asinine Airedale!" and "you Back-biting Beetle!" (An interesting and disturbing detail is a servant character named, variously, "Henry" and "Creosote." Played by white actor Tom

Wilson, the character, who is *not* in blackface, nonetheless speaks in minstrel patois, saying for example: "De landlord called fo' de rent but Ah didn't encourage him any," and offering to work for free if necessary. This vocal styling is akin to the "whiteface" minstrelsy of Sopher Tucker and other singers who appropriated Black vocal stylings in their "coon shouting" but never donned burnt cork.) Meanwhile, Henry has promised rich, pale-visaged dandy Percy Fairweather that he can marry Laura in return for a much-needed loan. Fairweather, whose "family tree was a poison oak," is coded as effeminate by his excessive decorum, white gloves, monocle, and satin top hat, a lanky, pallid Mr. Peanut. Eltinge's character flirts with Laura, thus cuckolding Percy, who accuses his rival of being a "fourflusher"—that is, a bluffer or a poser. Eltinge's Jack passes the masculine litmus test by refusing foppery while pretending and aspiring to be prosperous. The story inevitably leads to Jack crossdressing as the mysterious missing lady witness whom Seth and Henry respectively woo with great ardor.[12]

Most audiences would have seen *Madame Behave* through the lens of what they knew about Julian Eltinge. It's hard to tell who was more uncomfortable with the homoerotic humor: Seth and Henry, each of whom is asking a man to marry them, or Julian Eltinge, forced again into a role in which men find him desirable. Seth tells the crossdressed Jack, "I can see you're not a bit like other women," leading Henry to parry, "I'm a Boy Scout looking for a playmate." Later, Eltinge's dragged-up Jack strokes dandified Percy's head, saying, "What a beautiful nose! Just like the cow-catcher on the 'Iron Horse'!", an early locomotive.[13]

By the time of *Madame Behave*, few except other characters in the story would have mistaken Julian Eltinge's impersonation for a woman. The "counterfeit" women of his earlier years had become blowsy, dame-like, and "decidedly matronly." His renderings, like his own person, were increasingly "husky," both desexualized (in the eyes of many) and yet somehow closer to his actual self, the impersonator and his impersonations colliding in a way Julian Eltinge had long avoided. The only advantage to it all was that he could perhaps live more comfortably within his new baseline weight of 215 lbs. With *Madame Behave*, the actor was also finally free of needing to "claim to kinship with the fashion show." The once-Houdini-like, "ambisextrous" female impersonator couldn't play the beauty for mainstream audiences. He would star in only one more film and work in cabarets as top-shelf vaudeville faded into the past. The actor was in a holding pattern from which there was no escape, an "ambivalent diva." He would have no part of the "pansy

228 BEAUTIFUL

craze" of late 1920s, in which men, mostly gay, dragged openly in certain parts of New York and other cities. Julian Eltinge had long been a master of the middle ground. But as polarities began to widen he was at risk of ending up in a nether zone, at once invisible and vulnerable.[14]

Madame Behave, a six-reeler, was officially released in December 1925 but wouldn't enjoy widespread screenings until the following month. Audiences laughed, some apparently finding it "screamingly funny." The picture fit well into standardized programs that bundled it with comical shorts and newsreels. Whereas Eltinge himself had once been the erotic, stylish center-piece, his younger, female costars, notably Ann Pennington, now took over. In her diaphanous, chiffon dress and "unconcerned chapeau," Pennington made a "splendid foil" for the aging impersonator. It soon became clear that *Madame Behave*, whatever its charms, would not reignite Julian Eltinge's movie career. Within a few years, the picture had been "almost totally for-gotten in America" and was marketed to filmgoers in China, something that made more sense back when movies spoke in a silent tongue.[15]

* * *

The upside to *Madame Behave*'s relative failure is that it let the actor return to his newfound passion, the ranch-resort at Alpine. When the movie was through shooting, Eltinge packed up his things at the Hollywood Plaza Hotel where he'd been staying and headed back to the mountains and canyons. He snapped up more acreage to make it easier for Rancho guests to travel into town, and vice versa. When A. H. Woods offered him a musical whose very title, *That Blonde Lady*, suggested a nightmarish cliché, Eltinge politely said no and explained that he'd be down in San Diego County for the season. His onetime mentor got it; there was no bad blood. Early in the summer of 1927, Julian Eltinge's father, Joe Dalton, long a bit player in his son's life, passed away. Julia was free to spend her time with Billy/Julian out at the ranch or, every so often, at Villa Capistrano in Edendale/Silver Lake.[16]

The impersonator's life now followed a new script: work on building-out the Rancho, then whip up a quick, passably new tour to refill the coffers. The next offering would be *Fads & Fancies of the Fair Sex*, featuring the expectable if now burdensome "dazzling array of gowns, jewels and songs." Also expect-ably, *Fads & Fancies* was dubbed Eltinge's "ninety-ninth farewell tour"—which would be proven especially false when he took a warmed-over reboot of it on the road in the early 1930s.[17] Poking around for other employment, the impersonator was briefly attached to *The Golden Girls*, a musical by R. H. Burnside and *Crinoline Girl* composer Percy Wenrich. But he had to drop everything when his mother became ill. Julian Eltinge and A. H. Woods kept in touch, but their collaborations were by now the stuff of history.[18]

Vaudeville, incubator of Julian Eltinge's transvestic art, had also become the Sick Man of Entertainment. Movies were devouring what remained of its audiences and it was suffering labor problems. In order to attract anything approaching real talent, both the two-a-day and small-time circuits had to pay inflated salaries—up to $200 a week on average, up from $30–$50 when Eltinge started out—for even midlevel stars. Vaudeville was increasingly the destination for has-beens and never-wills, a bit like lesser Las Vegas hotels or cruise ships in our day. Julian Eltinge was bitter about it, despairing that vaudeville was "shot to pieces," no longer attracting "big names" (or even many smaller ones). As vaudeville scaled down, no longer able to keep talent from working in adjacent spaces, it began to share more in common with the cabaret and dinner-club venues where Eltinge and others found work. An industry once held proudly aloft and apart by B. F. Keith and E. F. Albee in effect acknowledged that it had to join what it could not beat. Eltinge split the bill with Mary Astor at the Boston Keith-Albee in December 1928. Astor, later in *The Maltese Falcon*, was a rising star thanks to *Romance of the Underworld*, a movie set in the speakeasies of gangland. While Eltinge spent hours making-up and taking-it-off, Astor could well be lounging on her divan at home or driving around town in her motorcar. The impersonator resented it. Astor's career, a beeline from vaudeville to movies, represented the future, the reverse of his. Indeed, that very year, 1928, the Keith-Albee company, which had already absorbed former rival the Orpheum chain, sold its approximately two hundred remaining major playhouses to the Radio Corporation of America. RCA in turn wired them all for the newly intro-duced talking motion pictures. Keith-Albee vaudeville as such was gone, replaced by the Radio-Keith-Orpheum movie concern—RKO for short. In 1932, RKO converted New York's Palace theatre, once the mecca of vaude-ville, to film. A former vaudevillian lamented that Hiram Brown, the new head of RKO, "knew a lot about leather [desk chairs] but nothing about show biz." If B. F. Keith had been alive, he might even have applauded the change as just the next, inevitable step in the commercial amusement industry. A few large, centrally run entities would dominate show business. Depending on which side of the desk you sat, this was either a good thing or a very bad thing. But it was the future.[19]

230 BEAUTIFUL

Julian Eltinge allowed that he'd be open to making movies, preferably dramas, but with the "hitch" that he not be asked to skirt-up, leading at least one observer to comment, stingingly, that "nothing could be funnier" than seeing Eltinge in a serious role. When nothing came his way, and with the Rancho (not to mention his mother) still in need of subsidy, Eltinge signed a four-picture deal with Hollywood publicist-turned-indie-producer Jesse Weil. They would eventually make but a single film. *Maid to Order* began production at Tec Art Studios, mostly used for Westerns and Rin-Tin-Tin serials, in October 1929, the very month when the stock market would begin the first of its precipitous crashes and pitch the United States (and much of the world) into the Great Depression. *Maid to Order*, Eltinge's first talkie, directed by Elmer Clifton and adapted for the screen by Grace Elliott from a story by Doris Dembow and A. J. L. Parsons, featured a few original songs to show off emergent sound technology. Eltinge played "Julian Eltinge," a onetime female-impersonation star and vaudeville headliner who knows two things about crime: how to commit it and how to solve it. The cops enlist Eltinge-qua-"Eltinge" to break a diamond-smuggling ring that uses a nightclub as a drop-point. Meta-Eltinge eventually ends up rooming with entertainer-turned-smuggler Lotti Lorraine, whom the Eltinge character himself has begun impersonating. Despite its potentially interesting, self-reflexive concept, *Maid to Order* had a hack script that "squeeze[d] out the last double meaning gag" anywhere it could. A B-minus movie at best, *Maid to Order*'s patter wasn't offensive but neither was it clever. To make matters worse, 1929 saw a glut of mediocre films churned out purely to exploit the newfangled sound technology. Eltinge's pictures, "none of them . . . what you might call top-notchers," in the opinion of influential columnist Louella Parsons, faded further into a blur of indistinction. *Maid to Order* resulted in its star becoming just another of those "one-talkie wonders" flopping about in the wake of technological and artistic developments that were still finding their way. Another filmland gossip writer, Robbin Coons, called the impersonation artist's career "very, very sad" by now. Indeed, *Maid to Order*'s producers cut short its initial release and held it for what they hoped would be a more opportune moment, eventually distributing it through a webwork of regional companies in 1931. But with the economy even worse by then, it fared no better. (Interestingly, *Maid to Order* costarred George Stone, who would later play a small, supporting role in the transvestic classic *Some Like It Hot*.[20])

Not only was Julian Eltinge nearing fifty—he looked "a trifle mature" according a theatre critic attempting to be politic—but he had also been in

Figure 9.1 An aging, silver-haired Julian Eltinge cuts a fine figure in pinstripes. America in 1940, when this picture was taken, was vastly different from what it had been when the impersonation artist first went pro at the turn of the century. Bigger changes yet were afoot, though Eltinge would not live to see them.
Credit: *Billy Rose Theatre Division, The New York Public Library for the Performing Arts.*

a serious car crash.[21] In July 1929, the actor and three showbiz pals were cruising around Los Angeles when they collided with a police car that was (ironically) on traffic-enforcement duty. Of the four persons in his vehicle, Eltinge was hurt the worst, suffering a concussion, deep lacerations in his scalp and elsewhere, and a scattering of ugly bruises and hematomas. The car carrying the impersonator and his friends was totaled. So was the cops'.

232   BEAUTIFUL

Officer H. B. Rich, the other vehicle's driver, alleged he smelled alcohol in the offending vehicle (which was actually owned by Eltinge's friend, actress Leonora Cosnova, and driven by yet another acting buddy, Mitchell Harris). The actor and his entourage were coming back from a long night of partying. The accident, which occurred at 6:30 in the morning, not only destroyed the police cruiser and injured a civilian passenger it carried, but also took out a telephone pole. After everyone was treated at the hospital, both factions began pointing bandaged, accusatory fingers at one other. Policeman Rich claimed the actors' car was traveling a then-speedy forty miles per hour, though Mitchell Harris claimed it was in fact the officer who had been "driving fast." Except for the headwounds and lacerations, it resembled a scene from *Madame Behave.*[22]

* * *

The auto mishap was the sort of sub-apocalyptic event that at once symbolized, resulted from, and contributed to the actor's growing pile of problems. Eltinge had had to drop everything to tend to his sick mother, then got tangled up in a nasty car crash, then found out that talkies weren't going to save his career after all. The artist continued to try his hand at radio, a medium hardly fit for a female impersonator no matter how tuneful his voice, singing some of his old hits and, on a separate occasion, talking about women's style on-air at KHJ–Los Angeles with renowned fashion editor Peggy Hamilton.[23] It was all just a passing fancy.

The comparatively expanded social liberties of the freewheeling 1920s, including the so-called pansy craze, later triggered what has been described as a "powerful backlash" against all things non-heteronormative. As the Depression metastasized fears of social collapse and exposed the weaknesses of capitalism, reactive forces saw vague but dangerous encroachments lurking everywhere below the fragile surface: Bolshevism in the ranks of unhappy laborers; perverts masquerading as seemingly conventional men— or worse yet, not even *pretending* to masquerade; and crossdressers tossing assumptions about gender, thought to be settled, out the window. The influential sexology research that had once heralded a new era of scientific liberality was becoming weaponized. The title character in Nathanael West's 1933 novella *Miss Lonelyhearts*, a man posing as a female advice columnist, barges into a restroom and, with a homophobic buddy, accosts an elderly man in a stall waiting for a hookup. "We're scientists. He's Havelock Ellis and I'm

Krafft-Ebing," they taunt, calling the old man a "pervert." What gives them the right to persecute him, wonders the old man who walks with a cane. "Science gives us the right," they shout. It is worth noting that Havelock Ellis, despite his legacy and the problematic nature of his writings, generally believed the law ought not to intrude on sexual matters, particularly among freely consenting adults. But fear ever lubricates the gears of regression. There were rumors to the effect that police officer Rich had purposely plowed into Julian Eltinge's car, though he of course denied intentionally trying to hit "the female impersonator's automobile."[24] Nonetheless, collisions, injuries, and fatalities of all kinds were becoming unavoidable.

To those paying closer attention, willing to see what others could yet ignore, there were ill omens even prior to the all-out economic collapse of 1929–1932, seedlings and precursors of sexual panic and gender hysteria. The literal and figurative trials of Mae West in the late 1920s provide a useful window into what was becoming acceptable and what would be deemed over-the-line. Because she came under scrutiny for producing, acting in, and sometimes coauthoring plays about sex, prostitution, female impersonation, and a growing gay subculture, West was a lightning rod for many of the forces with which Julian Eltinge had long had to contend (though each chose very different strategies). Press coverage of West's legal travails sometimes referred to Eltinge, either for humor or as a subtle counterpoint, as if to say, this is how a man may literally upend his gender while avoiding censure. At least one of West's biographers argues that Eltinge's approach to personal style influenced the edgy actress even if she played the rebellious daughter and he the compliant son.[25] What Mae West probably meant was that she appreciated not just Eltinge's but other impersonators' keen eye for attention-grabbing individuality. Whereas Eltinge had poured his energy into staying within the lines, others directed theirs toward breaching boundaries, leading to over-the-top caricatures that struck a different chord in audiences' minds. Mae West may well have admired Julian Eltinge's polish and precision, but she had too much of the rebel in her to abide by the same rules. She liked the carnivalesque, the sarcastic, and the outrageous, mixing such qualities with her own hyper-femininity, contributing to a camp aesthetic. To the extent that Julian Eltinge conformed onstage and off-, Mae West did the opposite. Though in some ways clearly homophobic and ill-informed, West's ironic, suggestive quips—like "Why don't you come up some time, see me?" and "When I'm caught between two evils, I generally like to take the one I've never tried"—owe a clear debt not to Julian Eltinge's restraint but

Figure 9.2 In this publicity still, Julian Eltinge resembles Mae West, whose scandals and trials said much about changing attitudes toward sex and gender in the late 1920s and early 1930s, and who remarked that she'd been influenced by Eltinge's style. In his way, the impersonator was more conservative than West, and she herself displayed complicated attitudes toward sexuality and gender, as much a product of her times as a rebel against them.
Credit: *Billy Rose Theatre Division, The New York Public Library for the Performing Arts.*

to "[o]utrageously campy" performers like Bert Savoy. Savoy, in fact, had become famous for his oft-repeated, comical catchphrases, including "You must come over," and the classic, "You don't know the half of it, dearie." Mae West was both hyperfeminine—seductive, sexual, and desirable—yet also cast as an anti-woman, libidinous and driven in a way women were not supposed to be. Some even referred to her as "the greatest female impersonator since Julian Eltinge."[26]

* * *

Mary Jane West was born in 1893, a generation after Julian Eltinge, to a working-class family in the then-tough neighborhood of Greenpoint, Brooklyn. Her mother, Matilda, was unhappily married to an irregularly employed inebriate named John West. Matilda—"Tillie" as she was known—determined to help the oldest of her surviving three children make it in show business, and it was to the girl who would soon be known as "Mae" that Tillie devoted her efforts. Tillie West was a "tough-minded stage mother," able to channel her energies and unrealized personal wishes into seeing Mae succeed. Matilda West refused to martyr herself to an alcoholic marriage. There is little doubt that Mae West learned a lot about power, sex, and coupling as she watched the sometimes-cold, often-hot war that was her parents' relationship.[27]

Tillie West encouraged her child not only to study but actually imitate the biggest female star in vaudeville, Eva Tanguay. Tanguay, also the ambitious, hugely talented child of an alcoholic father, conveyed a wild energy that made her a favorite in the two-a-day. Tanguay was known for some racy jokes and a merry narcissism, which many believed inappropriate for a woman (though admirable in a man). But while Eva Tanguay managed to stay on the right side of respectability—just barely at times, as she wrangled with censors and critics—Mae West did not, nor did she care to. She was overtly sexual and disregarded boundaries only prodded by Eva Tanguay. Tanguay was broadly libidinal and vivacious but not smutty, which made her a mainstream vaudeville star. Mae West on the other hand was regarded as "vulgar," leading her to leave the Keith circuit in the late 1910s and, after some success in musical comedy, appear on the Mutual Burlesque Wheel ("wheel" being the burlesque equivalent of a vaudeville "circuit") in the early 1920s.[28]

Tired of being at the whim of impresarios and producers—pretty much all of whom, it should be noted, were men—Mae West decided to try her hand and playwriting. It is widely believed that in order to make the transition from variety performer to playwright, West had help from seasoned ghost writers. But she stuck to her new calling and, in 1926, her first dramatic effort, *Sex*, debuted in Stamford, Connecticut, the very city where Eltinge's

236 BEAUTIFUL

The Elusive Lady had stalled out four years earlier. Despite writing that was considered by turns depraved and dull, *Sex* caught the public's attention. The main character, Margy LaMont, played by West herself, "presides over the roughest brothel in all of Montreal" before heading to Trinidad, Harlem, and other realms off the mainstream, white radar. There were calls to close the play down, but *Sex* managed to have a profitable run at Daly's on Broadway.[29]

In early 1927, when New York's corrupt, theatre-loving mayor Jimmy Walker took a break from patronizing the city's speakeasies to enjoy the Florida sun, conservatives jumped into action and shut down three shows alleged to be "corrupting the morals of the youth, or others." The plays in question were *Sex*; *The Virgin Man* (a seduction comedy about a Yale lad); and *The Captive*, a lesbian-themed work by French dramatist Edouard Bourdet. The moral fracas served only to heighten interest in plays dealing with perceived sexual deviancy. By the time it closed, *Sex* had become one of the longest-running plays then on Broadway. West's next work, *The Drag*, originally titled *The Wicked Queen*, explored the city's growing gay subculture and "pansy craze" of the late 1920s.[30]

While Mae West would later position herself as a student and protector of gay subculture, she appears to have been more interested in capitalizing on trends, exploiting controversy, and pushing the limits of public outrage. *The Drag* concerns Rolly Kingsbury, a wealthy judge's son whose marriage falls apart after it becomes clear that he is attracted to men. West hired gay men, many of them also crossdressing artists, to act in *The Drag*, and also for subsequent shows in which they would play *gay men*. West herself believed homosexuals, as they were now more commonly called, to be victims, not of social repression but rather of a disease that rendered them "inverts" from birth or "perverts" by dint of adverse experience. Influenced by the work of Karl Heinrich Ulrichs, West believed gay men possessed a woman's "soul" and informed police that when beating up a homosexual, "you're hitting a lady." Under new enforcement efforts and stricter laws, *Sex* faced a second trial. This time, its author was sentenced to ten days in New York City's Welfare Island prison. Despite offers to have physicians and other authority figures vet *The Drag* in previews, the play was unable to secure a New York production, in part because influential newspaperman William Randolph Hearst cited it as an example of all that was wrong with an unregulated theatre, "a disgusting . . . challenge to decency," after it previewed in Bridgeport, Connecticut.[31]

THE VELVET INQUISITION   237

Partly on the appeal of her scandalous reputation, but mostly due her evolving style and attitude, Mae West's next venture, *Diamond Lil*, became a huge hit in 1928. She was now a legitimate star. *Diamond Lil*, which would become the basis of the 1933 movie *She Done Him Wrong*, was set amid the slums and shady denizens of the Bowery, giving audiences the opportunity to do some slumming and underworld-peeping.[32]

* * *

But it was her next venture, *Pleasure Man*, that would end up associating Mae West with Julian Eltinge in the public mind and shed light on changing attitudes toward the drag in its various forms. In time, social and legal developments would force the artist to do something he had avoided his entire professional life: choose sides. Shifts in the cultural climate would make it impossible to inhabit a middle ground, which in any case would soon disappear.

Pleasure Man depicted the backstage and offstage lives of female impersonators, many of whom were also gay both in the show and, it was widely known in the business, in actual fact. The play culminated in a party scene marked by seductive, campy wordplay that gave respectable theatre patrons a glimpse into the supposed real lives of drag artists. After seeing a preview in the Bronx, *Variety* columnist Jack Conway called *Pleasure Man*, which was preparing to migrate to the Biltmore Theatre (now the Peter J. Friedman Theatre) in Times Square, "the queerest show you've ever seen" featuring "All of the Queens," plus plenty of drag hijinks and close-up views of a fascinating and presumably horrifying subculture. Alas, *Pleasure Man*'s run ended abruptly when policemen jumped onstage and literally placed their hands over the actors' mouths in October 1928 amid the usual charges of degeneracy and youth-corruption, piling most of the blame on playwright and director Mary Jane West.[33]

Mae West argued that *Pleasure Man*, which actually lifted some dialogue and characters from *The Drag*, wasn't primarily about homosexuality. Furthermore, even where it did involve same-sex coupling, the play did not condone it. According to its director-author, *Pleasure Man* was simply a naturalistic depiction of the lives and labors of professional female impersonators. Yes, she conceded, many of the play's male characters resembled effeminate stereotypes, with nicknames like Peaches and Bunny. But that was what female impersonators looked and sounded like in real life, or so she argued.

238 BEAUTIFUL

West said she sincerely believed doctors ought to "find a cure" for those poor, inverted or perverted souls. It was a medical matter, not a forensic one. West also pointed out, not incorrectly, that female-impersonating was a time-honored profession. If the law had a problem with these artists, why didn't it target those on "the Keith Circuit" or in the movies?[34]

Which of course put our protagonist in an uncomfortable, even untenable, position. His whole proposition had been that female-impersonating was a *profession*, manly in its precision and, in his case, its profitability. But it was no more related to his true self than, say, being an actuary was when said actuary was playing golf or at home with Mrs. Actuary and the kids. This argument necessitated sidestepping another pillar of modern manhood: super-identification with one's work. Indeed, understanding oneself *as* one's profession, as a skilled operative or expert, was one of the last vestiges of a shrinking male "sphere" and what made it unique from a qualitatively different female sphere (in which women could super-identify as "wife," "mother," and perhaps maid or nurse.) A man did not *conduct* accounting. Rather, he *was* an accountant, much as he did not just *go to* Harvard but was a "Harvard man."[35] In trying to separate and sanitize a professional group from a sexual subculture, Mae West ended up further conflating them. To many, it now seemed as if a sexually deviant Fifth Column had been hiding in plain sight, its ranks swelling, funded by the blindly happy buyers of vaudeville and movie tickets. The artist community parried but with limited success. *Billboard* argued that female impersonators were neither inverts nor perverts, calling *Pleasure Man* a "libelous and treacherous portrayal of show people," desperately (and, ultimately, ineffectively) throwing gay people under the bus, a betrayal of many of its rank-and-file. But the public could not unsee what it had long suspected: the female impersonation craft was but a cauldron of perversion. Something had to be done before it was too late, before society fell to the outsiders, the inverts, and the non-compliers. In a few short decades, entertainment had become a massive, centrally run, economic and social influence in need of proper stewardship.[36]

Nathan Burkan, the high-profile attorney defending Mae West, was a veteran of theatrical litigation. In 1910, he had secured an injunction against Edna Luby on behalf of vaudeville superstar Irene Franklin, giving Franklin the "exclusive right" to perform the song "I'm a-Bringing Up the Family," which Luby had tried to appropriate. Burkan now defended crossdressing as a respectable art form dating back to Shakespeare, much as Julian Eltinge had done. The counselor even indicated, no doubt to Julian Eltinge's horror, that he might call the famed impersonator himself as a witness. "It was not the play that was complained of," argued attorney Burkan in Judge Morris Koenig's court, "but rather the female impersonations which the police said dealt with sex perversion. From the earliest Shakespearian days there have been female impersonations on the stage and males have been called upon countless times to portray female roles."[37] Eltinge's name, as well as those of Bert Savoy and Jay Brennan, came up repeatedly during *voir dire* to find out what prospective jurors thought about female-impersonating. When Burkan asked a potential juror if he'd ever seen Savoy and Brennan, the latter said he didn't know, to which Burkan retorted, "You don't know the half of it." The case was a public spectacle, part humorous, part terrifying, collapsing female-impersonating and same-sex eroticism into a tangled, vulnerable target. Julian Eltinge's entire career had been predicated on keeping those phenomena apart. In the end, Mae West, charged with the difficult-to-prove crime of "parading degeneracy," denied all double-entendres and accusations of impropriety. The jury deadlocked, leaving the defendant free to go. But, as biographer Marybeth Hamilton notes, "female impersonation was not." The winds blew chillier. "I'm broke," Eltinge confessed to *Los Angeles Times* gossip columnist Grace Kingsley in late 1932 as he struggled to relaunch a scaled-down tour of *Fads & Fancies of the Fair Sex*. "The gradual decline of the female impersonator," syndicated columnist O. O. McIntyre wrote a few years later, "has come to a full stop. Such performers cannot be booked save in remote sections of honky-tonks." A classiness that once attended the art had vanished, the public no longer approving of "these androgynous antics." For Julian Eltinge, it was now just about survival.[38]

* * *

By the early 1930s, it was plainer to see that structural changes—in the economy, in social values, in politics—were well underway. Not only was Julian Eltinge struggling, even A. H. Woods, who had survived the turbulence of 1929–1930 relatively well, was left devastated by the utter bottoming of financial markets in 1932–1933. Lighting a cigar at his desk, Woods snapped at a reporter, "You're here to say, 'Well, Mr. Woods, aren't you *ever* going to produce another hit?'" If you ask that, explained the producer, *I'll toss you out onto Forty-Second Street*. "I was just wondering," the journalist said delicately, "if your season isn't one that might be called quiet." "Quiet!" bellowed the frustrated impresario. "It's not only quiet, it's lousy," he added, kicking

240   BEAUTIFUL

over a bronze clock given him by actress Hazel Dawn—once rumored in the press to be Julian Eltinge's fiancée—and exhaling a cloud of tobacco smoke. You could hardly blame Al Woods for being irritable. The Eltinge Theater turned into a seamy burlesque house in 1931 until a city ordinance led it to become the Laff Movie grindhouse in 1942, a decaying hulk whose frescoed renderings of its namesake were covered by grime and, in any case, hidden in a perpetually darkened cinema. In every way possible, the Julian Eltinge Theatre was decaying. When Woods died, in 1951, a longtime friend, actress Marie Doro, had to pay for his well-attended funeral.[39]

Nor could the human Julian Eltinge be blamed for bitterness. Social reality and the passage of time had undermined his lifelong business model. His world was getting smaller. People were done being tolerant for now and for decades to come. Rather than rage against the machine, like labor radicals or iconoclastic artists, though, our protagonist doubled down on a life-long strategy of conformism. He continued to criticize women who refused conventional social roles. "If I had a wife who came to breakfast with cold cream on her face, her hair in curlers, and a boudoir cap on, I would divorce her after breakfast!" he wrote in a guest column for a Canadian paper. "A woman must be immaculate," he insisted, "Morning, afternoon, and night." Marriages often failed, in his view, because women didn't dress for their husbands the way men dressed for their jobs. Everything was a transaction, a contract, which inadvertently suggested that his own profession, house-wifery, and prostitution were all in essence quite similar.[40]

Perhaps too he was feeling the pain of a life unlived, even within existing social constraints. In the mid-1930s, the impersonation artist befriended a young couple in Hollywood, John D. Lawrence and Marvel Retter. The two were said to have met when Utah-born Lawrence was passing through Marvel's home state of Kansas in 1933 on his way to the World's Fair in Chicago. Lawrence worked, variously, as an actor, show business execu-tive, and, rather ironically given Julian Eltinge's childhood, cartographer of "The Americana Treasure Map," which disclosed supposedly undiscovered treasures located in the US Southwest and Mexico. Eltinge offered the couple his Villa Capistrano for their wedding and walked the bride, whose father had died in the 1918 flu pandemic that nearly killed Eltinge himself, to the altar. Marvel wore a pink chiffon dress rather than a traditional bride's white, and the impersonation artist secured a Tin Pan Alley composer to score the ceremony. By 1936, John and Marvel Lawrence, who honeymooned at Eltinge's Rancho down in San Diego County, were living at the Villa

Capistrano, Marvel helping the actor and his mother manage their affairs. Judy Retter, a niece of Marvel's, said she believes Julian Eltinge was gay. Daniel Miller, the investigative reporter for the *Los Angeles Times* who wrote about the Lawrence treasure map and interviewed Judy Retter, suggests too that Marvel was a "beard" for her husband and the Villa Capistrano's owner with whom he was sexually involved. Marvel would later have a recurring bit part as "Nice Dress Nellie" on the hit TV series *The Andy Griffith Show* (CBS, 1960–1968).[41]

As the king lost his crown, so too his palace. The performer had to sell his beloved Villa Capistrano and put its extensive furnishings up for sale. The Persian rugs, the French furniture, and the Sheffield Silver—all of it had to go. Beverly Wilshire galleries held an estate sale in the spring of 1935. Like other embittered souls feeling adrift, Eltinge lashed out at another popular target: the government. Influenced by William Randolph Hearst's promise to spend less time in tax-heavy California, Eltinge insisted he'd follow suit. "Everything I have is for sale," said the actor (who still owned the ranch at Alpine); "I can't stand California taxes." Someone richer might have escaped to a tax haven like Arizona or Switzerland. But the truth was, if he was going to sustain himself, Julian Eltinge needed to be in Los Angeles or New York, where a few stages and audiences would still want him. All told, he had reportedly burned through some $3,000,000 in personal wealth over the years.[42]

With the proceeds from Villa Capistrano, the actor was able to purchase a modest home at 11284 Sunshine Terrace overlooking the San Fernando Valley, just north of Laurel Canyon's sprawling crags and gullies. True, he didn't have a semi-Moorish palazzo anymore. But word was, Errol Flynn was planning to build a place nearby so the neighborhood had something going for it. Eltinge tried to retain ownership of several lots adjacent to his former homestead, saying he'd sold them by accident and no doubt hoping they would skyrocket in value once the economy turned around (which it would not during his lifetime.) His mother, Julia, had been in charge of many facets of his financial life so, he averred, he wasn't aware of all the clauses and codicils of the Villa Capistrano sale. "I am very stupid, being an actor," he confessed, "dazed by it all," meaning the money stuff and, it seemed, a lot more. One of his pithy "Eltingegrams" had long ago advised, "A lean compromise is better than a fat lawsuit." But the attorney couple who bought his property had no interest in compromise and may have crafted a contract meant to slip some points cleverly by the actor and his mother. To this day, the lot

242   BEAUTIFUL

that holds Seven Terraces, the elegantly landscaped fountain assemblage that deposits water into a narrow, down-stepped channel amid cacti and aloe, remains in the possession of the Villa Capistrano's next-door neighbor. The owner, however, lets the current owner of the Villa (who is unrelated to the 1930s buyers) visit the lovely Seven Terraces via a formal arrangement—a compromise Julian Eltinge couldn't quite manage.[43]

* * *

Things weren't faring much better down in San Diego County. The Depression hit bookings hard, and a fire had scorched several acres and threatened buildings after a motorist tossed a match out their window onto the parched ground. Sierra Vista Rancho was never able to turn a profit. The property, once valued at $300,000, was put on the auction block for $40,000. It was unclear if it could fetch even that.[44]

His patience finally at an end, Julian Eltinge demanded a "straight role."[45] He beseeched A. H. Woods, but there was little the devastated producer could do. Then in 1935, he got his wish. It wouldn't be a grand production in New York, London, or Stockholm. But it was something . . . *maybe*? Eltinge got a costarring role in *Children of the Rich*, a satire about New York's moneyed set that played at Elsner's Little Theater in Hollywood, a venue founded by former Broadway director and sometime Noël Coward collaborator Edward Elsner. The run would be short, from late 1935 to early 1936. The longtime specialty player, now a legitimate thespian, fared well, cited as "an actor of power and delightful comic propensities," in the role of aging ne'er-do-well Uncle Remy. Julian Eltinge had finally been permitted to play a man. No skirts. No bathing suits. No faddish songs or snake dances. No rapid, backstage changes. No faking it as a Harvard grad talking about Wall Street stocks. *Children of the Rich* was over by late February 1936.[46] Eltinge was briefly cast in *The Adventures of Frank Merriwell*, a motion-picture serial about a college athlete in search of his missing father, but lost the gig. He was also briefly connected to what would become the movie titled *Klondike Annie*, a Mae West vehicle, but that too evaporated. He'd gotten to play the straight man in a proper drama with other professional actors. Finally. Then it was over.[47]

The once-famous impersonator retired to a domestic life. He watered his lawn. He and his neighbors petitioned the city to get connected to the sewage lines. He even gave a few tips to a lad named Wallace Palmer, son of a prominent Bay Area family, who was eager to learn about the increasingly clandestine art of female impersonation.[48]

Even if he had little desire to practice his craft save for the money, Julian Eltinge found himself nonetheless targeted by anti-drag/antigay forces. In 1940, a Los Angeles police commission led by John Kingsley sought to bar female-impersonation in nightclubs, taverns, and all public venues. The Kingsley faction had instead to settle for strict regulations, including one making drag artists obtain special work permits, which the commission promised would be "hard to get." In some cases, artists were required to pass a psychological exam, a "character analysis"—Krafft-Ebing's and Ellis's theorizing rarefied, re-engineered, and lethalized. Authorities further demanded that impersonators keep a distance of four feet from customers, and also outlawed "B-girls," young women—or cisgender males dressed as them—who solicited drinks for patrons and got a portion of the tab. Vice crusaders often used existing, more easily enforceable liquor laws to suppress drag and gay life, believing that many gay men and crossdressers earned side money as B-girl impersonators. A 1911 report by the Chicago Vice Commission found "supposed" women brokering booze at saloons and casinos, often persuading their woozy customers (without too much effort in many cases, it may be presumed) to pay for sex in nearby, private rooms. A few clever B-girls and B-boys in Los Angeles relocated to otherwise harmless soda fountains where they trafficked in "spiked" colas and shakes. (Some venues starting serving proper meals to avoid restrictions faced by drinking establishments, thus inaugurating the drag brunch and, quite possibly, drag dinner theatre.) Even Commissioner Kingsley admitted it would be difficult for the cops to prevent all that. As is well known by now, the New York State Liquor Authority used its muscle to shut down "homosexual haunts" well into the 1960s. In retrospect, this oughtn't be surprising given that the New York Academy of Medicine, which at the time considered the "aggressive homosexual" a public health menace, in 1964 reaffirmed homosexuality as "indeed an illness." What historian George Chauncey labels "the exclusion of homosexuality from the public sphere in the 1930s" had metastasized to a breaking point, as the Stonewall Riots would make clear before the 1960s were out.[49]

Things had gone too far, even for the politically avoidant Julian Eltinge. Cracking down on gay rathskellers and pansy-crazers was one thing. But when the artist himself was denied a permit to practice a trade he had practically invented, he demanded his day in court. In January 1940, Eltinge had been barred from working at a "known hangout for women who hold

244   BEAUTIFUL

women's hands and for men who hold men's hands." A few weeks later, he emceed a floorshow at the Hollywood Rendezvous club titled *The Spirit of the Gay Nineties*. (At the time, "gay" was not yet mainstream parlance for same-sex romance, though the term was widely used within queer/homosexual subculture.) The show's closure and ensuing penalties resulted in the entertainer's once again going before the Kingsley commission. It was a clever PR stunt, Julian Eltinge knowing full well that an eager press would be watching and reporting. "We thought we were to come before the commission again," said Anna Block who ran the Rendezvous. Commissioner Van M. Griffith reproached both Block and Eltinge, "I think you have had enough publicity out of this case to keep your business running for a couple of months," and ordered the matter concluded.[50] Eltinge briefly resorted to performances at the White Horse, described as "a sleazy Hollywood nightclub with a gay clientele," in which he stood next to a rack of his famous costumes as he sang and spoke. In the end, though, Eltinge got a special concession. He was no social rebel, and appearing before more judges and commissions was simply not in his DNA. By March 1940, he had been permitted to resume the drag based on his history of "clean artistry." It was a small reward for a lifetime of the most strenuous reinforcement of "the illusion of gender," to use words Judith Butler would write half a century later.[51]

* * *

At long last, Julian Eltinge allowed to play another role he'd also pretty much avoided his entire life: himself. The 1940 movie *If I Had My Way*, starring Bing Crosby and child actress Gloria Jean, featured a number of Broadway and vaudeville old-timers cast as themselves. Eltinge, his old friend and pseudo-love interest Blanche Ring, echoed their former glory, along with two-a-day veterans Trixie Friganza and Grace LaRue. A bit like a smartly dialogued Disney film, *If I Had My Way* was meant to appeal both to youthful audiences and the "oldsters." The plot centered on an orphan played by Gloria Jean who is brought to New York after her father plunges to his death while constructing the Golden Gate Bridge. A rich uncle rejects her, but a couple of former vaudevillians take the child in. In a related development, other retired two-a-day artists join forces to save a failing Swedish restaurant by turning it into a nightspot called the Tin Type Club. Vaudeville as a workable business model was as much a fantasy by this time as the notion of vaudevillians putting aside individual ambitions for the greater good. *The New Yorker*'s John

Mosher felt the picture suffered from a "fogginess" and that Crosby and his youthful costar were not in their best form. Mosher wrote that Julian Eltinge had "matured into a somewhat archiepiscopal type," a comment so coded it may reveal more about the author than the subject. It must have been hard for Julian Eltinge to watch the inimitable Bing Crosby sop up the spotlight while he, Blanche Ring, and the other "old-time vaudevillians" posed like dime museum effigies.[52]

Much like vaudeville, the artist's career was in its self-referential, backward-looking phase, obscuring recent ups and (mostly) downs in a nostalgic haze. Julian Eltinge's final gig was not really much different from one he might have had thirty-five years earlier: dressing up as a woman and singing songs in a variety show. Impresario and lyricist Billy Rose, famous for cowriting "It's Only a Paper Moon" with Harold Arlen and Yip Harburg, coaxed the impersonator back to New York to appear at his recently opened Billy Rose's Diamond Horseshoe, a nightspot on West 46th Street, in a revue called *Nights of Gladness*. Amid a worldwide depression and a war that looked like it might end with fascists taking over the planet, *Nights of Gladness* scented of "halcyon" days a quarter-century earlier, a brighter time when stars like Blanche Ring and Eddie Leonard—and Julian Eltinge—ruled the stage. The job would not only mark his final jog back East, but would also turn out to be the artist's last effort in a lifelong cycle of reducing as he shed 44 lbs. down to a stage-worthy 170. At least he'd only have to be onstage for ten minutes each show. Eltinge, nearing sixty, was back to being "one of the most interesting 'girls' still around," according to women's issues columnist Alice Hughes. "So here I am at the Diamond Horse Shoe [*sic*], on Broadway, right where I was 30 years ago," he remarked. New York film and culture critic Ben Crisler, one of the last to interview Eltinge, noticed a double-chin and crow's feet betraying an aging, and thus decidedly human, visage. The years had dissolved a carefully wrought porcelain mask that separated player from role to a degree that no other artist of his day had quite equaled.[53]

Legend has it that one day, the impersonation artist walked a few blocks south to the decaying burlesque house, now called the Empire, that once bore his name and drew bustling crowds of respectable theatergoers hungry for a lively comedy or a gripping melodrama. He sidled up to the box office and told the cashier he only had a twenty-dollar bill, which the cashier was reluctant to change. "I am Julian Eltinge," he explained, "The theater was named after me. Would you trust me for the 35 cents admission?" She would not. The king left his onetime nominal palace, an amusement hall that would soon

246 BEAUTIFUL

proffer a nearly endless stream of junky pictures including comical shorts and two-reelers with titles like *Mutiny on the Body* and *Mickey's Trailer*, the latter starring a well-known, androgynous cartoon mouse.[54]

He took an apartment in an Art Deco building at 333 West 57th Street, which, despite declining personal fortunes, he managed to decorate sumptuously, perhaps expectable for a veteran junkyard-hunter with a masterful design sense. The job at Billy Rose's club began in the fall of 1940 and ran into February of the following year. A few weeks later, on March 7, 1941, Eltinge fell ill with a kidney ailment. The artist asked a friend who was with him, onetime minstrel actor Earl Benham—now working as a celebrity tailor and stylist—to call their mutual friend of old, Jacques Pierre, one of Eltinge's former producers and now a theatrical manager living in Los Angeles. Eltinge wanted Pierre to get word to his mother who was living on what remained of the Sierra Vista Rancho at Alpine, that he was not doing well. As Benham explained the situation over the phone to Pierre, a physician who had been tending to the ailing, fifty-nine-year-old female-impersonation artist emerged from Eltinge's room and informed them that his patient had died.[55]

Some claimed Julian Eltinge's kidney troubles resulted from years of abusing diet pills and forcing himself into corsets. It was also later rumored that he had aided Death with a dose of sleeping pills. It surely couldn't have helped that the impersonator had long been a heavy drinker, endured life-threatening bouts of flu and appendicitis, and may have also suffered a stroke. Humorous though it may sound, Eltinge had also been badly injured in the early 1930s after being gored in the gut by a swordfish. He was out fishing with his friend, Dr. Earl O'Donnell, and wealthy socialite and boat-racing enthusiast Lazard Lippman on board Lippman's yacht off Point Vicente, not far from the San Pedro naval station where Eltinge had met and befriended Fred FitzGerald in 1918. The fish, which also injured O'Donnell, impaled Eltinge in the abdomen as he tried to haul it onboard. The affair was played up for laughs but the actor was hurt seriously enough to need "a major abdominal operation." How much this may have contributed to Julian Eltinge's demise will never be known. Some wounds fester over the years, even those inflicted by recalcitrant swordfish. After a viewing period for his body at the elegant Walter B. Cooke Funeral Chapel on Manhattan's Upper West Side, services were held at the historic Church of the Transfiguration in Manhattan's Chelsea neighborhood. Other theatrical luminaries, denied final rites at fancy churches that ill-judged the acting trade, had had funerals

THE VELVET INQUISITION   247

there including nineteenth-century acting giant (and brother of Abraham Lincoln's assassin) Edwin Booth, who had famously co-nicknamed it (along with famed thespian Joseph Jeffeson III) "The Little Church Round the Corner." The Rev. Dr. Randolph Ray and the rector, the Rev. Dr. Harold Le Moyne, of the Little Church officiated. But this last public event of Julian Eltinge's life was in fact a Lambs production. Some three hundred attendees, the deceased's recent costar Blanche Ring among them, watched pallbearers including William Gaxton and Victor Moore tend to their beloved, deceased fellow Lamb. The artist was cremated in Westchester County, just north of the city, and his ashes returned to California, the place where he seemed most hopeful, and most himself, whatever that was exactly. Julian Eltinge's earthly remains reside in the massive Great Mausoleum at Forest Lawn cemetery in Glendale, in the Columbarium of Rest, Niche 7310. But only family members are allowed to visit. Which means Julian Eltinge has a great deal of privacy for the remainder of eternity.[56]

* * *

In October 1938, the actor drew up a will directing that his entire estate go to his mother unless she predeceased him, in which case it was to be split between the Lambs Club and any legal heirs. Julia Dalton, now seventy-nine, thus became his sole inheritor barring any other claimants who might crawl out of the woodwork. At the time of his death, however, the artist's only significant asset was the ranch at Alpine or what was left of it, estimated now worth a measly $10,000. Julia Dalton had neither means nor interest in maintaining the place, so Benjamin T. Weinstein, Eltinge's lawyer, hatched an idea. The attorney asked the Lambs Club if it might, "[t]hrough your good offices," find a way to "dispose of the property," presumably by selling it for a pittance, and/or "make some arrangements for the maintenance of Mrs. Dalton." The ranchland was debt-free, it was true, but it didn't generate any income. Might the theatrical insiders' club therefore somehow find a way to help out a posthumous Lamb's aging mother? Lambs' treasurer Ralph Trier was at a loss. Both flattered and irritated, the treasurer explained there was little the club could do. Responding to Weinstein, Trier suggested that, "considering the late Julian Eltinge's great popularity throughout the entire country," maybe *you* could advertise the ranchland and attract a buyer; perhaps that "might bring some results." After all, there were at least a few people out there who recalled how a young man appeared on the American stage seemingly from nowhere forty years ago, and he didn't just *play* women but *became* them. Magically. Those who saw Julian Eltinge in his heyday, at a time when countless American men were dragging-up, had scratched their heads and wondered how it was possible for a man so convincingly to impersonate a woman that, for a few minutes, it seemed as if both man and woman could emanate from a single soul.[57]

# # #

Epilogue

So, Who Was Julian Eltinge Anyway? "Culture" is, if nothing else, a huge, interlocking web of agreements. We agree—or are urged to agree—on who is a man and who is a woman, and even that there will be such things as "man" and "woman." Anyone who violates an important agreement, particularly an agreement that connects to many others, usually gets punished. It also appears obvious that some people and groups have much greater say in big agreements, rendering those "agreements" closer to enforced rules. Some, perhaps many, as Freud observed, will be discontent, forced to surrender "possibilities of happiness."[1]

We have glimpsed how Julian Eltinge's life provides a lens through which to view struggles over important cultural agreements—about sex, gender, binarism, masculinity, normality, work, and so forth—as they coalesced and shifted in his day, forming the seeds of our own ongoing controversies and contortions. At present, a wave of not only anti-trans but, more to the point, anti-drag/anti-impersonation laws are being proposed or passed in many locales in the United States. To many, particularly those pushing the restrictions, something big but hard-to-define feels at stake. Fears of inversion abound once again.[2]

Similarly revealing are the ways in which various parties—journalists, popular authors, entertainers, and scholars—have represented Julian Eltinge's story, giving us a sense of changing cultural metrics from his day to ours. That Eltinge has let us know so little about his thoughts, wishes, and noncurated "private" life allowed the impersonator to become a screen onto which many judgments, speculations, and assertions have been projected over the years. But Eltinge's failure or refusal to tell us more about who he "really" was also misses the performer's most important trait: an intuitive, almost naïve understanding that surface and depth are inseparable in a marketplace culture like ours, and that trying to parse one from the other—via medico-scientific study, legal interrogation, exploratory writing, and so on—is a frustratingly circular, no-win scenario. Eltinge, mostly apolitical with a leavening of libertarianism, nonetheless brilliantly laid bare the extent to which the surface

Beautiful. Andrew L. Erdman, Oxford University Press. © Oxford University Press 2024.
DOI: 10.1093/9780197696361.003.0011

Figure E.1 Eltinge's publicity machine was almost as impressive as his female-impersonating skills, churning out scads of promotional cards, autographed shots, and character reproductions. Many exist in archives and private collections today, even as we have virtually nothing in the way of diaries, letters, or other autobiographical materials. Perhaps the preponderance of promotional literature and paucity of direct disclosure tells us what we really need to know about the man's inner life.
Credit: *Laurence Senelick Collection*.

is the depth and vice versa. As such, he fit well into an era shaped by P. T. Barnum, B. F. Keith, Sears and Roebuck, Henry Ford, and Teddy Roosevelt. Even those who sought to look below the surface and explain how the depth ultimately wins out—Freud, Ellis, Hirschfield, Weber, and others—could not help, ultimately, also revealing that *surface* and *depth* are not inseparable binaries but concepts to which our limited, human thinking must resort.

* * *

The discourse on Julian Eltinge has shifted notably in the years since his death, at times dividing into identifiable, sometimes overlapping camps. During the conservative 1940s and 1950s, Eltinge was barely spoken of in the press and popular writing. He was, after all, a vestige of an antediluvian era. Eltinge was someone who prospered in old-time vaudeville, an art form that had all but vanished. But postwar, midcentury commentators also wished to forget, or never knew, or never *wanted to know*, the extreme popularity of male drag shows, college musicals, womanless weddings, professional female impersonation, and the quarterbacks, wrestlers, and soldiers who delighted in skirting-up. In the early 1920s, Halsey Mills became the toast of Dartmouth as a "singer, eccentric dancer, and impersonator of female roles" in college theatricals. Mills won further acclaim as a backup quarterback, making Ivy League rival Harvard work extra hard to eke out a pyrrhic twelve-to-three victory. "Now he is basking in a double spotlight, that of the gridiron as well as the stage," according to a news report at the time.[3] It would be difficult to find similarly warm public regard in, say, 1950 (though not impossible). Mainstream American culture wished to shut the door on that section of its past, and that is where Julian Eltinge ever-so-artfully dwelt. Vaudeville memoirist and amateur historian Joe Laurie Jr. typified what was said about Eltinge during the 1940s and 1950s, setting the tone for decades to come, by reminding us that the impersonator was "never offensive." Laurie and others like him distilled the most sanitized, conservative interpretation of the performer, the image Eltinge himself cocreated with his handlers, the press, and the industry. "The only unobjectionable act of [its] kind . . . Not suggestive in word, action," wrote H. A. Daniels, manager of Keith's Philadelphia, in a 1905 report to company executives.[4]

With the liberalization of the 1960s, some began to utter Julian Eltinge's name differently. There was the same admiration of his artistic skills, but also room for an assumed homosexuality, a kind of liberal tolerance that softens

252   BEAUTIFUL

earlier blows and stretches things a little yet keeps the basic agreements intact. By the early 1960s, George Jessel could simultaneously *out* Eltinge as a "fairy" while insisting that the impersonator's sexual choices were "nobody's business." Julian Eltinge's and his fellow impersonators' potential homosexuality was becoming tolerated, a private matter to be sure, but somehow *essential to know* if one were to understand the man and his art. During the 1970s, historian Robert Toll argued that many of Eltinge's fans wondered whether impersonation artists indeed "were homosexuals and/or transvestites" offstage. Two decades later, famed entertainer Milton Berle said publicly that he believed Julian Eltinge to have been gay, calling Eltinge a "straight man" but only when it came to comedy scenes. (Berle made a similar, mildly homophobic joke about Bert Savoy.) By that time, the mid-1990s, being gay had coalesced into a distinct "identity" with cultural and political meaning, while at the same time becoming semi-normalized, a quality more worthy of understanding than censure, at least in liberal circles. But it now seemed quite important to determine whether or not Julian Eltinge was a "homosexual."[5]

In the post-Stonewall era, and particularly in the wake of the AIDS epidemic of the 1980s and 1990s, it also became essential to those in the LGBTQ community to know whether Julian Eltinge was gay, either to resuscitate him as a lost icon or to denounce him as a traitor who constantly tried to pass as a "respectable, confirmed bachelor."[6] The very titles of Eve Golden's 1995 *TheaterWeek* feature, "Julian Eltinge: The Queen of Old Broadway," and Brooks Peters's 1998 article "Gay Deceiver" in *Out* magazine reflected such inquiry. Christopher Connelly's profile of Eltinge in *Etc.* magazine, "The King of Drag," positions the actor as presumptively gay and heavily closeted, always busy "quelling any rumors of homosexuality." A more recent, apparently self-published, scrapbook-like biography by F. Michael Moore, *Julian Eltinge: Drag Diva of Broadway, Vaudeville & Hollywood* (2020), continues in this vein, resuscitating the artist as a pioneer of modern "gay and drag entertainments," though also linking him to a tradition "as old as theatre itself." (Julian Eltinge would of course have been horrified at the former and delighted at the latter.) Those outside an emergent LGBTQ community continued the liberal quest to name homosexuality and transvestism as such, not pejoratively but certainly not using what might now be considered a *queer* perspective. For instance, we have seen how a scholar in the 1990s sought "strong proof" of the performer's presumed homosexuality rather than relying on clichés like lifelong bachelorhood or enjoying a close relationship with his mother. The 2012 edition of the widely used reference book

Encyclopedia of Vaudeville considers the matter important enough to conclude that "there was never a public hint that [Julian Eltinge] was homosexual." This reinforces the more important idea that knowing someone's sexual desires and behaviors had become crucial, a viable "object of analysis" in theorist Michel Foucault's reckoning, to understanding their work.[7]

The coalescing of an "out" gay identity, permitted by the 1990s (especially with lifesaving medical advances that effectively turned HIV into a chronic, manageable condition for many), of course, coincided with a massive new wave of thinking about gender: Was it inherent? Performed? And how did it function, exactly? Judith Butler was and continues to be probably the most famous and influential thinker on the subject. But others have explored the ways in which crossdressing provokes primal, social anxiety by pointing out the inherently unstable nature of "man" and "woman." In her widely read 1992 book *Vested Interests*, Marjorie Garber, who calls Julian Eltinge the "most celebrated female impersonator of his time," explores the connections between blackface minstrelsy and female impersonation in the vaudeville era. For Garber, Eltinge's portrayals raised the "specter of transvestism" just as surely as his more openly inverted contemporaries and/or Japanese *onnagata* artists, a centuries-old tradition from the Noh and Kabuki stages. All such art, in Garber's view, inaugurates a "crisis" of trying to organize gender according to "category."[8] It has fallen to subsequent thinkers and writers to explain, *how*, exactly. Crossdressing, particularly in so exacting a manner as Julian Eltinge, clearly has the ability to stimulate strong feelings. But why do some find it pleasurable and others threatening?

* * *

In our present, fraught moment, the liberal-tolerance approach has been challenged not only by recurrent reactionary voices but more significantly by calls for "queer representation." To put it perhaps too simply, the queer framework questions not just gender binaries but the overall structure of social and cultural hierarchies, examining how they become enforced and whom they benefit (and harm). This provides a broader, more spacious perspective in which to ask questions such as, "Was Julian Eltinge gay?" because it simultaneously *questions the question itself*. As queer theory pioneer Eve Kosofsky Sedgwick asks: what if we lived in world where so many agreements, categories, and concepts were looser, giving people greater options to live their lives in bespoke, authentic fashion, or at least provide a better shot at it, rather

254 BEAUTIFUL

than forcing so many rigid notions like gender, sexuality, family, and so on somehow to "line up tidily with each other"?[9] In a sense, Julian Eltinge was a master of making categories line up tidily, responding perfectly to what culture was not so much asking but rather, insisting of him.

The desire to make Julian Eltinge a more broadly iconoclastic, proto-queer artist is an understandable outgrowth or at least correlate of such impulses. David Hajdu and John Carey's erudite graphic novel, *A Revolution in Three Acts: The Radical Vaudeville of Bert Williams, Eva Tanguay, and Julian Eltinge*, tells the story of three famous performers who each challenged cultural norms in their own respectively impactful ways. Hajdu and Carey depict Julian Eltinge as a complicated figure, one who reinforced a "feminine ideal" while betraying the "malleability of gender" as few artists could. Eltinge's art, in other words, was radical, even if he himself was not.[10] The UK's Sky History channel website, like many other mainstream media outlets in the era of monetized Gay Pride, used a similar approach in recuperating Julian Eltinge, publishing an old, colorized publicity shot of him as a Bathing Beauty within an article titled "A Brief but Glamorous History of Drag," part of the network's 2023 "LGBT+ History Month" celebration.[11]

Maybe the least fallible way we have to interpret Julian Eltinge is in the context he understood best: the theatre. The writings of Laurence Senelick, emeritus chair of the Tufts University theatre department, takes such a tack. Senelick, who sees gender-constructionist philosophy as predating Judith Butler, notably in the writings of sociologist Erving Goffman (1922–1982) and the plays of Swedish dramatist August Strindberg (1849–1912), believes that Julian Eltinge's clever guises, onstage and off-, do indeed shed light on "the nexus between popular entertainment and the social construction of gender." But for Senelick, as for others theatre artists and devotees, the stage is a world unto itself. Yes, it exists in a larger cultural context. Yes, it draws on that context, both shaping and reflecting it. But by its very nature, it manages to slip from our white-knuckled grip on reality, usually to our great relief. Socialist playwright Bertolt Brecht famously called upon the theatre to reshape the political and economic world by presenting the "natural" as "alien" in a way only the theatre may. For Senelick, the theatre, like an artist's canvas, provides a space where wishes, ideas, and impulses can become real in a powerful, embodied manner, engaging our perceptions, sensations, thoughts, and projections. In the theatre, we may glimpse how we wrestle with an illusion called gender or gain insight into the arbitrary nature of class division. But we can also assuredly gaze upon "something never seen on land or sea" and marvel at our ability to create, making space for our inchoate and unformed impulses to wear masks, costumes, and makeup and so enact wishes, fears, and fantasies in dreamlike, Freudian fashion. The rise of the titular Carrie Meeber in Theodore Dreiser's 1900 novel *Sister Carrie*, from sweatshop worker to celebrated actress, reflects an understanding that the performing arts may liberate us, if only between the rise and fall of the curtain. "Don't you think it's rather fine to be an actor?" muses Carrie. At about the same time Dreiser penned those words, a talented young man named William Dalton was toying with the stage name Julian Eltinge because he already very much knew the answer.[12]

# # #

Notes

Introduction

1. [The description of his act is an idealized composite for purposes of illustration, drawn chiefly from sources listed in this and next few Notes.] "Chatter about Theatrical Folk," *Buffalo Enquirer*, May 26, 1905, 2; "Albee on Vaudeville in 1912–13," *New York Clipper*, October 5, 1912, 10; "E. F. Albee, Co-Founder of Vaudeville," *New York Times*, March 23, 1930, ix: 6; "Keith's Boston Programme," *New York Dramatic Mirror*, February 20, 1904, 18.

2. "In Woman's Gorgeous Costumes," *St. Paul Globe* (MN), April 27, 1902, 16; Lois W. Banner, *American Beauty* (New York: Knopf, 1983), 154–155; Laurence Senelick, "Lady and the Tramp: Drag Differentials in the Progressive Era," in *Gender in Performance: The Presentation of Difference in the Performing Arts*, ed. Laurance Senelick (Hanover, NH: University Press of New England, 1992), 29; University of Iowa, Special Collections, Keith/Albee Collection, 11/28/1904–8/28/1905 (237), Box: 4, 183, 183a; Themista [pen name of: Wilshire, Ida], "He Fascinates the Women in His Feminine Finery," *Boston Globe*, March 1, 1901, 7; "Manages Skirts with Sang Froid," *Buffalo Courier*, November 18, 1907, 5; "Amusement Notes," *Brooklyn Daily Eagle*, July 30, 1907, 4 [22]; "Julian Eltinge," *Variety* October 12, 1907, 9; "Harry Lehr Has a Rival among the Boston 400," *Philadelphia Inquirer Sunday Magazine*, July 28, 1901, 37–38.

3. John Kemble and Lester Keith, "I'm Getting Fond of You," published in *Marion Daily Mirror* (OH), August 8, 1908, 10; "Keith's Theater: Vaudeville," *Boston Evening Transcript*, February 19, 1907, 13; University of Iowa, Special Collections, Keith/Albee Collection, 11/28/1904–8/28/1905 (237), Box: 4, 84, 84a; "Harry Lehr Has a Rival among the Boston 400"; Joe Laurie Jr., *Vaudeville: From the Honky-tonks to the Palace* (New York: Henry Holt & Co., 1953), 54–56, 251; "The Vaudeville Theaters," *Boston Evening Transcript*, December 7, 1909, 17; "How a Man Makes Himself a Beautiful Woman," *Chicago Tribune*, September 27, 1908, 48; W. F. A. [only name given], "Whitney Hall: Vaudeville," *Boston Evening Transcript*, May 22, 1901, 21.

4. "Take a Dip in the Ocean," from playscript of *The Fascinating Widow* by Otto Hauerbach (a.k.a. Otto Harbach), Otto Harbach Papers, Series III—Scripts, *T-Mss 1993-038, Box 11a, NYPL-PA-BRTC; "Brilliant Beginning of Fall Season of Refined Vaudeville," *Pittsburgh Post*, September 1, 1907, 30; University of Iowa, Special Collections, Keith/Albee Collection, 11/28/1904–8/28/1905 (237), Box 4: 84, 84a, 183a;

5. University of Iowa, Special Collections, Keith/Albee Collection, 11/28/1904–8/28/1905 (237), Box 4: 183a.

6. "Opening Night at Theaters," *Washington Post*, March 12, 1907, 5; University of Iowa, Special Collections, Keith/Albee Collection, Box 5: 9/4/1905–4/23/1906, 140; "Hammerstein's Roof," *Variety*, June 13, 1908, 15; Marybeth Hamilton, "*When I'm*

258 NOTES

Bad, I'm Better": Mae West, Sex, and American Entertainment (Berkeley: University of California Press, 1997), 141.

7. "Boston Has a Harry Lehr, Too! His Name is Julian Eltinge," *Boston Sunday Post*, August 11, 1901, 13; University of Iowa, Special Collections, Keith/Albee Collection, 11/28/1904–8/28/1905 (237), Box 4: 179; Themista, "He Fascinates the Women in His Feminine Finery"; James F. Wilson, "The Somewhat Different Diva: Impersonation, Ambivalence and the Musical Comedy Performances of Julian Eltinge," *Studies in Musical Theatre* 12, no. 1 (2018): 10.

8. Themista [pen name of: Wilshire, Ida], "Julian Eltinge: The Woman Impersonator," *Daily Province* (Vancouver, BC), January 29, 1910, 11 [127]; Themista, "He Fascinates the Women in His Feminine Finery"; University of Iowa, Special Collections, Keith/ Albee Collection, 11/28/1904–8/28/1905 (237), Box 4: 95.

9. Hilton Dresden, "L.A. Has Its Own History of Anti-Drag Laws," *Hollywood Reporter*, April 14, 2023, https://www.hollywoodreporter.com/news/politics-news/l-a-hist ory-anti-drag-laws-1235371248/.

10. Vern L. Bullough and Bonnie Bullough, *Cross Dressing, Sex, and Gender* (Philadelphia: University of Pennsylvania Press, 1993), 213; George Chauncey, *Gay New York: Gender, Urban Culture, and the Making of the Gay Male World, 1890–1940* (New York: Basic Books, 1994/2019), 26; University of Iowa, Special Collections, Keith/Albee Collection, 11/28/1904–8/28/1905 (237), Box: 4, 84, 84a; Jonathan Ned Katz, *The Invention of Heterosexuality* (New York: Dutton, 1995), 7, 55.

11. David Hajdu and John Carey, *A Revolution in Three Acts: The Radical Vaudeville of Bert Williams, Eva Tanguay, and Julian Eltinge* (New York: Columbia University Press, 2021); Bullough and Bullough, *Cross Dressing, Sex, and Gender*, 235; Wilson, "The Somewhat Different Diva," 10; Kathleen B. Casey, *The Prettiest Girl on Stage Is a Man: Race and Gender Benders in American Vaudeville* (Knoxville: University of Tennessee Press, 2015), 56, xxiii; Sophie Tucker, *Some of these Days: The Autobiography of Sophie Tucker* (Garden City, NY: Garden City Publishing, 1946), 1, 104.

12. Armond Fields, *Sophie Tucker: The First Lady of Show Business* (Jefferson, NC: McFarland & Co., 2003), 140; "Harry Lehr Has a Rival among the Boston 400."

13. Brooks Peters, "Gay Deceiver," *Out*, December 1998, 87; Hamilton, *"When I'm Bad, I'm Better"*; E. V. Durling, "Portraits in Words," *Pittsburgh Sun-Telegram*, July 19, 1944, 15; Trav S.D. *No Applause—Just Throw Money: The Book that Made Vaudeville Famous* (New York: Faber & Faber, 2005), 189–190; Sylvester [only name given], "Of the Stage," *Belvedere Daily Republican* [IL], March 4, 1911, 5; Simon Doonan, *Drag: The Complete Story* (London: Lawrence King Publishing, 2019), 137; Channing Gerard Joseph, "The First Drag Queen," *The Nation*, February 17, 2020, 25; Sarah Crocker, "Drag Shows Are Older than You Realize. Here's the Real Story," *Grunge*, March 30, 2023, https://www.grunge.com/1243587/drag-shows-older-realize-real-history/; Spick Hall, "Julian Eltinge Is Fascinating to the Last Degree," *Nashville Tennessean and Nashville American*, January 24, 1913, 10; George Freedley, "History of Female Impersonation," *New York Times*, December 16, 1956, ii: 5.

14. "On Professional Stage: Julian D. Eltinge, Famous Impersonator of Female Roles, to Abandon Amateur Work," *Boston Globe*, May 8, 1904, 7; "Harry S. Lehr Dies;

Once Social Leader," *New York Times*, January 4, 1929, 25; Banner, *American Beauty*, 193.

15. L. Wolfe Gilbert quoted in John Dimeglio, *Vaudeville U.S.A.* (Bowling Green, OH: Bowling Green University Popular Press, 1973), 32; Anthony Rotundo, *American Manhood: Transformations in Masculinity from the Revolution to the Modern Era* (New York: Basic Books, 1993), 224–226.

16. "Amusement Notes."

17. "Eltinge Says He Didn't," *Variety*, January 6, 1906, 12.

18. Michael Kimmel, *Manhood in America: A Cultural History* (New York: Free Press, 1996), 100; "Julian Eltinge Wants to Drop the Petticoats and Play Shylock," *Omaha Daily News*, September 16, 1910, 12; "Orpheum," *Reading News-Times* (PA), December 12, 1918, 7.

19. Timothy J. Gilfoyle, "Policing of Sexuality," in *Inventing Times Square: Commerce and Culture at the Crossroads of the World*, ed. William R. Taylor (Baltimore: Johns Hopkins University Press, 1991), 303; "Impersonations by Julian Eltinge, a Big, Husky Man," *Indianapolis News*, September 23, 1908, 8.

20. Senelick, "Lady and the Tramp," 32.

21. Sharon R. Ullman, " 'The Twentieth Century Way': Female Impersonation and Sexual Practice in Turn-of-the-Century America," *Journal of the History of Sexuality* 5, no. 4 (April 1995): 577; Christopher S. Connelly, "King of Drag," *Etc.*, September 6, 1996, 40; Robert C. Toll, *On with the Show: The First Century of Show Business in America* (New York: Oxford University Press, 1976), 240, 256, 260; Laurie, *Vaudeville: From the Honky-tonks to the Palace*, 87–95; Anthony Slide, *The Encyclopedia of Vaudeville* (Westport, CT: Greenwood Press, 2012), 93–94.

22. Renée M. Sentilles, *Performing Menken: Adah Isaacs Menken and the Birth of the American Celebrity* (Cambridge: Cambridge University Press, 2003), 106; Neil Harris, *Humbug: The Art of P. T. Barnum*, 169; Clare Sears, "Electric Brilliancy: Cross-Dressing Law and Freak Show Displays in Nineteenth-Century San Francisco," *Women's Studies Quarterly* 36, no. 3/4 (2008): 179; Kimmel, *Manhood in America*, 77; Elaine Frantz Parsons, *Ku-Klux: The Birth of the Klan During Reconstruction* (Chapel Hill: University of North Carolina Press, 2015), 92–93.

23. "Orpheum's Inauguration Bill Luminates with Bright Stars," *Courier* (Harrisburg, PA), January 15, 1991, 6; Slide, *Encyclopedia of Vaudeville*, 68.

24. "Temple—Vaudeville," *Detroit Free Press*, March 17, 1914, 4; "Theaters Present Array of Talents: Davis—Keith Vaudeville," *Pittsburgh Press*, December 18, 1921, 39.

25. Laurie, *Vaudeville: From the Honky-tonks to the Palace*, 91; Call Boy [*sic*], "The Call Boy's Chat," *Philadelphia Inquirer*, March 8, 1931, 6 [72]; "Footlight Flashes," *Philadelphia Inquirer*, February 22, 1931, 5 [69].

26. "Vardalan," *La Cross Tribune* (WI), April 30, 1910, 7; "Stables Club," *Miami Daily News*, December 10, 1937, 23; Slide, *Encyclopedia of Vaudeville*, 158; Connelly, "King of Drag," 40.

27. "Temple—Vaudeville," *Detroit Free Press*, March 17, 1914, 4; Annemarie Bean, "Transgressing the Gender Divide: The Female Impersonator in Nineteenth-Century Blackface Minstrelsy," in *Inside the Minstrel Mask: Readings in Nineteenth-Century*

260 NOTES

Blackface Minstrelsy, ed. Annemarie Bean, James Vernon Hatch, and Brooks McNamara (Hanover, NH: Wesleyan University Press, 1996), 249, 251; Toll, *On with the Show*, 242; "'Male Patti' [Stuart] to be Attraction," *Honolulu Star-Bulletin*, December 6, 1924, 14 [44]; "Coburn Minstrels Score Big Hit," *Dothan Eagle* (AL), December 13, 1920, 2; Laurence Senelick, *The Changing Room: Sex, Drag and Theatre* (New York: Routledge, 2000), 300–301; Mary Anne Long, "'All Our Girls Are Men': The Haresfoot Club and the Original College Musical" (PhD diss., University of Wisconsin–Madison, 20040, 111–113; Slide, *Encyclopedia of Vaudeville*, 158; Roger Baker, *Drag: A History of Female Impersonation on the Stage* (London: Triton, 1968), 174.

28. "Vaudeville Acts on Benefit Program," *St. Louis Post-Dispatch*, August 15, 1923, 15; Andrew Erdman, *Blue Vaudeville: Sex, Morals, and the Mass Marketing of Entertainment, 1885–1915* (Jefferson, NC: McFarland, 2004); for more on statuary see Mary Rita Fleischer, "Collaborative Projects of Symbolist Playwrights and Early Modern Dancers" (PhD diss., City University of New York Graduate Center, 1998).

29. "Rival for Julian," *Philadelphia Inquirer*, June 29, 1919, 17 [41]; "Excellent Bills on Current List," *Pittsburg [sic] Press*, February 22, 1920, 67; "'Lady Do' Has Merit as a Musical Play," *New York Times*, April 19, 1927, 24; Baker, *Drag*, 213; "Karyl Norman Tops Maryland Bill," *Evening Sun, Baltimore*, May 30, 1922, 6; Eleanor Barnes, "Male Soprano Voices Woes," *Illustrated Daily News, Los Angeles*, January 5, 1933, 16; David Monod, "Double-Voiced: Music, Gender, and Nature in Performance," *Journal of the Gilded Age and Progressive Era* 14, no. 2 (April 2015): 173, https://www.jstor.org/stable/43903078.

30. "'Julian Eltinge' of Orient Sets Style for Nippon Girls," *Omaha Daily News* (NE), June 12, 1919, 1; Senelick, *Changing Room*, 114. (Senelick uses the nomenclature "Mei Lanfang"); "Coming Over," *McCook Daily Gazette* (NE), February 2, 1927, 3; "Chinese Star Creates Stir," *Detroit Free Press*, February 2, 1930, iv: 6 [56]; "Roundabout," *Illustrated Daily News, Los Angeles*, November 21, 1934, 12; May Day Lo, "Chinese Julian Eltinge Is Thrilling Audiences Here," *Honolulu Star-Bulletin*, November 30, 1940, 7.

31. "The Chinese Julian Eltinge Gets Monthly Pay of $2,000," *Minneapolis Sunday Tribune*, February 4, 1917, 9 [33]; U.S. Inflation Calculator, January 10, 2022, https://www.usinflationcalculator.com/.

32. "Chinese 'Julian Eltinge' Slain," *San Francisco Chronicle*, August 29, 1921, 1.

33. "Mexican Julian Eltinge Arrested as Crosses River," *El Paso Herald*, September 18, 1918, 2.

34. [Advertisement.] *Daily News* (New York), April 25, 1929, 41 [185]; Edna Nahshon, ed., *New York's Yiddish Theater: From the Bowery to Broadway* (New York: Columbia University Press, 2016), 49; "Michalesko Coming Here," *Montreal Daily Star*, October 6, 1944, 15.

35. "Young Russian Female Impersonator May Tread Toes of Julian Eltinge," *Wichita Eagle* (KS), July 23, 1922, 29; Leone Cass Baer, "New Bills Open at Portland Theaters," from clipping file on microfilm at NYPL-PA-BRTC, ELTINGE, Julian; MWEZ+N.C. 9882 22,638 22,939#.

NOTES   261

36. "Wire Dancer Known as 'Eltinge of the Wire,'" *Paterson Morning Call* (NJ), May 8, 1922, 5; crossdressing in the circus went back at least as far as the 1840s according to Gillian M. Rodger, *Champagne Charlie and Pretty Jemima: Variety Theater in the Nineteenth Century* (Urbana: University of Illinois Press, 2010), 44; E. L. Warner, Jr., "Olympia Ice Carnival Finest in Club History," *Detroit Free Press*, March 15, 1936, 15.

37. Daniel Hurwitz, *Bohemian Los Angeles and the Making of Modern Politics* (Berkeley: University of California Press, 2007), 4, 34.

38. Rotundo, *American Manhood*, 2; Frederick Engels, *The Origin of the Family, Private Property and the State* (London: Penguin, 1927), 95 (original work published 1884); Laurence Senelick, "Mollies or Men of Mode? Sodomy and the Eighteenth-Century London Stage," *Journal of the History of Sexuality* 1, no. 1 (July 1990): 37.

39. Katz, *Invention of Heterosexuality*, 6, 13–14, 19, 38, 44–45; Chauncey, *Gay New York*, 118.

40. Senelick, *Changing Room*, 310; Geoffrey Hilsabeck, *American Vaudeville* (Morgantown: West Virginia University Press, 2021), 79, 84; A. S. Byatt, *Possession: A Romance* (New York: Vintage International, 1990), 10.

41. Toll, *On with the Show*, 249, 251; James Garbarino, *Children and Families in the Social Environment*, 2nd ed. (New York: Aldine de Gruyter, 1992), 23–25; Ceylan Swensen, "Julian Eltinge" presentation, virtual and at Northport Historical Society, Long Island, NY, June 26, 2022; Lee Alan Morrow, "More about Eltinge," *TheaterWeek*, September 11–17, 1995, 7.

42. Marjorie Garber, *Vested Interests: Cross-dressing and Cultural Anxiety* (New York: Routledge, 1997), 25–27; Sherrie Inness, "Girls Will Be Boys and Boys Will Be Girls: Cross-dressing in Popular Turn-of-the-Century College Fiction," *Journal of American Culture* 18, no. 2 (Summer 1995): 2.

43. Curtis Cate, *Friedrich Nietzsche* (Woodstock, NY: Overlook Press, 2002), 45–48, 202, 395.

44. Bertrand Russell, *A History of Western Philosophy* (New York: Simon & Schuster, 1945), 525–546.

45. George Herbert Mead, "The Working Hypothesis in Social Reform," *American Journal of Sociology* 5, no. 3 (November 1899): 369, 371.

46. Bullough and Bullough, *Cross Dressing, Sex, and Gender*, 204–205.

47. Michel Foucault, *The History of Sexuality*, Vol. 1: *An Introduction*, trans. Robert Hurley (New York: Vintage Books, 1980), 20–22; Ronnie Swartz, "Social Work Values in an Age of Complexity," *Journal of Social Work Values and Ethics* 4, no. 3 (2007), 65–80; Ullman, "'Twentieth Century Way,'" 576; Hamilton, *"When I'm Bad, I'm Better,"* 147.

48. Bullough and Bullough, *Cross Dressing, Sex, and Gender*, 204–205.

49. Bullough and Bullough, *Cross Dressing, Sex, and Gender*, 212–213; Havelock Ellis, *Studies in the Psychology of Sex: Sexual Inversion* (Philadelphia: P. A. Davis Co., 1901), 3, 55, 117, 227.

50. Bullough and Bullough, *Cross Dressing, Sex, and Gender*, 204–205, 207–213; Ellis, *Studies in the Psychology of Sex: Sexual Inversion*, x.

262 NOTES

51. Baker, *Drag*, 115, 118; William Nelson Taft, "Human Curios," *Evening State Journal* (NE), September 13, 1920, 4 [5].

52. Sigmund Freud, *The Basic Writings of Sigmund Freud*, ed. and trans. A. A. Brill (New York: Modern Library, 1938), 553–554. Sigmund Freud, "Three Contributions to the Theory of Sex," in *The Basic Writings of Sigmund Freud*, ed. and trans. A. A. Brill (New York: Modern Library, 1938), 553–554. (Original work published 1905; see Peter Gay, *Freud: A Life for Our Times*, New York: Anchor Books, 142.); Sara Flanders et al., "On the Subject of Homosexuality: What Freud Said," *International Journal of Psychoanalysis* 97 (2016): 934; Hamilton, "*When I'm Bad, I'm Better*," 145; New York Academy of Medicine, Committee on Public Health, "Homosexuality," *Bulletin of the New York Academy of Medicine* 40, no. 7 (July 1964): 576, 578; Bullough and Bullough, *Cross Dressing, Sex, and Gender*, 213–214.

53. New York Academy of Medicine, "Homosexuality," 576, 578; Freud, *Basic Writings*, 1938, 778, 758; Charlotte Suthrell, *Unzipping Gender: Sex, Cross-Dressing, and Culture* (Oxford: Berg, 2004), 147; Lenard R. Berlanstein, "Breeches and Breaches: Cross-Dress Theater and the Culture of Gender Ambiguity in Modern France," *Comparative Studies in Society and History* 38, no. 2 (April 1996): 338, https://www.jstor.org/stable/179132; Baker, *Drag*, 191.

54. Themista, "He Fascinates the Women in His Feminine Finery"; Chauncey, *Gay New York*, 55.

55. "Julian Eltinge's Imitator Held in Observation Ward," *New St. Louis Star*, June 22, 1914, 2; Robert J. Stoller, *Perversion: The Erotic Form of Hatred* (London: Karnac, 1975), 78–79; Robert J. Stoller, "Transsexualism and Transvestism," *Psychiatric Annals* 1, no. 4 (1971): 68; Hamilton, "*When I'm Bad, I'm Better*," 147; Suthrell, *Unzipping Gender*, 131; Otto Fenichel, *The Psychoanalytic Theory of Neurosis*, 50th anniversary ed. (London: Routledge, 1996), 344–345 (original work published 1946); M. Anupama, K. H. Gangadhar, Vardana B. Shetty, and P. Bhadja Dip, "Transvestism as a Symptom: A Case Series," *Indian Journal of Psychological Medicine* 38, no. 1 (January–February 2016): 79–80.

56. Juliet B. Rogers and Andreja Zevnik, "Symptoms of the Political Unconscious: Introduction to a Special Issue," *Political Psychology* 38, no. 4 (August 2017): 585.

57. Juan Perez Jr., "Republican States Are Fuming—and Legislating—over Drag Performances," *Politico*, February 25, 2023, https://www.politico.com/news/2023/02/05/drag-show-bans-gop-statehouses-00081193; Jacques Derrida, *Writing and Difference*, trans. A. Bass (Chicago: University of Chicago Press, 1978), 5; for an able explication of Derrida's often difficult writings on deconstruction see J. M. Balkin, "Deconstructive Practice and Legal Theory," *Yale Law Journal* 96 (1987), 744–786; Allen Rubin and Earl Babbie, *Research Methods for Social Work*, 4th ed. (Belmont, CA: Wadsworth/Thomson Learning, 2001), 151.

58. Judith Butler, "Performative Acts and Gender Constitution: An Essay in Phenomenology and Feminist Theory," *Theatre Journal* 40, no. 4 (December 1988): 519–520; Judith Butler, *Gender Trouble: Feminism and the Subversion of Identity* (New York: Routledge, 1990), 24–25; Senelick, *Changing Room*, 5–6; Naomi

NOTES 263

Gordon-Loebl, "Breaking Down the Binary," *The Nation*, December 26, 2022–January 2, 2023, 30.

59. Kathy Peiss, *Hope in a Jar: The Making of America's Beauty Culture* (New York: Metropolitan Books, 1998), 49; Long, "'All Our Girls Are Men,'" 120–121; Percy Hammond, "Notes of Plays and Players," *Chicago Daily Tribune*, March 23, 1910, 10; Connelly, "King of Drag," 40–43.

60. "Keith's Theater: Vaudeville"; Albert F. McLean Jr., *American Vaudeville as Ritual* (Lexington: University of Kentucky Press, 1965), 16–17; Theodore Dreiser, *An American Tragedy* (New York: New American Library, 2000), 484 (original work published 1925); Karl Marx, *Capital: A Critique of Political Economy*, Vol. 1: *The Process of Capitalist Production*, ed. Frederick Engels, trans. from the third German edition Samuel Moore and Edward Aveling (New York: International Publishers, 1967), 354 (original work published 1867).

61. US Bureau of the Census, *Historical Statistics of the Unites States, Colonial Times to 1970, Bicentennial Edition, Part 2* (Washington, DC: US Government Printing Office, 1975), 134, 138–139.

62. US Bureau of the Census, "Part II: Comparative Occupation Statistics, 1870–1930," 101, 110–121, 168, October 9, 2021, https://www2.census.gov/library/publications/decennial/1940/population-occupation/00312147ch2.pdf.

63. Henry S. Pritchett, "Introduction," in *Medical Education in the United States and Canada: A Report to the Carnegie Foundation for the Advancement of Teaching, Bulletin No. Four*, by Abraham Flexner (Boston: D. B. Updike, The Merrymount Press, 1910), viii, xiii, iii.

64. Boris Emmet and John E. Jeuck, *Catalogues and Counters: A History of Sears, Roebuck and Company* (Chicago: University of Chicago Press, 1950), 102.

65. Lorin F. Deland, "At the Sign of the Dollar," *Harper's Monthly Magazine*, March 1917, 526; Andrew L. Erdman, "Edward Bernays and the 'Golden Jubilee of Light': Culture, Performance, Publicity," *Theatre Annual* 49 (1996), 49, 51, 53.

66. Connelly, "King of Drag," 41; "How a Man Makes Himself a Beautiful Woman"; Frederick Tregelles, "Difficult Art of Stage Makeup Described by an Expert," *Times-Democrat* (Lima, OH), June 8, 1907, 12 [6]; Julian Eltinge, "When a Man Becomes a Woman: A Vaudeville Miracle," *Louisville, Kentucky Courier-Journal, Illustrated Sunday Magazine*, June 23, 1907, 2 [38]; Peiss, *Hope in a Jar*, 73; Senelick, "Lady and the Tramp," 32.

Chapter 1

1. Connelly, "King of Drag," 41; Long, "'All Our Girls Are Men,'" 118, cites: Laurence Senelick, "Julian Eltinge," in *American National Biography* (New York: Oxford University Press, 1999), 467; Casey, *Prettiest Girl on Stage*, xxii, 39; Gerald Bordman, *The Oxford Companion to American Theatre* (New York: Oxford University Press, 1984), 229; "Julian Eltinge, Impersonator, 57," *New York Times*, March 8, 1941, 19;

264 NOTES

"Julian Eltinge, 57, Famous Female Impersonator, Dies," *Boston Daily Globe*, March 7, 1941, 1, 8; for instances in which he actively lied to journalists about his age see "Chat with Eltinge," *Gazette* (Montreal), January 18, 1908, 6; "William Dalton Is Old Butte Boy," *Butte Inter Mountain* (MT), January 26, 1910, 2; Reman Norin, "Julian Eltinge, Coming into Manhood, at Age 51," *Daily Missoulian* (MT), January 8, 1936, 1.

2. Government records provided courtesy of Butte-Silver Bow Public Archives (Montana); scan of birth certificate from Newton, Massachusetts, official copy dated May 25, 1999, supplied courtesy of Anne Alison Barnet.

3. This is how he is identified in the aforementioned 1891 and 1892 school registration roles for his son.

4. "Death Takes Father of Julian Eltinge," *Los Angeles Record*, July 8, 1927, 15; FamilySearch.org, January 21, 2022, https://www.familysearch.org/tree/person/deta ils/L7CJ-SK2 (and links from this URL); certain details of the Dalton family are from the documentary film *Lady Bill: The Julian Eltinge Story, Part 1 (1881–1910)*, accessed on YouTube: https://www.youtube.com/watch?v=fr4WaBe7GjI&t=3s.

5. "Cambridge Aldermen," *Boston Daily Globe*, January 13, 1887, 2; *Butte City Directory*, 1890, provided courtesy of Butte-Silver Bow Public Archives (Montana) [BSBPA]; US Department of Labor and Commerce, *Statistical Abstract of the United States*, no. 32 (Washington, DC, 1909), 66.

6. "Welcome to the City of Newton Massachusetts," January 23, 2022, https://www.newtonma.gov/about.

7. M. F. Sweetser, *King's Handbook of Newton Massachusetts* (Boston: Moses King Corp., 1889), 15–16.

8. Sweetser, *King's Handbook of Newton*, 17–19.

9. Sweetser, *King's Handbook of Newton*, 22, 30, 32, 34, 36, 42, 131–132; *Newton Directory, Containing a General Directory of Citizens, a Business Directory, and the City Record* (Worcester, MA: Drew, Allis & Co., 1881), 13; film *Lady Bill: The Julian Eltinge Story, Part 1 (1881–1910)*; Rotundo, *American Manhood*, 3; *Atlas of the City of Newton Massachusetts* (New York: J. B. Beers, 1886), Secs. E–I; *Newton Directory*, 113; Leo Braudy, *The Frenzy of Renown: Fame and Its History* (New York: Vintage, 1997), 510–511; California's original mining boom, of course, focused on gold, mushrooming from a regional to an "international" frenzy in 1848–49, see: Kevin Starr, *California: A History* (New York: Modern Library, 2007), 79–81.

10. Rotundo, *American Manhood*, 3; details of Dalton's mother crossdressing him as a toddler are from the documentary film *Lady Bill: The Julian Eltinge Story, Part 1 (1881–1910)*.

11. Dorothy Kunhardt, "Little Lord Fauntleroy: This Is Centennial of His Creator's Birth," *Life*, December 5, 1949, 71–79; "Kate Kellaway's Frances Hodgson Burnett: The Unpredictable Life of the Author of The Secret Garden," [Book Review], *Observer* (London), April 4, 2004, 15; "Vivian Burnett, Son of Frances Hodgson Burnett," *Herald Tribune*, July 26, 1937, no page number supplied, from clipping file at NYPL-PA-BRTC; "Original 'Fauntleroy' Dies in Boat after Helping Rescue 4 in Sound," *New York Times*, July 26, 1937, 1, from clipping file at NYPL-PA-BRTC; *The Companion Story to "Fauntleroy,"* no other information supplied, from clipping file at

NOTES **265**

NYPL-PA-BRTC; Andrew Erdman, *Queen of Vaudeville: The Story of Eva Tanguay* (Ithaca, NY: Cornell University Press, 2012), 36; Hamilton, *"When I'm Bad, I'm Better,"* 8–9; "E. F. Albee, Co-Founder of Vaudeville"; Elbridge Gerry, "Children of the Stage," in *American Vaudeville as Seen by Its Contemporaries*, ed. Charles Stein (New York: Alfred A. Knopf, 1984), 138.

12. Peter Boag, *Re-Dressing America's Frontier Past* (Berkeley: University of California Press, 2011), 59, 62; Theodore Roosevelt, *The Winning of the West: An Account of the Exploration and Settlement of Our Country from the Alleghanies to the Pacific*, vol. 2, pt. 1 (New York: G. Putnam's Sons, 1889), no page numbers supplied, Project Guttenberg eBook, release date: April 7, 2004 [EBook #11941], https://www.gutenb erg.org/cache/epub/11941/pg11941.html; Barbara W. Tuchman, *The Proud Tower: A Portrait of the World before the War, 1890–1914* (New York: Random House, 2014), 304 (original work published 1962).

13. Kimmel, *Manhood in America*, 16–17; Garber, *Vested Interests*, 60; John Dos Passos, *U.S.A. 1919* (Boston: Houghton Mifflin, 1946), 166 (original work published 1930); "Dowry for Each Daughter," *Washington Post*, March 12, 1907, 5.

14. Kimmel, *Manhood in America*, 88, 181–182; Braudy, in *The Frenzy of Renown*, calls Teddy Roosevelt the clear "heir of the post–Civil War self-made man," 552; Farnsworth, *Ziegfeld Follies*, no page number supplied.

15. Ann Douglas, *The Feminization of American Culture* (New York: Noonday Press, 1977), 57; Beryl Satter, *Each Mind a Kingdom: American Women, Sexual Purity, and the New Thought Movement, 1875–1920* (Berkeley: University of California Press, 1999), 5, 15, 35; Mary Baker Eddy, *Science and Health with Key to the Scriptures* (Boston: First Church of Christ, Scientist, 1971), 44.

16. "Harry Lehr Has a Rival among the Boston 400"; Themista, "He Fascinates the Women in His Feminine Finery"; Walter Anthony, "Julian and Not Julia, Eltinge Speaks," *San Francisco Call*, November 10, 1912, 31; "Julian Eltinge Makes Game Fight for Life after Operation," *San Francisco Chronicle*, August 9, 1921, ii: 1 [13].

17. Myron Brinig, *Wide Open Town* (Helena, MT: Sweetgrass Books, 1993), 5, 29 (original work published in 1931); Earl Ganz, "Introduction," in *Wide Open Town*, by Myron Brinig, xviii; "Cigarette Law Pains Eltinge," *Salt Lake Telegram*, June 16, 1921, ii: 1 [2]; "Willard Mack Is Busily Engaged in Three Big Stage Productions," *Salt Lake Tribune*, October 16, 1921, 4; Themista, "He Fascinates the Women in His Feminine Finery"; Gail Bederman, *Manliness & Civilization: A Cultural History of Gender and Race in the United States, 1880–1917* (Chicago: University of Chicago Press, 1995), 170, quoted in Long, " 'All Our Girls Are Men,' " 78.

18. Michael P. Malone, *The Battle for Butte: Mining and Politics on the Northern Frontier, 1864–1906* (Seattle: University of Washington Press, 1981), 34, 58, 63; "Western Mining History: Butte, Montana," accessed January 12, 2023, https://westernmininghistory.com/ towns/montana/butte/#:~:text=Butte%20went%20from%20the%20handful,close%20 to%20100%2C000%20in%201917; "Montana Connections: Ten Quick Facts about Butte, Montana," accessed January 12, 2023, https://montanaconnectionspark.com/ 2020/08/18/10-quick-facts-about-butte-montana/#:~:text=Butte%20Once%20 Had%20over%20100%2C000,population%20was%20over%20100%2C000%20people.

266 NOTES

19. Malone, *Battle for Butte*, 21, 28, 30–31, 62; Michael C. Freeman, *A Brief History of Butte, Montana: The World's Greatest Mining Camp* (Chicago: Henry O. Shepard Co., 1900), 16.

20. Freeman, *Brief History of Butte*, 6, 8,10 28; Malone, *Battle for Butte*, 3–4; Brinig, *Wide Open Town*, 3; Ganz, "Introduction," in *Wide Open Town*, xv; US Bureau of the Census, *Historical Statistics, Part 2*, 139, 166; Stanley Lebergott, "Labor Force and Employment, 1800–1960," in *Output, Employment, and Productivity in the United States after 1800*, ed. Dorothy S. Brady (Washington, DC: National Bureau of Economic Research, 1966), 122.

21. Dee Brown, *Bury My Heart at Wounded Knee: An Indian History of the American West* (New York: Henry Holt, 1970), 320–321; Malone, *Battle for Butte*, 83; Robert W. Rydell, *All the World's a Fair* (Chicago: University of Chicago Press, 1984), 25; Long, "'All Our Girls Are Men,'" 79; Kimmel, *Manhood in America*, 183; US Department of Labor and Commerce, *Statistical Abstract of the United States*, no. 32 (Washington, DC, 1909), 34.

22. "Behind the Footlights," *Butte Daily Miner*, November 13, 1893, 6.

23. "The Calhoun Company," *Butte Daily Miner*, January 5, 1895, 5; Freeman, *Brief History of Butte*, 3–4, 18–19, 28, 35–37, 107–109, 112; Toll, *On with the Show*, 199; S.D., *No Applause—Just Throw Money*, 69; Malone, *Battle for Butte*, 63, 73; "Look Who's with Us, Yes, Charlie Burke," *Anaconda Standard*, January 8, 1914, 14; "Montana," *New York Clipper*, August 19, 1899, 489; Brinig, *Wide Open Town*, 5, 102.

24. Butte city directory pages, 1895, 1896 eds., provided courtesy of BSBPA.

25. US Library of Congress, Image 13 of Sanborn Fire Insurance Map from Butte, Silver Bow County, Montana, accessed December 27, 2021, https://www.loc.gov/resou rce/g4254bm.g4254bm_g049501900/?sp=13&r=0.128,0.098,0.363,0.171,0 (links to and assistance with Sanborn maps provided by BSBPA); "A Casino Case," *Daily Inter Mountain Butte, Montana*, December 16, 1895, 5; "Marion and Barnett," *Butte Daily Miner*, April 12, 1894, 5; Rodger, *Champagne Charlie and Pretty Jemima*, 17; Robert W. Snyder, *The Voice of the City: Vaudeville and Popular Culture in New York* (New York: Oxford University Press, 1989), 3–4; Laurie, *Vaudeville: From the Honky-tonks to the Palace*, 452–453; Armond Fields and L. Marc Fields, *From the Bowery to Broadway: Lew Fields and the Roots of American Popular Theater* (New York: Oxford University Press, 1993), 92; Isabel Wilkerson, *Caste: The Origins of our Discontents* (New York: Random House, 2020), 49.

26. "Butte Stage Star Dies in New York: Julian Eltinge Succumbs," *Montana Standard, Butte*, March 11, 1941 (morning ed.), 12; Tracy Thornton, "The Great Pretender," *Montana Standard*, April 16, 2000, C1; links and documents provided courtesy of Butte-Silver Bow Public Archives; Morrow, "More about Eltinge."

27. Thornton, "Great Pretender"; Malone, *Battle for Butte*, 21; photos and maps provider courtesy of BSBPA.

28. "William Dalton Is Old Butte Boy"; Anthony, "Julian and Not Julia, Eltinge Speaks"; "Cigarette Law Pains Eltinge"; Butte city directory pages provided courtesy of BSBPA. The childhood friend from whom Eltinge says he borrowed his name is variously called "Charles" and "Will" or "Willie" in later news articles, further underscoring

the mutability of names in an era of print journalism relying on handwritten notes, staticky wireline communications, and a more evident expectation of the human, and therefore fallible, mind as the center of public discourse rather than its location in a verifiable "object" truth, that could be "checked" and "balanced"; Kurt Gänzl, *Lydia Thompson: Queen of Burlesque* (New York: Routledge, 2002), 118; Sentilles, *Performing Menken*, 273; Harley Erdman, *Staging the Jew: The Performance of and American Ethnicity, 1860–1920* (New Brunswick, NJ: Rutgers University Press, 1997), 70; "Billy J. Dalton in Reminiscences," *Anaconda Standard*, February 14, 1919, 5; "George K. Fortescue Dead," *New York Times*, January 14, 1914, 11; "Julian Mitchell Dies; Directed 13 Follies," *New York Times*, June 24, 1926 (the connection between Mitchell and Eltinge suggested by David Armstrong, *David Armstrong's Broadway Nation*, "Cole Porter & the Queers Who Invented Broadway," accessed June 15, 2023, https://broadwaypodcastnetwork.com/podcast/broadway-nation/); "A Few Minutes with Julian Mitchell and the Chorus," *Inter Ocean*, October 8, 1905, morning ed., 3 [23].

29. Thornton, "Great Pretender"; "Butte Stage Star Dies in New York."

30. "Look Who's with Us, Yes, Charlie Burke"; Charles C. Cohan, "Montanans Crash Films," *Los Angeles Times*, June 23, 1929, iii: 23 [53]. In this article, Burke refers to Eltinge as "Jimmy Dalton" rather than Billy. While this may cause concern over the veracity of the narrative, it is entirely possible that Burke merely made a verbal slip, or that the reporter misremembered or misrecorded Julian Eltinge's childhood name, or further errors occurred on the publishing side; Peters, "Gay Deceiver," 84; "Julian Eltinge Wanted to Perform Like Al Jolson," *Brooklyn Citizen*, May 13, 1923, 17.

31. Alan Dale, "Why Women Are Greater Actors than Men," *Cosmopolitan*, September 1906, 517; George Jessel, *Elegy in Manhattan* (New York: Holt, Rinehart, & Winston, 1961), 121.

32. "In the Old Butte Days," *Anaconda Standard*, February 9, 1919, 2 [38]; " 'Eltinge' was Butte's Tough Kid," *San Francisco Examiner*, January 3, 1919, 19.

33. Tania Modleski, "A Woman's Gotta Do . . . What a Man's Gotta Do: Cross-dressing in the Western," *Signs* 22, no. 3 (Spring 1997): 523.

34. Boag, *Re-Dressing America's Frontier Past*, 59; Gregory D. Smithers, " 'Two Spirits': Gender, Ritual, and Spirituality in the Native South," *Early American Studies* 14, no. 3 (Fall 2014): 626–627, 630, https://www.jstor.org/stable/24474873.

35. Senelick, "Lady and the Tramp," 33; Hajdu and Carey, *Revolution in Three Acts*, 15; Boag, *Re-Dressing America's Frontier Past*, 67; Long, " 'All Our Girls Are Men,'" 128.

36. "Martha and A. G.," *The Skirmisher, St. John's Military School, Salina, Kansas*, April 25, 1919, 1.

37. Julia Lee Brown, "School Activities," *El Paso Morning Times*, March 2, 1917, 17; "Max Heyman Is Julian Eltinge of American Legion 'Jollies,'" *Okmulgee Daily Democrat* (OK), January 18, 1924, vi: B [14]; Sam Raddon Jr., "Looking Backward," *Park Record* (UT), February 10, 1944, 1, 4; Senelick, *Changing Room*, 350; Elaina Patton, Jillian Eugenios, Ellie Rudy, Brooke Sopelsa, and Jay Valle, "Pride 30: Drag Performers Who Made 'Herstory,'" *NBCnews.com*, June 1, 2023, https://www.nbcnews.com/specials/pride-month-2023-drag-performers-who-made-herstory/index.html.

268 NOTES

38. Sears, "Electric Brilliancy," 172; Senelick, *Changing Room*, 6; Amy Sueyoshi, *Discriminating Sex: White Leisure and the Making of the American "Oriental"* (Champaign: University of Illinois Press, 2018), 115, 117; Alexandra Scholten, "Drag Performance in Minnesota Theater from the 1880s through the 1920s," *MinnPost. com*, June 5, 2023, https://www.minnpost.com/mnopedia/2023/06/drag-performance-in-minnesota-theater-from-the-1880s-through-the-1920s/; Dresden, "L.A. Has Its Own History of Anti-Drag Laws"; W. L. McConnell, "New Orleans," *San Francisco Dramatic Review*, December 5, 1908, 7.

39. In part from documents and clippings provided courtesy of BSBPA; Rennold Wolf, "The Sort of Fellow Julian Eltinge Really Is," *The Green Book Magazine*, November 1913, 793, 798; *Butte Daily Post*, December 18, 1894; "Filed for Record," *Butte Miner*, October 22, 1895; "Stockholders' Meeting," *Butte Daily Post*, February 4, 1899; Themista, "He Fascinates the Women in His Feminine Finery"; "World's Foremost Imitator of Women," *Spokesman-Review* (Spokane, WA), June 30, 1907, v: 1.

40. US Bureau of the Census, *Historical Statistics of the Unites States, 1789 to 1945: A Supplement to the Statistical Abstract of the United States* (Washington, DC: US Government Printing Office, 1949), 29; Brown, *Bury My Heart at Wounded Knee*, 439–445, 449.

41. Walter LaFeber, *The American Age: United States Foreign Policy at Home and Abroad since 1750* (New York: W. W. Norton, 1989), 165, 184; Emily S. Rosenberg, *Spreading the American Dream: American Economic and Cultural Expansion, 1890–1945* (New York: Hill & Wang, 1982), 14; Strong quote in Michael Hunt, *Ideology and U.S. Foreign Policy* (New Haven, CT: Yale University Press, 1987), 37; LaFeber, *American Age*, 93, 160–161, 205 (LaFeber puts the foreign-investment figures at $700 million in 1897 and $3.5 billion in 1914, *American Age*, 221); Willis J. Abbot, *Soldiers of the Sea: The Story of the United States Marine Corps* (New York: Dodd, Mead & Co., 1919), 288–289; Marine Corps University, "Marine Corps Fiscal Year End Strengths, 1798–2015," accessed January 14, 2023, https://www.usmcu.edu/Research/Marine-Corps-History-Division/Research-Tools-Facts-and-Figures/End-Strengths/; "Jardin De Paris: 'Follies of 1909'," *Theatre Magazine*, August 1909, 37; Rosenberg, *Spreading the American Dream*, 24, 25, 39, 68, 111; Fred V. Carstensen, *American Enterprise in Foreign Markets* (Chapel Hill: University of North Carolina Press, 1984), 5; Hunt, *Ideology and U.S. Foreign Policy*, 90, 129; Danielle Mireles, "College Chorus 'Girls',": Drag at Male College and University Campuses during the Progressive Era" (MA thesis, University of California–Riverside, 2017), 13–14.

42. Richard Slotkin, *The Fatal Environment: The Myth of the Frontier in the Age of Industrialization* (New York: Atheneum, 1985), 5; Malone, *Battle for Butte*, 132–133; "Censorship in Chicago," *New York Dramatic Mirror*, March 21, 1908, 15.

43. Marx, *Capital*, 332; William C. Kessler, "Business Organization and Management," in *The Growth of the American Economy*, ed. Harold F. Williamson (New York: Prentice-Hall, 1951), 605, 609; Slotkin, *Fatal Environment*, 8; Chester W. Wright, *Economic History of the United States* (New York: McGraw-Hill Book Group, 1949), 496–497, 607; Alfred D. Chandler, "The Rise of Big Business," in *United States Economic History: Selected Readings*, ed. Harry N. Schreiber (New York: Knopf, 1964),

345–346, 352, 355–356, 358, 364; Thomas C. Cochran, *200 Years of American Business* (New York: Basic Books, 1977), 51, 79–88; Leach, *Land of Desire*, 161; Themista, "He Fascinates the Women in His Feminine Finery," 7.

44. LaFeber, *American Age*, 254; Slotkin, *Fatal Environment*, 5; Malone, *Battle for Butte*, 132–133.

Chapter 2

1. "World's Foremost Imitator of Women"; census data provided courtesy of BSBPA.

2. "How Billy Dalton of Butte Got His Start as Actor," *Sacramento Bee* (CA), March 10, 1917, 28; "Liberty," *Pittsburgh Sunday Post*, November 18, 1917, v: 4 [36]; William Leach, *Land of Desire: Merchants, Power, and the Rise of a New American Culture* (New York: Vintage, 1993), 147; Banks, "The Man Who's Tired of Wearing Skirts"; "World's Foremost Imitator of Women"; Wolf, "The Sort of Fellow Julian Eltinge Really Is," 798.

3. "Feminine New York," *Boston Evening Transcript*, November 24, 1900, 19.

4. Themista, "He Fascinates the Women in His Feminine Finery"; "Girl Seeking Disguise May Be Lost Heiress," *Evening World, Evening Edition* (NY), January 26, 1911, 1; "Buffalo Searched for Girl," *Buffalo Evening Times*, January 30, 1911, 1; James E. Lough, "Why Wearing Skirts Makes a Man Effeminate," *Minneapolis Sunday Tribune*, January 9, 1916, Feature Section: 1 [58]; Long, "'All Our Girls Are Men,'" 139.

5. Horatio Alger Jr., *Ragged Dick or, Street Life in New York with the Boot Blacks* (New York: Penguin Books, 1990), 183 (original work published 1868).

6. Banner, *American Beauty*, 164.

7. David Krasner, *Resistance, Parody, and Double Consciousness in African American Theatre, 1895–1910* (New York: St. Martin's Press, 1997), 76–77.

8. F. Scott Fitzgerald, *The Great Gatsby* (Planet eBook, February 7, 2022, https://www.planetebook.com/free-ebooks/the-great-gatsby.pdf), 8 (original work published 1925).

9. When Wyman died in 1944, several obituaries listed her as ninety years old, making her year of birth 1854 (see citations); however, a family genealogy website lists her birth year as 1859: https://www.wyman.org/getperson.php?personID=I63840&tree=Wyman&sitever=standard; "Noted Dancing Teacher, 90, Dies," *San Francisco Examiner*, May 15, 1944, 10; "'Grand Duchess of Dance,' Lilla Viles Wyman Is Dead," *Boston Daily Globe*, April 14, 1944, 26.

10. Toll, *On with the Show*, 246; Themista, "He Fascinates the Women in His Feminine Finery"; K. G. Tallqvist, "Behind Scene Views of Vaudeville's Vamp Man," *Arkansas Democrat*, January 18, 1922, 5; Oscar G. Brockett, *History of the Theatre*, 6th ed. (Boston: Allyn & Bacon, 1991), 433; *Variety*, January 27, 1906, 7; Philip Furia, "Irving Berlin: Troubadour of Tin Pan Alley," in *Inventing Times Square*, 196–197; [Advertisement.] *Los Angeles Record*, July 25, 1917, 5; "World's Foremost Imitator of Women."

270 NOTES

11. Historic New England, "Tremont Theatre, Boston Mass," accessed February 9, 2022, https://www.historicnewengland.org/explore/collections-access/capobject/?refd=PC001.03.01.TMP.138; Anne Alison Barnet, *Extravaganza King* (Boston: Northeastern University Press, 2004), 120.

12. Eugenia Everett, "Men of the Dancing First," in *Performing Arts Resources: Taking the Pledge and Other Public Amusements*, ed. Barbara Naomi Cohen-Stratyner (New York: Public Theatre Library Association, 1991), 124.

13. Themista, "He Fascinates the Women in His Feminine Finery," 7; "The Cadets and 'Tabasco'," *Boston Home Journal*, February 3, 1894, no page number supplied, from clipping file at NYPL-PA-BRTC; all additional information from Cadet programs from MWEZ+n.c.2261 also at NYPL-PA-BRTC.

14. Themista, "He Fascinates the Women in His Feminine Finery."

15. Themista, "He Fascinates the Women in His Feminine Finery"; Barnet, *Extravaganza King*, xiv; "Julian Eltinge Popular Star," *Quad City Times* (Davenport, IA), February 18, 1912, 17.

16. "Harry Lehr Has a Rival among the Boston 400." In one of the few major magazine features on the performer during his prime, "The Sort of Fellow Julian Eltinge Really Is," by Rennold Wolf in *The Green Book Magazine* (November 1913), it is suggested that Eltinge only sought out instruction with Ms. Wyman after his placement in *Miladi*. From a logistical standpoint, this makes little sense: why train an unknown to fill a role he would not have merited in the first place? More likely, Eltinge wanted to further construct the story that he reluctantly entered crossdressing but had been "forced . . . by circumstances" into the field—that is, the culturally acceptable allure of recognition and remuneration. (See Casey, *Prettiest Girl on Stage*, 47.)

17. Robert M. Lewis, ed., *From Traveling Show to Vaudeville: Theatrical Spectacle in America*, 1830–1910 (Baltimore: Johns Hopkins University Press, 2003), 197; Gänzl, *Lydia Thompson*, 34, 86, 94, 154–155; Garber, *Vested Interests*, 10, 135; Rodger, *Champagne Charlie and Pretty Jemima*, 130, 162; Sentilles, *Performing Menken*, 184; Allen, *Horrible Prettiness: Burlesque and American Culture* (Chapel Hill: University of North Carolina Press, 1991), 169; University of Iowa, Special Collections, Keith/Albee Collection, Box 8, 9/23/1907–3/12/1908, 50, 50a; Katie Normington, *Gender and Medieval Drama* (Suffolk, UK: D. S. Brewer, 2004), 63.

18. Lewis, *From Traveling Show to Vaudeville*, 195–197; Toll, *On with the Show*, 173–175; Dimeglio, *Vaudeville U.S.A.*, 48; Peter G. Buckley, "Boundaries of Respectability: Introduction," in *Inventing Times Square*, 294–295; Marybeth Hamilton, "Mae West Live: 'SEX, The Drag, and 1920s Broadway'," *TDR* 36, no. 4 (Winter 1992): 87–88, https://www.jstor.org/stable/1146217. For a good sense of what the Ziegfeld *Follies* offered audiences, and how women and their bodies fit into the entire production scheme, the 1941 movie *Ziegfeld Girl* (dirs. Robert Z. Leonard and Busby Berkeley) is an interesting and at times amusing (and, often, troubling) artifact.

19. "Boston Gets a Wind Storm," *Boston Evening Transcript*, February 5, 1900, 1.

20. Everett, "Men of the Dancing First," 124; "Victoria—My Lady," *New York Dramatic Mirror*, February 23, 1901, 16.

NOTES 271

21. Everett, "Men of the Dancing First," 125; Casey, *Prettiest Girl on Stage*, 49.

22. See Jen-Christophe Agnew, "Times Square: Secularization and Sacralization," in *Inventing Times Square*, 10, especially where he discusses Levine and how popular culture has become "canonized" in the twentieth century; Pierre Bourdieu, *Distinction: A Social Critique of the Judgment of Taste*, trans. Richard Nice (Cambridge, MA: Harvard University Press, 1984), 6; Ethel Barrymore, *Memories: An Autobiography* (New York: Harper & Brothers, 1955), 177.

23. "He Dances for Boston Society"; Long, "'All Our Girls Are Men,'" 119; "Amusement Notes"; Sime Silverman, "Shows of the Week by Sime: Keith's," *Variety*, January 6, 1906, 8; George H. Picard, "The Drama and Those Who Present It," *Wichita Eagle*, January 30, 1910, 27; "George K. Fortescue Dead"; "At the Theaters: B. F. Keith's—Vaudeville," *Washington Herald*, June 29, 1920, 12; Harris, *Humbug*.

24. Everett, "Men of the Dancing First," 123; Barnet, *Extravaganza King*, 2; "Short History of the Cadet Theatricals," from clipping file at NYPL-PA-BRTC; Barnet, *Extravaganza King*, xiii, 4; Eric Lott, *Love and Theft: Blackface Minstrelsy and the American Working Class* (Oxford: Oxford University Press, 1993), 6–7; Boston Literary District, "Tremont Temple," accessed February 13, 2022, http://bostonlitdistrict.org/venue/tremont-temple/.

25. Barnet, *Extravaganza King*, 9; Anne Alison Barnet (paternal great-granddaughter and biographer of Robert Ayres Barnet), phone interview by author, March 3, 2023; engagement letter dated June 22, 1879, as well as other Barnet family history facts, generously provided by Alison Anne Barnet.

26. Everett, "Men of the Dancing First," 124; Barnet, *Extravaganza King*, 17, 19; "Short History of the Cadet Theatricals"; "The Cadets and 'Tabasco'"; "How Is the Armory Getting On?," from clipping file at NYPL-PA-BRTC; Cadet Theatricals [program], *Cinderella & The Prince*, 1904, from clipping file at NYPL-PA-BRTC.

27. Cadet Theatricals [program], *Injured Innocents*, from clipping file at NYPL-PA-BRTC, MWEZ+N.C. 2261; Barnet, *Extravaganza King*, 30; Senelick, *Changing Room*, 30–31; the Cadets created a backstage space reflecting Senelick's notion of a "changing room," a place of "metamorphosis" and freedom from social strictures.

28. Rydell, *All the World's a Fair*, 46; Barnet, *Extravaganza King*, xv, 39; Chauncey, *Gay New York*, 15; Cadet Theatricals [program], *1492*, 1892, from clipping file at NYPL-PA-BRTC, MWEZ+N.C. 2258; "The Cadet Property," in Cadet Theatricals [program], *Cinderella & The Prince*, 1904, from clipping file at NYPL-PA-BRTC, MWEZ+N.C. 2258.

29. Baker, *Drag*, 161–162; Inness, "Girls Will Be Boys and Boys Will Be Girls," 8; Mireles, "College Chorus 'Girls,'" 150; Kathy Peiss, *Cheap Amusements: Working Women and Leisure in Turn-of-the-Century New York* (Philadelphia: Temple University Press, 1986), 5.

30. "Julian Eltinges of 'Den' Are Jealous," *Omaha Daily News*, February 11, 1912, 7C; Rydell, *All the World's a Fair*, 109, 111. "Elks' Minstrels Pull Out Mirth," *Butte Miner*, February 28, 1919, 9.

31. "One Close Shave and Then Another," *Anaconda Standard*, April 16, 1914, 13; Everett, "Men of the Dancing First," 123, 127; Barnet, *Extravaganza King*, xiv, 123;

272 NOTES

"Rainmaking and Love," *Boston Sunday Globe*, January 16, 1898, 26; "Coreopsis Sung in Malden," *Boston Globe*, December 18, 1901, 5.

32. "Famous Woman Impersonator Is Featured," *Visalia Daily Times* (CA), April 7, 1926, 5; "Harry Lehr Has a Rival among the Boston 400"; Themista, "He Fascinates the Women in His Feminine Finery."

33. "Harry Lehr Has a Rival among the Boston 400"; "Harry Lehr's Boston Rival," *Buffalo Courier*, November 11, 1902, 3; "Boston Has a Harry Lehr, Too! His Name Is Julian Eltinge"; Kimmel, *Manhood in America*, 52, 120; Winifred Aydelotte, "Julian Eltinge Is Back after Two Years of Vacation," *Los Angeles Record*, July 11, 1931, ii: 1 [7]; Alger, *Ragged Dick*, 98–99; Bill [only byline given], "Julian Eltinge, He-Man to Quit Feminine Role," *Los Angeles Evening Express*, September 4, 1924, 7.

34. Harry Lawson Heartz, "But He Said It So Politely," *Vocal Gems: Miss Simplicity* [score] (Boston: White-Smith Music Publishing, 1901), 3, NYPL-PA-BRTC, MWEZ+N.C. 9882 22,638 22,939#; Barnet, *Extravaganza King*, 125.

35. "Bright and Merry Children in a Carnival of Fun," *Boston Sunday Globe*, May 6, 1900, 9; Themista, "He Fascinates the Women in his Feminine Finery."

36. "Bright and Merry Children in a Carnival of Fun"; Themista, "He Fascinates the Women in His Feminine Finery"; "Coreopsis Sung in Malden."

37. "Malden Auditorium: 'The Omero," *Boston Evening Transcript*, October 23, 1900, 11; Themista, "He Fascinates the Women in His Feminine Finery"; "Harry Lehr Has a Rival among the Boston 400"; Boston Public Library, *Allen A. Brown Collection of Books Relating to the Stage in the Public Library of the City of Boston* (Boston: Trustees [of the Boston Public Library], 1919), 639; "Coreopsis Sung in Malden."

38. Banks, "The Man Who's Tired of Wearing Skirts," 5 [115]; Charles Welton, "This Man a Martyr to the Modiste," *Pittsburgh Press Illustrated Magazine Section*, March 3, 1918, 91; "Music and Musicians," *Boston Sunday Globe*, April 28, 1901, 17; "Table Gossip," *Boston Sunday Globe*, May 12, 1901, 38; W. F. A., "Whitney Hall: Vaudeville."

39. "He Dances for Boston Society"; "Whitney Hall: Vaudeville"; "Social World News: Sunday at the Commonwealth Club," *Boston Sunday Post*, May 18, 1902, 26; "Table Gossip."

40. Anthony, "Julian and Not Julia, Eltinge Speaks"; "Wants to Take Stage Name," *Santa Ana Register* (CA), November 27, 1918, ii: 1 [7]; "Julian Eltinge Popular Star," *Davenport Democrat and Leader* (IA), February 18, 1912, 17; "William Dalton Is Old Butte Boy."

41. See Geoffrey Hilsabeck, *American Vaudeville*, featuring Laurence Senelick, accessed May 2, 2022, https://vimeo.com/571349404.

42. Bill [only byline given], "Julian Eltinge, He-Man to Quit Feminine Role"; Mary Pickford, "Daily Talks by Mary Pickford: Personalities I Have Met—Julian Eltinge," *Birmingham News* (AL), October 10, 1916, 7; Miles Kreuger, founder and manager of the Institute for the American Musical, who knew an Eltinge associate, actress Blanche Ring, argues that the name ought to end with a soft "g"; Anne Alison Barnet, great-granddaughter and biographer of Robert Barnet, believes the proper pronunciation is with a hard "g" (phone interview by author, March 3, 2023); Tino Balio, "Stars

NOTES   273

in Business: The Founding of United Artists," in *The American Film Industry*, rev. ed., ed. Tino Balio (Madison: University of Wisconsin Press, 1985), 154.

43. Raymond [only name given], "Some Stage Reflections," *Philadelphia Times*, October 23, 1898, 22; Lindsey Perlman, "Mask and Wig, Penn's All-Male Comedy Troupe, Will Welcome All Genders in 2022," *Daily Pennsylvanian*, October 10, 2021, accessed May 18, 2022, https://www.thedp.com/article/2021/10/mask-wig-gender-inclusive-penn-comedy.

44. "On Professional Stage: Julian D. Eltinge, Famous Impersonator of Female Roles, to Abandon Amateur Work"; "He Dances for Boston Society."

45. "Mr. Eltinge Is Popular," *Morning News, Wilmington* (DE), March 31, 1905, 6; "Temple Theater: Adgie and Her Lions—Other Fine Attractions," *Detroit Free Press*, May 14, 1905, iv: 7 [47]; "World's Foremost Imitator of Women"; "Womanly Photographs of a Manly, Athletic Harvard Grad, Who, When He Dons Skirts, Fools Even His Own Manager: Athlete in Gowns Stage Sensation," *St. Louis Post-Dispatch*, July 5, 1907, 16; "Another 'Girl' Question," *Washington Times*, December 16, 1908, 11; McKim Garrison, *An Illustrated History of Hasty Pudding Club Theatricals* (Cambridge, MA: Hasty Pudding Club, 1897), 284, 286, 290; *Thirteenth Catalogue & a History of the Hasty Pudding Club*, 249; Garrison, *An Illustrated History of the Hasty Pudding Club Theatricals* (Cambridge, MA: Hasty Pudding Club, 1897); Email communication from Harvard University Archives (Cambridge MA: Pusey Library—Harvard Yard), October 20, 2021.

46. Rydell, *All the World's a Fair*, 57; Frances Cabanne Scovel, "Society," *St. Louis Post-Dispatch*, May 25, 1913, 5.

47. "New York Day by Day," *Richmond Palladium and Sun-Telegram* (IN), June 3, 1927, 6; "From Harvard Student to Stage Celebrity," *Washington Times*, February 26, 1909, 8; "Agnes Booth Again Married," *New York Times*, February 5, 1885, 5.

48. "Amusement Notes"; Richard deCordova, *Picture Personalities: The Emergence of the Star System in America* (Chicago: University of Chicago Press, 1990), 117–151; Casey, *Prettiest Girl on Stage*, 39–40; Connelly, "King of Drag," 40–41; Garrison, *Illustrated History of Hasty Pudding Club Theatricals*, 284, 286, 290; *Thirteenth Catalogue & a History of the Hasty Pudding Club*, 249; Cambridge Hasty Pudding Club, *An Illustrated History of the Hasty Pudding Club Theatricals*; Rydell, *All the World's a Fair*, 57; Email communication from Harvard University Archives (Cambridge MA: Pusey Library—Harvard Yard), October 20, 2021.

49. Barnet, *Extravaganza King*, xvi; Long, "'All Our Girls Are Men,'" 9.

50. US Bureau of the Census, *Historical Statistics of the Unites States, Colonial Times to 1970, Bicentennial Edition, Part 2* (Washington, DC: US Government Printing Office, 1975), 139–140; US Bureau of the Census, "Part II: Comparative Occupation Statistics, 1870–1930," 100, 168, October 9, 2021, https://www2.census.gov/library/publications/decennial/1940/population-occupation/00312147ch2.pdf; Long, "'All Our Girls Are Men,'" 69.

51. Garrison, *Illustrated History of Hasty Pudding Club Theatricals*, 11–12, 34; *Thirteenth Catalogue & a History of the Hasty Pudding Club* (New York: Riverside Press, 1907), 3–6, 14–16; Long, "'All Our Girls Are Men,'" 3–6, 11; Garber, *Vested Interests*, 60.

274 NOTES

52. Long, "'All Our Girls Are Men,'" 98; Willa Silbert Cather, *My Ántonia* (Hollywood, FL: Simon & Brown, 2011), 10 (original work published 1918).

53. Garrison, *An Illustrated History of Hasty Pudding Club Theatricals*, 34; *Thirteenth Catalogue & a History of the Hasty Pudding Club*, 16; Garber, *Vested Interests*, 60; Mireles, "College Chorus 'Girls,'" 29; "Has Prettiest Pair of Eyes at Harvard," *Boston Sunday Post*, March 13, 1921, 6; "At the New York Theaters," *Hartford Courant*, March 22, 1914, 4 [34].

54. Lough, "Why Wearing Skirts Makes a Man Effeminate"; Mead, "The Working Hypothesis in Social Reform," 369; Senelick, *Changing Room*, 358; Kimmel, *Manhood in America*, 187; Berlanstein, "Breeches and Breaches," 358; Destination Paris Saclay, "Point Gamma at the Ecole Polytechnique," accessed January 16, 2023, https://www.destination-paris-saclay.com/en/events-calendar/not-to-be-missed/point-gamma-polytechnique/; Corbin Patrick, "Songs, Dances, Humor of 'Tarantella' Reveal Some Future Julian Eltinges," *Indianapolis Star*, March 29, 1928, 10.

55. Mireles, "College Chorus 'Girls,'" 3; "College Julian Eltinges Fool Faculty Members," *Inter Ocean* (Chicago), May 23, 1913, 2; Garber, *Vested Interests*, 63; Senelick, *Changing Room*, 358; Long, "'All Our Girls Are Men,'" 139–140.

56. Long, "'All Our Girls Are Men,'" 11, 161; "Julian Eltinge Show," *South Bend Tribune* (IN), January 26, 1909, 9; Clarence J. Bulleit, "Next Notable Juliet a Mere Man," *Indianapolis Sunday Star*, January 22, 1911, 32; Senelick, *Changing Room*, 358; Banner, *American Beauty*, 141, 160; Mireles, "College Chorus 'Girls,'" 34; Long, "'All Our Girls Are Men,'" 161; Jessel, *Elegy in Manhattan*, 122; "Gridiron Star Also Wins Fame as Impersonator of Female Roles," *Olean Evening Times* (NY), January 20, 1923, 17; Garber, *Vested Interests*, 63; "Dramatic Arts at Dartmouth," *Boston Evening Transcript*, November 26, 1913, 7 (thanks to Lou Lumenick for introducing the author to this connection).

57. "He Dances for Boston Society"; "Music and Drama: 'Baron Humbug' Rehearsed," *Boston Evening Transcript*, January 30, 1903, 9.

58. Leach, *Land of Desire*, 18; Peiss, *Cheap Amusements*, 6; Theodore Dreiser, *Sister Carrie*, (New York: Penguin Classics, 1981), 3, 499; "Plays and Players," *The Theatre*, July 1902, 6; "New York—Chaperones," *New York Dramatic Mirror*, June 14, 1902, 14.

59. Barnet, *Extravaganza King*, 134.

Chapter 3

1. Barnet, *Extravaganza King*, 45, 48; Toll, *On with the Show*, 177; Long, "'All Our Girls Are Men'"; "Obituary: One-Time Famous Impersonator Dies of Pneumonia," *News* (Daily News, NYC), February 20, 1920, 15; Welton, "This Man a Martyr to the Modiste"; "George K. Fortescue Dead"; for the "exhibitionistic" appeal of certain acts in vaudeville and silent film see Tom Gunning, "The Cinema of Attractions: Early Film, Its Spectator and the Avant-Garde," in *Early Cinema: Space, Frame, Narrative*,

NOTES   275

ed. Thomas Elsaesser (London: British Film Institute, 1990), 57; Barnet, *Extravaganza King*, xiv; "First Corps to Give 'Ye Old Folks' Concert,'" *Boston Globe*, May 6, 1932, 10.

2. Barnet, *Extravaganza King*, xvi.

3. "Caught, Clipped, and Pasted," *Fall River Daily Herald* (MA), September 4, 1904, 4; "'Mr. Wix of Wickham' at New Haven," *New York Times*, September 13, 1904, 6.

4. "Pretty Girls in 'Wix of Wickham,'" *Hartford Courant*, November 16, 1904, 7; Mantle, "He Wore Skirts for a Living." A fragmentary clipping from the *Denver Times* in the NYPL-PA-BRTC dated December 22, 1912, reported Eltinge got just $13 a week with Rice, which seems unlikely—it also mislabeled the production *Mr. Wicks of Wickham*—or, perhaps, Eltinge's pay was quickly raised when Rice realized that the impersonator was one of the few things theatergoers actually liked about his show; "Caught, Clipped, and Pasted."

5. Banner, *American Beauty*, 180.

6. Banner, *American Beauty*, 175, 181–182; In the 1941 movie *Ziegfeld Girl* (dirs. Robert Z. Leonard & Busby Berkeley), Lana Turner (as Sheila Reagan) dines with a wealthy admirer at just such an establishment. A Brooklyn-born woman who worked as an elevator operator at Macy's, Sheila insists on "a stack o' wheats" rather than, say, lobster or Châteaubriand. Eventually, she is persuaded to order "crèpe suzette"; Dimeglio, *Vaudeville U.S.A.*, 176; Susan A. Glenn, *Female Spectacle: The Theatrical Roots of Modern Feminism* (Cambridge, MA: Harvard University Press, 2000), 197; Scholten, "Drag Performance in Minnesota Theater."

7. Excerpted in "The Stage: Amusements for the Week," *Spokesman-Review, Spokane* (WA), October 16, 1904, 2 [14].

8. [Advertisement.] *Philadelphia Inquirer*, November 20, 1904, iii: 2 [34]; The History Project, *Improper Bostonians* (Boston: Beacon Press, 1998), 111–112; Burns Mantle and Garrison P. Sherwood, eds., *The Best Plays of 1899–1909 and the Yearbook of Drama in America* (New York: Dodd, Mead & Co., 1944), 466; Dreiser, *Sister Carrie*, 93, 115.

9. Freeman, *Brief History of Butte*, 106–112; Leach, *Land of Desire*, 57–59, 91, 143–144; David Nasaw, *Going Out: The Rise and Fall of Public Amusements* (New York: Basic Books, 1993), 20; "Vaudeville's Clearing House," *New York Clipper*, November 29, 1913, 1; E. F. Albee, "Twenty Years of Vaudeville," *Theatre Magazine*, May 1920, 408; "Plays and Players," *The Theatre*, July 1912, 6.

10. "Fun and Good Music," *Harrisburg Telegraph* (PA), December 9, 1904, 10 [26]; The History Project, *Improper Bostonians*, 111–112; "The Merry Shopgirls," *Harrisburg Telegraph* (PA), December 15, 1904, 2.

11. "Fulton Opera House: 'Mr. Wix of Wickham' Lacks Action," *New Era—Lancaster* (PA), December 17, 1904, 2; *Denver Times*, December 22, 1912, no other attribution or page number, from clipping file at NYPL-PA-BRTC, Robinson Locke Collection, ser. 2: Eli-Yet; "Affairs of the Theater," *Brooklyn Daily Eagle*, December 25, 1904, 8 [16]; "'The Merry Shopgirls,'" *Boston Sunday Globe*, January 15, 1905, 33; "He Wore Skirts for a Living"; Toll, *On with the Show*, 202; Burns Mantle, "Professional Career of 40 Years Ended with Eltinge Death," *Sunday Journal-Herald Spotlight* (Dayton, OH), March 16, 1941, 56 [3].

276 NOTES

12. Cadet Theatricals [program], *Miss Po-Ko-Hon-Tas*, from clipping file at NYPL-PA-BRTC, MWEZ+N.C. 2261; Barnet, *Extravaganza King*, xiv; "First Corps to Give 'Ye Old Folks' Concert.'"

13. Berlanstein, "Breeches and Breaches," 350–351.

14. Inness, "Girls Will Be Boys and Boys Will Be Girls," 2; Garber, *Vested Interests*, 21–22; Leach, *Land of Desire*, 148; Cadillac advertisement reproduced in James Playstead Wood, *The Story of Advertising* (New York: Ronald Press, 1958), 310; Weber quoted in Kimmel, *Manhood in America*, 104; John Fiske, *Understanding Popular Culture* (Boston: Unwin Hyman, 1989), 41.

15. Brockett, *History of the Theatre*, 18, 24; Jill Gentile with Michael Macrone, *Feminine Law: Freud, Free Speech, and the Voice of Desire* (London: Karnac, 2016), 69, 173.

16. Peter Ackroyd, *Dressing Up: Transvestism and Drag: The History of an Obsession* (New York: Simon & Schuster, 1979), 89; Brockett, *History of the Theatre*, 22; Archer quoted in Sylvan Barnet, Morton Berman, and William Burto, "Medieval and Renaissance English Drama: An Introduction," in *The Genius of the Early English Theater*, ed. Sylvan Barnet, Morton Berman, and William Burto (New York: Signet, 1962), 8–9.

17. Averil Cameron, *The Later Roman Empire* (Cambridge, MA: Harvard University Press, 1993), 131; Brockett, *History of the Theatre*, 46, 69.

18. Barnet, Berman, and Burto, "Medieval and Renaissance English Drama," 11; Suthrell, *Unzipping Gender*, 126; Barnet, Berman, and Burto, "Medieval and Renaissance English Drama," 12–14; Brockett, *History of the Theatre*, 15–17, 94–97, 100.

19. Ackroyd, *Dressing Up*, 89–91; Normington, *Gender and Medieval Drama*, 58.

20. Ackroyd, *Dressing Up*, 92; Brockett, *History of the Theatre*, 164, 170–171, 181.

21. Bernard Capp, "Playgoers, Players, and Cross-Dressing in Early Modern London," in *Moral Panics, the Media and the Law in Early Modern England* (London: Palgrave Macmillan, 2009), 160; Anne Herrmann, "Travesty and Transgression: Transvestism in Shakespeare, Brecht, and Churchill," *Theatre Journal* 41, no. 2 (1989): 135–136; Normington, *Gender and Medieval Drama*, 59; see also Anna Bayman, "Cross-Dressing and Pamphleteering in Early Seventeenth-Century London," in *Moral Panics, Media, and the Law in Early Modern England*, ed. David Lemmings and Clare Walker (London: Palgrave Macmillan, 2009), 63–77.

22. Baker, *Drag*, 16, 52–53; Phyllis Rackin, "Androgyny, Mimesis, and the Marriage of the Boy Heroine on the English Renaissance Stage," *PMLA* 102, no. 1 (January 1987): 29.

23. Herrmann, "Travesty and Transgression," 135–136.

24. Ackroyd, *Dressing Up*, 95; Brockett, *History of the Theatre*, 109.

25. Brockett, *History of the Theatre*, 285, 305; Ackroyd, *Dressing Up*, 96; "Greenroom, Stage, and Foyer," *Los Angeles Herald Sunday Magazine*, January 10, 1909, 4 [48].

26. Baker, *Drag*, 63; Lesley Ferris, "Introduction: Current Crossings," in *Crossing the Stage: Controversies on Cross-Dressing* (New York: Routledge, 1993), 81.

27. Senelick, "Mollies or Men of Mode?," 38; Brockett, *History of the Theatre*, 288–290; Ackroyd, *Dressing Up*, 101; Landis, "Julian Eltinge's Manly Transformation," 16.

28. See Lawrence W. Levine, *Highbrow/Lowbrow: The Emergence of Cultural Hierarchy in America* (Cambridge, MA: Harvard University Press, 1988), "One: William

NOTES 277

Shakespeare in America," 11–82; Esther Newton, *Mother Camp: Female Impersonators in America* (Englewood Cliffs, NJ: Prentice Hall, 1972), 58.

29. "Eltinges of Queen Elizabeth's Time as Shakespeare Heroines," *Detroit Free Press*, February 11, 1912, 12 [63].

30. Anthony, "Julian and Not Julia, Eltinge Speaks"; Senelick, "Mollies or Men of Mode?," 39–40, 53; "Eltinge Harks Back Three Centuries," *Sun, Baltimore*, March 4, 1913, 5; "He Wears a Corset," *Sunday Telegram, Clarksburg, W.Va.*, May 23, 1915, 30.

31. [Advertisement.] *Boston Evening Transcript*, February 11, 1905, 29.

32. "Albee on Vaudeville in 1912–13"; "E. F. Albee, Co-Founder of Vaudeville"; "Keith's Boston Programme"; "The Keith Anniversary," *New York Clipper*, November 29, 1913, 6; E. F. Albee, "The Future of Show Business," *Billboard*, December 19, 1914, 38; Harris, *Humbug*, 113; Toll, *On with the Show*, 265; Barrymore, *Memories*, 177.

33. [Advertisement.] *Boston Evening Transcript*, February 11, 1905, p. 29; University of Iowa, Special Collections, Keith/Albee Collection, Box 4: 11/28/1904–8/28/1905, 84a.

34. "Temple Theater—Adgie and Her Lions—Other Fine Attractions"; "The Stage," *Detroit Free Press*, May 16, 1905, 4; "Amusement Notes"; "Manhattan Theaters," *Brooklyn Citizen*, June 11, 1905, 15; "Roof Garden Seasons Now," *Sun* (NY), June 4, 1905, 7 [31]; Dan Dietz, *The Complete Book of 1900s Broadway Musicals* (Lanham, MD: Rowman & Littlefield, 2022), 289; Peters, in "Gay Deceiver," 85–86, writes the Eltinge appeared in *Lifting the Lid* rather than that he adapted a character from it, as seems to have been the case.

35. Keith/Albee Collection, Box 4: 11/28/1904–8/28/1905, 84a; for more on Stuart see Bean, 249; Jolin quote in Peters, "Gay Deceiver," 85.

36. Keith/Albee Collection, Box 4: 11/28/1904–8/28/1905, 95; "At the Buffalo Theaters," *Buffalo Illustrated Times*, May 21, 1905, 34 [38].

37. Lewis, "Traveling Show," 9.

38. Nasaw, *Going Out*, p. 19; Toll, *On with the Show*, 265; Wilson quote in Slide, *Encyclopedia of Vaudeville*, front matter, no page number.

39. S.D., *No Applause—Just Throw Money*, 40–41, 52–53; Rodger, *Champagne Charlie and Pretty Jemima*, 11–17, 47, 59; Laurie, *Vaudeville: From the Honky-tonks*, 10–11; Luc Sante, *Low Life* (New York: Vintage Books, 1991), 85; Snyder, *Voice of the City*, 4; Parker R. Zellers, "The Cradle of Variety: The Concert Saloon," *Educational Theatre Journal* 20, no. 4 (December 1968): 580, 584; Brockett, *History of the Theatre*, 385–386.

40. "B. F. Keith, The Man Who Dared and Won," *New York Star*, October 24, 1903, no page number given, from clipping file at NYPL-PA-BRTC; "'Tony' Pastor," *New York Clipper*, September 5, 1908, 722; Snyder, *Voice of the City*, 13; Toll, *On with the Show*, 29, 51–55, 268; "Dean of Vaudeville Celebrities," *Variety*, March 4, 1906, 5; Tony Pastor, "Tony Pastor Recounts the Origin of American 'Vaudeville," *Variety*, December 15, 1906, 17; *New York Dramatic Mirror*, January 1, 1898, 16; *New York Clipper*, March 12, 1898, 24; *New York Clipper*, September 16, 1899, 582; S.D., *No Applause—Just Throw Money*, 68; Chauncey, *Gay New York*, 58; Zellers, "The Cradle of Variety," 581; Douglas Gilbert, *American Vaudeville: Its Life and*

278 NOTES

Times (New York: Dover Publications, 1940), 10; [Advertisement.] "Tony Pastor's New 14th St. Theatre" and "Pastor Looks Far Back: Stars the Dean of Music Halls Has Discovered," both from clipping files on microfilm at NYPL-PA-BRTC, MWEZ+ n.c. 4547.

41. Braudy, *Frenzy of Renown*, 13; "Albee on Vaudeville in 1912–13"; regarding Albee and Keith receiving startup money from the Catholic church, see Laurie, *Vaudeville: From the Honky-tonks*, 342–343; Charles Samuels and Louise Samuels, *Once upon a Stage: The Merry World of Vaudeville* (New York: Dodd, Mead & Co., 1974), 39; and Stein, ed., *American Vaudeville as Seen by Its Contemporaries*, 99; Gilbert, *American Vaudeville*, 205.

42. Hartley Davis, "In Vaudeville," *Everybody's Magazine*, August 1905, 231–232; Laurie, *Vaudeville: From the Honky-tonks*, 398–399; "Evolution of Cheap Vaudeville," *Variety*, December 14, 1907, 10; Neal Gabler, *An Empire of Their Own: How the Jews Invented Hollywood* (New York: Anchor Books, 1988), 2; see also David Bordwell, Janet Staiger, and Kristin Thompson, *The Classical Hollywood Cinema: Film Style and Mode of Production to 1960* (New York: Columbia University Press, 1985).

43. Nasaw, *Going Out*, 20; Noël Burch, "A Primitive Mode of Representation?," in *Early Cinema: Space, Frame, Narrative*; Brockett, *History of the Theatre*, 385; "The Keith Anniversary"; Harris, *Humbug*, 163–164; "B. F. Keith Dead"; "Albee on Vaudeville in 1912–13."

44. Laurie, *Vaudeville: From the Honky-tonks*, 340; "E. F. Albee, Co-Founder of Vaudeville"; "E. F. Albee Dies at Palm Beach," *New York Times*, March 12, 1930, 32.

45. "E. F. Albee, Co-Founder of Vaudeville"; "E. F. Albee Dies at Palm Beach"; Robert W. Snyder, "Vaudeville and the Transformation of Popular Culture," in *Inventing Times Square*, 133; Samuels and Samuels, *Once upon a Stage*, 38.

46. Samuels and Samuels, *Once upon a Stage*, 38, 233; Fleischer, "Collaborative Projects of Symbolist Playwrights and Early Modern Dancers"; University of Iowa, Special Collections, Keith/Albee Collection, Box 4: 11/28/1904–8/28/1905, 165; Gilbert, *American Vaudeville*, 200; Snyder, *Voice of the City*, 27, 198.

47. It is generally agreed that the term "vaudeville" derives from a genre of lively ballads and drinking songs associated with troubadour Olivier Basselin who brought his musical stylings to Normandy's Vire river valley—the *val de vire* or *vau de vire* in French—in the fifteenth century. Robert Snyder argues that when these types of songs and associated entertainments eventually migrated and urbanized in France, a new artistic sensibility known as *voix de ville* or a "voice of the city" emerged. As we have seen, there were instances of North American producers using the term "vaudeville" before Keith & Albee. (Dimeglio cites a Boston saloon being the first to deploy the word, back in 1840.) But there is little doubt that it was the latter team that heavily leveraged the term to burnish their product in the marketplace and disaggregate it from "variety," "concert saloon," and, increasingly, "burlesque." An act called "The Representative Vaudeville Company of America" toured to acclaim in 1887, and at least one newspaper was covering the "Vaudeville Stage" by 1896, though through much of the 1890s, the trade paper the *New York Clipper* still referred to the entertainment as "variety" in regular columns and reviews. See: Pastor, "Tony Pastor Recounts

NOTES 279

the Origin of American 'Vaudeville'"; Joseph M. Schenck, "Inside Vaudeville," *Variety*, December 20, 1912, 33; Snyder, *Voice of the City*, 12, 27; Brockett, *History of the Theatre*, 385; S.D., *No Applause—Just Throw Money*, 20; Leigh Woods, "Sarah Bernhardt and the Refining of American Vaudeville," *Theatre Research International* 18 (Spring 1993): 16; Dimeglio, *Vaudeville U.S.A.*, 19; various clippings, New York Public Library for the Performing Arts, Billy Rose Theatre Collection; "Variety," *New York Clipper*, January 18, 1890, 740; "Variety," *New York Clipper*, January 4, 1896, 692.

48. "Pastor Looks Far Back"; "The Keith Anniversary"; Albee, "Future of Show Business," 38; Snyder, *Voice of the City*, 31–32, 64; Snyder, "Vaudeville and the Transformation of Popular Culture," 134; Stein, ed., *American Vaudeville as Seen by Its Contemporaries*, 99; Gilbert, *American Vaudeville*, 205; *New York Dramatic Mirror*, August 25, 1900, 8; theatrical journalists were also learning the new rules, including one who chided theatergoers who "laughed very impolitely" at what seemed an inappropriate moment. Taste meant power, increasingly, and vice versa; see "Proctor's Thérèse," *New York Dramatic Mirror*, May 27, 1899, 18.

49. One report indicated that the UBO was offering sixty-eight-week contracts by 1907, see "United Managers in One Big Corporation," *Variety*, June 22, 1907, 6; Schenck, "Inside Vaudeville"; *Fortune* magazine credited as author, "Metro-Goldwyn-Mayer," in *American Film Industry*, rev. ed., 311–333; "State Senate Passes Voss Bill," *New York Clipper*, May 8, 1909, 319; Gilbert, *American Vaudeville*, 228–230; Samuels and Samuels, *Once upon a Stage*, 23, 45; Harvey Alexander Higgins Jr., "The Origin of Vaudeville," *New York Dramatic Mirror*, May 13, 1919, 720; Peter A. Davis, "The Syndicate/Shubert War," in *Inventing Times Square*, 150–153.

50. [Advertisement.] *New York Clipper*, June 30, 1900, 403; *New York Dramatic Mirror*, April 8, 1905; *New York Dramatic Mirror*, March 4, 1905, 20; "The Big Merger Completed," *New York Dramatic Mirror*, June 13, 1906, 1; Sam M'Kee, "Something of E. F. Albee," *New York Telegraph*, October 10, 1905, no page number, from clipping file at NYPL-PA-BRTC; "Vaudeville by Wholesale," *Variety*, March 9, 1907, 2; "Percy Williams Houses Sold," *Variety*, April 6, 1912, 3; "Williams Sells Theatres," *New York Clipper*, May 4, 1912, 10; "Sale of Hammerstein Stock," *New York Clipper*, October 31, 1914, 1; [Advertisement.] *New York Clipper*, February 23, 1907, 30; Laurie, *Vaudeville: From the Honky-tonks*, 353–358; "Williams Goes with Keith," *Variety*, February 16, 1907, 2; Samuels and Samuels, *Once upon a Stage*, 25; "The Keith Anniversary"; "United Booking Offices Cleans Up All 'Big Time,'" *Variety*, May 4, 1912, 5; "Another Big Keith Deal," *New York Clipper*, September 6, 1913, 1; *New York Clipper*, November 8, 1913, 1; S.D., *No Applause—Just Throw Money*, 147; Tucker, *Some of These Days*, 88; "No More 'Continuous,'" *New York Dramatic Mirror*, December 8, 1906, 16; University of Iowa, Special Collections, Keith/Albee Collection, Box 4: 11/28/1904–8/28/1905, 37, 216.

51. [Advertisement.] *New York Clipper*, June 1, 1912, 9; "Vaudeville's Clearing House"; "Evolution of Cheap Vaudeville"; *New York Clipper*, August 19, 1905, 655; *New York Clipper*, August 7, 1909, 653; Stein, ed., *American Vaudeville as Seen by Its Contemporaries*, 109, 124; "E. F. Albee, Co-Founder of Vaudeville"; M. Alison

280 NOTES

Kibler, *Rank Ladies: Gender and Cultural Hierarchy in American Vaudeville* (Chapel Hill: University of North Carolina Press, 1999), 18; Gilbert, *American Vaudeville*, 206; McLean, *American Vaudeville as Ritual*, 47; "Vaudeville and Minstrel," *New York Clipper*, November 6, 1897, 611.

52. "Attorney General Asked to Dissolve the U.B.O.," *Variety*, October 11, 1912, 1; "Marinelli Loses," *New York Clipper*, January 24, 1914, 1; "United Booking Offices Win Another Suit," *New York Clipper*, November 13, 1915, 8; Laurie, *Vaudeville: From the Honky-tonks*, 37, 311; [Advertisement.] *New York Clipper*, June 1, 1912, 9; "Vaudeville's Clearing House"; "Evolution of Cheap Vaudeville"; *New York Clipper*, August 19, 1905, 655; *New York Clipper*, August 7, 1909, 653; Stein, ed., *American Vaudeville as Seen by Its Contemporaries*, 109, 124; "E. F. Albee, Co-Founder of Vaudeville"; Kibler, *Rank Ladies*, 18, 171 (Kibler's chapter on the White Rats provides an excellent, succinct overview and interpretation of vaudeville's labor struggles); Snyder, *Voice of the City*, 37–40; Gilbert, *American Vaudeville*, 206; McLean, *American Vaudeville as Ritual*, 47; Letter to "Walter," written from Shubert Theatre, Kansas City, MO, February 9, 1914, otherwise unattributed, from clipping file at NYPL-PA-BRTC.

53. "Albee on Vaudeville in 1912–1913"; University of Iowa, Special Collections, Keith/Albee Collection, Box 4: 11/28/1904–8/28/1905, 6; *New York Clipper*, November 6, 1897, 594.

54. "Albee on Vaudeville in 1912–1913"; University of Iowa, Special Collections, Keith/Albee Collection, Box 4: 11/28/1904–8/28/1905, 26, 179; *New York Clipper*, November 6, 1897, 594; S. Ziegler, "Review of Show & Stage Report," *Variety*, April 10, 1909, 10; A. Herbert, "Week's Vaudeville Bills in New York," *New York Star*, July 4, 1914, no page number, from clipping file at NYPL-PA-BRTC.

55. Schenck, "Inside Vaudeville"; Dimeglio, *Vaudeville U.S.A.*, 11; Samuels and Samuels, *Once upon a Stage*, 4–5; Stein, ed., *American Vaudeville as Seen by Its Contemporaries*, 129; Allen, "Vaudeville and Film, 1895–1915," 24; E. F. Albee, "Keith Vaudeville," *New York Clipper*, February 15, 1913, viii; *B. F. Keith's Theatre News*, no. 31, vol. 25, April 9, 1923, no page number, from clipping file at NYPL-PA-BRTC.

56. Hasan Ali, "Trans in Pakistan," *The Nation*, January 23–30, 2023, 28; Slide, *Encyclopedia of Vaudeville*, 158; Kimmel, *Manhood in America*, 52–54; "Harry Lehr's Boston Rival"; University of Iowa, Special Collections, Keith/Albee Collection, Box 4: 11/28/1904–8/28/1905, 84a, 179, Box 5: 5/4/1905–4/23/1906, 92, 92a, Box 8, 9/23/1907–3/12/1908, 39, 78; George Wallace, "Julian Eltinge, the Fascinating Widow," *Northport Journal*, March 2, 1995, 1+.

57. Allen, "Vaudeville and Film, 1895–1915," 153; Snyder, *Voice of the City*, 105; University of Iowa, Special Collections, Keith/Albee Collection, Box 4: 11/28/1904–8/28/1905, 64, 93, 93a, 100, 116, 116a, Box 5: 5/4/1905–4/23/1906, 26.

58. "Temple Theater: Adgie and Her Lions—Other Fine Attractions"; "Vaudeville at the Temple," *Detroit Free Press*, May 16, 1905, 4; Senelick, *Changing Room*, 334–337; [Advertisement.] *San Francisco Examiner*, September 17, 1905, 11; "Playhouses and Players: Orpheum," *Los Angeles Daily Times*, March 10, 1905, ii: 13 [17]; [Advertisement.] *Sunday Star, Washington*, February 11, 1906, ii: 7 [23];

NOTES 281

[Advertisement.] *Baltimore Sun*, February 20, 1906, 1; University of Iowa, Special Collections, Keith/Albee Collection, Box 5: 9/4/1905–4/23/1906, 140.

59. Wolf, "The Sort of Fellow Julian Eltinge Really Is," 801, 798; "Athlete in Gowns Stage Sensation," *St. Louis Post-Dispatch*, July 5, 1907, 16; "Amusement Notes"; "Impersonations by Julian Eltinge, a Big, Husky Man"; Gilbert, *American Vaudeville*, 19; William Sage, "Albee Talks Vaudeville," *Cleveland Leader*, date-stamped December 28, 1912, no page number, from clipping file at NYPL-PA-BRTC; "Keith Orders Bigger Shows for His New York Theatres," *Variety*, October 4, 1912, 4; University of Iowa, Special Collections, Keith/Albee Collection, Box 4: 11/28/1904–8/28/1905, 76, 76a, 77; Wolf, "The Sort of Fellow Julian Eltinge Really Is," 800.

60. "Amusement Notes"; "Manages Skirts with Sang Froid"; [Advertisement.] *Washington Times*, February 3, 1912, 3; Silverman, "Shows of the Week by Sime: Keith's"; Slide, *The Encyclopedia of Vaudeville*, 68–69; communication from J. J. Shubert to P. S. Mattox provided by Sylvia Wang, curator of the Shubert Archive, New York; Hajdu and Carey, *Revolution in Three Acts*, 111.

61. *New York Dramatic Mirror*, January 5, 1901, 16; *New York Dramatic Mirror*, September 15, 1900, 18; "What Greater Vaudeville Promises This Winter," *New York Times*, September 1, 1907, vi: 2; Tucker, *Some of These Days*, 219.

62. *Variety*, March 6, 1906, 6 [57], "Eltinge in Demand Abroad," *Variety*, March 6, 1906, 5; "Julian Eltinge Booked Abroad," *Variety*, April 28, 1906, 5; "Julian Eltinge in 'The Widow's Might,' at Clune's Broadway," *Los Angeles Record*, March 9, 1918, 5; "Vaudeville Notes," *Hartford Daily Courant*, August 21, 1906, 5; "Eltinge's Return Delayed," *Variety*, September 22, 1906, 6; *Variety*, December 15, 1906, 3; "Eltinge for Broadway," *Variety*, February 24, 1906; *Minneapolis Tribune*, September 26, 1906, 25; *Sunday Times, Chattanooga* (TN), January 6, 1907, 23; *Variety*, January 19, 1907, 3; [Advertisement.] *Boston Globe*, February 17, 1907, 26; "Julian Eltinge's Real Monaker [*sic*]," *Fort Wayne Daily News* (IN), May 1, 1911, 2; "The Bearded American Belle," *Variety*, December 14, 1907, 44 [81]; "Who Would You Rather Be?," February 21, 1912, typed draft, no further attributions, in NYPL-PA-BRTC.

63. Connelly, "King of Drag," 41; "'Lucky Lucy' Floors a Surprised Stagehand," *Pittsburg Press*, April 10, 1907, 16; "Julian Eltinge Dies; Famous in Feminine Roles," *Chicago Daily Tribune*, March 8, 1941, 20; the exchange rate of US\$5 per UK£1 sterling at the time is about correct: https://www.exchangerates.org.uk/articles/1325/the-200-year-pound-to-dollar-exchange-rate-history-from-5-in-1800s-to-todays.html.

64. "Brilliant Beginning of Fall Season of Refined Vaudeville"; "Julian Eltinge's Real Monaker [*sic*]"; "Julian Eltinge Again Sees Rialto from Busy Post," no other attribution, from a clipping file at NYPL-PA-BRTC, MWEZ+N.C. 9882 22,638 22,939#; Eltinge, "When a Man Becomes a Woman"; Sarah Mitchell, Research Room and Enquiries Assistant, Royal Archives/Private Secretary's Office, Windsor, UK, email to author, October 12, 2021; Golden, "Julian Eltinge: The Queen of Old Broadway," 21; Thornton, "Great Pretender"; Erdman, *Blue Vaudeville*, 91.

282 NOTES

Chapter 4

1. "Plays & Playfolk: Julian Eltinge and Some Other Good Things on Chase Bill," *Washington Herald*, March 10, 1907, 4 [24]; "Opening Night at Theaters"; "World's Foremost Imitator of Women"; "The Week at Local Theatres: Chase's—Julian Eltinge, Gibson Girl Impersonator," *Washington Post*, March 10, 1907, 2 [19]; New England Historical Society, "Maxine Elliot, the Maine Starlet and Winston Churchill," June 9, 2022, https://www.newenglandhistoricalsociety.com/maxine-elliott-maine-starlet-winston-churchill/.
2. "Keith's Theater: Vaudeville"; Banner, *American Beauty*, 155–156; "The Week at Local Theatres: Chase's—Julian Eltinge, Gibson Girl Impersonator"; Nasaw, *Going Out*, 20; "Amusement Notes"; "Julian Eltinge," *Variety*, October 12, 1907, 9 [52].
3. Tregelles, "Difficult Art of Stage Makeup"; Eltinge, "When a Man Becomes a Woman."
4. Eltinge, "When a Man Becomes a Woman."
5. "Four Views of Mr. Julian Eltinge," *Variety*, December 14, 1907, 9; "At the Playhouses: Vaudeville at Bennett's," *Gazette Montreal*, January 14, 1908, 9; Ernest L. Waitt, "Boston," *Variety*, February 22, 1908, 27; "Cleveland O.," *Variety*, February 8, 1908, 31.
6. Laurie, *Vaudeville: From the Honky-tonks to the Palace*, 53–54; "Chat with Eltinge"; *Variety*, January 18, 1908, 11; "Eltinge Quits Skirts," *Variety*, April 18, 1908, 9; Bullough and Bullough, *Cross Dressing, Sex, and Gender*, 235; Baker, *Drag*, 212.
7. "Eltinge: A Mystery," *Variety*, October 26, 1907, 7 [130]; "Four Views of Mr. Julian Eltinge."
8. "General Grand Chapter: Order of the Eastern Star," Order of the Eastern Star, June 11, 2022, https://easternstar.org/about-oes/our-history/; "Disguised as Woman," *Boston Globe*, February 20, 1908, 8.
9. "Disguised as Woman."
10. Banner, *American Beauty*, 160.
11. Kimmel, *Manhood in America*, 136–137; Casey, *Prettiest Girl on Stage*, 60.
12. "Chat with Eltinge"; *Variety*, April 4, 1908, 5; "Eltinge Quits Skirts"; Wolf, "The Sort of Fellow Julian Eltinge Really Is," 795.
13. Many thanks to a personal communication from Mr. Peter Sullivan in July 2022, with information about his home, the former Eltinge/Dalton property; 1909 map provided by Ceylan Swensen of the Northport Historical Society, Long Island, NY (see following note); "Spotlight on Stars of the Stage," *Buffalo Courier*, March 15, 1908, 6 [2]; *Variety* (April 4, 1908, 5) identified the seller slightly more accurately as "John Henschel."
14. Wallace, "Julian Eltinge, the Fascinating Widow," 1+; "Eltinge Quits Skirts."
15. "Music and Drama Notes," *Vancouver World*, July 29, 1911; unidentified clip regarding "house warming" provided courtesy of Northport Historical Society's Julian Eltinge archival materials.
16. "In Just a Minute," *Boston Globe*, February 13, 1911, 3; "One Close Shave and Then Another."
17. "Wants to Take Stage Name."

18. Thirteenth Census, Huntington Township, Suffolk County, New York State, provided courtesy of BSBPA; "The Theatre," *Sunday Star, Washington, DC*, ii: 3 [21]; "Julian Eltinge Is a Regular Farmer," *Buffalo Courier*, March 9, 1913, 42; information regarding the Henschels courtesy of Terry Reid of the Northport Historical Society and Ceylan Swensen, "Julian Eltinge," presentation, virtual and at Northport Historical Society, Long Island, NY, June 26, 2022; Senelick, *Changing Room*, 353–354; Scholten, "Drag Performance in Minnesota Theater."

19. *Variety*, April 4, 1908, 5; *Brooklyn Citizen*, July 23, 1908, 7; Ceylan Swensen, researcher and educator at the Northport Historical Society (NHS), provided substantial assistance with various details pertaining to Julian Eltinge's Ft. Salonga purchase, and the author is grateful: Ceylan Swensen, "Julian Eltinge" presentation, virtual and at NHS, June 26, 2022.

20. Wolf, "The Sort of Fellow Julian Eltinge Really Is," 801.

21. Silverman, "Shows of the Week by Sime, Keith's"; "Julian Eltinge's Success," *Sun, Baltimore*, February 20, 1906, 12; University of Iowa, Special Collections, Keith/Albee Collection, Box 5: 9/4/1905–4/23/1906, 100, 113; Box 8: 9/23/1907–3/12/1908, 25, 46, 46a.

22. For weather history see www.weather.gov, accessed January 24, 2023, https://www.weather.gov/media/okx/Climate/CentralPark/monthlyannualtemp.pdf; Snyder, *Voice of the City*, 86–91; "Hammerstein's Roof"; "Julian Eltinge," *Variety*, July 24, 1909, 4.

23. Toll, *On with the Show*, 191; "Smokes in Woman's Attire," prepublication article manuscript, no other attribution or page number, from clipping file at NYPL-PA-BRTC; "One Dancer among 500 Boys," *Variety*, May 23, 1908, 7; Wolf, "The Sort of Fellow Julian Eltinge Really Is," 801.

24. Lott, *Love and Theft*, 6–7.

25. Snyder, *Voice of the City*, 5; Rydell, *All the World's a Fair*, 236; Hannah Arendt, *The Origins of Totalitarianism*, new edition with added prefaces (New York: Harcourt, Brace Jovanovich, 1979), 192 (original work published 1951).

26. Toll, *On with the Show*, 81–82, 84, 87.

27. S.D., *No Applause—Just Throw Money*, 37–38.

28. In Lewis, ed., *From Traveling Show to Vaudeville*, 74–76.

29. Toll, *On with the Show*, 89; Rodger, *Champagne Charlie and Pretty Jemima*, 15.

30. Bean, "Transgressing the Gender Divide," 246–247; Lewis, ed., *From Traveling Show to Vaudeville*, 68; Laurie, *Vaudeville: From the Honky-tonks*, 88; Toll, *On with the Show*, 243.

31. Laurie, *Vaudeville: From the Honky-tonks*, 88; Lott, *Love and Theft*, 164; Bean, "Transgressing the Gender Divide," 249; Senelick, *Changing Room*, 275–276; Garber, *Vested Interests*, 276; Erdman, *Queen of Vaudeville*, 212; Laurie, *Vaudeville: From the Honky-tonks*, 89; Toll, *On with the Show*, 240; Long, "'All Our Girls Are Men,'" 34–35.

32. Casey, *Prettiest Girl on Stage*, xxiii, 42; Peiss, *Hope in a Jar*, 33; Pamela Brown Lavitt, "First of the Red Hot Mamas: 'Coon Shouting' and the Jewish Ziegfeld Girl," *American Jewish History* 87, no. 4 (December 1999), 262–272, https://www.jstor.org/stable/23886224; University of Iowa, Special Collections, Keith/Albee Collection,

284   NOTES

Box 4: 11/28/1904–8/28/1905, 27a, 53; Edward Said, *Culture and Imperialism* (New York: Vintage Books, 1993), xi.

33. Snyder, *Voice of the City*, 120; Laurie, *Vaudeville: From the Honky-tonks*, 141; University of Iowa, Special Collections, Keith/Albee Collection, Box 4: 11/28/1904–8/28/1905, 35, 50, 58; "Julian Eltinge Says His Great Boyhood Ambition Was to Be a Blackface Comedian," *New Orleans Item*, December 4, 1921, no page number given, from clipping file at NYPL-PA-BRTC; Gilbert, *American Vaudeville*, 83; Dimeglio, *Vaudeville U.S.A.*, 72.

34. Laurie, *Vaudeville: From the Honky-tonks*, 141; University of Iowa, Special Collections, Keith/Albee Collection, Box 4: 11/28/1904–8/28/1905, 53a, 60, 192a; Erdman, *Queen of Vaudeville*, 9; Joe Laurie Jr., "A Thumbnose Sketch: Jack Norworth," *New York Herald Tribune*, March 5, 1944, no page number given, from clipping file at NYPL-PA-BRTC.

35. Glenn, *Female Spectacle*, 111; "New Acts of the Week," *Variety*, May 30, 1908, 13 [158]; Toll, *On with the Show*, 191–194.

36. Toll, *On with the Show*, 195–196; "Frank L. Perley's Comedians," no other attribution or page number, from clipping file at NYPL-PA-BRTC, Robinson Locke Collection; "Andrew Mack in 'Tom Moore'," *Brooklyn Eagle*, November 4, 1902, 14; "Why Authors Go Crazy," *New York Times*, March 23, 1930, ix: 4.

37. Kibler, *Rank Ladies*, 171 (Kibler's chapter on the White Rats provides an excellent, succinct overview and interpretation of vaudeville's labor struggles); Laurie, *Vaudeville: From the Honky-tonks*, 311; Snyder, *Voice of the City*, 37–40; Marx, *Capital*, 338; "Stage Stars Sued in $500,000 Case," *Boston Globe*, August 12, 1919, 13; "Julian Eltinge Shied Clear of Actors' Strike," *Sunday Times, Chattanooga* (TN), September 7, 1919, 7; Toll, *On with the Show*, 192–193, 197; Dos Passos, *U.S.A. Nineteen Nineteen*, 197; "Cigarette Law Pains Eltinge"; Boag, *Re-Dressing America's Frontier Past*, 75–76; Brinig, *Wide Open Town*, 153; Rydell, *All the World's a Fair*, 4; *Lady Bill: The Story of Julian Eltinge*, directed by WHO/Soapbox Productions, 2014, https://www.youtube.com/watch?v=fr4WaBe7GjI&t=3s.

38. Toll, *On with the Show*, 106; Lewis, ed., *From Traveling Show to Vaudeville*, 69; Allen, *Horrible Prettiness*, 165; Rodger, *Champagne Charlie and Pretty Jemima*, 158–160; "One Dancer among 500 Boys"; Connelly, "King of Drag," 43; [Advertisement.] *Variety*, May 30, 1908, 17 [88]; "Julian Eltinge Dies in East," *Hollywood Citizen-News*, March 7, 1941, 1; "Earl Benham Dies; Actor, Song Writer," *New York Times*, March 23, 1976, 34; "In all the years I have been with the William Morris Agency," wrote Sophie Tucker, "there has never been a piece of paper between us" (Tucker, *Some of These Days*, 87).

39. [Advertisement.] *New York Dramatic Mirror*, date-stamped September 26, 1908, 17, NYPL-PA-BRTC ELTINGE, Julian; "New Acts of the Week," *Variety*, May 30, 1908, 13 [158]; "Cohan 'Explains' Split with Harris," *New York Times*, Monday April 9, 1934, 20; MWEZ+N.C. 9882 22,638 22,939#; "Fifth Avenue," *Variety*, June 6, 1908, 14 [16]; "Hammerstein's Roof"; Harris, *Humbug*, 77; University of Iowa, Special Collections, Keith/Albee Collection, Box 8: 9/23/1907–3/12/1908, 69; Box 4: 11/28/1904–8/28/1905, 84, 84a; Laurie, *Vaudeville: From the Honky-tonks*, 88.

NOTES   285

40. "How a Man Makes Himself a Beautiful Woman"; University of Iowa, Special Collections, Keith/Albee Collection, Box 8: 9/23/1907–3/12/1908, 78; Lavitt, "First of the Red Hot Mamas," 275; "Impersonations by Julian Eltinge, a Big, Husky Man"; "The Art of Makeup," *Butte Miner*, January 17, 1909, 17; Glenn, *Female Spectacle*, 111; "Plays and Players: About Julian Eltinge," *Nashville Banner*, January 22, 1910, 3 [21].

41. "The Call of Salome," *New York Times*, August 16, 1908, 36.

42. Feliz Cherniavsky, *The Salome Dancer: The Life of Maud Allan* (Toronto: McClelland & Stewart, 1991), 141–142; Richard Bizot, "The Turn-of-the-Century Salome Era: High- and Pop-Culture Variations on the Dance of the Seven Veils," *Choreography and Dance* 2, pt. 3 (1992): 72; John Southworth, *The English Medieval Minstrel* (Suffolk: Boydell & Brewer, 1989), 6–7; Betsy Prioleau, *Seductress: The Women Who Ravished the World and Their Lost Art of Love* (New York: Viking, 1993), 20.

43. Hank [only name given], "La Dance des Nymphes," *New York Clipper*, March 19, 1910, 131; Cherniavsky, *Salome Dancer*, 142; Bizot, "Turn-of-the-Century Salome Era," 72–73.

44. Laurie, *Vaudeville: From the Honky-tonks*, 41; "The Call of Salome"; *New York Clipper*, February 2, 1907, 1322; "New Acts of the Week: Dance of the Seven Veils," *Variety*, February 2, 1907, 10; [Advertisement.] *New York Clipper*, February 9, 1907, 1360; Bizot, "Turn-of-the-Century Salome Era," 78; "A School for Salomes," *New York Dramatic Mirror*, August 26, 1908, 17.

45. S.D., *No Applause—Just Throw Money*, 131; "The Call of Salome"; Edward B. Marks and Abbott J. Lieberling, *They All Sang: From Tony Pastor to Rudy Vallée* (New York: Viking Press, 1934), 172; *Spokane Review*, date-stamped October 25, 1908, no other attribution or page number, from clipping file at NYPL-PA-BRTC, Robinson Locke Collection, no. 450.

46. Charles Darnton, "The Visitation of Salome," *New York Evening World*, August 9, 1908, 7; "All about 'Salome,'" *Variety*, August 1, 1908, 7; Samuels and Samuels, *Once upon a Stage*, 52; *Variety*, August 8, 1908, 15; "'Who Is It?' A Salome Dance," *New York Clipper*, August 29, 1908, 701; Bizot, "Turn-of-the-Century Salome Era," 78; Toll, *On with the Show*, 321; Rush, "New Acts of the Week," *Variety*, December 12, 1908, 14; "The Call of Salome"; Laurie, *Vaudeville: From the Honky-tonks*, 41.

47. "All about 'Salome'"; Laurie, *Vaudeville: From the Honky-tonks*, 34, 41.

48. Glenn, *Female Spectacle*, 111; "This Man Is to Marry This Woman," *Pittsburgh Press*, August 29, 1908, 4.

49. "Julian Eltinge's Latest," *New York Dramatic Mirror*, August 7, 1909, 19; "Another Salome Heralded," *New York Dramatic Mirror*, August 1, 1908, 14.

50. [Advertisement.] *Variety*, January 1, 1915, 22–23; [Advertisement.] *Variety*, October 3, 1908, 2; *Brooklyn Citizen*, July 23, 1908, 7; "Manhattan Stage Notes," *Brooklyn Citizen*, August 16, 1908, 12; "How a Man Makes Himself a Beautiful Woman."

51. "Autumnal Attractions at Buffalo Theaters," *Buffalo Courier*, October 20, 1908, 7; "Amusements," *Times-Democrat* (New Orleans), November 23, 1908, 4; "Julian Eltinge in His Impersonations of Salome with Cohan & Harris Minstrels Monday Evening," *Fort Wayne Journal-Gazette* (IN), September 27, 1908, 19; Rydell, *All the World's a Fair*, 87.

286 NOTES

52. "Amusements," *Times-Democrat*; "Autumnal Attractions at Buffalo Theaters".

53. "Amusements," *Times-Democrat*; Banner, *American Beauty*, 129–131; Glenn, *Female Spectacle*, 112.

54. Bizot, "Turn-of-the-Century Salome Era," 72; Toll, *On with the Show*, 302; "Salome Barred in New Jersey," *New York Dramatic Mirror*, August 26, 1908, 17; "Salomes under Observation," *New York Dramatic Mirror*, September 5, 1908, 19.

55. Thomas Laquer, "Sexual Desire and the Market Economy during the Industrial Revolution," in *Discourses of Sexuality: From Aristotle to AIDS*, ed. Donna Stanton (Ann Arbor: University of Michigan Press, 1992), 186; Anne Hollander, *Seeing through Clothes* (New York: Viking, 1978), 330, 340; "Withdraw 'Salome' after Police Fiat," *New York Times*, November 30, 1910, 11; "No 'Salomes' on Orpheum Circuit," *Variety*, September 12, 1908, 1; Laurie, *Vaudeville: From the Honky-tonks*, 359–361; *New York Clipper*, February 26, 1910, 57; Will H. Low and Kenyon Cox, "The Nude in Art," *Scribner's Magazine*, December 1892, 741–749; Laurie, *Vaudeville: From the Honky-tonks to the Palace*, 359–360; A. A. Brill, "Introduction," in *The Basic Writings of Sigmund Freud*, trans. and ed. A. A. Brill (New York: Modern Library, 1938), 16.

56. *New York Dramatic Mirror*, October 24, 1908, 17; "Conditions on the Stage," *New York Times*, February 14, 1909, v: 8; Joseph I. C. Clarke, "The Sunday Question in Seattle," *New York Dramatic Mirror*, August 26, 1908, 17; Glenn, *Female Spectacle*, 3; Kathleen B. Casey, "Sex, Savagery, and the Woman Who Made Vaudeville Famous," *Frontiers* 36, no. 1 (2015): 87–89; Samuels and Samuels, *Once upon a Stage*, 90–97; S.D., *No Applause—Just Throw Money*, 261; Dimeglio, *Vaudeville U.S.A.*, 146; "The Sunday Question," *New York Dramatic Mirror*, December 15, 1906, 16; "Sunday Crusader Threatened," *New York Dramatic Mirror*, March 16, 1907, 18; *New York Dramatic Mirror*, June 5, 1909, 11; "Ministers on Sunday Question," *New York Dramatic Mirror*, February 9, 1907, 17; "Supreme Court Decides Sunday Shows Illegal," *Variety*, December 7, 1907, 2; "Sunday Vaudeville Crusade," *New York Times*, December 3, 1908, 9; "War on Sunday Vaudeville," *New York Times*, December 1, 1908, 9; "The 'Salome' Dance Gets into Politics," *New York Times*, August 24, 1908, 2; "Says Salome Spirit Pervades Theatre," *New York Times*, February 22, 1909, 9; Bayman, "Cross-Dressing and Pamphleteering in Early Seventeenth-Century London," 63; "Will Withdraw 'Salome'," *New York Times*, February 18, 1909, 1.

57. See Erdman, *Queen of Vaudeville*; Caroline Caffin, *Vaudeville: The Book* (New York: Mitchell Kennerly, 1914), 35–36.

58. Gilbert, *American Vaudeville*, 327; Samuels and Samuels, *Once upon a Stage*, 54; Crowley, Aleister, "Drama Be Damned!" The International 12, issue 4 (April 1918), accessed July 4, 2022, https://hermetic.com/crowley/international/xii/4/the-drama-eva-tanguay.

59. Marks and Lieberling, *They All Sang*, 178–179; Emily Wortis Leider, *Becoming Mae West* (Boston: Da Capo, 2000), 41–42, 63; "The Truth about Tanguay," *Pittsburgh Post*, May 5, 1912, 8; Marybeth Hamilton, *"When I'm Bad, I'm Better,"* 40, 43; Marybeth Hamilton, "Mae West Live: 'SEX, The Drag, and 1920s Broadway'," 82.

60. Casey, "Sex, Savagery, and the Woman Who Made Vaudeville Famous," 87–90; Glenn, *Female Spectacle*, 109; "All about 'Salome' "; Hank, "Eva Tanguay as 'Salome'",

New York Clipper, August 15, 1908, 653; Harriet Coffin, "All Sort and Kinds of Salomes," *Theatre*, April 1909, 132–133; "Eva Tanguay Makes Broad Claim," *New York Dramatic Mirror*, September 26, 1908, 17; [Advertisement.] *Variety*, October 3, 1908, 2.

61. "Julian Eltinge May Wed Tanguay," *Washington Times*, August 16, 1908, 2 [22].

62. "Eva Tanguay's Coming Wedding Talk of the Stage," *Evening World* (NY), August 17, 1908, 3; Chauncey, *Gay New York*, 76.

63. Daniel Boorstin, *The Image: A Guide to Pseudo-Events in America* (New York: Vintage, 1992), 11 (original work published 1962); "When Girl-Boy Weds Boy-Girl, Who'll Be the Boss?" *St. Louis Post-Dispatch*, August 18, 1908, 2; Lowry, *Vaudeville Humor*, 171.

64. "Eva Tanguay Will Wed Julian Eltinge," *Minneapolis Tribune*, August 19, 1908, 4; "The Press' Saturday Woman's Page," *Pittsburgh Press*, August 29, 1908, 4; "This Man Is to Marry This Woman."

65. "The Theaters," *Cincinnati Enquirer*, September 6, 1908, iii & iv, 1; Erdman, *Queen of Vaudeville*, 134; "Eva Tanguay Will Not Marry There," poss. *New York Telegraph*, but otherwise unattributed article in clipping file at NYPL-PA-BRTC, dated August 30, 1908.

66. *New York Clipper*, March 5, 1910, 81; *New York Clipper*, August 27, 1910, 697; *The Sambo Girl* script from the Eva Tanguay Collection, acc. no. 2006.9, the Henry Ford, Dearborn, Michigan.

67. "Eva Tanguay," likely *New York Dramatic Mirror*, but otherwise unattributed article in clipping file at NYPL-PA-BRTC, dated March 26, 1913; Mimi Aguglia letter from Shubert Archive, dated December 17, 1913.

68. Themista, "Julian Eltinge: The Woman Impersonator"; "At the Newark Theatre," *Montclair Times*, February 26, 1910, 2.

Chapter 5

1. Tucker, *Some of These Days*, 36; "Julian Eltinge Wants to Drop the Petticoats and Play Shylock"; "A Dressing Room Marvel," *Variety*, December 11, 1909, 28; "Chat with Eltinge"; Tregelles, "Difficult Art of Stage Makeup"; "CIP Inflation Calculator," accessed October 3, 2022, https://www.in2013dollars.com/us/inflation/1907?amount=900; Kerrera, a "famous international female character impersonator" who claimed (falsely, but with gusto) to be "the only recognized successful rival of Julian Eltinge," promoted the $5,000 gown he wore onstage ([Advertisement.] *Knoxville Sentinel* [TN], February 7, 1912), 10; Connelly ("King of Drag," 4) writes that it was Eltinge's "incredible wardrobe, then valued at $25,000, [that] audiences came to see," which seems to confuse present-day value with that of the past.

2. Exactly when Eltinge engaged Ko Shima's services is, like much about the artist's life, unclear. The latter is mentioned as early as September 1908 ("How a Man Makes Himself a Beautiful Woman"); a March 1918 article refers to Shima's "eleven years of continuous service" (Welton, "This Man a Martyr to the Modiste"), while a January

288 NOTES

1922 interview, by which time Eltinge had switched dressers, refers to Shima having provided "twelve years" of assistance beginning around 1905 (Tallqvist, "Behind Scene Views of Vaudeville's Man Vamp").

3. Mari Uyehara, "The Western Strategy," *Nation*, August 23, 2021, 17–81.

4. "Hans Hanke, Carter DeHaven, Shea's Big Hits," *Buffalo Courier*, September 21, 1909, no page number supplied, from clipping file at NYPL-PA-BRTC.

5. "He Had Learned," *Miami Herald*, December 5, 1912, 8; *New York Telegraph*, date-stamped November 11, 1912, no page number, from clipping file at NYPL-PA-BRTC.

6. Sueyoshi, *Discriminating Sex*, 115.

7. In Rydell, *All the World's a Fair*, 50, 181.

8. University of Iowa, Special Collections, Keith/Albee Collection, Box 4: 11/28/1904–8/28/1905, 20, 37, 89, 109, 109a, 177, 177a.

9. Rydell, *All the World's a Fair*, 205.

10. Themista, "Julian Eltinge: The Woman Impersonator"; Shima was apparently a bachelor when he came into Eltinge's employ, though he later is reported to have gotten "married" (Tallqvist, "Behind Scene Views of Vaudeville's Man Vamp").

11. "Julian Eltinge Wants to Drop the Petticoats and Play Shylock"; "A 'Close-up' of Julian Eltinge," *Wichita Beacon* (KS), November 6, 1917, 9.

12. *Vicksburg Evening Post*, January 6, 1913, 6.

13. Welton, "This Man a Martyr to the Modiste"; Landis, "Julian Eltinge's Manly Transformation," 17–18.

14. "Wichita Women Meet Eltinge," *Wichita Eagle* (KS), November 16, 1919, 6.

15. Landis, "Julian Eltinge's Manly Transformation," 18.

16. M. E. Edsberg, "Risque Rally Rouses Wrath," *Richmond Item* (IN), November 22, 1923, 3.

17. Ullman, "'Twentieth Century Way," 593.

18. Harry Lauder, *Between You and Me* (New York: James McCann, 1919), 163–164.

19. Julian Johnson, "The Drama—Playhouses, Players, Theatrical Chit-Chat," *Los Angeles Times*, January 2, 1910, 29 [III, 1]; Laurie, *Vaudeville: From the Honky-tonks to the Palace*, 372.

20. Tucker, *Some of These Days*, 86; Laurie, *Vaudeville: From the Honky-tonks to the Palace*, 340.

21. Laurie, *Vaudeville: From the Honky-tonks to the Palace*, 372; "Morris Makes Announcement," *New York Dramatic Mirror*, March 14, 1908, 13; *New York Clipper*, July 3, 1909, 536.

22. "Vaudeville of the Year"; Dudley Field Malone, [open letter], *Variety*, October 27, 1926, 46; "William Morris Invades Pacific Coast," *New York Clipper*, July 31, 1909, 635. (Estimates of modern-day monetary values from *MeasuringWorth.com*, accessed October 7, 2022.)

23. Sime Silverman, "William Morris' Only Failure," *Variety*, October 27, 1910, 110; Sam M'Kee, *New York Telegraph*, October 10, 1909, no page number, from clipping file at NYPL-PA-BRTC; "American Music Hall," *Press, Kansas City, Kansas*, January 21, 1910, 2; Charles J. Ross, "The Building and Repairing of Vaudeville Sketches," *New York Dramatic Mirror*, July 5, 1911, 5.

NOTES 289

24. Lauder, *Between You and Me*, 198–199; Snyder, *Voice of the City*, 145; Lauder, *Roamin' in the Gloamin'* (New York: Grosset & Dunlap, 1928), 148, 169; Erdman, *Staging the Jew*, 21.

25. Lauder, *Between You and Me*, 16; Lauder, *Roamin' in the Gloamin'*, 139; "Butte School Boy with Lauder," *Butte Inter Mountain*, January 18, 1910, 8; Walter Anthony, "Lauder Charms Los Angeles," *San Francisco Call*, January 10, 1910, 5.

26. W. Herbert Blake, "Harry Lauder Delights Scots," *Los Angeles Herald*, January 7, 1910, 10.

27. Anthony, "Lauder Charms Los Angeles"; Lauder, *Roamin' in the Gloamin'*, 136; Blake, "Harry Lauder Delights Scots"; Johnson, "The Drama—Playhouses, Players, Theatrical Chit-Chat."

28. Tucker, *Some of These Days*, 88; Johnson, "The Drama—Playhouses, Players, Theatrical Chit-Chat"; Wolf, "The Sort of Fellow Julian Eltinge Really Is," 802; "Mr. Ettinge [*sic*] Isn't Huffy Now," *Kansas City Star* (MO), February 1, 1910, 2 [4]; in an advertisement from the *Los Angeles Herald* (January 7, 1910, 2), Lauder's name is some five times larger than Eltinge's, making disparity look almost humorous, though no doubt the latter didn't find it funny; Lauder, *Between You and Me*, 212; *Roamin' in the Gloamin'*, 192; Ida Wilshire, "Julian Eltinge: Then and Now—An Appreciation," *Daily Province, Vancouver, British Columbia*, February 24, 1923, 12; One source reports the tour was four, not fourteen, weeks, though this seems very likely a typographical error: "Plays and Players: About Julian Eltinge"; Themista, "Julian Eltinge: The Woman Impersonator."

29. "Plays and Players: About Julian Eltinge"; "American Music Hall"; Lauder, *Roamin' in the Gloamin'*, 168.

30. Blake, "Harry Lauder Delights Scots"; Al C. Joy, "Harry Lauder? Yes, He's the Laugh King," *San Francisco Examiner*, January 11, 1910, 3 [1].

31. Lauder, *Between You and Me*, 17, 201, 211, 214; *Roamin' in the Gloamin'*, 147; Anthony, "Julian and Not Julia, Eltinge Speaks."

32. Lauder, *Between You and Me*, 17, 201, 211, 214; *Roamin' in the Gloamin'*, 147; Anthony, "Julian and Not Julia, Eltinge Speaks"; Blake, "Harry Lauder Delights Scots"; Themista, "Julian Eltinge: The Woman Impersonator"; Joy, "Harry Lauder? Yes, He's the Laugh King"; Lynn Linton, "The Wild Women as Social Insurgents," *Nineteenth Century*, October 1891, 596–601; Casey, "Sex, Savagery, and the Woman Who Made Vaudeville Famous," 87–88.

33. Anthony, "Julian and Not Julia, Eltinge Speaks"; "Lauder Jealous for Once," *Brooklyn Citizen*, June 11, 1911, 17.

34. "Mr. Ettinge [*sic*] Isn't Huffy Now"; "Lauder Jealous for Once"; Anthony, "Julian and Not Julia, Eltinge Speaks"; Hurwitz, *Bohemian Los Angeles*, 30.

35. Anthony, "Julian and Not Julia, Eltinge Speaks."

36. Nasaw, *Going Out*, 19; "Eltinge at the American," *Boston Globe*, May 3, 1910, 11; "News of the Theaters," *Brooklyn Daily Eagle*, 8 [18]; "Theatrical Notes," *San Francisco Examiner*, July 10, 1910, 64; "Julian Eltinge Heads Vaudeville Company," *Indianapolis Star*, July 10, 1910, 35 [43].

37. "Julian Eltinge Heads Vaudeville Company"; "Julian Eltinge Will Tour the West," *Tacoma Daily News* (WA), July 16, 1910, 8; "Frohman Sets a Hard Pace for the Others," *Idaho Statesman*, July 24, 1910, 2 [18].

290 NOTES

38. "Julian Eltinge Heads Vaudeville Company"; "Eltinge at the American"; *Evening Free Press* (Winfield, KS), March 26, 1910, 4; "Julian Eltinge Sings 'Come Over on My Veranda,'" *Post-Crescent* (Appleton, WI), March 2, 1910, 7; [Advertisement.] *Indianapolis News*, February 18, 1910, 5; "Plays and Players: About Julian Eltinge."

39. Golden ("Julian Eltinge: The Queen of Old Broadway," 21) writes that Julian Eltinge "never played women; he played men playing women." This was obviously not the case, but his biggest successes, as we are about to see, came in such roles and represented a major change in his career; Erdman, *Staging the Jew*, 18; "Julian Eltinge Wants to Drop the Petticoats and Play Shylock."

40. "Notes of the Stage," *South Bend Tribune* (IA), January 8, 1910, 6; "The Theater," *Sunday Star, Washington, DC* July 31, 1910, II, 5 [23]; "The Stage: Trouble for Eltinge," *Anaconda Standard* (MT), August 28, 1910, 11 [31].

41. The *New York Times* claimed Woods was "born in this city," though he was Hungarian-born: "A. H. Woods Dead; Producer Was 81," *New York Times*, April 25, 1951, 29; Sidney Skolsky, "Tintypes," *Sunday News* (*Daily News*, NY), April 12, 1931, 42 [183]; Erdman, *Staging the Jew*, 99; Fields and Fields, *From the Bowery to Broadway*, 92; Fields, *Sophie Tucker*, 7; Rotundo, *American Manhood*, 3, 195; Ruth Gordon, "'You'll Fracture 'Em, Sweetheart,'" *New York Times*, August 31, 1969, ii: 1, 3.

42. "Why Authors Go Crazy," *New York Times*, March 23, 1930, ix: 4.

43. B. Zorina Khan and Kenneth Sokoloff, "History Lessons: The Early Development of Intellectual Property Institutions in the United States," *Journal of Economic Perspectives* 15, no. 3 (Summer 2001): 233, 236–237; Skolsky, "Tintypes"; Gordon, "'You'll Fracture 'Em, Sweetheart'"; Nasaw, *Going Out*, 36–37; "A. H. Woods Dead; Producer Was 81"; *Julian Eltinge Magazine* [courtesy Northport Historical Society].

44. Skolsky, "Tintypes."

45. Skolsky, "Tintypes"; "A. H. Woods Dead; Producer Was 81"; Gordon, "'You'll Fracture 'Em, Sweetheart.'"

46. Skolsky, "Tintypes"; Gordon, "'You'll Fracture 'Em, Sweetheart.'"

47. Skolsky, "Tintypes"; Gordon, "'You'll Fracture 'Em, Sweetheart.'"

48. Skolsky, "Tintypes"; "Julian Eltinge Popular Star," *Quad City Times*.

49. "The Theater," *Sunday Star, Washington, DC*, July 31, 1910, ii: 5 [23]; "Julian Eltinge Wants to Drop the Petticoats and Play Shylock"; "Bills of the Week: Ford's," *Sun, Baltimore*, November 27, 1910, 12; "The Stage: Trouble for Eltinge"; [Advertisement.] *New York Times*, September 11, 1910, 26.

50. "The Theater," *Sunday Star, Washington, DC*, July 31, 1910, ii: 5 [23]; "Julian Eltinge Wants to Drop the Petticoats and Play Shylock"; "Bills of the Week: Ford's"; "The Stage: Trouble for Eltinge"; [Advertisement.] *New York Times*, September 11, 1910, 26.

51. "Offerings at the Local Theaters: Columbia—Julian Eltinge in 'The Fascinating Widow,'" *Washington Post*, November 22, 1910, 4.

52. Otto Hauerbach [Harbach] and Karl Hoschna, *The Fascinating Widow*, playscript NYPL-PA-BRTC, Otto Harbach Papers; "Offerings at the Local Theaters: Columbia—Julian Eltinge in 'The Fascinating Widow.'"

53. Rotundo, *American Manhood*, 53, 180, 204, 249; Long, "'All Our Girls Are Men,'" 94.

NOTES 291

54. US Bureau of the Census, *Historical Statistics of the United States, Colonial Times to 1970, Bicentennial Edition, Part 2* (Washington, DC: US Government Printing Office, 1975), 55; Allan Pinkerton, *Allan Pinkerton's Detective Stories* (Toronto: Belford Brothers, 1877), 60 (thanks to Sarah Marshall and her podcast *You're Wrong About* in which she mentioned this tale: "Thanksgiving Bonus Episode: The Pinkertons," November 21, 2021); *Sir Jonah Barrington, Personal Sketches of His Own Times*, Vol. I (London: Henry Colburn & Richard Bentley, 1830), 238, Project Gutenberg, accessed November 22, 2022, https://www.gutenberg.org/files/49792/49792-h/49792-h.htm; "Beware of Widows," *Butte Miner*, August 29, 1912, 4.

55. "'Widow Bedott' Has Enemies," *New York Times*, March 7, 1887, 1; Sarah Jones, "Pinkertons Still Never Sleep," *New Republic*, March 23, 2018, accessed October 22, 2022, https://newrepublic.com/article/147619/pinkertons-still-never-sleep; Mantle and Sherwood, eds., *The Best Plays of 1899–1909*, 466.

56. "Offerings at the Local Theaters: Columbia—Julian Eltinge in 'The Fascinating Widow'"; Amy Leslie, "Lets Audience Guess," date-stamped December 8, 1910, no other attribution, from clipping file at NYPL-PA-BRTC; Snyder, *Voice of the City*, 117; "Mr. Eltinge at Ford's," *Sun, Baltimore*, November 29, 1910, 11; "Bills of the Week: Ford's."

57. "Offerings at the Local Theaters: Columbia—Julian Eltinge in 'The Fascinating Widow'"; "Julian Eltinge, 'Widow,' Is Truly Fascinating," *Washington Times*, November 22, 1910, 7.

58. "Mr. Eltinge at Ford's"; "Morning Performance of 'Fascinating Widow'," *Buffalo Enquirer*, January 27, 1911, 7; "Last Week of Julian Eltinge at the Boston," *Boston Sunday Globe*, February 26, 1911, 52; "Three Stars Coming," *Butte Miner*, May 28, 1911, 16; "Shows at the Box Office in New York and Chicago," *Variety*, November 1, 1912, 10.

59. "Julian Eltinge at the Boston," *Boston Globe*, February 7, 1911, 15; in History Project, *Improper Bostonians*, 111–112.

60. "Female Impersonator in Musical Comedy," *Pittsburgh Gazette Times*, January 31, 1911, 10; Rotundo, *American Manhood*, 269–270; "Victoria—My Lady." "Mrs. Nation" refers to Caroline Amelia "Carrie" Nation (1846–1911), famed temperance crusader who led the charge against alcohol in the United States. While Nation was fiery and bombastic—in 1903 she charged onto a vaudeville stage in Tennessee and smashed a prop bottle of iced tea she mistakenly believed was real whiskey, declaring, "You can't make this little girl do any drinking when Carrie is around"—she also became a highly gendered symbol of prudishness and unreasonable censure. Plenty of men inveighed against liquor at the time and were taken dead seriously, such as medical educator Dr. John Madden who insisted, "The greatest anomaly of our present day civilization is our attitude of indifference toward the existing wholesale poisoning of our people by alcohol," in *Scientific American*. Similarly, writing in the popular periodical *McClure's* Dr. Henry Smith Williams and other medical authorities estimated that 25–33 per cent of all state asylum admissions of the day were linked to alcohol use. (See: *New York Dramatic Mirror*, August 1, 1903, 10; John Madden, "Is Alcohol a Food, a Poison, or Both?," *Scientific American Supplement*, August 3, 1901,

292   NOTES

21401–21402; Henry Smith Williams, "Alcohol and the Community," *McClure's Magazine*, December 1908, 154–161.)

61. Sylvester, "Of the Stage"; Rotundo, *American Manhood*, 270–271, 273; "Eltinge Announced for Week at Century," *St. Louis Star*, March 7, 1912, 14; "Julian Eltinge at the Boston"; "Julian Eltinge and Some of His Costumes as a Fascinating Widow," *Washington Herald*, November 20, 1910, 9; "How Does He Do It! The Problem Successfully Solved," *Pittsburgh Gazette Times*, January 26, 1911, 3; Banner, *American Beauty*, 48, 129; "Eltinge Says Women Have Much to Learn," *Pittsburg [sic] Press*, January 27, 1911, 24.

62. "Julian Eltinge and Some of His Costumes as a Fascinating Widow"; "How Does He Do It!"

63. "'In Just a Minute'"; "Julian Eltinge, 'Widow,' Is Truly Fascinating"; "No One Can Take His Place," *Boston Globe*, February 10, 1911, 9.

64. "Theatre and Vaudeville Bills," *Lexington Herald* (KY), June 25, 1911, 3 [25]; Gordon, "'You'll Fracture 'Em, Sweetheart'"; Robert Grau, "How Performers Spend Their 'Real' Money," *San Francisco Examiner*, January 15, 1911, 68; "Julian Eltinge Popular Star," *Davenport Democrat and Leader*; "Julian Eltinge Receives Pierce Arrow Machine," *Spokane Daily Chronicle*, July 8, 1911, 8; dollar conversions from https://www.in2013dollars.com/us/inflation/1910?amount=1 (accessed January 29, 2023).

65. Gordon, "'You'll Fracture 'Em, Sweetheart'"; "Vaudeville's Clearing House"; Gimlet [only name given], "Imaginary Interview No. 2," *The Standard and Vanity Fair*, June 13, 1912, 12; Ward Morehouse Papers, NYPL-PA-BRTC; Farnsworth, *Ziegfeld Follies*, chapter 1, no page numbers supplied; Skolsky, "Tintypes."

66. Mary C. Henderson, *The City and the Theatre* (New York: Back Stage Books, 2004), 241.

67. "Mr. Eltinge's Heavy Heart," otherwise unattributed clipping from NYPL-PA-BRTC ELTINGE, Julian, MWEZ+N.C. 9882 22,638 22,939#.

68. "Great Loves," *Visalia Daily Times* (CA), October 5, 1927, 4.

69. "Made Good with Lillian," *Morning Register* (Eugene, OR), July 16, 1911, 11; Lillian Russell, "Lillian Russell's Answers to Her Inquirers," *Buffalo Evening Times*, July 17, 1911, 3.

70. Gilbert, *American Vaudeville*, 113; "Tony Pastor Recounts the Origin of American 'Vaudeville'"; "Dean of Vaudeville Celebrities"; S.D., *No Applause—Just Throw Money*, 69; Harris, *Humbug*, 77; Lavitt, "First of the Red Hot Mamas," 87, 264; "What Greater Vaudeville Promises This Winter."

71. Banner, *American Beauty*, 5; Jessel, *Elegy in Manhattan*, 141; History Project, *Improper Bostonians*, 111.

72. Banner, *American Beauty*, 136; "World's Foremost Imitator of Women"; Tregelles, "Difficult Art of Stage Makeup"; "Julian Eltinge and Some of His Costumes as a Fascinating Widow"; "Didn't Want to Don Feminine Attire," *Buffalo Enquirer*, January 23, 1911, 3.

73. Welton, "This Man a Martyr to the Modiste"; Celeste Rau, "Julian Eltinge—An Interview," *Buffalo Enquirer*, May 21, 1919, 9; Banner, *American Beauty*, 135–136; S.D., *No Applause—Just Throw Money*, 69; Lillian Russell, "Lillian Russell's

Remembrances," *Cosmopolitan*, 1922, in Stein, ed., *American Vaudeville as Seen by Its Contemporaries*, 11.

74. *A Winsome Widow*, program, November 25, 1912, NYPL-PA-BRTC; Rotundo, *American Manhood*, 200–202; Julia Lee Brown, "Society: School Activities," *El Paso Morning Times*, March 2, 1917, 7.

Chapter 6

1. Many details of Julian Eltinge's activities from May to August 1911 come from a postcard in the Northport Historical Society archive, Long Island, New York.

2. "More Profitable to Be Eltinge than President," *Butte Miner*, September 22, 1912, 16.

3. "Manager Woods Has Plays from Europe," *New York Times*, May 20, 1911, 13; "Julian Eltinge's Real Monaker [*sic*]"; "The Drama," *Joliet Evening Herald* (IL), August 18, 1911, 9; "More Profitable to Be Eltinge than President"; "Julian Eltinge for Australia," *Daily Ledger, Tacoma, Washington*, August 27, 1911, 32.

4. "Julian Eltinge Popular Star," *Quad City Times*; "More Profitable to Be Eltinge than President"; "Who Would You Rather Be?" unpublished draft from archives of NYPL-PA-BRTC;

5. [Untitled], *Omaha Daily News*, July 12, 1911, 4.

6. "Gossip of the Players," *Indianapolis Star*, August 27, 1911, 32 [51].

7. "Theatre for A. H. Woods," *New York Times*, August 15, 1911, 9; Henderson, *The City and the Theatre*, 240–241; Rydell, *All the World's a Fair*, 62–64; "Brief but to the Point Resume of the Best Things of This Week's Playbills," *Philadelphia Inquirer*, February 16, 1912, 37; "Julian Eltinge, Impersonator, 57"; Christopher Gray, "A Film Restores a bit of 42nd Street—in Faux Decay," *New York Times*, March 28, 1993, x: 7.

8. "Brief but to the Point Resume of the Best Things of This Week's Playbills"; "First Eltinge Theatre Bill," *New York Times*, June 7, 1912, 13; Henderson, *The City and the Theatre*, 238–239; John Hutchens, "The Times Square Narrative, in Lights," *New York Times*, October 19, 1930, ix: 2; Gordon, "You'll Fracture 'Em, Sweetheart"; "Now Honky Tonks Occupy Theaters' 'Gold Coast,'" *Wisconsin State Journal, Madison*, August 6, 1944, 24; "Julian Eltinge Hennepin Star," *Minnesota Daily Star*, January 20, 1923, 6.

9. "A Film Restores a bit of 42nd Street—in Faux Decay"; Margaret Knapp, "Introductory Essay," in *Inventing Times Square*, 127; Douglas Gomery, *Shared Pleasures: A History of Movie Presentation in the United States* (Madison: University of Wisconsin Press, 1992), 73; John Holusha, "A Theater's Muses, Rescued: Mural Figures Recall Celebrity of a (Well-Painted) Face," *New York Times*, March 1, 1998, B1, B6; "Our Theatres To-Day and Yesterday," 76, no other attribution, book page from archive at the Institute for the American Musical, Los Angeles, CA.

10. "Eltinge Beauty Parlor," *Spokesman-Review* (Spokane, WA), June 2, 1912, 2 [42]; [Advertisement.] "Most Beautiful Woman in the World is a Man!", *Chicago Sunday Tribune*, July 2, 1911, H4 [38].

294 NOTES

11. "Advice to the Fat," *Anaconda Standard* (MT), July 9, 1911, 11 [35]; Julia Chandler Manz, "Julian Eltinge Gives Away Secret of His Rapid Flesh Reduction," *Washington Herald*, January 3, 1912, 6; Julian Eltinge, "Let Your Mirror Be Your Beauty Critic," *San Francisco Call*, November 17, 1913, 9; Marguerite Moores Marshall, "Julian Eltinge's Battle against Flesh," *Akron Times*, August 14, 1914, 4; Manz, "Julian Eltinge Gives Away Secret of His Rapid Flesh Reduction."

12. *Julian Eltinge Magazine*, from clipping file on microfilm at NYPL-PA-BRTC, ELTINGE, Julian, NAFR + Ser. 3 v. 432.

13. Jean-Philippe Chaput and Angelo Tremblay, "Adequate Sleep to Improve Treatment of Obesity," *Canadian Medical Association Journal* 184, no. 18 (December 11, 2012): 1975–1976, doi: 10.1503/cmaj.120876.

14. "Well, There's Julian Eltinge," *Boston Globe*, September 8, 1915, 16.

15. Eltinge, "Let Your Mirror Be Your Beauty Critic"; "Eltinge Says Women Have Much to Learn," *Pittsburg [sic] Press*, January 27, 1911, 24.

16. "Eltinge's Ingrowing Wisdom," *Inter Ocean*, March 26, 1911, 11 [37]; History Project, *Improper Bostonians*, 111.

17. References to *Julian Eltinge Magazine* come from archival materials at the Northport Historical Society, Long Island, New York.

18. "Actor on Boxing," *Philadelphia Inquirer*, February 23, 1913, 6.

19. [Advertisement.] *Pittsburg [sic] Press*, September 3, 1912, 5; Peiss, *Hope in a Jar*, 73, 101.

20. Welton, "This Man a Martyr to the Modiste"; Senelick, *Changing Room*, 114; Slide, *Encyclopedia of Vaudeville*, 160; "Foyer Gossip," *Enquirer, Cincinnati*, September 5, 1915, iii: 2 [2]; Peters, "Gay Deceiver," 87.

21. Peters, "Gay Deceiver," 87; "News in Gossip Form," *Buffalo Times*, December 4, 1911, 11; "Julian Eltinge's Hobby Is Collecting Shoes," *Boston Sunday Globe*, January 20, 1918, 39; "Julian Eltinge Has No Lady's Taste for Sport," *Minneapolis Morning Tribune*, August 28, 1916, 16; Harriette Underhill, "Julian Eltinge on Keeping One's Lines," *New York Tribune*, December 2, 1917, iv: 4 [32]; "Lingerie, Cigars Are All Alike to Julian Eltinge," *Fresno Bee*, February 3, 1926, 3 W [17]; "Made Trouble for Joe Humphreys," *Boston Globe*, January 8, 1909, 16.

22. "Plays and Players," *New York Times*, July 28, 1911, 64; [Advertisement.], *Sun* (NY), May 14, 1911, 13 [29]; "Friars' Frolic Tonight," *New York Daily Tribune*, May 28, 1911, iv: 6 [50]; "Programme at the Frolic," *Chicago Examiner*, June 4, 1911, 41; "Dramatic," *Butte Miner*, July 2, 1911, 16; "Crinoline Girl Due to Lambs' Gambol," *Washington Times*, February 16, 1914, 5; "Lambs' Gambol in Brooklyn," *Brooklyn Life*, May 20, 1916, 20.

23. Bullough and Bullough, *Cross Dressing, Sex, and Gender*, 235; Rotundo, *American Manhood*, 192; "Lambs' Gambol in Brooklyn."

24. Lambs Club Constitution, from archive at the Institute for the American Musical, Los Angeles, CA.

25. *The Lambs: Certificate of Incorporation, Constitution, By-Laws and Rules, Members and Committees, 1944–1952* (The Lambs: New York, 1952), 2, 4, 16; Eric Lampard, "Introductory Essay," in *Inventing Times Square: Commerce and Culture at the*

Crossroads of the World, ed. William R. Taylor (Baltimore: Johns Hopkins University Press, 1991), 17–18; Grace Kingsley, "Stella Hears about Europe," *Los Angeles Sunday Times*, August 28, 1927, 4 [126]; Andrew Erdman, "From Frank Fay to Jimmy Stewart: Broadway, Hollywood, and the Construction of Creativity," *Theatre Studies* 41 (1996): 13–28; Miles Kreuger, interviews by author, October 19, 2022, and May 22, 2023, Institute for the American Musical; accusations of Fay's abuse of Stanwyck are widespread, both in printed and electronic sources, see, e.g., "The Warped, Hateful Father of Stand-Up Comics: Frank Fay," *Stories from Classic Hollywood: The Life and Times of Hollywood*, accessed January 30, 2023, https://thelifeandtimesofhollywood.com/the-warped-hateful-father-of-stand-up-comics-frank-fay/.

26. Mantle and Sherwood, eds., *The Best Plays of 1899–1909*, 450; Henderson, *The City and the Theatre*, 241; "Julian Eltinge Popular Star," *Davenport Democrat and Leader*; "Theatrical Notes: Julian Eltinge: 'The Fascinating Widow,'" *Shreveport Journal*, January 1, 1913, 3; Julia Murdock, "Julia Murdock Says Julian Eltinge Is Best Looking 'Woman' on Stage," *Washington Times*, February 10, 1913, 10; Julia Chandler, "Old, Old Problem of Sex Furnishes Theme for New Drama by Feminine Playwrights," *Washington Herald*, January 30, 1916, ii: 1 [17].

27. "'The Fascinating Widow,'" *Brooklyn Citizen*, September 12, 1911, 7; Murdock, "Julia Murdock Says Julian Eltinge Is Best Looking 'Woman' on Stage"; "Star Buys $1,800 Dinner," *Washington Post*, October 18, 1914, 2; "Actor's $1,500 Gems Gone," *York Daily* (PA), September 11, 1911; "Eva Tanguay to Walk's Rescue," article date-stamped December 26, 1907 from *New York Telegraph*, no other attribution, from clipping file at NYPL-PA-BRTC; "Stillman Gifts Stolen, She Says," *New York Times*, February 25, 1922, 5; Erdman, *Queen of Vaudeville*, 161; Budd Schulberg, *What Makes Sammy Run?* (New York: Random House, 1993), 106 (original work published 1941); "Eltinge Will Pay $2,000 Income Tax," *Washington Times*, February 7, 1914, 8; "Julian Eltinge Has His Teeth Insured," *Oregon Sunday Journal, Portland*, March 23, 1913, 2 [38]; "Weeks' Weddings," *Cecil Whig* (Elkton, MD), June 15, 1912, 1; Thorstein Veblen (1857–1929) was a famously influential, early critic of capitalism and consumerism, credited with coining the term "conspicuous consumption" in his book *The Theory of the Leisure Class: An Economic Study of Institutions*, originally published in 1899. Veblen was especially reproachful of the emerging class of brokers and intermediaries—agents, middlemen, financiers, and salesmen—who, in his view, enriched themselves without actually producing useful items or services, effectively procuring "something for nothing" (quoted in Leach, *Land of Desire*, 232-233, which also provides a good overview of Veblen's ideas).

28. "Ravishing Toilets Worn by Mr. Julian Eltinge," *Minneapolis Sunday Tribune*, September 15, 1912, 29 [49]; "Columbia," *Evening Star* (Washington, DC), January 2, 1912, 3.

29. "Queerest Woman in the World," *Omaha Daily News*, October 1, 1911, 8B [20]; "Orpheum's Inauguration Bill Illuminates with Bright Stars."

30. Golden, "Julian Eltinge: The Queen of Old Broadway," 21; James T. Metcalfe, "The Theaters," *Sunday State Journal* (Lincoln, NE), March 22, 1914, 4B [16].

31. "Julian Eltinge for Australia."

296 NOTES

32. "Our Theatres To-Day and Yesterday," 76, no other attribution, book page from archive at the Institute for the American Musical, Los Angeles, CA; Vanderheyden Fyles, "Vanderheyden Fyles' Letter of New York Theatrical News," *Times-Democrat* (New Orleans), March 22, 1914, 2 [16]; "Eltinge Succeeds in 'Crinoline Girl,'" *New York Times*, March 17, 1914, 11.

33. J.O.L. [only name given], "The Three Arts," *Evening Sun, Baltimore*, January 21, 1914, 4; [Advertisement.] *Washington Herald*, January 15, 1914, 9 [21]; "One Close Shave and Then Another"; "Eltinge Succeeds in 'Crinoline Girl.'"

34. "Knickerbocker: 'The Crinoline Girl,'" *The Theatre*, 1914, no other attribution, book page from archive at the Institute for the American Musical, Los Angeles, CA; "Eltinge Succeeds in 'Crinoline Girl'"; Metcalfe, "The Theaters"; "Julian Eltinge in Skirts and Trousers," *Boston Globe*, November 10, 1914, 6; Ralph E. Mooney, "Julian Eltinge, as Old-Fashioned Girl, Super-Fascinating," *St. Louis Star*, January 26, 1915, 4; "The Story of Jeanne Eagels," *Spokesman-Review* (Spokane, WA), May 17, 1931, 47; "'Woman Is Only Ten Percent Nature, the Rest is Art,'" *San Francisco Examiner*, April 12, 1914, 36.

35. "New Heights Scaled in 'Crinoline Girl' by Great Impersonator," *Oregon Sunday Journal, Portland*, March 29, 1914, 2 [34]; Metcalfe, "The Theaters"; "One Close Shave and Then Another"; Bullough and Bullough, *Cross Dressing, Sex, and Gender*, vii, 155, 207–212; "'Woman Is Only Ten Percent Nature, the Rest is Art.'"

36. "Knickerbocker: 'The Crinoline Girl,'" *The Theatre*; "'Woman Is Only Ten Percent Nature, the Rest Is Art'"; Lewis Erenberg, "Impresarios of Broadway Nightlife," in *Inventing Times Square*, 166–167; Sante, *Low Life*, 164–165; "Julian Eltinge, as Old-Fashioned Girl, Super-Fascinating"; Katherine Richardson, "Julian Eltinge in a New Comedy and Sweet Irish Play, Next Bills," *St. Louis Star*, January 23, 1915, 6.

37. Roswell Dague, "Klein's Last Farce Is But Vehicle for Girl Impersonator," *Oakland Tribune*, September 19, 1915, 30; "Many Klein Plays Called Valueless," *New York Times*, July 2, 1916, 8; "Julian Eltinge in a Chas. Klein Play," *Brooklyn Daily Eagle*, August 28, 1915, 2.

38. "Theatrical News: Star Theatre," *Buffalo Commercial*, October 5, 1915, 14; "National—Julian Eltinge in 'Cousin Lucy,'" *Washington Herald*, February 1, 1916, 1 [4]; "Julian Eltinge in a Chas. Klein Play."

39. "Julian Eltinge in a Chas. Klein Play"; Heywood Broun, "Eltinge Every Inch a Lady," *New York Tribune*, August 28, 1915, 7; "Klein's Last Farce Is But Vehicle for Girl Impersonator"; "Julian Eltinge in Klein's Last Play," *New York Times*, August 28, 1915, 7; "'Cousin Lucy' is Clever," *Brooklyn Daily Times*, August 28, 1915, 4.

40. "Julian Eltinge in Klein's Last Play"; Broun, "Eltinge Every Inch a Lady"; Chandler, "Old, Old Problem of Sex Furnishes Theme for New Drama by Feminine Playwrights."

41. Broun, "Eltinge Every Inch a Lady"; George St. George, "Julian Eltinge," *Evening Express*, Los Angeles, March 2, 1917, 9.

42. "'Cousin Lucy' Almost New Show, Very Entertaining," *Buffalo Evening News*, November 14, 1916, 15; "'Cousin Lucy' Displays Fashions and Julian Eltinge"; "Julian Eltinge in Klein's Last Play."

43. *Cousin Lucy* playbill, George M. Cohan Theatre, from clipping file on microfilm at NYPL-PA-BRTC, ELTINGE, Julian; MWEZ+N.C. 9882 22,638 22,939#; "Julian

NOTES 297

Eltinge in Klein's Last Play"; [Advertisement.] *Long Branch Daily Record*, August 19, 1915, 12; Charles Darnton, "'Cousin Lucy' Displays Fashions and Julian Eltinge," *Arkansas Gazette, Little Rock*, September 5, 1915, 9 [29]; "Theatrical News: Star Theatre"; "Julian Eltinge in Skirts and Trousers."

44. Peters, "Gay Deceiver," 86; Chandler, "Old, Old Problem of Sex Furnishes Theme for New Drama by Feminine Playwrights"; "National—Julian Eltinge in 'Cousin Lucy'"; "Julian Eltinge and Company Opens Season at the Court," *Wheeling Intelligencer*, September 16, 1916, 11; "In 'Cousin Lucy' at the Star Next Week," *Buffalo Enquirer*, November 11, 1916, 7; "Julian Eltinge as 'Cousin Lucy,'" *Brooklyn Daily Eagle*, January 2, 1917, 12; "Star Theater: Julian Eltinge," *Buffalo Enquirer*, November 14, 1916, 9; "'Cousin Lucy' Almost New Show, Very Entertaining."

45. "'Cousin Lucy' Displays Fashions and Julian Eltinge"; "Foyer Gossip"; "Julian Eltinge Has No Lady's Taste for Sport"; Bullough and Bullough, *Cross Dressing, Sex, and Gender*, 116.

46. Looker-On [only name given], "The Passing Show," *Charlotte News*, January 28, 1917, 4; Rotundo, *American Manhood*, 168.

47. [Classified advertisement.] *Los Angeles Sunday Times*, August 16, 1914, x: 1 [53]; "Julian Eltinge Will Open at the Victoria," *Dayton Herald*, September 2, 1916, 7; "Amusements: At the Theatres Tomorrows: Academy: Julian Eltinge in 'Cousin Lucy,'" *Charlotte News* (NC), January 28, 1917, 10; "Julian Eltinge Can't Find Suitable Play," *San Francisco Examiner*, November 24, 1925, 19; [Advertisement.] *Anniston Evening Star and Daily Hot Blast* (AL), August 8, 1917, 7; "Hal Russell in the 'Fascinating Widow,'" *Allentown Democrat*, September 19, 1917, 11.

48. Barnet, *Extravaganza King*, 30; C.L.T., "Julian Eltinge Has Interview with 'Cousin Lucy,'" *Brooklyn Daily Eagle, New York*, January 7, 1917, 3 [15]; "More Profitable to Be Eltinge than President" (also, unpublished draft of apparently same article, titled "Smokes in Women's Attire" / "Who Would You Rather Be?", from clipping file on microfilm at NYPL-PA-BRTC); Rotundo, *American Manhood*, 282.

Chapter 7

1. "Julian Eltinge's Trunks," *Fresno Morning Republican* (CA), August 5, 1917, 9.

2. Harley Erdman, "Caught in the 'Eye of the Eternal': Justice, Race, and the Camera, from 'The Octoroon' to Rodney King," *Theatre Journal* 45, no. 3 (October 1993): 339; A. R. Fulton, "The Machine," in *American Film Industry*, rev. ed., 30; David Bordwell and Kristin Thompson, *Film Art: An Introduction*, 6th ed. (New York: McGraw-Hill, 1993), 14.

3. Robert C. Allen, "Contra the Chaser Theory," *Wide Angle*, 3, no. 1 (1979): 4–11; University of Iowa, Special Collections, Keith/Albee Collection, Box 5: 9/4/1905–4/23/1906, 26, 26a, 32; Laurie, *Vaudeville: From the Honky-tonks to the Palace*, 4; Gunning, "The Cinema of Attractions"; Charles Musser, "The Early Cinema of Edwin Porter," *Cinema Journal* 19, no. 1 (1979): 3–5; Hajdu and Carey, *Revolution in Three Acts*, 137; deCordova, *Picture Personalities*, 26.

298 NOTES

4. Robert C. Allen, "The Movies in Vaudeville: Historical Context of the Movies as Popular Entertainment," and Balio, "Part I: A Novelty Spawns a Small Business, 1894–1908," both in *The American Film Industry*, rev. ed., 21, 75–76; Gomery, *Shared Pleasures*, 5–6; Gordon Hendricks, "The History of the Kinetoscope," in *The American Film Industry*, rev. ed., 43–48.

5. Allen, "The Movies in Vaudeville," 77; deCordova, *Picture Personalities*, 25; see also Rick Altman, *Silent Film Sound* (New York: Columbia University Press, 2004), 181–201; Balio, "Part I: A Novelty Spawns a Small Business, 1894–1908," 20, Russell Merritt, "Nickelodeon Theaters, 1905–1914: Building an Audience for the Movies," 86, 96–97, and Tino Balio, "Part II: Struggles for Control, 1908–1930," in *The American Film Industry*, rev. ed., 144; Gomery, *Shared Pleasures*, 31, 59; Thomas Schatz, *The Genius of the System: Hollywood Filmmaking in the Studio Era* (New York: Pantheon Books, 1988), 19.

6. Balio, "Part II: Struggles for Control, 1908–1930," 114–115, 117; Gomery, *Shared Pleasures*, 57; Schatz, *The Genius of the System*, 21; Gabler, *An Empire of Their Own*, 75–76; David C. Hammack, "Developing for Commercial Culture," in *Inventing Times Square*, 48; Harriette Underhill, "Lasky Says a Number of Things," *New York Tribune*, November 25, 1917, iv: 6 [36]; "Nat Goodwin Cancels Route to Remain in Picture Plays," *Variety*, July 30, 195, 3; deCordova, *Picture Personalities*, 79.

7. "Eltinge, Anna Held in Unique Movie Cast 'Romeo-Juliet' Film Novelty Is Arranged," *Los Angeles Express*, November 6, 1913, ii: 1 [13]; "Intensely Interesting Pictures Shown at Lyceum Theater," *Scranton Republican* (PA), September 9, 1915, 6; deCordova, *Picture Personalities*, 98–99; Anthony Slide, "The Silent Closet," *Film Quarterly* 52, no. 4 (Summer 1999): 24–32; Connelly, "King of Drag," 43.

8. *American Film Institute Catalog of Motion Pictures Produced in the United States: Feature Films, 1911–1920*, (Berkeley: University of California Press, 1989), F1.0812, 167; "Julian Eltinge in 'The Countess Charming' at Shea's Hippodrome," *Buffalo Sunday Times*, September 23, 1917, 54; "Julian Eltinge 'Ountee Charming' Princess July 16th," *Copper Era* (Clifton, AZ), July 11, 1919, 8; J. Keeley, *Photoplay Journal*, October 1917, no page number supplied, from clipping file at NYPL-PA-BRTC.

9. "Eltinge a Film," *Los Angeles Daily Times*, June 14, 1917, 15; "'Mrs. Raffles's Career' for Julian Eltinge," *El Paso Herald*, June 26, 1917, 7; *AFI Catalogue, 1911–1920*, 167; Daisy Dean, "News and Notes from Movieland," *Hutchinson News* (KS), September 18, 1917, 4; "First Production Is Selected for Julian Eltinge," *Edmonton Journal*, July 7, 1917, 10; "Julian Eltinge in Movies," *New York Times*, September 17, 1917, 11; "Julian Eltinge," *Janesville Daily Gazette* (WI), August 19, 1917, 6; "Filmed Julian Eltinge in 'Princess Charming' a Big Rialto Success," *Evening World* (NY), September 18, 1917, 13.

10. "Attractions at Playhouses in the City," *Daily News and Independent* (Santa Barbara, CA), September 21, 1917, 6; "Shea's Hippodrome Presents Julian Eltinge," *Buffalo Courier*, September 24, 1917, 4; "The Good and Bad on Monday's Bills," *Wichita Daily Eagle*, September 30, 1917, 60; "Theaters: Elko Tonight," *Bemidji Daily Pioneer* (MN),

January 2, 1918, 3; P. H. A. [only name given], "Screen Screenings," *Wichita Beacon*, February 9, 1918, 10.

11. "Grand Double Attraction," *Ogden Standard* (UT), November 10, 1917, 10; "Week at Des Moines Film Houses," *Des Moines Register* (IA), October 21, 1917, 7 [38]; "Julian Eltinge in 'Clever Mrs. Carfax' at the Zoe," *Houston Daily Post*, November 11, 1917, 46; George Blaisdell, " 'The Clever Mrs. Carfax,'" *Moving Picture World*, November 17, 1917, 1034.

12. "Eltinge Comes Here to Make Photoplay," *Oregon Sunday Journal*, Portland, August 12, 1917, 10; "Julian Eltinge as a Broncho Buster," *Victoria Daily Times*, January 8, 1918, 6; "Stage for Four Day Program of Greeters Ready," *Oregon Daily Journal*, Portland, June 23, 1919, 5; "Ladies' Night with the Knights of Columbus," *Long Beach Daily Telegram*, July 24, 1919, 9.

13. Bullough and Bullough, *Cross Dressing, Sex, and Gender*, 147; Senelick, *Changing Room*, 355; "Who'd a Thunk It? John Tobin as an Austin April Bride," *Austin American*, March 24, 1918, 5; " 'The Womanless Wedding' Put Over Big by Members of Knights of Columbus," *Daily Messenger* (Canandaigua, NY), June 19, 1923, 1; "The Womanless Wedding," *Windsor Review* (MO), March 13, 1924, 1.

14. "Who's Who in the Movies," *Goodwin's Weekly*, September 8, 1917, 12; deCordova, *Picture Personalities*, 98; "Julian Eltinge in 'Clever Mrs. Carfax' at the Zoe"; "Clever Julian Eltinge at the Hippodrome," *Allentown Morning Call* (PA), January 18, 1918, 10.

15. "Julian Eltinge to Talk at Auditorium," *Los Angeles Record*, September 17, 1917, 7; Gabler, *An Empire of Their Own*, ch. 8.

16. "Julian Eltinge to Talk at Auditorium."

17. deCordova, *Picture Personalities*, 108–109; "Latest Gossip of the Movies," *Butte Miner*, August 19, 1917, 5 [37]; "Filmograms," *Sunday Star, Washington, DC*, August 12, 1917, 2 [18]; "A 'Close-up' of Julian Eltinge"; Underhill, "Julian Eltinge on Keeping One's Lines."

18. Underhill, "Julian Eltinge on Keeping One's Lines"; Pickford, "Daily Talks by Mary Pickford: Personalities I Have Met—Julian Eltinge."

19. deCordova, *Picture Personalities*, 107; "Airdome: Saturday, May 8, Julian Eltinge in 'The Clever Mrs. Carfax,'" *Randolph Enterprise, Randolph, Kansas*, May 6, 1920, 3; [Untitled.] *Sunday Star, Washington, DC*, August 5, 1917, ii: 2 [18]; "Eltinge Prefers Life in the Open Air," *Pittsburgh Press*, November 6, 1921, Theatrical and Photoplay Section, 2 [38].

20. Mae Tinée, "Ask Me, Ask Me, Ask Me," *Chicago Sunday Tribune*, January 12, 1919, vii: 5 [36]; " 'Dazed' Thespian Wants Lots Back," *Hollywood Citizen-News*, December 17, 1938, 3 [2]; "Eltinge in Court," *Hollywood Citizen-News*, February 27, 1939, 1.

21. "A 'Close-up' of Julian Eltinge"; for an interesting, recent overview see Barry Lank, "The Silent Era's Best Cross-Dresser, and His Silver Lake Estate," *The Eastsider*, March 24, 2023, https://www.theeastsiderla.com/neighborhoods/silver_lake/the-sil ent-eras-best-cross-dresser-and-his-silver-lake-estate/article_f65bcd7a-c795-11ed-aad0-6f18fd898a8b.html.

300 NOTES

22. "Open Meeting Is Planned," *Pasadena Post*, October 31, 1930, 6; Louella O. Parsons, "Is Julian Eltinge, Impersonator of Women, Going to Wed?" *Herald-Republican, Salt Lake City, Utah*, December 16, 1917, 31; [Untitled.] *Escanaba Morning Press* (CA), September, 15, 1918, 4; "Julian Eltinge in His Home," *Daily Times* (Davenport, IA), December 21, 1918, 9; [Advertisement.] *Los Angeles Times*, May 12, 1935, 10; [Advertisement.] *Los Angeles Times*, June 2, 1935, i: 11 [11]; Peters, "Gay Deceiver," 86.

23. Connelly, "King of Drag," 44; "Julian Eltinge in His Home"; *New York Star*, October 30, 1918, otherwise unattributed clipping from NYPL-PA-BRTC, ELTINGE, Julian, MWEZ+N.C. 9882 22,638 22,939#; "Notable Buildings," *Los Angeles Sunday Times*, February 29, 1920, v: 5 [89]; "Stucco Type of Architecture," *Fall River Evening News* (MA), July 14, 1923, [4]; Schulberg, *What Makes Sammy Run?*, 263.

24. "Southern California Modernizes, Modifies, Old Spanish Architecture," *Minneapolis Sunday Tribune*, May 13, 1923, 11; "Stucco Type of Architecture."

25. My thanks to Tony Castaneda, current facilities manager for owner Charles Knill, for Mr. Castaneda's generous tour of Villa Capistrano on May 17, 2023, and the information he provided; Peters, "Gay Deceiver," 86; *Architectural Record* quotation from: Daniel Miller, "Is Gold Hidden under a California Peak?," *Los Angeles Times* (online), April 13, 2023, https://www.latimes.com/california/story/2023-04-13/la-col1-treasure-map-california-actor-mystery.

26. "Eltinge Has to Stay in 'Soft' Condition," *Santa Cruz Evening News*, July 18, 1919, 6; "Impersonator in New Role," *Daily Times* (Davenport, IA), December 13, 1918, 11.

27. deCordova, *Picture Personalities*, 106; *New York Star*, October 30, 1918, otherwise unattributed clipping from NYPL-PA-BRTC, ELTINGE, Julian, MWEZ+N.C. 9882 22,638 22,939#; Parsons, "Is Julian Eltinge, Impersonator of Women, Going to Wed?"; "About Eva Tanguay," *Telegram*, otherwise unattributed clippings from NYPL-PA-BRTC, Edward V. Darling scrapbook, 1909–1952.

28. Welton, "This Man a Martyr to the Modiste"; Barbara Tuchman, *The Guns of August* (New York: Dell, 1962), 198–199; "Adopt Belgian Orphan," *Los Angeles Times*, November 15, 1918, ii: 3 [11]; "Last Will and Testament," Julian D. Eltinge, October 13, 1938, from NYPL-PA-BRTC archive.

29. "Julian Eltinge Entertains Japanese; Wife Watches Hubby Imitate Her Sex," *Muskogee Daily Phoenix*, March 1, 1920, 3.

30. deCordova, *Picture Personalities*, 107; Kenneth McGaffey, "Clothes Do Not Make the Woman," *Photoplay*, January 1918, 135.

31. Wendy Arevalo, "The Navy at San Pedro: Terminal Island, California," *Naval Command History and Heritage*, published January 21, 2022, https://www.history.navy.mil/browse-by-topic/organization-and-administration/historic-bases/san-pedro.html; "Fred FitzGerald Will Be Host to Julian Eltinge," *Santa Rosa Press Democrat*, October 30, 1923, 2 [20]; "Julian Eltinge Visits Burbank," *Santa Rosa Republican* (CA), November 6, 1923, 8; "Fred Fitzgerald to Return to Vallejo," *Santa Rosa Republican*, November 26, 1923, 7.

32. "Merchants Present Plans and Purposes at Meeting of the Progressive Club," *Santa Rosa Republican*, December 23, 1921, ii: 1 [7]; Cecil W. Etheredge, "Fitzgerald Egg Plant Is Doing Remarkable Work for the Egg Men," *Santa Rosa Republican*, July 12,

NOTES   301

1923, 7; "Fred FitzGerald Will Be Host to Julian Eltinge"; "Twenty Years Ago Today," *News-Pilot, San Pedro, California*, July 29, 1938, 5.

33. Quoted in Kimmel, *Manhood in America*, 183;

34. Rotundo, *American Manhood*, 274–275; Chauncey, *Gay New York*, 142–143.

35. Bullough and Bullough, *Cross Dressing, Sex, and Gender*, 116.

36. Senelick, *Changing Room*, 360; "Dumbells Coming," *Victoria Daily Times* (BC), January 25, 1921, 11.

37. "'Rose of Queretaro' Creating Much Interest," *San Francisco Examiner*, August 23 1918, 7; Kimmel, *Manhood in America*, 111.

38. H. H. Niemeyer, "St. Louisan, Trucker, A. E. F. Show 'Leading Lady'," *St. Louis Post-Dispatch*, December 31, 1918, 6; Barbara Tuchman, *A Distant Mirror: The Calamitous Thirteenth Century* (New York: Ballantine Books, 1978), 32.

39. "St. Louisan, Trucker, A. E. F. Show 'Leading Lady'"; "Decatur Soldier Leading Lady of A. E. F. in France," *Decatur Herald*, January 6, 1919, 10;

40. William A. McCracker, "354th Infantry," *Trench and Camp*, January 19, 1918, 2; "American Soldiers Overseas Developing into Army of Souvenir Enthusiasts," *Buffalo Courier*, May 4, 1919, iv: 1 [17].

41. "Days at Camp Custer Found the Real Thing," *Enquirer and Evening News* (Battle Creek, MI), November 23, 1918, 3; Maggie Baska, "The Long History of Drag—from Vaudeville to Reagan—and Why Right-Wing Outrage Is Nonsense," *ThePinkNews.com*, April 8, 2023, https://www.thepinknews.com/2023/04/08/drag-history-thea tre-art-movies-tv-pop-culture-ban-lgbtq/.

42. "Yank, Second Julian Eltinge, to Appear in 'Chicken' Role," *Des Moines Register*, June 12, 1919, 7.

43. "Baltimoreans in Cast," *Sun, Baltimore*, June 22, 1919, 12.

44. Gladys Hall, "The Widow's Might (Paramount)," no other attribution, book page from archive at the Institute for the American Musical, Los Angeles, CA; "Beware of Widows"; *American Film Institute Catalog of Motion Pictures Produced in the United States: Feature Films, 1911–1920* (Berkeley: University of California Press, 1989), F1.4974, 1036; "Alice Brady and Julian Eltinge on Garden Bill," *Paterson Morning Call* (NJ), February 2, 1918, 14; "Eltinge Picture at Clune's Proves Strong Attraction," *Evening Express, Los Angeles*, March 11, 1918, 6 [8].

45. *American Film Institute Catalog of Motion Pictures Produced in the United States: Feature Films, 1911–1920* (Berkeley: University of California Press, 1989), F1.4974, 1036; P. H. A. [only name given], "Screen Screenings," *Wichita Beacon*; "Eltinge Picture at Clune's Proves Strong Attraction"; "Julian Eltinge Makes Tremendous Hit at the Alhambra," *Ogden Standard* (UT), March 21, 1918, 10. In newspapers of the era, both De Mille brothers' names were spelled to with a capital "D." (See, e.g., "New Bill at Clemmer is Replete with Thrills," *Spokesman-Review, Spokane, Washington*, January 20, 1919, 5.) Since then, however, some scholarly sources, such as the *American Film Institute Catalog*, use a lower-case "de" for William and a capital "De" for Cecil.

46. "Julian Eltinge Tells Why He'll Stick to Photodrama," *Los Angeles Record*, March 9, 1918, 5; Katherine Richardson, "Julian Eltinge to Quit Stage This Week," *St. Louis*

302 NOTES

Star, March 19, 1918, 8; "The Crescent," *Ithaca Journal* (NY), February 1, 1918, 2; Barrett quote in Slide, *Encyclopedia of Vaudeville*, 159; Richardson, "Julian Eltinge to Quit Stage This Week."

47. Hall, "The Widow's Might (Paramount)"; Ullman, "'Twentieth Century Way,'" 593, 599; [Advertisement.] *Long Beach Daily Telegram*, June 7, 1920, 16; "Ladies' Night with the Knights of Columbus."

48. Connelly, "King of Drag," 44; "Julian Eltinge at Palace," *New York Times*, January 8, 1918, 13; "Eltinge Quits Screen for 'Vode' Jan. 6," *Evening Express, Los Angeles*, October 24, 1918, 8; "Filmland Gossipings," *Washington Herald*, November 24, 1918, ii: 1 [11]; "Julian Eltinge at Tacoma Soon," *Tacoma Daily Ledger*, January, 29, 1919, 7; "Keith's Vaudeville Bills in New York: Weekly Laugh Bulletin," *New York Star*, date-marked January 13, 1918, no page number, from NYPL-PA-BRTC archive; "Julian Eltinge, Noted Female Impersonator, Lets Men of Omaha In on 'Women's Ten Mysteries,'" *Omaha Daily News*, January 31, 1919, 12; "Julian Eltinge a Big Hit at Keith's," *Evening Public Ledger, Philadelphia*, February 5, 1918, 9; "Lessons in Movies," *Anaconda Standard* (MT), January 27, 1918, 37.

49. "Julian Eltinge," *Sunday Star, Washington, DC*, February 3, 1918, ii: 4 [18]; Ullman, "'Twentieth Century Way,'" 592; Tallqvist, "Behind Scene Views of Vaudeville's Man Vamp"; Faye E. Dudden, *Women in the American Theatre: Actresses & Audiences 1790–1870* (New Haven, CT: Yale University Press), 85.

50. "'No More Skirts' Says Julian Eltinge," *Sheboygan Press* (WI), June 2, 1917, 5.

51. [Advertisement.] *Salt Lake Tribune*, December 24, 1918, 11; Gomery, *Shared Pleasures*, 61; "Eltinge, in Skirts, Awaits Eagerly the Coming of Old Age," *Sunday Express: Los Angeles*, December 29, 1918, iv: 4 [44].

Chapter 8

1. deCordova, *Picture Personalities*, 35, 54; "Lessons in Movies"; "No More Pictures for Julian," *Capital Times* (Madison, WI), August 27, 1919, 8.

2. "Enter High Cost of Entertaining as Damper upon Society's Gayety; Hallowe'en Promises 'Better Times,'" *Muskogee Daily Phoenix* (OK), October 19, 1919, ii: 3 [15].

3. "The Race Is Getting Warmer[;] Picture Favorites Are Getting Votes," *Leavenworth Post* (KS), December 30, 1920, 8.

4. Minnie Alper, "Julian Eltinge's 'Perfect 36' Is Somewhat Extended When He Is Not on Stage," *McAlester News-Capital* (OK), October 15, 1919, 3; Edna Irvine, "Stage and Screen," *Oregon Daily Journal, Portland*, November 30, 1917, 8; [Advertisement.] *Theatre*, date-marked February 1918, no page number, from clipping file at NYPL-PA-BRTC.

5. *American Film Institute Catalog of Motion Pictures Produced in the United States: Feature Films, 1911–1920* (Berkeley: University of California Press, 1989), F1.4983, 1037–1038.

NOTES   303

6. "Eva Tanguay Has Notable Support," *Moving Picture World*, August 18, 1917, 1098; "The Screen Shows a New Eva Tanguay," *Moving Picture World*, September 22, 1917, 1872.

7. Golden, "Julian Eltinge: The Queen of Old Broadway," 21; Henry Jenkins argues that the Marx Brothers and others who made a leap from vaudeville to film combined narrative storylines with a "vaudeville aesthetic," which is to say, gags, pratfalls, and other stimulating disruptions prized in their own right, giving such movies an "anarchistic" quality (see Henry Jenkins, *What Made Pistachio Nuts: Early Sound Comedy and the Vaudeville Aesthetic* [New York: Columbia University Press, 1992], 22); Bert O. States, "The Dog on the Stage: Theater as Phenomenon," *New Literary History* 14, no. 2 (Winter 1983): 373, https://www.jstor.org/stable/468691.

8. "Eltinge at Orpheum," *Brooklyn Daily Times*, January 2, 1918, 8; "Eltinge Breaks Records," New York Star, date-marked February 6, 1918, otherwise unattributed clippings from NYPL-PA-BRTC; "Julian Eltinge's Career," *Brooklyn Citizen*, December 30, 1917, 16; "Julian Eltinge in 'The Widow's Might,' at Clune's Broadway."

9. Baer, "New Bills Open at Portland Theaters," and "Julian Eltinge Proves Winner," otherwise unattributed clippings from NYPL-PA-BRTC, ELTINGE, Julian; MWEZ+ N.C. 9882 22,638 22,939#.

10. New National Theatre, May 11, 1919, partial program, NYPL-PA-BRTC, ELTINGE, Julian; MWEZ+N.C. 9882 22,638 22,939#.

11. "News of the Theaters," *Pittsburgh Gazette Times*, April 24, 1919, 10; "Ford's—The Eltinge Revue," *Evening Sun, Baltimore*, May 3, 1919, 9; Laurie, *Vaudeville: From the Honky-tonks*, 177; Julian Eltinge (as related to Marion Van B. Sturges), "What I Would Do If I Were Really a Woman," *Metropolitan*, September 1923, 37; "Julian as Five Women," *Washington Herald*, May 9, 1919, 2 [28].

12. "Julian Eltinge Is Going on a Trip around the World," *Minneapolis Sunday Tribune*, May 25, 1919, 14 [46]; Alper, "Julian Eltinge's 'Perfect 36' is Somewhat Extended When He Is Not on Stage"; [Advertisement.] *Los Angeles Evening Express*, August 4, 1919, 11; "Julian Eltinge, Ably Supported, Delights Austin Audience," *Statesman* (Austin, TX), October 5, 1919, 10 [26]; "Julian Eltinge Seems to Have Changed Mind," *Oregon Sunday Journal, Portland*, July 20, 1919, 4 [42].

13. [Advertisement.] *Richmond Palladium and Sun-Telegram* (IN), March 24, 1920, 7.

14. "Julian Eltinge Entertains Japanese; Wife Watches Hubby Imitate Her Sex"; [Untitled.] *Wichita Eagle*, April 4, 1920, 33; "K. C. Orient Head Safe, Message Said," *Green Bay Press-Gazette*, April 10, 1920, 1; "Eltinge Actress Dies," *Oregon Daily Journal, Portland*, May 13, 1920, 15; "Men and Women of the Stage," *Wichita Eagle*, May 30, 1920, 5 [37]; "Report of the Death of an American Citizen: American Consular Service," Peking, China, March 12, 1920, document posted on https://www.flickr.com/photos/puzzlemaster/5676212928, accessed December 5, 2022; Alper, "Julian Eltinge's 'Perfect 36' Is Somewhat Extended When He Is Not on Stage"; "Woman Infatuated with Julian Eltinge Is Divorced," *San Francisco Chronicle*, September 20, 1922, 7.

15. "Eltinge Quits Screen for 'Vode' Jan. 6"; [Advertisement.] *Evening Record* (Hackensack, NJ), April 27, 1918, 3; "Julian Eltinge Says America Will Set Fashions

304 NOTES

for Women," *Visalia Daily Times* (CA), March 28, 1917, 3; "Julian Eltinge Drags the Market for Bathing Bells," *Fort Wayne Journal-Gazette* (IN), May 30, 1920, 8B.

16. "Shadows on the Screen," *New York Tribune*, October 20, 1918, 5 [37].

17. "Julian Eltinge as Statue of Liberty," *Daily News and the Independent* (Santa Barbara, CA), January 16, 1919, 5; "Julian Eltinge to Serve R. C. Luncheon," *San Francisco Chronicle*, January 19, 1919, 12; "No Man's Land," *Jacobin* 48 (Winter 2023): 65–66; "Dollars for Doughnuts," *Buffalo Evening Times*, May 22, 1919, 4.

18. "Eltinge in New War Picture," *Oregon Daily Journal, Portland*, September 22, 1918, 2 [30]; *American Film Institute Catalog of Motion Pictures Produced in the United States: Feature Films, 1911–1920* (Berkeley: University of California Press, 1989), F1.0029, 7; Vito Russo, *The Celluloid Closet: Homosexuality in the Movies* (New York: Harper & Row, 1981), 15; "The Screen," *Reno Evening Gazette*, March 1, 1919, 12; Fred J. Balshofer and Arthur C. Miller, *One Reel a Week* (Berkeley: University of California Press, 1967), 139.

19. *American Film Institute Catalog of Motion Pictures Produced in the United States: Feature Films, 1911–1920* (Berkeley: University of California Press, 1989), F1.0029, 7; "Republic Distributing Announces Six Feature Productions for March Release," *Moving Picture World*, March 6, 1920, no page number supplied, from AMPAS archive; "Garden: Julian Eltinge in 'An Adventuress,'" *Morning Call* (Paterson, NJ), June 10, 1920, 5.

20. *American Film Institute Catalog of Motion Pictures Produced in the United States: Feature Films, 1911–1920* (Berkeley: University of California Press, 1989), F1.0029, 7; [Advertisement for *An Adventuress*.] from clipping file on microfilm at NYPL-PA-BRTC, ELTINGE, Julian; MWEZ+N.C. 9882 22,638 22,939#; "Eltinge Stars in New Comedy," *Tacoma Sunday Ledger*, February 29, 1920, E-5 [57]; "Julian Eltinge, World's Premier Female Impersonator, and His Wonderful Costumes, Tonight," *Carson City Daily Appeal* (NV), May 5, 1920, 1; Balshofer and Miller, *One Reel a Week*, 139.

21. *American Film Institute Catalog of Motion Pictures Produced in the United States: Feature Films, 1921–30* (Berkeley: University of California Press, 1997), F2.2759, 388; "Photoplays This Week: LEADER—'The Isle of Love,'" *Sunday Star, Washington, DC*, September 10, 1922, iii: 3 [49]; "Fotosho Today—Rodolph Valentino and Julian Eltinge in 'The Isle of Love,'" *Herald, Miami, Florida*, January 2, 1923, A 7 [19].

22. Rodney Q. Selby, "Eltinge Show at Princess Theater," *Des Moines Register*, January 17, 1921, 10; Arthur Quincy, "Here's Closeup of Movie Players and It's Not Written by Press Agents," *Sacramento Star*, January 19, 1921, 2; "New Moves Show Large Evolution in Screen Films," *New York Herald*, February 6, 1921, 9; Gomery, *Shared Pleasures*, 53–64; "Julian Eltinge on Stock-Selling Tour," *Los Angeles Evening Express*, March 5, 1921, ii: 5 [13]; "In the Movies," *St. Louis Star*, March 16, 1921, 17; "Eltinge Forms Film Company," *Los Angeles Daily Times*, November 24, 1920, iii: 4 [32]; "Julian Eltinge in Keith Feature Act," *Boston Globe*, May 10, 1921, 3.

23. Monroe Lathrop, "Plays, Pictures, and Players," *Los Angeles Evening Express*, June 2, 1921, 23; "Julian Eltinge in Keith Feature Act"; "Eltinge Declines," *Dayton Daily*

News, June 5, 1921, ii: 2 [21]; "Rival of Eltinge in Aero Benefit," *Birmingham News* (AL), May 10, 1921, 16.

24. "Julian Eltinge, Well Known Actor, Is 'Flu' Victim," *Fall River Daily Globe* (MA), October 23, 1918, 6; "Bulletins," *Noblesville Daily Ledger* (IN), October 23, 1918, 1; "Sprained Ankle No Handicap for Julian Eltinge," *Albuquerque Morning Journal*, August 13, 1919, 4; "Late Julian Eltinge Planned to Visit Here," *Paris News, Paris, Texas*, March 14, 1941, 3; "Death Calls R M Clement," *Paris News*, March 18, 1935, 5; "Dozen a Day," *Tulsa Tribune*, August 26, 1944, 10; Smithsonian, National Museum of African American History and Culture, "Scene at Convention Hall (Tulsa Race Riot, June 1st 1921)," https://nmaahc.si.edu/object/nmaahc_2011.175.5.

25. "Julian Eltinge Makes Game Fight for Life after Operation."

26. "Julian Eltinge to Headline Bill at Orpheum," *Salt Lake Telegram*, October 4, 1921, 4 [20].

27. Linton Wells, "Amusements," *Record* (Los Angeles), September 6, 1921, 15; "At the Theater Last Night," *Pittsburgh Press*, September 6, 1921, 6; "Eltinge Prefers Life in the Open Air."

28. Erenberg, "Impresarios of Broadway Nightlife," 159, 163.

29. Rotundo, *American Manhood*, 275; Senelick, "Lady and the Tramp," in *Gender in Performance*, 37, 39; Bullough and Bullough, *Cross Dressing, Sex, and Gender*, 177, 183; Ann Douglas, *Terrible Honesty: Mongrel Manhattan in the 1920s* (New York: Farrar, Straus & Giroux, 1995), 8.

30. G. A. Martin, "Pickups and Comment," *Santa Maria Times* (CA), January 13, 1938, 1.

31. "Julian Eltinge Arrested for Having Liquor," *Sacramento Bee*, February 27, 1923, 4; "Julian Eltinge Case Is Dropped," *Tacoma Daily Ledger*, March 1, 1923, 12; "Jury Exonerates Julian Eltinge," *Boston Globe*, March 3, 1923, 8.

32. "Plays, Pictures and Players," *Los Angeles Evening Express*, June 16, 1922, 27; "Julian Eltinge Resting Quietly after Operation," *Buffalo Times*, August 1, 1922, 1; "Manages Skirts with Sang Froid"; "Miss Shalek Sings Carmen at the Teck," *Buffalo Courier*, October 20, 1908, 7; Sylvester, "Of the Stage"; see Sears, "Electric Brilliancy," 170; "Julian Eltinge Has Serious Operation," *Fall River Evening News* (MA), August 2, 1922, 2; "Operate Here on Julian Eltinge," *Buffalo Courier*, August 2, 1922, 16.

33. [Program.] *The Elusive Lady*, Stamford Theatre, Stamford, Connecticut, November 22, 1922, from clipping archive at NYPL-PA-BRTC, ELTINGE, Julian; MWEZ+N.C. 9882 22,638 22,939#; "Stage and Screen Bits," *Philadelphia Inquirer*, June 18, 1922, 30; "News and Views of Theaters," *Pittsburgh Gazette*, July 30, 1922, 56; " 'Elusive Lady' Shares Honors with 'Bride'," *Sun, Baltimore*, October 1, 1922, iv: 4 [42]; "Cute Little Beaute from Butte, Montana," *Butte Miner* (MT), October 9, 1922, 3; "Eltinge at Majestic in Comedy, The Elusive Lady," *Illustrated Buffalo Express*, October 22, 1922, vii: 2 [65]; " 'The Elusive Lady' Is Typically Eltinge," *Buffalo Evening News*, October 24, 1922, 2.

34. [Program.] *The Elusive Lady*, Stamford Theatre, Stamford, Connecticut; " 'Elusive Lady' Shares Honors with 'Bride' "; "Julian Eltinge to Give Radio Concert," *Buffalo Evening News*, October 21, 1922, 3.

306 NOTES

35. " 'The Elusive Lady' Is Typically Eltinge"; Toll, *On with the Show*, 203–206.
36. "Decatur Soldier Leading Lady of A. E. F. in France"; *Variety* report 1923 in Bullough and Bullough, *Cross Dressing, Sex, and Gender*, 236; "Karyl Norman Tops Maryland Bill"; "Strangest of Engagements Has Been Broken Off," *Indianapolis Star*, September 3, 1922, 74; "Coburn's Minstrels Pleases Audience that Packs Court," *Fort Myers Press*, January 4, 1923; "Fields' Company at Fulton Theatre," *Lancaster Examiner* (PA), January 9, 1923, 3.
37. "Julian Eltinge Teaches Harvard Hasty Pudding Boys to Be 'Perfect Ladies,'" April 13, 1924, B-3, no other publication information, from clipping file on microfilm at NYPL-PA-BRTC; "Original Burlesque to Be Staged at Stanford," *Monrovia Daily News* (CA), March 12, 1920, 2.
38. "Pretty? Yes, But 'She's' a 'He,'" *Bee, Danville* (VA), November 8, 1923, 4.
39. Long, " 'All Our Girls Are Men,'" 5, 27, 298; "At the New York Theaters"; " 'Her' Name is Albert; 'She's' a College Ingenue," *Anaconda Standard*, January 2, 1917, 2; "College Actors Stage Success," *Kenosha Evening News* (WI), April 22, 1920, 3; "Julian Eltinge Praises Haresfoot Performers While in Madison," *Racine Journal-News* (WI), April 8, 1924, 4; Winifred Van Duzer, "Why 'Iron Mike' Became 'Miss Fluffy Ruffles,'" *Zanesville Times Signal* (OH), October 11, 1925, 38.
40. "Julian Eltinge to Sponsor His Greatest Rival," *Wisconsin State Journal*, March 8, 1924, 7; Senelick, *Changing Room*, 61.
41. "Adela Verne Shows Great Art at Piano," *Los Angeles Evening Express*, September 27, 1926, 8; [Untitled.] *Detroit Free Press Gravure Supplement*, April 10, 1927, 131; "New York Day by Day," *Richmond Palladium and Sun-Telegram* (IN), June 3, 1927, 6.
42. Katz, *Invention of Heterosexuality*, 15; "Old Impersonator, Julian Eltinge, Dies," *Wisconsin State Journal, Madison*, March 8, 1941, 2.
43. "Philharmonic Auditorium—Black and White Revue of 1924," *Los Angeles Evening Express*, September 15, 1923, 10; "His Trousseau," *Los Angeles Sunday Times*, September 16, 1923, iii: 23 [57]; "Julian Eltinge Revue Entirely Satisfactory," *Sacramento Star*, October 26, 1923, 2.
44. "Julian Eltinge Discovers Gem: Miss Norma Gregg," *Los Angeles Daily Times*, September 25, 1923, ii: 6 [24]; "Vogel's Minstrels," *Coshocton Tribune* (OH), August 4, 1920 [3]; "Women Envy This Fellow for His Clever Costumes," *Illustrated Daily News* (Los Angeles), May 5, 1926, 16; "Julian Eltinge to Play in This City for One Night Only," *Visalia Morning Delta* (CA), September 26, 1923, 5; William Foster Elliot, "Black and White Revue Mixture of Dates," *Fresno Bee*, October 3, 1923, 4; Furia, "Irving Berlin: Troubadour of Tin Pan Alley," 196–197; Rosetta and Vivian Duncan, "Big Company in the 'Black and White Revue,'" *San Francisco Examiner*, October 29, 1923, 10; [Untitled.] *Morning Sun, Yuma* (AZ), November 9, 1923, 5; "Julian Eltinge Began Stage Career at College," *Capital Times* (WI), March 7, 1924, 6.
45. (See prior note for some sources); "Julian Eltinge to Headline Bill at Orpheum"; various unattributed or undated clips from NYPL-PA-BRTC; "Julian Eltinge's Future," *Pittsburgh Press*, May 17, 1923, 12; Senelick, "Lady and the Tramp," 35.

Chapter 9

1. "Buys Ranch," *Daily News* (NY), October 16, 1923, 20; [Advertisement.] *San Francisco Examiner*, September 30, 1926, 30; Kingsley, "Eltinge Would Be Bill Dalton"; "Eltinge Plans to Continue His Feminine Roles," *Los Angeles Daily Times*, April 25, 1925, 7; Aydelotte, "Julian Eltinge Is Back after Two Years of Vacation"; "Eltinge Buys Up Tract to Add to Artists' Colony," *Los Angeles Sunday Times*, August 23, 1925, iii: 20 [64]; Brockett, *History of the Theatre*, 494, 544. Some reporting locates Eltinge's ranch in the vicinity of the Imperial Valley; however, the latter is located over a hundred miles further east, close to the Mexico border.

2. Kingsley, "Eltinge Would Be Bill Dalton"; Aydelotte, "Julian Eltinge Is Back after Two Years of Vacation."

3. Edwards Roberts, "Ramona's Home: A Visit to the Camulos Ranch, and to Scenes Described by 'H.H.,'" December 19, 2022, https://scvhistory.com/scvhistory/edw ardsroberts_ramonashome.htm; Kingsley, "Eltinge Would Be Bill Dalton"; "Julian Eltinge Buys Convent Finishings," *Salinas Daily Index* (CA), May 7, 1925, 4; for more on Ramona and the "Mission Myth" see: Kevin Starr, *California: A History* (New York: Modern Library, 2007), 47, 148.

4. Bill [only name given], "Julian Eltinge, He-Man to Quit Feminine Role."

5. George Tucker, "In New York," *Monroe News-Star* (LA), May 31, 1940, 4.

6. Bill [only name given], "Julian Eltinge, He-Man to Quit Feminine Role"; Kingsley, "Eltinge Would Be Bill Dalton"; Bullough and Bullough, *Cross Dressing, Sex, and Gender*, 161; Tregelles, "Difficult Art of Stage Makeup"; Casey, *Prettiest Girl on Stage*, xxiii. (For discussion of the makeup industry's marketing to white, versus Black, women see Peiss, *Hope in a Jar*, 33, 89.)

7. Kingsley, "Eltinge Would Be Bill Dalton"; "Eltinge Buys Up Tract to Add to Artists' Colony"; [Advertisement.] *Los Angeles Daily Times*, May 4, 1926, ii: 22 [42]; [Advertisement.] *San Francisco Examiner*, September 30, 1926, 30; "Eltinge Plans to Continue His Feminine Roles"; Connelly, "King of Drag," 44; "Julian Eltinge Craves to Grow Hair on Chest," *Progress, Pomona* (CA), October 7, 1924, 2; "World's Biggest Cosmetic User," *Andalusia Star* (Alabama), May 29, 1928, 1.

8. US Department of Commerce, *Statistical Abstract of the United States*, no. 52 (Washington, DC, 1930), 320; "Eltinge Plans to Continue His Feminine Roles"; Alice Hughes, "Today's Woman," article hand-dated September 23, 1940, and identified as from "*New York Post*," from clipping file on microfilm at NYPL-PA-BRTC, ELTINGE, Julian; MWEZ+N.C. 9882 22,638 22,939#; Grace Kingsley, "Hobnobbing in Hollywood: Julian Eltinge Comes Back," *Los Angeles Times*, December 16, 1932, i: 13 [13].

9. Erdman, "Edward Bernays and the 'Golden Jubilee of Light': Culture, Performance, Publicity," 53; "Julian Eltinge Brings Lots of Gowns to L.A.," *Los Angeles Evening Express*, April 21, 1925, 8.

10. O. O. McIntyre, "New York Letter," *Dayton Daily News*, May 31, 1924, 4; Hutchens, "The Times Square Narrative, in Lights"; "Eltinge Plans Theater in L.A.," *Los Angeles Record*, April 25, 1925, 12 [10].

308 NOTES

11. "A. H. Woods Dead; Producer Was 81"; "Julian Eltinge Can't Find Suitable Play"; "Eltinge Plans to Continue His Feminine Roles"; [Untitled.] *Montpelier Morning Journal*, June 4, 1913, 4; Hugh H. Huhn, "Decline of the Nerve-Wracking Drama," *Commercial Appeal, Memphis*, 22 [56]; [Untitled.] *Record-Journal* (Meriden, CT), September 19, 1913, 10; "Julian Eltinge Here," *Los Angeles Daily Times*, February 3, 1926, ii: 9 [25]; Una H. H. Cool, "Book Page of the Sunday Call: 'Wally,'" *San Francisco Sunday Call*, October 12, 1911, 7.

12. *American Film Institute Catalog of Motion Pictures Produced in the United States: Feature Films, 1921–30* (Berkeley: University of California Press, 1997), F2.3326, 471; "Julian Eltinge Here"; "Eltinge Buys Up Tract to Add to Artists' Colony"; "Exits and Entrances," *Oakland Tribune*, July 1, 1925, 12; "Julian Eltinge a Cousin to 'Charley's Aunt'?," *Los Angeles Sunday Times*, August 2, 1925, [sec.] "Acts and Actors: 1," 63; "Julian Eltinge to Be Here Friday," *Modesto News-Herald* (CA), January 1, 1926, 7; "California Tonight," *Venice Evening Vanguard* (CA), January 23, 1926, 2; see Lavitt, "First of the Red Hot Mamas"; Bullough and Bullough, *Cross Dressing, Sex, and Gender*, 237.

13. Bullough and Bullough, *Cross Dressing, Sex, and Gender*, 237.

14. Connelly, "King of Drag," 44; "Made Good with Lillian"; Walter Prichard Eaton, "Alexander Kirkland and Miss Edith Barrett Will Give 'Romeo and Juliet,'" *Berkshire Evening Eagle* (MA), July 12, 1930, 5; Senelick, "Lady and the Tramp," 34; "Julian Eltinge's Future"; "Julian Eltinge a Cousin to 'Charley's Aunt'?"; Hamilton, *"When I'm Bad, I'm Better,"* 141; James F. Wilson, "The Somewhat Different Diva," 21; Chauncey, *Gay New York*, 239, 315.

15. *American Film Institute Catalog of Motion Pictures Produced in the United States: Feature Films, 1921–30* (Berkeley: University of California Press, 1997), F2.3326, 471; "Julian Eltinge to Be Here Friday"; "Madame Behave at Second Week at the Figueroa," *Los Angeles Sunday Times*, January 17, 1926, iii: 29 [77]; "Stage and Screen," *Santa Ana Daily Register* (CA), January 27, 1926, 10; [Untitled.] *Provo Evening Herald* (UT), May 6, 1929, 5.

16. "Eltinge Buys Up Tract to Add to Artists' Colony"; Wood Soanes, "Curtain Calls," *Oakland Tribune*, July 1, 1926, B: 31 [30]; "Julian Eltinge Here"; "Death Takes Father of Julian Eltinge Father"; Long says Eltinge had moved to Florida by 1927 ("'All Our Girls Are Men,'" 125), but there is little evidence to support this other than an apparent error in the *New York Times*: "'Lady Do' Has Merit as a Musical Play." Eltinge did travel to Florida to deep-sea fish, socialize, and get away from the grind of work, and the Florida city was beginning to host its own homegrown female-impersonators such as Johnny Magnum (see Ben Prout, "For Your Amusement," *Miami Daily News*, December 9, 1932, 4.) But Eltinge did not have a permanent home of any sort in Florida, as best as can be discerned. Interestingly, New York's corrupt, charismatic former vaudevillian mayor, Jimmy Walker, vacationed in Florida, and it was on one of his Floridian holidays in 1927 when some of his conservative foes acted to close down theatres with shows they deemed unfit for morally fragile youth (see Leider, *Becoming Mae West*, 155.)

NOTES 309

17. "Julian Eltinge in Classy New Togs," *Illustrated Daily News* (Los Angeles, CA), September 1, 1926, 17; "Eltinge Is a Fair Charmer in a New Turn," *Los Angeles Evening Express*, October 5, 1926, 29; [Advertisement.] *Hollywood Citizen-News*, November 28, 1932, 7.

18. "Eltinge Show," *Daily News* (NY), March 27, 1928, 35, [143]; "Eltinge Delays His Musical Play," *Sunday News* (Daily News, NY), April 29, 1928, 50; "Buys London Play," *Daily News* (NY), March 27, 1928, 35, [143]; Hugh Walpole, *Portrait of a Man with Red Hair* (New York: International Magazine Co., 1925), 3.

19. "Pretty Soft Now for the Vaudeville Guy," *Public Opinion* (Chambersberg, PA), August 31, 1928, 8; Wood Soanes, "Curtain Calls," *Oakland Tribune*, December 13, 1927, 30 E [28]; "Julian Eltinge at Keith-Albee," *Boston Globe*, December 4, 1928, 29; Douglas Gomery, "The Coming of Sound," in *The American Film Industry*, rev. ed., 248; Laurie, *Vaudeville: From the Honky-tonks*, 482–483.

20. "Eltinge Bids Skirts Goodbye," *Border Cities Star, Windsor, Ontario*, June 4, 1927, 5 [21]; "Exits and Entrances," *Oakland Tribune*, March 18, 1928, 8 [42]; Jimmy Starr, "Weil Signs Stage Star," *Los Angeles Record*, July 23, 1929, 3; Louella O. Parsons, "Powell's First Starring Film Called 'Color of Money,'" *Morning Post, Camden* (NJ), October 1, 1929, 20; "Maid to Order (with Songs)," date-stamped May 17, 1932 and attributed to Film Daily Yearbook, no page number, from AMPAS clipping archive; *American Film Institute Catalog of Motion Pictures Produced in the United States: Feature Films, 1931–40* (Berkeley: University of California Press, 1993), F3.2658, 1282; Henry Jenkins, *What Made Pistachio Nuts: Early Sound Comedy and the Vaudeville Aesthetic*; Robbin Coons, "Hollywood Sights and Sounds," *News-Palladium* (Benton Harbor, MI), January 11, 1930, 5; "At the Strand," *Santa Rosa Republican* (CA), March 20, 1931, 4.

21. "Park Theatre: 'Maid to Order,'" *Boston Globe*, September 21, 1931, 4.

22. "Julian Eltinge, Actor, Hurt," *Boston Globe*, July 10, 1929, 6; "Julian Eltinge Badly Hurt in Crash," *Colton Courier* (CA), July 10, 1929, 1; "Stage Folk Hurt in Crash," *Los Angeles Times*, July 11, 1929, ii: 1, 20 [40].

23. "Eltinge Delays His Musical Play"; Wayne Miller, "Varied Radio Programs Announced for Tonight," *Pasadena Post*, November 20, 1929, 5; "Radio Program Standard Rises," *Los Angeles Times*, October 23, 1929, ii: 7 [27].

24. Chauncey, *Gay New York*, 331–332; Nathanael West, *Miss Lonelyhearts & The Day of the Locust* (New York: New Directions, 1962), 17 (original work published 1933); Celia Haddon, *The Sensuous Lie* (New York: Stein & Day, 1983), 25–26; "Let Us Be Tolerant," *San Francisco Examiner*, August 3, 1929, 30.

25. Leider, *Becoming Mae West*, 63.

26. Wilson, "The Somewhat Different Diva," 21; Senelick, "Lady and the Tramp," 37; John Chapman, "Go West, Milady, for a Love Guide," *Daily News* (New York), September 26, 1944, 27M.

27. Leider, *Becoming Mae West*, 20; Hamilton, *"When I'm Bad, I'm Better,"* 8.

28. Casey, "Sex, Savagery, and the Woman Who Made Vaudeville Famous," 87; Hamilton, *"When I'm Bad, I'm Better,"* 47.

29. Leider, *Becoming Mae West*, 151; Hamilton, *"When I'm Bad, I'm Better,"* 49.

310 NOTES

30. Leider, *Becoming Mae West*, 156–157; Hamilton, *"When I'm Bad, I'm Better,"* 69, 75.

31. Hamilton, *"When I'm Bad, I'm Better,"* 57–59, 102; Leider, *Becoming Mae West*, 156–157, 166.

32. Leider, *Becoming Mae West*, 184–185; Hamilton, *"When I'm Bad, I'm Better,"* 108–109.

33. Hamilton, *"When I'm Bad, I'm Better,"* 136–137; Leider, *Becoming Mae West*, 204–205.

34. Leider, *Becoming Mae West*, 204; Hamilton, *"When I'm Bad, I'm Better,"* 138.

35. Rotundo, *American Manhood*, 248.

36. Hamilton, "'I'm Queen of the Bitches': Female Impersonation and Mae West's Pleasure Man," in *Crossing the Stage: Controversies on Cross-Dressing*, ed. Lesley Ferris (New York: Routledge, 1993), 111.

37. "Mae West's Lawyer Quotes Shakespeare," *Daily News* (NY), October 19, 1928, 26 [358]; Dixie Tighe, "Mae West Fills Minor Role in Jury Picking," *Standard Union* (Brooklyn), March 18, 1930, 4.

38. [Advertisement.] *New York Clipper*, January 8, 1910, 1217; Kingsley, "Hobnobbing in Hollywood: Julian Eltinge Comes Back"; McIntyre, "New York Letter," 4.

39. "'You'll Fracture 'Em, Sweetheart'"; Ward Morehouse Papers, NYPL-PA-BRTC; Gray, "A Film Restores a bit of 42nd Street—in Faux Decay"; John Holusha, "3,700-Ton Theater to Move to New Role, and Address," *New York Times*, November 30, 1997; 9 [254]; Golden, "Julian Eltinge: Queen of Old Broadway," 23, refers to the venue as the "Laff House."

40. Julian Eltinge (as told to Diana Dare), "My Ideal Girl," *Border Cities Star, Windsor, Ontario*, March 3, 1927, 12 [28]; Wilson, "The Somewhat Different Diva," 18; O. O. McIntyre, "New York Day by Day," *Daily Messenger, Madisonville, Kentucky* April 3, 1935, 4.

41. Miller, "Is Gold Hidden under a California Peak?"; Daniel Miller, phone interview with author, May 17, 2023.

42. [Advertisement.] *Los Angeles Times*, May 12, 1935, 10; [Advertisement.] *Los Angeles Times*, June 2, 1935, i: 11; Lloyd Pantages, "Heavy Taxes Force Eltinge to Sell Property," *San Francisco Examiner*, November 4, 1935, 18; "Julian Eltinge Flees Tax Hike," *Arizona Republican, Phoenix*, January 6, 1936, 3; "Julian Eltinge, Foremost Female Impersonator, Dies," *Wilmington Morning News* (DE), March 8, 1941, 24.

43. "New York Theater Owner Buys Residential Realty Here," *Los Angeles Times*, May 23, 1937, v: 1 [81]; Banks, "The Man Who's Tired of Wearing Skirts"; "Sewer Tie-In Asked," *Los Angeles Times*, November 8, 1937, ii: 2 [18]; "'Dazed' Thespian Wants Lots Back"; "Valley Views," *San Fernando Valley Times*, February 16, 1939, 1, 12; "Eltinge in Court"; "Eltingegram" from Julian Eltinge archival files at NYPL-BRTC-PA, NAFR+ ser. 3 v. 432; current legal status and arrangement regarding Seven Terraces courtesy of Tony Castaneda, facilities manager of Villa Capistrano, onsite interview with person, May 17, 2023.

44. [Untitled.] *San Bernardino Daily Sun*, November 9, 1935, 12; Tucker, "In New York"; "Eltinge, Famed Female Impersonator, Passes," *Los Angeles Times*, March 8, 1941, 2.

45. Katherine T. Von Blon, "Julian Eltinge 'Straight'," *Los Angeles Times*, December 15, 1935, iii: 2 [50]; Harold W. Cohen, "The Drama Desk," *Pittsburgh Post-Gazette*, January 27, 1936, 8.

NOTES 311

46. Von Blon, "Julian Eltinge 'Straight'"; "Julian Eltinge Cast in Drama," *Los Angeles Times*, January 14, 1936, i: 11; Katherine T. Von Blon, "Julian Eltinge Great Trouper," *Los Angeles Times*, January 26, 1936, iii: 2 [44]; Monroe Lathrop, "Fay Bainter to Have New Play on Her Return," *Los Angeles Evening Express*, June 27, 1930, 13.

47. Edwin Schallert, "Group of Juniors in 'Frank Merriwell," *Los Angeles Times*, October 8, 1935, i: 13 [13]; [Untitled.] *Oakland Tribune*, October 21, 1935, 10.

48. Banks, "The Man Who's Tired of Wearing Skirts"; "Sewer Tie-In Asked"; "Wallace Palmer Entertained at Programs in the South," *Burlingame—The Times and Daily News Leader—San Mateo, Calif.*, September 7, 1938, 5.

49. "Impersonators Face Cleanup," *Hollywood Citizen-News*, January 9, 1940, 3; Senelick, "Lady and the Tramp," 32; Connelly, "King of Drag," 45; Hurwitz, *Bohemian Los Angeles*, 147; Emily Chudy, "Drag Was Once Billed as Dinner Theater to Skirt Crossdressing Laws. That's How Drag Brunch Was Born," *LGBTQ Nation*, October 16, 2023, https://www.lgbtqnation.com/2023/10/drag-was-once-billed-as-dinner-thea ter-to-skirt-cross-dressing-laws-thats-how-drag-brunch-was-born/; "Commission Hears about New 'B-Girl' Racket," *Los Angeles Times*, January 10, 1940, i: 4 [16]; Katz, *Invention of Heterosexuality*, 107; New York Academy of Medicine, "Homosexuality," 576, 578; Chauncey, *Gay New York*, 331.

50. Connelly, "King of Drag," 45; "Impersonators Face Cleanup"; "Julian Eltinge Fails to Get L.A. Permit," *San Bernardino Daily Sun*, January 17, 1940, 2; [Advertisement.] *Hollywood Citizen-News*, January 20, 1940, 3; Chauncey, *Gay New York*, 14–15; "Female Impersonator Barred in Los Angeles," *Herald, Miami, Florida*, January 25, 1940, c: 2 [26].

51. "Julian Eltinge Again to Don Women's Garb," *San Fernando Valley Times*, February 1, 1940, 6; Butler, "Performative Acts," 528; Peters, "Gay Deceiver," 168; Eltinge's economic motivations were similar to those that undermined vaudeville's labor union, the White Rats. For more, see Kibler, *Rank Ladies*, 171–198; Laurie, *Vaudeville: From the Honky-tonks*, 311; Snyder, *Voice of the City*, 37–40; Slide, *Encyclopedia of Vaudeville*, 161.

52. "Blanche Ring Returns," *San Francisco Examiner*, March 11, 1940, 11; Harold Levy, "Bing Crosby, Gloria Jean Preview Here," *Oakland Tribune*, April 15, 1940; "Bing Crosby and Gloria Jean in Centre Musical," *Ottawa Journal*, May 18, 1940, 22; John Mosher, *New Yorker*, May 18, 1940, otherwise unattributed, and plot summary from various materials, some partly unattributed, in the AMPAS archive; *American Film Institute Catalog of Motion Pictures Produced in the United States: Feature Films, 1931–40* (Berkeley: University of California Press, 1993), F3.2087, 1003.

53. Alice Hughes, "A Woman's New York," *Fort Worth Star-Telegram*, October 5, 1940, 4; Tucker, "In New York"; [Untitled.] *Daily News* (NY), February 15, 1941, 21-M [85]; "Julian Eltinge Dies; Female Impersonator," *Brooklyn Eagle*, March 7, 1941, 1; Mantle, "Professional Career of 40 Years Ended with Eltinge Death"; "News of Nightclubs," *New York Times*, May 5, 1940, 155 [2], "Julian Eltinge, Foremost Female Impersonator, Dies."

54. "Julian Eltinge, Foremost Female Impersonator, Dies"; March 8, 1941, 24; NYC LGBT Historic Sites Project, "235 West 46th Street, Manhattan: Billy Rose's Diamond

312   NOTES

Horseshoe Nightclub," accessed June 14, 2023, https://www.nyclgbtsites.org/site/billy-roses-diamond-horseshoe-nightclub/; [Advertisement.] *Daily News* (NY), August 17, 1942, 355 [35B].

55. "Julian Eltinge, Foremost Female Impersonator, Dies"; "Julian Eltinge Dies in East"; Peters, "Gay Deceiver," 168; "Julian Eltinge, Impersonator, 57."

56. Peters, "Gay Deceiver," 168; "Julian Eltinge Dies at 59; 'Venus de Milo's Brother," *Pittsburgh Sun-Telegraph*, March 7, 1941, 21; "Fish Injures Actor," *North Adams Transcript*, October 19, 1931, 4; "Operation Saves Eltinge, Knifed by Swordfish," *Daily News* (NY), October 17, 1931, 27 [99]; "Julian Eltinge and Doctor Injured by Big Swordfish," *Los Angeles Evening Express*, October 17, 1931, 3; "Swordfish Stabs Julian Eltinge," *Okmulgee Daily Times* (OK), October 17, 1931, 1; "Deaths in Miami and Elsewhere," *Miami Daily News*, March 9, 1941, 7 D [43]; Alice Hughes and Leonard Hall, "Brian Boru O'Hall Fixes His Kelly Green Cravat," *Akron Beacon-Journal*, March 17, 1941, 8; "300 at Eltinge Funeral," *New York Times*, March 10, 1944, 17; information regarding Forest Lawn from author's visit, May 22, 2023; Eltinge had long admired the so-called Little Church Around the Corner. Indeed, there had been an article about it in *Julian Eltinge Magazine*: "The Little Church Around the Corner: Sixty-Three Years of Existence and Known the World Over," ca. 1912, 38–40 (no other information, courtesy of Northport Historical Society).

57. "Julian Eltinge Leaves His Estate to His Mother," *Modesto Bee* (CA), March 26, 1941, 7; will, estate, and related letters and documents from Julian Eltinge archival files at NYPL-BRTC-PA; "Eltinge Bequeaths Entire Estate to His Mother," *Citizen-News* (Hollywood, CA), March 25, 1941, 3.

Epilogue

1. Raymond Williams, "Base and Superstructure in Marxist Cultural Theory," *New Left Review* [*NLR*] 82, no. 1 (November/December, 1973): 3–16; Sigmund Freud, *Civilization and Its Discontents*, ed. and trans. James Strachey (New York London: W. W. Norton, 1961), 73 (original work published 1930).

2. Rick Rojas, Emily Cochrane, Ava Sasani, and Michael Paulson, "Tennessee Laws Limiting 'Cabaret' Shows Raises Uncertainty about Drag Events," *New York Times*, March 5, 2023, https://www.nytimes.com/2023/03/05/us/tennessee-law-drag-shows.html; Suzanne Nossel, "The Drag Show Bans Sweeping the US Are a Chilling Attack on Free Speech," *Guardian*, March 10, 2023, https://www.theguardian.com/culture/commentisfree/2023/mar/10/drag-show-bans-tennessee-lgbtq-rights.

3. "Gridiron Star Also Wins Fame as Impersonator of Female Roles."

4. Laurie, *Vaudeville: From the Honky-tonks*, 91; University of Iowa, Special Collections, Keith/Albee Collection, Box 4: 11/28/1904–8/28/1905, 188, 188a.

5. Connelly, "King of Drag," 45, 42; Eve Golden, "Julian Eltinge: The Queen of Old Broadway," *TheaterWeek*, July 31, 1995, 20; Peters, "Gay Deceiver," 83; Soledad Santiago, "The King of TV Is Queen for a Day: Milton Berle Wigs Out at This Week's

NOTES   313

Dragfest," *Newsday* (NY), June 20, 1994, ii: 4 [prepublication draft, courtesy of Northport Historical Society, NY]; Slide, *Encyclopedia of Vaudeville*, 160; Toll, *On with the Show*, 249, 251; Rotundo, *American Manhood*, 276.

6. Connelly, "King of Drag," 45.

7. Golden, "Julian Eltinge: The Queen of Old Broadway," 20; Peters, "Gay Deceiver," 83; Soledad Santiago, "The King of TV Is Queen for a Day"; Connelly, "King of Drag," 45, 42; F. Michael Moore, *Julian Eltinge: Drag Diva of Broadway, Vaudeville & Hollywood* ([No Location.] Everleigh Books: A Broken Shoestring Production, 2020), 1–2; Morrow, "More about Eltinge"; Slide, *Encyclopedia of Vaudeville*, 160; Foucault, *The History of Sexuality*, Vol. 1: *An Introduction*, 26.

8. Garber, *Vested Interests*, 32, 276 (Garber is not quite right in asserting that Julian Eltinge began his career in George M. Cohan's minstrel troupe; he had already been a renowned semiprofessional and full-on professional for close to a decade before he joined the Cohan ensemble); for helpful background on *onnagata*, see Baker, *Drag*, 149–155, and Senelick, *Changing Room*, 79–100.

9. Ceylan Swensen, "Julian Eltinge" presentation, virtual and at Northport Historical Society, Long Island, NY, 26 June 2022; Eve Kosofsky Sedgwick, "Queer and Now," in *Literary Theories: A Reader and Guide*, ed. Julian Wolfreys (Edinburgh: Edinburgh University Press, 1999), 539.

10. Hajdu and Carey, *Revolution in Three Acts,* 55, 111; Erdman, *Queen of Vaudeville*.

11. Baker, *Drag*, 18; Moore, *Julian Eltinge: Drag Diva*, 1–2; "A Brief but Glamorous History of Drag," accessed February 13, 2023, https://www.history.co.uk/articles/a-brief-but-glamorous-history-of-drag.

12. Senelick, *Changing Room*, 5, 10, 12, 307, 308, 310; Bertolt Brecht, *Brecht on Theatre: The Development of an Aesthetic*, trans. and ed. John Willett (New York: Hill & Wang, 1957), 190–192; Dreiser, *Sister Carrie*, 336; Alger, *Ragged Dick*, 123; Sigmund Freud, "The Interpretation of Dreams," in *The Basic Writings of Sigmund Freud*, ed. and trans. by A. A. Brill (New York: Modern Library, 1938), 181–549 (original work published 1900).

Select Bibliography

"300 at Eltinge Funeral." *New York Times*, 10 March 1944, 17.

"A. H. Woods Dead; Producer Was 81." *New York Times*, 25 April 1951, 29.

Abbot, Willis J. *Soldiers of the Sea: The Story of the United States Marine Corps.* New York: Dodd, Mead & Co., 1919.

Ackroyd, Peter. *Dressing Up: Transvestism and Drag: The History of an Obsession.* New York: Simon & Schuster, 1979.

"Actor on Boxing." *Philadelphia Inquirer*, 23 February 1913, 6.

"Adopt Belgian Orphan." *Los Angeles Times*, 15 November 1918, ii: 3 [11].

"Advice to the Fat." *Anaconda Standard* (MT), 9 July 1911, 11 [35].

Agnew, Jean-Christophe. "Times Square: Secularization and Sacralization." In *Inventing Times Square: Commerce and Culture at the Crossroads of the World*, edited by William R. Taylor, 2–13. Baltimore: Johns Hopkins University Press, 1991.

"Airdome: Saturday, May 8, Julian Eltinge in 'The Clever Mrs. Carfax.'" *Randolph Enterprise, Randolph, Kansas*, 6 May 1920, 3.

"Albee on Vaudeville in 1912–13." *New York Clipper*, 5 October, 1912, 10.

Albee, E. F. "The Future of Show Business." *Billboard*, 19 December 1914, 38.

Albee, E. F. "Keith Vaudeville." *New York Clipper*, 15 February 1913, viii.

Albee, E. F. "Twenty Years of Vaudeville." *Theatre Magazine*, May 1920, 408.

Alger, Horatio, Jr., *Ragged Dick or, Street Life in New York with the Boot Blacks.* New York: Penguin Books, 1990. (Original work published 1868.)

Alper, Minnie. "Julian Eltinge's 'Perfect 36' Is Somewhat Extended When He Is Not on Stage." *McAlester News-Capital* (OK), 15 October 1919, 3.

Ali, Hasan. "Trans in Pakistan." *The Nation*, 23–30 January, 2023, 26–31.

"Alice Brady and Julian Eltinge on Garden Bill." *Paterson Morning Call* (NJ), 2 February 1918, 14.

"All about 'Salome.'" *Variety*, 1 August 1908, 7.

Allen, Robert C. "Contra the Chaser Theory." *Wide Angle*, 3, no. 1 (1979): 4–11.

Allen, Robert C. *Horrible Prettiness: Burlesque and American Culture.* Chapel Hill: University of North Carolina Press, 1991.

Allen, Robert C. "The Movies in Vaudeville: Historical Context of the Movies as Popular Entertainment." In *The American Film Industry, rev. ed.*, edited by Tino Balio, 57–82. Madison: University of Wisconsin Press, 1985.

Allen, Robert C. *Vaudeville and Film, 1895–1915: A Study in Media Interaction.* PhD diss., University of Iowa, 1977.

Altman, Rick. *Silent Film Sound.* New York: Columbia University Press, 2004.

American Film Institute Catalog of Motion Pictures Produced in the United States: Feature Films, 1911–1920. Berkeley: University of California Press, 1989.

American Film Institute Catalog of Motion Pictures Produced in the United States: Feature Films, 1921–30. Berkeley: University of California Press, 1997.

American Film Institute Catalog of Motion Pictures Produced in the United States: Feature Films, 1931–40. Berkeley: University of California Press, 1993.

316   SELECT BIBLIOGRAPHY

"American Music Hall." *Press, Kansas City, Kansas*, 21 January 1910, 2.

"Amusement Notes." *Brooklyn Daily Eagle*, 30 July 1907, 4 [22].

"Amusements." *Times-Democrat* (New Orleans), 23 November 1908, 4.

"Amusements: At the Theatres Tomorrows: Academy: Julian Eltinge in 'Cousin Lucy.'" *Charlotte News* (NC), 28 January 1917, 10.

"Another Big Keith Deal." *New York Clipper*, 6 September 1913, 1.

"Another 'Girl' Question." *Washington Times*, 16 December 1908, 11.

"Another Julian Eltinge?" *Hartford Courant*, 23 May 1937, 8 [72].

Anthony, Walter. "Julian and Not Julia, Eltinge Speaks." *San Francisco Call*, 10 November 1912, 31.

Anthony, Walter. "Lauder Charms Los Angeles." *San Francisco Call*, 10 January 1910, 5.

Anupama, M., K. H. Gangadhar, Vardana B. Shetty, and P. Bhadja Dip. "Transvestism as a Symptom: A Case Series." *Indian Journal of Psychological Medicine* 38, no. 1 (January–February 2016): 78–80.

Arendt, Hannah. *The Origins of Totalitarianism*, new ed. with added prefaces. New York: Harcourt, Brace Jovanovich, 1979. (Original work published 1951.)

Armstrong, David. "Cole Porter & the Queers Who Invented Broadway," *David Armstrong's Broadway Nation*, accessed June 15, 2023. https://broadwaypodcastnetwork.com/podcast/broadway-nation/.

"The Art of Makeup." *Butte Miner*, 17 January 1909, 17.

"Athlete in Gowns Stage Sensation." *St. Louis Post-Dispatch*, 5 July 1907, 16.

"Attorney General Asked to Dissolve the U.B.O." *Variety*, 11 October 1912, 1.

"Attractions at Playhouses in the City." *Daily News and Independent* (Santa Barbara, CA), 21 September 1917, 6.

"Autumnal Attractions at Buffalo Theaters." *Buffalo Courier*, 20 October 1908, 7.

Aydelotte, Winnifred. "Julian Eltinge Is Back after Two Years of Vacation." *Los Angeles Record*, 11 July 1931, ii: 1 [7].

"B. F. Keith Dead." *New York Clipper*, 4 April 1914, 1.

Bach, Sheldon. *The Language of Perversion and the Language of Love*. Northvale, NJ: Jason Aronson, 1991.

"Back to the Two-a-Day." *Brooklyn Citizen*, 3 April 1921, 10.

Baker, Roger. *Drag: A History of Female Impersonation on the Stage*. London: Triton, 1968.

Balio, Tino, ed. *The American Film Industry*, rev. ed. Madison: University of Wisconsin Press, 1985.

Balio, Tino, ed. "Part I: A Novelty Spawns a Small Business, 1894–1908." In *The American Film Industry*, rev. ed., edited by Tino Balio, 3–26. Madison: University of Wisconsin Press, 1985.

Balio, Tino, ed. "Part II: Struggles for Control, 1908–1930." In *The American Film Industry*, rev. ed., edited by Tino Balio, 103–132. Madison: University of Wisconsin Press, 1985.

Balio, Tino, ed. "Stars in Business: The Founding of United Artists." In *The American Film Industry*, rev. ed., edited by Tino Balio, 153–172. Madison: University of Wisconsin Press, 1985.

Balshofer, Fred J., and Arthur C. Miller. *One Reel a Week*. Berkeley: University of California Press, 1967.

"Baltimoreans in Cast." *Sun, Baltimore*, 22 June 1919, 12.

Banks, Louis. "The Man Who's Tired of Wearing Skirts." *Los Angeles Times Sunday Magazine*, 12 September 1937, 14 [115].

Banner, Lois W. *American Beauty*. New York: Knopf, 1983.

SELECT BIBLIOGRAPHY   317

Barnet, Anne Alison. *Extravaganza King*. Boston: Northeastern University Press, 2004.

Barnet, Sylvan, Morton Berman, and William Burto. "Medieval and Renaissance English Drama: An Introduction." In *The Genius of the Early English Theater*, edited by Sylvan Barnet, Morton Berman, and William Burto, 7–19. New York: Signet, 1962.

Barrymore, Ethel. *Memories: An Autobiography*. New York: Harper & Brothers, 1955.

Baska, Maggie. "The Long History of Drag—from Vaudeville to Reagan—and Why Right-Wing Outrage Is Nonsense." *ThePinkNews.com*, 8 April 2023. https://www.thepinkn ews.com/2023/04/08/drag-history-theatre-art-movies-tv-pop-culture-ban-lgbtq/.

Bayman, Anna. "Cross-Dressing and Pamphleteering in Early Seventeenth-Century London." In *Moral Panics, Media, and the Law in Early Modern England*, edited by David Lemmings and Clare Walker, 63–77. London: Palgrave Macmillan, 2009.

Bean, Annemarie. "Transgressing the Gender Divide: The Female Impersonator in Nineteenth-Century Blackface Minstrelsy." In *Inside the Minstrel Mask: Readings in Nineteenth-Century Blackface Minstrelsy*, edited by Annemarie Bean, James Vernon Hatch, and Brooks McNamara, 245–256. Hanover, NH: Wesleyan University Press, 1996.

"The Bearded American Belle." *Variety*, 14 December 1907, 44 [81].

Bederman, Gail. *Manliness & Civilization: A Cultural History of Gender and Race in the United States, 1880–1917*. Chicago: University of Chicago Press, 1995.

"Behind Scene Views of Vaudeville's Vamp Man." *Arkansas Democrat*, 18 January 1922, 5.

Berlanstein, Lenard R. "Breeches and Breaches: Cross-Dress Theater and the Culture of Gender Ambiguity in Modern France." *Comparative Studies in Society and History* 38, no. 2 (April 1996): 338–369.

"Bert Baker Admits He's Not a Julian Eltinge." *Buffalo Express*, 13 January 1916, 7.

"Beware of Widows." *Butte Miner*, 29 August 1912, 4.

Bill [only name given]. "Julian Eltinge, He-Man to Quit Feminine Role." *Los Angeles Evening Express*, 4 September 1924, 7.

"Billy J. Dalton in Reminiscences." *Anaconda Standard*, 14 February 1919, 5.

Bizot, Richard. "The Turn-of-the-Century Era: High- and Pop-Culture Variations on the Dance of the Seven Veils." *Choreography and Dance* 2, pt. 3: 71–87.

Blaisdell, George. "'The Clever Mrs. Carfax.'" *Moving Picture World*, 17 November 1917, 1034.

Blake, W. Herbert. "Harry Lauder Delights Scots." *Los Angeles Herald*, 7 January 1910, 10.

Boag, Peter. *Re-Dressing America's Frontier Past*. Berkeley: University of California Press, 2011.

Boorstin, Daniel. *The Image: A Guide to Pseudo-Events in America*. New York: Vintage, 1992. (Original work published 1962.)

Bordman, Gerald. *The Oxford Companion to American Theatre*. New York: Oxford University Press, 1984.

Bordwell, David, Janet Staiger, and Kristin Thompson. *The Classical Hollywood Cinema: Film Style and Mode of Production to 1960*. New York: Columbia University Press, 1985.

Bordwell, David, and Kristin Thompson. *Film Art: An Introduction*, 6th ed. New York: McGraw-Hill, 1993.

Bourdieu, Pierre. *Distinction: A Social Critique of the Judgment of Taste*. Translated by Richard Nice. Cambridge, MA: Harvard University Press, 1984.

"Boston Has a Harry Lehr Too! And His Name Is Julian Eltinge." *Boston Sunday Post*, 11 August 1901, 13.

318 SELECT BIBLIOGRAPHY

Braudy, Leo. *The Frenzy of Renown: Fame and Its History*. New York: Vintage, 1997.

Brill, A. A. "Introduction." In *The Basic Writings of Sigmund Freud*, translated and edited by A. A. Brill, 3–32. New York: Modern Library, 1938.

Brockett, Oscar G. *History of the Theatre*, 6th ed. Boston: Allyn & Bacon, 1991.

Broun, Heywood. "Eltinge Every Inch a Lady." *New York Tribune*, 28 August 1915, 7.

Brown, Dee. *Bury My Heart at Wounded Knee: An Indian History of the American West*. New York: Henry Holt, 1970.

Brecht, Bertolt. *Brecht on Theatre: The Development of an Aesthetic*. Edited and translated by John Willett. New York: Hill & Wang, 1957.

Bregg, Charles M. "Note and Comment." *New York Dramatic Mirror*, 11 December 1909, 19.

Brinig, Myron. *Wide Open Town*. Helena, MT: Sweetgrass Books, 1993.

Buckley, Peter G. "Boundaries of Respectability: Introduction." In *Inventing Times Square: Commerce and Culture at the Crossroads of the World*, edited by William R. Taylor, 286–296. Baltimore: Johns Hopkins University Press, 1991.

Bulleit, Clarence J. "Next Notable Juliet a Mere Man." *Indianapolis Sunday Star*, 22 January 1911, 32.

Bullough, Vern L., and Bonnie Bullough. *Cross Dressing, Sex, and Gender*. Philadelphia: University of Pennsylvania Press, 1993.

Burch, Noël. "A Primitive Mode of Representation?" In *Early Cinema: Space, Frame, Narrative*, edited by Thomas Elsaesser, 220–227. London: British Film Institute, 1990.

Butler, Judith. *Gender Trouble: Feminism and the Subversion of Identity*. New York: Routledge, 1990.

Butler, Judith. "Performative Acts and Gender Constitution: An Essay in Phenomenology and Feminist Theory." *Theatre Journal* 40, no. 4 (December 1988): 519–531.

"Butte School Boy with Lauder." *Butte Inter Mountain*, 18 January 1910, 8.

"Butte Stage Star Dies in New York: Julian Eltinge Succumbs." *Montana Standard, Butte*, 11 March 1941, 12.

Caffin, Caroline (and artwork by Marius de Zayas). *Vaudeville: The Book*. New York: Mitchell Kennerly, 1914.

"California Tonight." *Venice Evening Vanguard* (CA), 23 January 1926, 2.

"The Call of Salome." *New York Times*, 16 August 1908, 36.

Capp, Bernard. "Playgoers, Players, and Cross-Dressing in Early Modern London." *The Seventeenth Century* 18, no. 2 (2003): 159–171. doi: 10.1080/0268117X.2003.10555524.

Carstensen, Fred V. *American Enterprise in Foreign Markets*. Chapel Hill: University of North Carolina Press, 1984.

Casey, Kathleen B. *The Prettiest Girl on Stage Is a Man: Race and Gender Benders in American Vaudeville*. Knoxville: University of Tennessee Press, 2015.

Casey, Kathleen B. "Sex, Savagery, and the Woman Who Made Vaudeville Famous." *Frontiers* 36, no. 1 (2015): 87–112.

Cather, Willa Silbert. *My Ántonia*. New York: Houghton Mifflin, 1918.

Chandler, Alfred D. "The Rise of Big Business." In *United States Economic History: Selected Readings*, edited by Harry N. Schreiber, 334–367. New York: Knopf, 1964.

Chandler, Julia. "Old, Old Problem of Sex Furnishes Theme for New Drama by Feminine Playwrights." *Washington Herald*, 30 January 1916, ii: 1 [17].

Chapman, John. "Go West, Milady, for a Love Guide." *Daily News* (New York), 26 September 1944, 27M.

"Chat with Eltinge." *Gazette* (Montreal), 18 January 1908, 6.

SELECT BIBLIOGRAPHY   319

"Chatter about Theatrical Folk." *Buffalo Enquirer*, 26 May 1905, 2.

Chauncey, George. *Gay New York: Gender, Urban Culture, and the Making of the Gay Male World, 1890–1940*. New York: Basic Books, 1994/2019.

Cherniavsky, Felix. *The Salome Dancer: The Life and Times of Maud Allan*. Toronto: McClelland & Stewart, 1991.

"The Chinese Julian Eltinge Gets Monthly Pay of $2,000." *Minneapolis Sunday Tribune*, 4 February 1917, 9 [33].

"Chinese 'Julian Eltinge' Slain." *San Francisco Chronicle*, 29 August 1921, 1.

Chudy, Emily. "Drag Was Once Billed as Dinner Theater to Skirt Crossdressing Laws. That's How the Drag Brunch Was Born." *LGBTQ Nation*, 16 October 2023, https://www.lgbtqnation.com/2023/10/drag-was-once-billed-as-dinner-theater-to-skirt-cross-dressing-laws-thats-how-drag-brunch-was-born/.

"Cigarette Law Pains Eltinge." *Salt Lake Telegram*, 16 June 1921, ii: 1 [2].

"Clever Julian Eltinge at the Hippodrome." *Allentown Morning Call* (PA), 18 January 1918, 10.

"A 'Close-up' of Julian Eltinge." *Wichita Beacon* (KS), 6 November 1917, 9.

C.L.T. "Julian Eltinge Has Interview with 'Cousin Lucy'." *Brooklyn Daily Eagle, New York*, 7 January 1917, 3 [15].

Cochran, Thomas C. *200 Years of American Business*. New York: Basic Books, 1977.

Coffin, Harriet. "All Sorts and Kinds of Salomes." *Theatre*, April 1909, 130–133.

Cohan, Charles C. "Montanans Crash Films." *Los Angeles Times*, 23 June 1929, iii: 23 [53].

"College Julian Eltinges Fool Faculty Members." *Inter Ocean* (Chicago), 23 May 1913, 2.

"A Colored Julian Eltinge at Orpheum." *Omaha Daily News*, 30 January 1911, 5.

Connelly, Christopher S. "The King of Drag." *Etc*, 6 September 1996, 40–46.

Coons, Robbin. "Hollywood Sights and Sounds." *News-Palladium* (Benton Harbor, MI), 11 January 1930, 5.

"'Cousin Lucy' Almost New Show, Very Entertaining." *Buffalo Evening News*, 14 November 1916, 15.

"'Cousin Lucy' Is Clever." *Brooklyn Daily Times*, 28 August 1915, 4.

"Crinoline Girl Due to Lambs' Gambol." *Washington Times*, 16 February 1914, 5.

Crocker, Sarah. "Drag Shows Are Older than You Realize. Here's the Real Story." *Grunge*, 30 March 2023. https://www.grunge.com/1243587/drag-shows-older-realize-real-history/.

"Cute Little Beaute from Butte, Montana." *Butte Miner* (MT), 9 October 1922, 3.

Dague, Roswell. "Klein's Last Farce Is But Vehicle for Girl Impersonator." *Oakland Tribune*, 19 September 1915, 30.

Dale, Alan. "Why Women Are Greater Actors than Men." *Cosmopolitan*, September 1906, 517–524.

Darnton, Charles. "'Cousin Lucy' Displays Fashions and Julian Eltinge." *Arkansas Gazette, Little Rock*, 5 September 1915, 9 [29].

Darnton, Charles. "The Visitation of Salome." *New York Evening World*, 9 August 1908, 7.

Davis, Hartley. "In Vaudeville." *Everybody's Magazine*, August 1905, 231–240.

Davis, Peter A. "The Syndicate/Shubert War." In *Inventing Times Square: Commerce and Culture at the Crossroads of the World*, edited by William R. Taylor, 147–157. Baltimore: Johns Hopkins University Press, 1991.

"'Dazed' Thespian Wants Lots Back." *Hollywood Citizen-News*, 17 December 1938, 3 [2].

"Dean of Vaudeville Celebrities." *Variety*, 4 March 1906, 5.

"Death Takes Father of Julian Eltinge." *Los Angeles Record*, 8 July 1927, 15.

320 SELECT BIBLIOGRAPHY

"Decatur Soldier Leading Lady of A. E. F. in France." *Decatur Herald*, 6 January 1919, 10.

deCordova, Richard. *Picture Personalities: The Emergence of the Star System in America*. Chicago: University of Chicago Press, 1990.

Deland, Lorin F. "At the Sign of the Dollar." *Harper's Monthly Magazine*, March 1917, 525–533.

Derrida, Jacques. *Writing and Difference*. Translated by A. Bass. Chicago: University of Chicago, 1978.

"Didn't Want to Don Feminine Attire." *Buffalo Enquirer*, 23 January, 1911, 3.

Dietz, Dan. *The Complete Book of 1900s Broadway Musicals*. Lanham, MD: Rowman & Littlefield, 2022.

Dimeglio, John. *Vaudeville U.S.A*. Bowling Green, OH: Bowling Green University Popular Press, 1973.

"Disguised as Woman." *Boston Globe*, 20 February 1908, 8.

Doonan, Simon. *Drag: The Complete Story*. London: Lawrence King Publishing, 2019.

Dos Passos, John. *U.S.A. 1919*. Boston: Houghton Mifflin, 1946. (Original work published 1930.)

Douglas, Ann. *The Feminization of American Culture*. New York: Noonday Press, 1977.

Douglas, Ann. *Terrible Honesty: Mongrel Manhattan in the 1920s*. New York: Farrar, Straus & Giroux, 1995.

"Drake U. Man Tries a Bit of Impersonation: a la Julian Eltinge." *Des Moines Tribune*, 15 January 1927, 14.

"The Drama." *Joliet Evening Herald* (IL), 18 August 1911, 9.

"Dramatic." *Butte Miner*, 2 July 1911, 16.

Dreiser, Theodore. *An American Tragedy*. New York: New American Library, 2000. (Original work published 1925.)

Dreiser, Theodore. *Sister Carrie*. New York: Penguin Classics, 1981. (Original work published 1900.)

Dresden, Hilton. "Hollywood Has Its Own History of Anti-Drag Laws." *Hollywood Reporter*, 14 April 2023. https://www.hollywoodreporter.com/news/politics-news/l-a-history-anti-drag-laws-1235371248/.

Dudden, Faye E. *Women in the American Theatre: Actresses & Audiences, 1790–1870*. New Haven, CT: Yale University Press, 1994.

Duncan, Rosetta, and Vivian Duncan. "Big Company in the 'Black and White Revue." *San Francisco Examiner*, 29 October 1923, 10.

Durling, E. V. "Portraits in Words." *Pittsburgh Sun-Telegram*, 19 July 1944, 15.

"E. F. Albee, Co-Founder of Vaudeville." *New York Times*, 23 March 1930, ix: 4.

"E. F. Albee Dies at Palm Beach," *New York Times*, 12 March 1930, 32.

"Earl Benham Dies; Actor, Song Writer." *New York Times*, 23 March 1976, 34.

"Easy for Him to 'Doll Up' and Fool Patrons of Keith's." *Dayton Daily News* (OH), 12 December 1918, 12.

Eddy, Mary Baker. *Science and Health with Key to the Scriptures*. Boston: First Church of Christ, Scientist, 1971.

Edsberg, M. E. "Risque Rally Rouses Wrath." *Richmond Item* (IN), 22 November 1923, 3.

Elliot, William Foster. "Black and White Revue Mixture of Dates." *Fresno Bee*, 3 October 1923, 4.

Ellis, Havelock. *Studies in the Psychology of Sex: Sexual Inversion*. Philadelphia: P. A. Davis Co., 1901.

Elsaesser, Thomas. "The New Film History." *Sight and Sound* 55 (1986): 246–251.

SELECT BIBLIOGRAPHY 321

Elsaesser, Thomas, ed. *Early Cinema: Space, Frame, Narrative*. London: British Film Institute, 1990.

"Eltinge a Film." *Los Angeles Daily Times*, 14 June 1917, 15.

"Eltinge: A Mystery." *Variety*, 26 October 1907, 7 [130].

"Eltinge, Anna Held in Unique Movie Cast: 'Romeo-Juliet' Film Novelty Is Arranged." *Los Angeles Express*, 6 November 1913, ii: 1 [13].

"Eltinge Announced for Week at Century." *St. Louis Star*, 7 March 1912, 14.

"Eltinge at Majestic in Comedy, The Elusive Lady." *Illustrated Buffalo Express*, 22 October 1922, vii: 2 [65].

"Eltinge at Orpheum." *Brooklyn Daily Times*, 2 January1918, 8.

"Eltinge at the American." *Boston Globe*, 3 May 1910, 11.

"Eltinge Beauty Parlor." *Spokesman-Review* (Spokane, WA), 2 June 1912, 2 [42].

"Eltinge Bequeaths Entire Estate to His Mother." *Citizen-News* (Hollywood, CA), 25 March 1941.

"Eltinge Bids Skirts Goodbye." *Border Cities Star, Windsor, Ontario*, 4 June 1927, 5 [21].

"Eltinge Buys Up Tract to Add to Artists' Colony." *Los Angeles Sunday Times*, 23 August 1925, iii: 20 [64].

"Eltinge Comes Here to Make Photoplay." *Oregon Sunday Journal*, Portland, 12 August 1917, 10.

"Eltinge Declines." *Dayton Daily News*, 5 June 1921, ii: 2 [21].

"Eltinge, Famed Female Impersonator, Passes." *Los Angeles Times*, 8 March 1941, 2.

"Eltinge for Broadway." *Variety*, 24 February 1906.

"Eltinge Forms Film Company." *Los Angeles Daily Times*, 24 November 1920, iii: 4 [32].

"Eltinge Harks Back Three Centuries." *Sun, Baltimore*, 4 March 1913, 5.

"Eltinge Has to Stay in 'Soft' Condition." *Santa Cruz Evening News*, 18 July 1919, 6.

"Eltinge in Court." *Hollywood Citizen-News*, February 27, 1939, 1.

"Eltinge in Demand Abroad." *Variety*, 3 March 1906, 6.

"Eltinge in New War Picture." *Oregon Daily Journal, Portland*, 22 September 1918, 2 [30].

"Eltinge, in Skirts, Awaits Eagerly the Coming of Old Age." *Sunday Express: Los Angeles*, 29 December 1918, iv: 4 [44].

"Eltinge Is a Fair Charmer in a New Turn." *Los Angeles Evening Express*, 5 October 1926, 29.

"Eltinge Picture at Clune's Proves Strong Attraction." *Evening Express, Los Angeles*, 11 March 1918, 6 [8].

"Eltinge Plans Theater in L.A." *Los Angeles Record*, 25 April 1925, 12 [10].

"Eltinge Plans to Continue His Feminine Roles." *Los Angeles Daily Times*, 25 April 1925, 7.

"Eltinge Prefers Life in the Open Air." *Pittsburgh Press*, 6 November 1921, Theatrical and Photoplay Section, 2 [38].

"Eltinge Quits Screen for 'Vode' Jan. 6." *Evening Express, Los Angeles*, 24 October 1918, 8.

"Eltinge Quits Skirts." *Variety*, 18 April 1908, 9.

"Eltinge Says He Didn't." *Variety*, 6 January 1906, 12.

"Eltinge Says Women Have Much to Learn." *Pittsburg [sic] Press*, 27 January 1911, 24.

"Eltinge Stars in New Comedy." *Tacoma Sunday Ledger*, 29 February 1920, E-5 [57].

"Eltinge Succeeds in 'Crinoline Girl.'" *New York Times*, 17 March 1914, 11.

"'Eltinge' Was Butte's Tough Kid." *San Francisco Examiner*, 3 January 1919, 19.

"Eltinge Will Pay $2,000 Income Tax." *Washington Times*, 7 February 1914, 8.

"Eltinge's Ingrowing Wisdom." *Inter Ocean*, 26 March 1911, 11 [37].

"Eltinges of Queen Elizabeth's Time as Shakespeare Heroines." *Detroit Free Press*, 11 February 1912, 12 [63].

322   SELECT BIBLIOGRAPHY

"Eltinge's Return Delayed." *Variety*, 22 September 1906, 6.

Eltinge, Julian. "Let Your Mirror Be Your Beauty Critic." *San Francisco Call*, 17 November 1913, 9.

Eltinge, Julian (as related to Marion Van B. Sturges). "What I Would Do If I Were Really a Woman," *Metropolitan*, September 1923, 37.

Eltinge, Julian. "When a Man Becomes a Woman: A Vaudeville Miracle." *Louisville, Kentucky Courier-Journal, Illustrated Sunday Magazine*, 23 June 1907, 2 [38].

Eltinge, Julian, and Diana Dare. "My Ideal Girl." *Border Cities Star, Windsor, Ontario*, 3 March 1927, 12 [28].

"'The Elusive Lady' Is Typically Eltinge." *Buffalo Evening News*, 24 October 1922, 2.

"'Elusive Lady' Shares Honors with 'Bride.'" *Sun, Baltimore*, 1 October 1922, iv: 4 [42].

Emmet, Boris, and John E. Jeuck. *Catalogues and Counters: A History of Sears, Roebuck and Company*. Chicago: University of Chicago Press, 1950.

Engels, Frederick. *The Origin of the Family, Private Property and the State*. London: Penguin, 1972. (Original work published 1884.)

Erdman, Andrew. *Blue Vaudeville: Sex, Morals, and the Mass Marketing of Entertainment, 1885–1915*. Jefferson, NC: McFarland, 2004.

Erdman, Andrew. "Edward Bernays and the 'Golden Jubilee of Light': Culture, Performance, Publicity." *Theatre Annual* 49 (1996): 49–64.

Erdman, Andrew. "From Frank Fay to Jimmy Stewart: Broadway, Hollywood, and the Construction of Creativity." *Theatre Studies* 41 (1996): 13–28.

Erdman, Andrew. *Queen of Vaudeville: The Story of Eva Tanguay*. Ithaca, NY: Cornell University Press, 2021.

Erdman, Harley. "Caught in the 'Eye of the Eternal': Justice, Race, and the Camera, from 'The Octoroon' to Rodney King." *Theatre Journal* 45, no. 3 (October 1993): 333–348. https://www.jstor.org/stable/3208358.

Erdman, Harley. *Staging the Jew: The Performance of an American Ethnicity, 1860–1920*. New Brunswick, NJ: Rutgers University Press, 1997.

Erenberg, Lewis. "Impresarios of Broadway Nightlife." In *Inventing Times Square: Commerce and Culture at the Crossroads of the World*, edited by William R. Taylor, 158–190. Baltimore: Johns Hopkins University Press, 1991.

"Eva Tanguay Will Wed Julian Eltinge." *Minneapolis Tribune*, 19 August 1908, 4.

"Eva Tanguay's Coming Wedding Talk of the Stage." *Evening World* (NY), 17 August 1908, 3.

Everett, Eugenia. "Men of the Dancing First." In *Performing Arts Resources: Taking the Pledge and Other Public Amusements*, edited by Barbara Naomi Cohen-Stratyner, 121–129. New York: Public Theatre Library Association, 1991.

"Evolution of Cheap Vaudeville." *Variety*, 14 December 1907, 10.

"Famous Woman Impersonator Is Featured." *Visalia Daily Times* (CA), 7 April 1926, 5.

Farnsworth, Marjorie. *The Ziegfeld Follies*. New York: Bonanza Books, 1956.

"'The Fascinating Widow.'" *Brooklyn Citizen*, 12 September 1911, 7.

"Female Impersonator Barred in Los Angeles." *Herald, Miami, Florida*, 25 January 1940, c: 2, 26.

"Female Impersonator in Musical Comedy." *Pittsburgh Gazette Times*, 31 January 1911, 10.

Fenichel, Otto. *The Psychoanalytic Theory of Neurosis, 50th Anniversary Edition*. London: Routledge, 1996. (Original work published 1946.)

Ferris, Lesley. "Introduction: Current Crossings." In *Crossing the Stage: Controversies on Cross-Dressing*, edited by Lesley Ferris, 1–19. New York: Routledge, 1993.

SELECT BIBLIOGRAPHY   323

Ferris, Lesley, ed. *Crossing the Stage: Controversies on Cross-Dressing*. New York: Routledge, 1993.

Fields, Armond L. *Sophie Tucker: The First Lady of Show Business*. Jefferson, NC: McFarland & Co., 2003.

Fields, Armond L., and Marc Fields. *From the Bowery to Broadway: Lew Fields and the Roots of American Popular Theater*. New York: Oxford University Press, 1993.

"Fifth Avenue," *Variety*, June 6, 1908, 14 [16].

"Filmed Julian Eltinge in 'Princess Charming' a Big Rialto Success." *Evening World* (NY), 18 September 1917, 13.

"First Eltinge Theatre Bill." *New York Times*, 7 June 1912, 13.

"First Production Is Selected for Julian Eltinge." *Edmonton Journal*, 7 July 1917, 10.

"Fish Injures Actor." *North Adams Transcript*, 19 October 1931, 4.

Fiske, John. *Understanding Popular Culture*. Boston: Unwin Hyman, 1989.

Fitzgerald, F. Scott. *The Great Gatsby*. Planet eBook, accessed 7 February 2022. https://www.planetebook.com/free-ebooks/the-great-gatsby.pdf. (Original work published 1925.)

Flanders, Sara, Francois Ladame, Anders Carlsberg, Petra Heymanns, Despina Naziri, and Denny Panitz. "On the Subject of Homosexuality: What Freud Said." *International Journal of Psychoanalysis* 97 (2016): 933–950. doi: 10.1111/1745-8315.12520.

Fleischer, Mary Rita. "Collaborative Projects of Symbolist Playwrights and Early Modern Dancers." PhD diss., City University of New York Graduate Center, 1998.

"Ford's—The Eltinge Revue." *Evening Sun, Baltimore*, 3 May 1919, 9.

Fortune magazine. "Metro-Goldwyn-Mayer." In *American Film Industry*, rev. ed., edited by Tino Balio, 311–333. Madison: University of Wisconsin Press, 1985.

"Fotosho Today—Rodolph Valentino and Julian Eltinge in 'The Isle of Love.'" *Herald, Miami, Florida*, 2 January 1923, A 7 [19].

Foucault, Michel. *The History of Sexuality*, Vol. 1: *An Introduction*. Translated by Robert Hurley. New York: Vintage Books, 1980.

"Four Views of Mr. Julian Eltinge." *Variety*, 14 December 1907, 9.

"Fred FitzGerald Will Be Host to Julian Eltinge," *Santa Rosa Press Democrat*, 30 October 1923, 2 [20].

Freedley, George. "History of Female Impersonation." *New York Times*, 16 December 1956, ii: 5.

Freeman, Michael C. *A Brief History of Butte, Montana: The World's Greatest Mining Camp*. Chicago: Henry O. Shepard Co., 1900.

Freud, Sigmund. *The Basic Writings of Sigmund Freud*. Edited and translated by A. A. Brill. New York: Modern Library, 1938.

Freud, Sigmund. *Civilization and its Discontents*. Edited and translated by James Strachey. New York: W. W. Norton, 1961. (Original work published 1930.)

Freud, Sigmund. "The Interpretation of Dreams." In *The Basic Writings of Sigmund Freud*, edited and translated by A. A. Brill, 181–549. New York: Modern Library, 1938. (Original work published 1900.)

Freud, Sigmund. "Three Contributions to the Theory of Sex." In *The Basic Writings of Sigmund Freud*, edited and translated by A. A. Brill, 553–629. New York: Modern Library, 1938. (Original work published 1905.)

"Friars' Frolic Tonight." *New York Daily Tribune*, 28 May 1911, iv: 6 [50].

"From Harvard Student to Stage Celebrity." *Washington Times*, 26 February 1909, 8.

Fulton, A. R. "The Machine." In *American Film Industry*, rev. ed., edited by Tino Balio, 27–42. Madison: University of Wisconsin Press, 1985.

324 SELECT BIBLIOGRAPHY

"Fulton Opera House: 'Mr. Wix of Wickham' Lacks Action." *New Era—Lancaster* (PA), 17 December 1904, 2.

Furia, Philip. "Irving Berlin: Troubadour of Tin Pan Alley." In *Inventing Times Square: Commerce and Culture at the Crossroads of the World*, edited by William R. Taylor, 191–211. Baltimore: Johns Hopkins University Press, 1991.

Fyles, Vanderheden. "Letter of New York Theatrical News." *Times-Democrat* (New Orleans, LA), 22 March 1914, 2 [16].

Gabler, Neal. *An Empire of Their Own: How the Jews Invented Hollywood*. New York: Anchor Books, 1988.

Ganz, Earl. "Introduction." In *Wide Open Town*, by Myron Brinig, xii–xix. Helena, MT: Sweetgrass Books, 1993.

Gänzl, Kurt. *Lydia Thompson: Queen of Burlesque*. New York: Routledge, 2002.

Garber, Marjorie. *Vested Interests: Cross-dressing and Cultural Anxiety*. New York: Routledge, 1997.

"Garden: Julian Eltinge in 'An Adventuress.'" *Morning Call* (Paterson, NJ), 10 June 1920, 5.

Garrison, McKim. *An Illustrated History of Hasty Pudding Club Theatricals*. Cambridge, MA: Hasty Pudding Club, 1897.

Gay, Peter. *Freud: A Life for Our Times*. New York: Anchor Books, 1988.

Gentile, Jill, with Michael Macrone. *Feminine Law: Freud, Free Speech, and the Voice of Desire*. London: Karnac, 2016.

"George K. Fortescue Dead." *New York Times*, 14 January 1914, 11.

"George Walker Says Julian Eltinge Is Very Rare Artist." *Austin American*, 19 February 1917, 6.

Gilbert, Douglas. *American Vaudeville: Its Life and Times*. New York: Dover Publications, 1940.

Gilfoyle, Timothy J. "Policing of Sexuality." In *Inventing Times Square: Commerce and Culture at the Crossroads of the World*, edited by William R. Taylor, 297–314. Baltimore: Johns Hopkins University Press, 1991.

Glenn, Susan A. *Female Spectacle: The Theatrical Roots of Modern Feminism*. Cambridge, MA: Harvard University Press, 2000.

Glickman, Lawrence. *A Living Wage: American Workers and the Making of a Consumer Society*. Ithaca, NY: Cornell University Press, 1997.

Golden, Eve. "Julian Eltinge: The Queen of Old Broadway." *TheaterWeek*, 31 July 1995, 20–23.

Gomery, Douglas. "The Coming of Sound: Technological Change in the American Film Industry." In *American Film Industry*, rev. ed., edited by Tino Balio, 229–251. Madison: University of Wisconsin Press.

Gomery, Douglas. *Shared Pleasures: A History of Movie Presentation in the United States*. Madison: University of Wisconsin Press, 1992.

"The Good and Bad on Monday's Bills." *Wichita Daily Eagle*, 30 September 1917, 60.

Gordon, Ruth. "'You'll Fracture 'Em, Sweetheart.'" *New York Times*, 31 August 1969, ii: 1, 3.

Gordon-Loebl, Naomi. "Breaking Down the Binary." *The Nation*, 26 December 2022–2 January 2023, 29–31+.

"Grand Double Attraction." *Ogden Standard* (UT), 10 November 1917, 10.

"'Grand Duchess of Dance,' Lilla Viles Wyman Is Dead." *Boston Daily Globe*, 14 April 1944, 26.

Grau, Robert. "How Performers Spend Their 'Real' Money." *San Francisco Examiner*, 15 January 1911, 68.

SELECT BIBLIOGRAPHY   325

Gray, Christopher. "A Film Restores a bit of 42nd Street—in Faux Decay." *New York Times*, 28 March 1993, x: 7.

"Greenroom, Stage, and Foyer." *Los Angeles Herald Sunday Magazine*, 10 January 1909, 4 [48].

"Gridiron Star Also Wins Fame as Impersonator of Female Roles." *Olean Evening Times* (NY), 20 January 1923, 17.

Gunning, Tom. "The Cinema of Attractions: Early Film, Its Spectator and the Avant-Garde." In *Early Cinema: Space, Frame, Narrative*, edited by Thomas Elsaesser, 56–62. London: British Film Institute, 1990.

Haddon, Celia. *The Sensuous Lie*. New York: Stein & Day, 1983.

Hajdu, David, and John Carey, *A Revolution in Three Acts: The Radical Vaudeville of Bert Williams, Eva Tanguay, and Julian Eltinge*. New York: Columbia University Press, 2021.

"Hal Russell in 'The Fascinating Widow.'" *Allentown Democrat* (PA), 9 September 1917, 11.

Hall, Spick. "Julian Eltinge Is Fascinating to the Last Degree." *Nashville Tennessean and Nashville American*, 24 January 1913, 10.

Hamilton, Marybeth. " 'I'm Queen of the Bitches': Female Impersonation and Mae West's Pleasure Man." In *Crossing the Stage: Controversies on Cross-Dressing*, edited by Lesley Ferris, 107–119. New York: Routledge, 1993.

Hamilton, Marybeth. "Mae West Live: 'SEX, The Drag, and 1920s Broadway.'" *TDR* 36, no. 4 (Winter 1992): 82–100. https://www.jstor.org/stable/1146217.

Hamilton, Marybeth. *"When I'm Bad, I'm Better": Mae West, Sex, and American Entertainment*. Berkeley: University of California Press, 1997.

Hammack, David C. "Developing for Commercial Culture." In *Inventing Times Square: Commerce and Culture at the Crossroads of the World*, edited by William R. Taylor, 36–50. Baltimore: Johns Hopkins University Press, 1991.

"Hammerstein's Roof." *Variety*, 13 June 1908, 15.

Hammond, Percy. "Notes of Plays and Players." *Chicago Daily Tribune*, 23 March 1910, 10.

Hank [only name given]. "Eva Tanguay as 'Salome.'" *New York Clipper*, 15 August 1908, 653.

Harris, Neil. *Humbug: The Art of P. T. Barnum*. Chicago: University of Chicago Press, 1973.

Harrison, Patricia King, exec. ed. *The American Film Institute Catalog of Motion Pictures Produced in the United States: Feature Films: 1911–1920*. Berkeley: University of California Press, 1988.

"Harry Lehr Has a Rival among the Boston 400." *Philadelphia Inquirer Sunday Magazine*, 28 July 1901, 37–38.

"Harry Lehr's Boston Rival." *Buffalo Courier*, 11 November 1902, 3.

"Harry S. Lehr Dies; Once Social Leader." *New York Times*, 4 January 1929, 25.

"Has Prettiest Pair of Eyes at Harvard." *Boston Sunday Post*, 13 March 1921, 6.

"He Dances for Boston Society." *Kansas City Star*, 20 April 1902.

"He Had Learned." *Miami Herald*, 5 December 1912, 8.

"He Wears a Corset." *Sunday Telegram, Clarksburg, W. Va.*, 23 May 1915, 30.

Henderson, Mary C. *The City and the Theatre*. New York: Back Stage Books, 2004.

Hendricks, Gordon. "The History of the Kinetoscope." In *The American Film Industry*, in *American Film Industry*, rev. ed., edited by Tino Balio, 43–56. Madison: University of Wisconsin Press, 1985.

Herrmann, Anne. "Travesty and Transgression: Transvestism in Shakespeare, Brecht, and Churchill." *Theatre Journal* 41, no. 2 (1989): 133–154.

Higgins, Harvey Alexander, Jr. "The Origin of Vaudeville." *New York Dramatic Mirror*, 13 May 1919, 719–720.

326 SELECT BIBLIOGRAPHY

Hilsabeck, Geoffrey. *American Vaudeville*. Morgantown: West Virginia University Press, 2021.

"His Trousseau." *Los Angeles Sunday Times*, 16 September 1923, iii: 23 [57].

The History Project (U.S.). *Improper Bostonians*. Boston: Beacon Press, 1998.

Hollander, Anne. *Seeing through Clothes*. New York: Viking, 1978.

Holusha, John. "3,700-Ton Theater to Move to New Role, and Address." *New York Times*, 30 November 1997, 9 [254].

Holusha, John. "A Theater's Muses, Rescued: Mural Figures Recall Celebrity of a (Well-Painted) Face." *New York Times*, 1 March 1998, B1, B6.

"How a Man Makes Himself a Beautiful Woman." *Chicago Tribune*, 27 September 1908, 48.

"How Billy Dalton of Butte Got His Start as Actor." *Sacramento Bee* (CA), 10 March 1917, 28.

"How Does He Do It! The Problem Successfully Solved." *Pittsburgh Gazette Times*, 26 January 1911.

Hughes, Alice. "A Woman's New York." *Fort Worth Star-Telegram*, 5 October 1940, 4.

Hunt, Michael. *Ideology and U.S. Foreign Policy*. New Haven, CT: Yale University Press, 1987.

Hurwitz, Daniel. *Bohemian Los Angeles and the Making of Modern Politics*. Berkeley: University of California Press, 2007.

Hutchens, John. "The Times Square Narrative, in Lights." *New York Times*, 19 October 1930, ix: 2.

"Impersonations by Julian Eltinge, a Big, Husky Man." *Indianapolis News*, 23 September 1908, 8.

"Impersonator in New Role." *Daily Times* (Davenport, IA), 13 December 1918, 11.

"Impersonators Face Cleanup." *Hollywood Citizen-News*, 9 January 1940, 3.

"In 'Cousin Lucy' at the Star Next Week." *Buffalo Enquirer*, 11 November 1916, 7.

"'In Just a Minute.'" *Boston Globe*, 13 February 1911, 3.

"In Woman's Gorgeous Costumes." *St. Paul Globe* (MN), 27 April 1902, 16.

Inness, Sherrie. "Girls Will Be Boys and Boys Will Be Girls: Crossdressing in Popular Turn-of-the-Century College Fiction." *Journal of American Culture* 18, no. 2 (Summer 1995): 15–23.

"Jean Malin Dies as Car Jumps Pier." *Daily News* (NY), 11 August 1933, 4.

Jenkins, Henry. *What Made Pistachio Nuts: Early Sound Comedy and the Vaudeville Aesthetic*. New York: Columbia University Press, 1992.

Jessel, George. *Elegy in Manhattan*. New York: Holt, Rinehart, & Winston, 1961.

Johnson, Julian. "The Drama—Playhouses, Players, Theatrical Chit-Chat." *Los Angeles Times*, 2 January 1910, 29 [iii, 1].

Joseph, Channing Gerard. "The First Drag Queen." *Nation*, 17 February 2020, 23–26.

Joy, Al C. "Harry Lauder? Yes, He's the Laugh King." *San Francisco Examiner*, 11 January 1910, 3 [1].

"Julian as Five Women." *Washington Herald*, 9 May 1919, 2 [28].

"Julian Eltinge." *Variety*, October 12, 1907, 9 [52].

"Julian Eltinge, 57, Famous Female Impersonator, Dies." *Boston Daily Globe*, 7 March 1941, 1, 8.

"Julian Eltinge a Big Hit at Keith's." *Evening Public Ledger, Philadelphia*, 5 February 1918, 9.

"Julian Eltinge a Cousin to 'Charley's Aunt'?" *Los Angeles Sunday Times*, 2 August 1925, [sec.] "Acts and Actors: 1," 63.

SELECT BIBLIOGRAPHY 327

"Julian Eltinge, Ably Supported, Delights Austin Audience." *Statesman* (Austin, TX), 5 October 1919, 10 [26].

"Julian Eltinge, Actor, Hurt." *Boston Globe*, 10 July 1929, 6.

"Julian Eltinge Again to Don Women's Garb." *San Fernando Valley Times*, 1 February 1940.

"Julian Eltinge and Company Opens Season at the Court." *Wheeling Intelligencer*, 16 September 1916, 11.

"Julian Eltinge and Doctor Injured by Big Swordfish." *Los Angeles Evening Express*, 17 October 1931, 3.

"Julian Eltinge and Some of His Costumes as a Fascinating Widow." *Washington Herald*, 20 November 1910, 9.

"Julian Eltinge Arrested for Having Liquor." *Sacramento Bee*, 27 February 1923, 4.

"Julian Eltinge as a Broncho Buster." *Victoria Daily Times*, 8 January 1918, 6.

"Julian Eltinge as 'Cousin Lucy.'" *Brooklyn Daily Eagle*, 2 January 1917, 12.

"Julian Eltinge as Statue of Liberty." *Daily News and the Independent* (Santa Barbara, CA), 16 January 1919, 5.

"Julian Eltinge at Keith-Albee." *Boston Globe*, 4 December 1928, 29.

"Julian Eltinge Hennepin Star." *Minnesota Daily Star*, 20 January 1923, 6.

"Julian Eltinge at Palace." *New York Times*, 8 January 1918, 13.

"Julian Eltinge at Tacoma Soon." *Tacoma Daily Ledger*, 29 January 1919, 7.

"Julian Eltinge at the Boston." *Boston Globe*, 7 February 1911, 15.

"Julian Eltinge Back in Female Portrayals." *New York Times*, 1 November 1927, 20.

"Julian Eltinge Badly Hurt in Crash." *Colton Courier* (CA), 10 July 1929, 1.

"Julian Eltinge Began Stage Career at College." *Capital Times* (Madison, WI), 7 March 1924, 6.

"Julian Eltinge Booked Abroad." *Variety*, 28 April 1906, 5.

"Julian Eltinge Brings Lots of Gowns to L.A." *Los Angeles Evening Express*, 21 April 1925, 8.

"Julian Eltinge Can't Find Suitable Play." *San Francisco Examiner*, 24 November 1925, 19.

"Julian Eltinge Case Is Dropped." *Tacoma Daily Ledger*, 1 March 1923, 12.

"Julian Eltinge Craves to Grow Hair on Chest." *Progress, Pomona* (CA), 7 October 1924, 2.

"Julian Eltinge Dies; Famous in Feminine Roles," *Chicago Daily Tribune*, 8 March 1941, 20.

"Julian Eltinge Dies; Female Impersonator." *Brooklyn Eagle*, 7 March 1941, 1.

"Julian Eltinge Dies at 59; 'Venus de Milo's Brother.'" *Pittsburgh Sun-Telegraph*, 7 March 1941, 21.

"Julian Eltinge Dies in East." *Hollywood Citizen-News*, 7 March 1941, 1.

"Julian Eltinge Drags the Market for Bathing Belles." *Fort Wayne Journal-Gazette* (IN), 30 May 1920, 8B.

"Julian Eltinge Entertains Japanese; Wife Watches Hubby Imitate Her Sex." *Muskogee Daily Phoenix*, 1 March 1920, 3.

"Julian Eltinge Fails to Get L.A. Permit." *San Bernardino Daily Sun*, 17 January 1940, 2.

"Julian Eltinge Flees Tax Hike." *Arizona Republican, Phoenix*, 6 January 1936, 3.

"Julian Eltinge for Australia." *Daily Ledger, Tacoma, Washington*, 27 August 1911, 32.

"Julian Eltinge, Foremost Female Impersonator, Dies." *Wilmington Morning News* (DE), 8 March 1941, 24.

"Julian Eltinge Has His Teeth Insured." *Oregon Sunday Journal, Portland*, 23 March 1913, 2 [38].

"Julian Eltinge Has Interview with 'Cousin Lucy.'" *Brooklyn Daily Eagle*, 7 January 1917, 3 [15].

328   SELECT BIBLIOGRAPHY

"Julian Eltinge Has No Lady's Taste for Sport." *Minneapolis Morning Tribune*, 28 August 1916, 16.

"Julian Eltinge Has Serious Operation." *Fall River Evening News* (MA), 2 August 1922, 2.

"Julian Eltinge Heads Vaudeville Company." *Indianapolis Star*, 10 July 1910, 35 [43].

"Julian Eltinge, He-Man to Quit Feminine Role." *Los Angeles Evening Express*, 4 September 1924, 7.

"Julian Eltinge Hennepin Star." *Minnesota Daily Star*, 20 January 1923, 6.

"Julian Eltinge Here." *Los Angeles Daily Times*, 3 February 1926, ii: 9 [25].

"Julian Eltinge, Impersonator, 57." *New York Times*, 8 March 1941, 19.

"Julian Eltinge in a Chas. Klein Play." *Brooklyn Daily Eagle*, 28 August 1915, 2.

"Julian Eltinge in Classy New Togs." *Illustrated Daily News* (Los Angeles, CA), 1 September 1926, 17.

"Julian Eltinge in His Impersonations of Salome with Cohan & Harris Minstrels Monday Evening." *Fort Wayne Journal-Gazette* (IN), 27 September 1908, 19.

"Julian Eltinge in Keith Feature Act." *Boston Globe*, 10 May 1921, 3.

"Julian Eltinge in Klein's Last Play." *New York Times*, 28 August 1915, 7.

"Julian Eltinge in Movies." *New York Times*, 17 September 1917, 11.

"Julian Eltinge in Skirts and Trousers." *Boston Globe*, 10 November 1914, 6.

"Julian Eltinge in 'The Countess Charming' at Shea's Hippodrome," *Buffalo Sunday Times*, 23 September 1917, 54.

"Julian Eltinge in 'The Widow's Might,' at Clune's Broadway." Los Angeles Record , 9 March 1918, 5.

"Julian Eltinge Is a Regular Farmer." *Buffalo Courier*, 9 March 1913, 42.

Julian Eltinge Is Going on a Trip around the World." *Minneapolis Sunday Tribune*, 25 May 1919, 14 [46].

"Julian Eltinge Leaves His Estate to His Mother." *Modesto Bee* (CA), 26 March 1941, 7.

"Julian Eltinge Makes Game Fight for Life after Operation." *San Francisco Chronicle*, 9 August 1921, ii: 1 [13].

"Julian Eltinge Makes Tremendous Hit at the Alhambra." *Ogden Standard* (UT), 21 March 1918, 10.

"Julian Eltinge May Wed Tanguay." *Washington Times*, 16 August 1908, 2 [22].

"Julian Eltinge, Noted Female Impersonator, Lets Men of Omaha in on 'Women's Ten Mysteries'." *Omaha Daily News*, 31 January 1919, 12.

" 'Julian Eltinge' of Orient Sets Style for Nippon Girls." *Omaha Daily News* (NE), 12 June 1919, 1.

"Julian Eltinge on Stock-Selling Tour." *Los Angeles Evening Express*, 5 March 1921, ii: 5 [13].

"Julian Eltinge 'Ountee Charming' Princess July 16th." *Copper Era* (Clifton, AZ), 11 July 1919, 8.

"Julian Eltinge Popular Star." *Davenport Democrat and Leader* (IA), 18 February 1912, 1.

"Julian Eltinge Popular Star." *Quad City Times* (Davenport, IA), 18 February 1912, 17.

"Julian Eltinge Praises Haresfoot Performers While in Madison." *Racine Journal-News* (WI), 8 April 1924, 4.

"Julian Eltinge Resting Quietly after Operation." *Buffalo Times*, 1 August 1922, 1.

"Julian Eltinge Revue Entirely Satisfactory." *Sacramento Star*, 26 October 1923, 2.

"Julian Eltinge Says America Will Set Fashions for Women." *Visalia Daily Times* (CA), 28 March 1917, 3.

SELECT BIBLIOGRAPHY   329

"Julian Eltinge Seems to Have Changed Mind." *Oregon Sunday Journal, Portland*, 20 July 1919, 4 [42].

"Julian Eltinge Shied Clear of Actors' Strike." *Sunday Times, Chattanooga*, 7 September 1919, 7.

"Julian Eltinge Show." *South Bend Tribune* (IN), 26 January 1909, 9.

"Julian Eltinge Sings 'Come Over on My Veranda.'" *Post-Crescent* (Appleton, WI), 2 March 1910, 7.

"Julian Eltinge Tells Why He'll Stick to Photodrama." *Los Angeles Record*, 9 March 1918, 5.

"Julian Eltinge, the 'Beautiful Man Who Appears as Most Beautiful Woman." *St. Louis Post-Dispatch*, 8 November 1908, 9.

"Julian Eltinge to Be Here Friday." *Modesto News-Herald* (CA), 1 January 1926, 7.

"Julian Eltinge to Give Radio Concert." *Buffalo Evening News*, 21 October 1922, 3.

"Julian Eltinge to Headline Bill at Orpheum." *Salt Lake Telegram*, 4 October 1921, 4 [20].

"Julian Eltinge to Play in this City for One Night Only." *Visalia Morning Delta* (CA), 26 September 1923, 5.

"Julian Eltinge to Serve R. C. Luncheon." *San Francisco Chronicle*, 19 January 1919, 12.

"Julian Eltinge to Sponsor His Greatest Rival." *Wisconsin State Journal*, 8 March 1924, 7.

"Julian Eltinge to Talk at Auditorium." *Los Angeles Record*, 17 September 1917, 7.

"Julian Eltinge Visits Burbank." *Santa Rosa Republican* (CA), 6 November 1923, 8.

"Julian Eltinge Wanted to Perform Like Al Jolson." *Brooklyn Citizen*, 13 May 1923, 17.

"Julian Eltinge Wants to Drop the Petticoats and Play Shylock." *Omaha Daily News*, 16 September 1910, 12.

"Julian Eltinge, Well Known Actor, Is 'Flu' Victim." *Fall River Daily Globe* (MA), 23 October 1918, 6.

"Julian Eltinge, Who Comes to the Columbia Next Week with the Cohan & Harris Minstrels." *Washington Times*, 16 December 1908, 11.

"Julian Eltinge, 'Widow,' Is Truly Fascinating." *Washington Times*, 22 November 1910, 7

"Julian Eltinge Will Open at the Victoria." *Dayton Herald*, 2 September 1916, 7.

"Julian Eltinge Will Tour the West." *Tacoma Daily News* (WA), 16 July 1910, 8.

"Julian Eltinge, World's Premier Female Impersonator, and His Wonderful Costumes, Tonight." *Carson City Daily Appeal* (NV), 5 May 1920, 1.

"Julian Eltinge's Career." *Brooklyn Citizen*, 30 December 1917, 16.

"Julian Eltinge's Future." *Pittsburgh Press*, 17 May 1923, 12.

"Julian Eltinge's Hobby Is Collecting Shoes." *Boston Sunday Globe*, 20 January 1918, 39.

"Julian Eltinge's Imitator Held in Observation Ward." *New St. Louis Star*, 22 June 1914, 2.

"Julian Eltinge's Latest." *New York Dramatic Mirror*, 7 August 1909, 19.

"Julian Eltinge's Success." *Sun, Baltimore*, 20 February 1906, 12.

"Julian Eltinge's Trunks." *Fresno Morning Republican* (CA), 5 August 1917, 9.

"Julian Eltinges of 'Den' Are Jealous." *Omaha Daily News*. 11 February 1912, 7C.

"Jury Exonerates Julian Eltinge." *Boston Globe*, 3 March 1923, 8.

"Karyl Norman Tops Maryland Bill." *Evening Sun, Baltimore*, 30 May 1922, 6.

Kasson, John. *Houdini, Tarzan, and the Perfect Man: The White Male Body and the Challenge of Modernity in America*. New York: Hill & Wang, 2001.

Katz, Jonathan Ned. *The Invention of Heterosexuality*. New York: Dutton, 1995.

"The Keith Anniversary." *New York Clipper*, 29 November 1913, 6.

Keith, B. F. "What Pleases in Vaudeville." *Criterion*, September 1900, 24.

"Keith's Boston Programme." *New York Dramatic Mirror*, 20 February 1904, 18.

330   SELECT BIBLIOGRAPHY

"Keith's Theater: Vaudeville." *Boston Evening Transcript*, 19 February 1907, 13.

Kessler, William C. "Business Organization and Management." In *The Growth of the American Economy*, edited by Harold F. Williamson, 602–615. New York: Prentice-Hall, 1951.

Khan, B. Zorina, and Kenneth L. Sokoloff. "History Lessons: The Early Development of Intellectual Property Institutions in the United States." *Journal of Economic Perspectives* 15, no. 3 (Summer 2001): 233–246.

Kibler, M. Alison. *Rank Ladies: Gender and Cultural Hierarchy in American Vaudeville*. Chapel Hill: University of North Carolina Press, 1999.

Kimmel, Michael. *Manhood in America: A Cultural History*. New York: Free Press, 1996.

Kingsley, Grace. "Eltinge Would Be Bill Dalton." *Los Angeles Sunday Times*, 7 September 1924, "Stage and Screen: 1": 13–14 [45].

Kingsley, Grace. "Hobnobbing in Hollywood: Julian Eltinge Comes Back." *Los Angeles Times*, 16 December 1932, i: 13 [13].

Kingsley, Grace. "Stella Hears about Europe." *Los Angeles Sunday Times*, 28 August 1927, 4 [126].

Knapp, Margaret. "Introductory Essay." In *Inventing Times Square: Commerce and Culture at the Crossroads of the World*, edited by William R. Taylor, 120–132. Baltimore: Johns Hopkins University Press, 1991.

Krasner, David. *Resistance, Parody, and Double Consciousness in African American Theatre, 1895–1910*. New York: St. Martin's Press, 1997.

Kunhardt, Dorothy. "Little Lord Fauntleroy: This Is Centennial of His Creator's Birth." *Life*, 5 December 1949, 71–79.

"'Lady Do' Has Merit as a Musical Play." *New York Times*, 19 April 1927, 24.

LaFeber, Walter. *The American Age: United States Foreign Policy at Home and Abroad since 1750*. New York: W. W. Norton, 1989.

"Lambs' Gambol in Brooklyn." *Brooklyn Life*, 20 May 1916, 20.

Lampard, Eric. "Introductory Essay." In *Inventing Times Square: Commerce and Culture at the Crossroads of the World*, edited by William R. Taylor, 16–35. Baltimore: Johns Hopkins University Press, 1991.

Landis, Kevin. "Julian Eltinge's Manly Transformation." *Gay & Lesbian Review Worldwide* 14, no. 5 (September/October 2007): 16–18.

Lank, Barry. "The Silent Era's Best Cross-Dresser, and His Silver Lake Estate." *The Eastsider*, 24 March 2023. https://www.theeastsiderla.com/neighborhoods/silver_l ake/the-silent-eras-best-cross-dresser-and-his-silver-lake-estate/article_f65bcd7a-c795-11ed-aad0-6f18fd898a8b.html.

Laquer, Thomas. "Sexual Desire and the Market Economy during the Industrial Revolution." In *Discourses of Sexuality: From Aristotle to AIDS*, edited by Donna Stanton, 185–215. Ann Arbor: University of Michigan Press, 1992.

"Last Week of Julian Eltinge at the Boston." *Boston Sunday Globe*, 26 February 1911, 52.

"Late Julian Eltinge Planned to Visit Here." *Paris News, Paris, Texas*, 14 March 1941, 3

Lathrop, Monroe. "Plays, Pictures, and Players." *Los Angeles Evening Express*, 2 June 1921, 23.

Lauder, Harry. *Between You and Me*. New York: James McCann, 1919.

Lauder, Harry. *Roamin' in the Gloamin'*. New York: Grosset & Dunlap, 1928.

"Lauder Jealous for Once." *Brooklyn Citizen*, 11 June 1911, 17.

Laurie, Joe, Jr., *Vaudeville: From the Honky-tonks to the Palace*. New York: Henry Holt & Co., 1953.

SELECT BIBLIOGRAPHY 331

Lavitt, Pamela Brown. "First of the Red Hot Mamas: 'Coon Shouting' and the Jewish Ziegfeld Girl." *American Jewish History* 87, no. 4 (December 1999): 253–290. https://www.jstor.org/stable/23886224.

Leach, William. *Land of Desire: Merchants, Power, and the Rise of a New American Culture.* New York: Vintage, 1993.

Lebergott, Stanley. "Labor Force and Employment, 1800–1960." In *Output, Employment, and Productivity in the United States after 1800,* edited by Dorothy S. Brady, 117–204. Washington, DC: National Bureau of Economic Research, 1966.

Leider, Emily Wortis. *Becoming Mae West.* Boston: Da Capo Press, 1997.

Lemmings, David, and Clare Walker, eds. *Moral Panics, Media, and the Law in Early Modern England.* London: Palgrave Macmillan, 2009.

"Lessons in Movies." *Anaconda Standard* (MT), 27 January 1918, 37.

Levine, Lawrence W. *Highbrow/Lowbrow: The Emergence of Cultural Hierarchy in America.* Cambridge, MA: Harvard University Press, 1988.

Lewis, Robert M., ed. *From Traveling Show to Vaudeville: Theatrical Spectacle in America, 1830–1910.* Baltimore: Johns Hopkins University Press, 2003.

"Lillian Russell Is the Model Julian Eltinge Tries to Copy When He Becomes a Dazzling Beauty." *St. Louis Post-Dispatch,* 11 November 1908, ii: 1 [9].

"Lingerie, Cigars Are All Alike to Julian Eltinge." *Fresno Bee,* 3 February 1926, 3 W [17].

Linton, E. Lynn. "The Wild Women as Social Insurgents." *Nineteenth Century,* October 1891, 596–605.

Long, Mary Ann. *"All Our Girls Are Men": The Haresfoot Club and the Original College Musical.* PhD diss., University of Wisconsin–Madison, 2004.

Looker-On. "The Passing Show." *Charlotte News,* 28 January 1917, 4.

Lott, Eric. *Love and Theft: Blackface Minstrelsy and the American Working Class.* Oxford: Oxford University Press, 1993.

Lough, James E. "Why Wearing Skirts Makes a Man Effeminate." *Minneapolis Sunday Tribune,* 9 January 1916, Feature Section: 1 [58].

Low, Will H., and Kenyon Cox. "The Nude in Art." *Scribner's Magazine,* December 1892, 741–749.

Lowry, Ed. *Vaudeville Humor.* Edited by Paul M. Levitt. Carbondale: Southern Illinois University Press, 2002.

" 'Lucky Lucy' Floors a Surprised Stagehand." *Pittsburg Press,* 10 April 1907, 16.

"Madame Behave at Second Week at the Figueroa." *Los Angeles Sunday Times,* 17 January 1926, iii: 29 [77].

"Made Good with Lillian." *Morning Register* (Eugene, OR), 16 July 1911, 11.

"Made Trouble for Joe Humphreys." *Boston Globe,* 8 January 1909, 16.

"Mae West's Lawyer Quotes Shakespeare." *Daily News* (NY), 19 October 1928, 26 [358].

Malone, Michael P. *The Battle for Butte: Mining and Politics on the Northern Frontier, 1864–1906.* Seattle: University of Washington Press, 1981.

"Manager Woods Has Plays from Europe." *New York Times,* 20 May 1911, 13.

"Manages Skirts with Sang Froid." *Buffalo Courier,* 18 November 1907, 5.

"Manhattan Stage Notes." *Brooklyn Citizen,* 16 August 1908, 12.

Mantle, Burns. "He Wore Skirts for a Living." *Sunday [Daily] News* (NY), 16 March 1941, C38 [78].

Mantle, Burns. "Professional Career of 40 Years Ended with Eltinge Death." *Sunday Journal-Herald Spotlight* (Dayton, OH), 16 March 1941, 56 [3].

332   SELECT BIBLIOGRAPHY

Mantle, Burns, and Garrison P. Sherwood, eds. *The Best Plays of 1899–1909 and the Yearbook of Drama in America*. New York: Dodd, Mead & Co., 1944.

Manz, Julia Chandler. "Julian Eltinge Gives Away Secret of His Rapid Flesh Reduction." *Washington Herald*, 3 January 1912, 6.

Marble, Anna. "Women in Variety." *Variety*, 22 December 1906, 14.

Marks, Edward B., and Abbott J. Lieberling. *They All Sang: From Tony Pastor to Rudy Vallée*. New York: Viking Press, 1934.

Marshall, Marguerite Moores. "Julian Eltinge's Battle against Flesh." *Akron Times*, 14 August 1914, 4.

Martin, G. A. "Pickups and Comment." *Santa Maria Times* (CA), 13 January 1938, 1.

Marx, Karl. *Capital: A Critique of Political Economy*, Vol. 1: *The Process of Capitalist Production*. Edited by Frederick Engels. Translated from the third German edition by Samuel Moore and Edward Aveling. New York: International Publishers, 1967. (Original work published 1867.)

"Max Heyman Is Julian Eltinge of American Legion 'Jollies.'" *Okmulgee Daily Democrat (OK)*, 18 January 1924, vi: B [14].

May Day Lo. "Chinese Julian Eltinge Is Thrilling Audiences Here." *Honolulu Star-Bulletin*, 30 November 1940, 7.

McConnell, W. L. "New Orleans." *San Francisco Dramatic Review*, 5 December 1908, 7.

McGaffey, Kenneth. "Clothes Do Not Make the Woman." *Photoplay*, January 1918, 84–87, 135.

McIntyre, O. O. "New York Day by Day." *Daily Messenger, Madisonville, Kentucky*, 3 April 1935, 4.

McIntyre, O. O. "New York Letter." *Dayton Daily News*, 31 May 1924, 4.

McLean, Albert F., Jr. *American Vaudeville as Ritual*. Lexington: University of Kentucky Press, 1965.

Mead, George Herbert. "The Working Hypothesis in Social Reform." *American Journal of Sociology* 5, no. 3 (November 1899): 367–371.

Merritt, Russell. "Nickelodeon Theaters, 1905–1914: Building an Audience for the Movies." In *The American Film Industry*, rev. ed., edited by Tino Balio, 83–102. Madison: University of Wisconsin Press, 1985.

"'The Merry Shopgirls.'" *Boston Sunday Globe*, 15 January 1905, 33.

"The Merry Shopgirls." *Harrisburg Telegraph* (PA), 15 December 1904, 2.

Metcalfe, James T. "The Theaters." *Sunday State Journal* (Lincoln, NE), 22 March 1914, 4B [16].

Miller, Daniel. "Is Gold Hidden under a California Peak?" *Los Angeles Times* (online), 13 April 2023. https://www.latimes.com/california/story/2023-04-13/la-col1-treasure-map-california-actor-mystery.

"Ministers on the Sunday Question." *New York Dramatic Mirror*, 9 February 1907, 17.

Mireles, Danielle. "College Chorus 'Girls': Drag at Male College and University Campuses During the Progressive Era." MA thesis, University of California–Riverside, 2017.

"Miss Shalek Sings Carmen at the Teck." *Buffalo Courier*, 20 October 1908, 7.

Modleski, Tania. "A Woman's Gotta Do . . . What a Man's Gotta Do: Cross-dressing in the Western." *Signs* 22, no. 3 (Spring 1997): 519–544.

Monod, David. "Double-Voiced: Music, Gender, and Nature in Performance." *Journal of the Gilded Age and Progressive Era* 14, no. 2 (April 2015): 173–193. https://www.jstor.org/stable/43903078.

Mooney, Ralph E. "Julian Eltinge, as Old-Fashioned Girl, Super-Fascinating." *St. Louis Star*, 26 January 1915, 4.

Moore, F. Michael. *Julian Eltinge: Drag Diva of Broadway, Vaudeville & Hollywood*. Everleigh Books: A Broken Shoestring Production, 2020.

SELECT BIBLIOGRAPHY   333

"More Profitable to Be Eltinge than President." *Butte Miner*, 22 September 1912, 16.

"Morning Performance of 'Fascinating Widow'." *Buffalo Enquirer*, 27 January 1911, 7.

Morrow, Lee Alan. "More about Eltinge." *TheaterWeek*, 11–17 September 1995, 7.

"Mr. Eltinge at Ford's." *Sun, Baltimore*, 29 November 1910, 11.

"Mr. Eltinge Is Popular." *Morning News, Wilmington* (DE), 31 March 1905, 6.

"Mr. Ettinge [*sic*] Isn't Huffy Now." *Kansas City Star* (MO), 1 February 1910, 2 [4].

" 'Mr. Wix of Wickham' at New Haven." *New York Times* 13 September 1904, 6.

" 'Mrs. Raffles's Career' for Julian Eltinge." *El Paso Herald*, 26 June 1917, 7.

Murdock, Julia. "Julia Murdock Says Julian Eltinge Is Best Looking 'Woman' on Stage." *Washington Times*, 10 February 1913, 10.

"Music and Drama: 'Baron Humbug' Rehearsed." *Boston Evening Transcript*, 30 January 1903, 9.

Musser, Charles. "The Early Cinema of Edwin Porter." *Cinema Journal* 19, no. 1 (Fall 1979): 1–38.

" 'My Lady,' a Showy Burlesque." *Brooklyn Eagle*, 7 May 1901, 6.

Nahshon, Edna, ed. *New York's Yiddish Theater: From the Bowery to Broadway.* New York: Columbia University Press, 2016.

Nasaw, David. *Going Out: The Rise and Fall of Public Amusements.* New York: Basic Books, 1993.

"National—Julian Eltinge in 'Cousin Lucy'." *Washington Herald*, 1 February 1916, 1 [4].

"New Acts of the Week: Dance of the Seven Veils." *Variety*, 2 February 1907, 10.

New England Historical Society. "Female Impersonator Julian Eltinge Gets His Start in Boston's Gay '90s," New England Historical Society, accessed 18 July 2021. https://www.newenglandhistoricalsociety.com/female-impersonator-julian-eltinge-gets-his-start-in-bostons-gay-90s/.

New England Historical Society. "Maxine Elliot, the Maine Starlet and Winston Churchill." New England Historical Society, accessed 9 June 2022. https://www.newenglandhistoricalsociety.com/maxine-elliott-maine-starlet-winston-churchill/.

"New Heights Scaled in 'Crinoline Girl' by Great Impersonator." *Oregon Sunday Journal, Portland*, 29 March 1914, 2 [34].

New York Academy of Medicine, Committee on Public Health. "Homosexuality." *Bulletin of the New York Academy of Medicine* 40, no. 7 (July 1964): 576–580.

"New York—Chaperones." *New York Dramatic Mirror*, 14 June 1902, 14.

"News of Nightclubs." *New York Times*, 5 May 1940, 155 [2].

Newton, Esther. *Mother Camp: Female Impersonators in America.* Englewood Cliffs, NJ: Prentice Hall, 1972.

Niemeyer, H. H. "St. Louisan, Trucker, A. E. F. Show 'Leading Lady'." *St. Louis Post-Dispatch*, 31 December 1918, 6.

"No More Pictures for Julian." *Capital Times* (Madison, WI), 27 August 1919, 8.

" 'No More Skirts' Says Julian Eltinge." *Sheboygan Press* (WI), 2 June 1917, 5.

"No One Can Take His Place." *Boston Globe*, 10 February 1911, 9.

"No 'Salomes' on Orpheum Circuit," *Variety*, September 12, 1908, 1.

Norin, Reman. "Julian Eltinge, Coming into Manhood, at Age 51." *Daily Missoulian* (MT), 8 January 1936, 1.

Normington, Katie. *Gender and Medieval Drama.* Suffolk: D. S. Brewer, 2004.

Nossel, Suzanne. "The Drag Show Bans Sweeping the US Are a Chilling Attack on Free Speech." *Guardian*, 10 March 2023. https://www.theguardian.com/culture/commentisfree/2023/mar/10/drag-show-bans-tennessee-lgbtq-rights.

"Noted Dancing Teacher, 90, Dies." *San Francisco Examiner*, 15 May 1944, 10.

334   SELECT BIBLIOGRAPHY

"Now Honky Tonks Occupy Theaters' 'Gold Coast.'" *Wisconsin State Journal, Madison*, 6 August 1944, 24.

"Obituary: One-Time Famous Impersonator Dies of Pneumonia." *News* (Daily News, NYC), 20 February 1920, 15.

"Offerings at the Local Theaters: Columbia—Julian Eltinge in 'The Fascinating Widow.'" *Washington Post*, 22 November 1910, 4.

"Old Impersonator, Julian Eltinge, Dies." *Wisconsin State Journal, Madison*, 8 March 1941, 2.

"On Professional Stage: Julian D. Eltinge, Famous Impersonator of Female Roles, to Abandon Amateur Work." *Boston Globe*, 8 May 1904, 7.

"One Close Shave and Then Another." *Anaconda Standard*, 16 April 1914, 13.

"Operate Here on Julian Eltinge." *Buffalo Courier*, 2 August 1922, 16.

Operation Saves Eltinge, Knifed by Swordfish." *Daily News* (NY), 17 October 1931, 27 [99].

"Orpheum's Inauguration Bill Illuminates with Bright Stars." *Courier* (Harrisburg, PA), 15 January 1911, 6.

Pantages, Lloyd. "Heavy Taxes Force Eltinge to Sell Property." *San Francisco Examiner*, 4 November 1935, 18.

"Park Theatre: 'Maid to Order.'" *Boston Globe*, 21 September 1931, 4.

Parsons, Elaine Frantz. *Ku-Klux: The Birth of the Klan During Reconstruction*. Chapel Hill: University of North Carolina Press, 2015.

Parsons, Louella O. "Is Julian Eltinge, Impersonator of Women, Going to Wed?" *Herald-Republican, Salt Lake City, Utah*, 16 December 1917, 31.

Parsons, Louella O. "Powell's First Starring Film Called 'Color of Money.'" *Morning Post, Camden* (NJ), 1 October 1929, 20.

Pastor, Tony. "Tony Pastor Recounts the Origin of American 'Vaudeville.'" *Variety*, 15 December 1906, 17.

Patrick, Corbin. "Songs, Dances, Humor of 'Tarantella' Reveal Some Future Julian Eltinges." *Indianapolis Star*, 29 March 1928, 10.

Patton, Elaina, Jillian Eugenios, Ellie Rudy, Brooke Sopelsa, and Jay Valle. "Pride 30: Drag Performers Who Made 'Herstory.'" *NBCnews.com*, 1 June 2023. https://www.nbcnews.com/specials/pride-month-2023-drag-performers-who-made-herstory/index.html.

"Paul Maurmonts." *Shreveport Times* (LA), 8 October 1919, 14.

Peiss, Kathy. *Cheap Amusements: Working Women and Leisure in Turn-of-the-Century New York*. Philadelphia: Temple University Press, 1986.

Peiss, Kathy. *Hope in a Jar: The Making of America's Beauty Culture*. New York: Metropolitan Books, 1998.

Perez, Juan, Jr. "Republican States Are Fuming—and Legislating—Over Drag Performances," *Politico*, 25 February 2023. https://www.politico.com/news/2023/02/05/drag-show-bans-gop-statehouses-00081193.

Perlman, Lindsay. "Mask and Wig, Penn's All-Male Comedy Troupe, Will Welcome all Genders in 2022." *Daily Pennsylvanian*, 10 October 2021. https://www.thedp.com/article/2021/10/mask-wig-gender-inclusive-penn-comedy.

Peters, Brooks. "Gay Deceiver." *Out*, December 1998, 83–87+.

"Photoplays this Week: LEADER—'The Isle of Love.'" *Sunday Star, Washington, DC*, 10 September 1922, iii: 3 [49].

Picard, George H. "The Drama and Those Who Present It." *Wichita Eagle*, 30 January 1910, 27.

SELECT BIBLIOGRAPHY 335

Pickford, Mary. "Daily Talks by Mary Pickford: Personalities I Have Met—Julian Eltinge." *Birmingham News* (AL), 10 October 1916, 7.

"Plays and Players: About Julian Eltinge." *Nashville Banner*, 22 January 1910, 3 [21].

"Plays & Playfolk: Julian Eltinge and Some Other Good Things on Chase Bill." *Washington Herald*, March 10. 1907, 4 [24].

"Pretty? Yes, but 'She's' a 'He.'" *Bee, Danville* (VA), 8 November 1923, 4.

"Pretty Girls in 'Wix of Wickham.'" *Hartford Courant*, 16 November 1904, 7.

Prioleau, Betsy. *Seductress: Women Who Ravished the World and Their Lost Art of Love.* New York: Penguin, 1993.

"Programme at the Frolic." *Chicago Examiner*, 4 June 1911, 41.

"Queerest Woman in the World." *Omaha Daily News*, 1 October 1911, 8B [20].

Rackin, Phyllis. "Androgyny, Mimesis, and the Marriage of the Boy Heroine on the English Renaissance Stage." *PMLA* 102, no. 1 (January 1987): 29–41. https://www.jstor.org/stable/462490.

Rau, Celeste. "Julian Eltinge—An Interview." *Buffalo Enquirer*, 21 May 1919, 9.

"Ravishing Toilets Worn by Mr. Julian Eltinge." *Minneapolis Sunday Tribune*, 15 September 1912, 29 [49].

Raymond [only name given]. "Some Stage Reflections." *Philadelphia Times*, 23 October 1898, 22.

Richardson, Katherine. "Julian Eltinge in a New Comedy and Sweet Irish Play, Next Bills." *St. Louis Star*, 23 January 1915, 6.

Richardson, Katherine. "Julian Eltinge to Quit Stage This Week." *St. Louis Star*, 19 March 1918, 8.

"Rival for Julian." *Philadelphia Inquirer*, 29 June 1919, 17 [41].

"Rival of Eltinge in Aero Benefit." *Birmingham News* (AL), 10 May 1921, 16.

Rodger, Gillian M. *Champagne Charlie and Pretty Jemima: Variety Theater in the Nineteenth Century.* Urbana: University of Illinois Press, 2010.

Rogers, Juliet B., and Andreja Zevnik. "Symptoms of the Political Unconscious: Introduction to a Special Issue." *Political Psychology* 38, no. 4 (August 2017): 581–589.

Rojas, Rick, Emily Cochrane, Ava Sasani, and Michael Paulson. "Tennessee Laws Limiting 'Cabaret' Shows Raises Uncertainty about Drag Events." *New York Times*, 5 March 2023. https://www.nytimes.com/2023/03/05/us/tennessee-law-drag-shows.html.

Roosevelt, Theodore. *The Winning of the West: An Account of the Exploration and Settlement of Our Country from the Alleghanies to the Pacific*, vol. 2, pt. 1. New York: G. Putnam's Sons, 1889.

" 'Rose of Queretaro' Creating Much Interest." *San Francisco Examiner*, 23 August 1918, 7.

Rosenberg, Emily S. *Spreading the American Dream: American Economic and Cultural Expansion, 1890–1945.* New York: Hill & Wang, 1982.

Ross, Charles J. "The Building and Repairing of Vaudeville Sketches." *New York Dramatic Mirror*, 5 July 1911.

Rotundo, Anthony. *American Manhood: Transformations in Masculinity from the Revolution to the Modern Era.* New York: Basic Books, 1993.

Russell, Lillian. "Lillian Russell's Answers to Her Inquirers." *Buffalo Evening Times*, 17 July 1911, 3.

Russo, Vito. *The Celluloid Closet: Homosexuality in the Movies.* New York: Harper & Row, 1981.

Rydell, Robert W. *All the World's a Fair.* Chicago: University of Chicago Press, 1984.

336 SELECT BIBLIOGRAPHY

S.D., Trav. *No Applause—Just Throw Money: The Book That Made Vaudeville Famous.* New York: Faber & Faber, 2005.

Said, Edward. *Culture and Imperialism.* New York: Vintage Books, 1993.

St. George, George. "Julian Eltinge." *Evening Express,* Los Angeles, 2 March 1917, 9.

"Salome Barred in New Jersey." *New York Dramatic Mirror,* 26 August 1908, 17.

"The 'Salome' Dance Gets into Politics." *New York Times,* August 24, 1908, 2.

"Salomes under Observation." *New York Dramatic Mirror,* 5 September 1908, 19.

Samuels, Charles, and Louise Samuels. *Once upon a Stage: The Merry World of Vaudeville.* New York: Dodd, Mead, & Co., 1974.

Sante, Luc. *Low Life.* New York: Vintage Books, 1991.

Santiago, Soledad. "The King of TV Is Queen for a Day: Milton Berle Wigs Out at This Week's Dragfest." *Newsday* (NY), 20 June 1994, ii: 4.

Satter, Beryl. *Each Mind a Kingdom: American Women, Sexual Purity, and the New Thought Movement, 1875–1920.* Berkeley: University of California Press, 1999.

"Says Salome Spirit Pervades Theatre." *New York Times,* 22 February 1909, 9.

Schatz, Thomas. *The Genius of the System: Hollywood Filmmaking in the Studio Era.* New York: Pantheon Books, 1988.

Schenck, Joseph M. "Inside Vaudeville." *Variety,* 20 December 1912, 33.

Scholten, Alexandra. "Drag Performance in Minnesota Theater from the 1880s through the 1920s." *MinnPost.com,* 5 June 2023. https://www.minnpost.com/mnopedia/2023/06/drag-performance-in-minnesota-theater-from-the-1880s-through-the-1920s/.

Schreiber, Harry N., ed. *United States Economic History: Selected Readings.* New York: Knopf, 1964.

Schulberg, Budd. *What Makes Sammy Run?* New York: Random House, 1993. (Original work published 1941.)

Schweitzer, Marlis. "A Failed Attempt at World Domination." *Theatre History Studies* 32 (2012): 53–79.

Scott, John. "Lure of Stage Brings Eltinge from Ranch." *Los Angeles Times,* 19 July 1931, iii: 13 [35].

"The Screen Shows a New Eva Tanguay." *Moving Picture World,* 22 September 1917, 1872.

Sears, Clare. "Electric Brilliancy: Cross-Dressing Law and Freak Show Displays in Nineteenth-Century San Francisco." *Women's Studies Quarterly* 36, no. 3/4 (2008): 170–187.

"Seattle Has Real Contender for Julian Eltinge Honors." *Seattle Star,* 10 November 1921, 10.

Sedgwick, Eve Kosofsky. "Queer and Now." In *Literary Theories: A Reader and Guide,* edited by Julian Wolfreys, 537–552. Edinburgh: Edinburgh University Press, 1999.

Selby, Rodney Q. "Eltinge Show at Princess Theater." *Des Moines Register,* 17 January 1921, 10.

Senelick, Laurence. *The Changing Room: Sex, Drag and Theatre.* New York: Routledge, 2000.

Senelick, Laurence. "Lady and the Tramp: Drag Differentials in the Progressive Era." In *Gender in Performance: The Presentation of Difference in the Performing Arts,* edited by Laurence Senelick, 26–45. Hanover, NH: University Press of New England, 1992.

Senelick, Laurence. "Mollies or Men of Mode? Sodomy and the Eighteenth-Century London Stage." *Journal of the History of Sexuality* 1, no. 1 (July 1990): 33–67.

Senelick, Laurence, ed. *Gender in Performance: The Presentation of Difference in the Performing Arts.* Hanover, NH: University Press of New England, 1992.

SELECT BIBLIOGRAPHY 337

Sentilles, Renée M. *Performing Menken: Adah Isaacs Menken and the Birth of the American Celebrity*. Cambridge: Cambridge University Press, 2003.

"Shea's Hippodrome Presents Julian Eltinge." *Buffalo Courier*, 24 September 1917, 4.

"Shows at the Box Office in New York and Chicago." *Variety*, 1 November 1912, 10.

Silverman, Sime. "Shows of the Week by Sime, Keith's." *Variety*, 6 January 1906, 8.

Silverman, Sime. "William Morris' Only Failure." *Variety*, 27 October 1910, 74, 110.

Skolsky, Sidney. "Tintypes." *Sunday News* (*Daily News*, NY), 12 April 1931, 42 [183].

Slide, Anthony. *The Encyclopedia of Vaudeville*. Westport, CT: Greenwood Press, 2012.

Slide, Anthony. "The Silent Closet." *Film Quarterly* 52, no. 4 (Summer 1999): 24–32.

Slotkin, Richard. *The Fatal Environment: The Myth of the Frontier in the Age of Industrialization*. New York: Atheneum, 1985.

Smithers, Gregory D. "'Two Spirits': Gender, Ritual, and Spirituality in the Native South." *Early American Studies* 14, no. 3 (Fall 2014): 626–651. https://www.jstor.org/stable/24474873.

Snyder, Robert W. "Vaudeville and the Transformation of Popular Culture." In *Inventing Times Square: Commerce and Culture at the Crossroads of the World*, edited by William R. Taylor, 133–146. Baltimore: Johns Hopkins University Press, 1991.

Snyder, Robert W. *The Voice of the City: Vaudeville and Popular Culture in New York*. New York: Oxford University Press, 1989.

Soanes, Wood. "Curtain Calls." *Oakland Tribune*, 1 July 1926, B: 31 [30].

Soanes, Wood. "Curtain Calls," *Oakland Tribune*, 13 December 1927, 30 E [28].

Southworth, John. *The English Medieval Minstrel*. Suffolk: Boydell & Brewer, 1989.

"Sprained Ankle No Handicap for Julian Eltinge." *Albuquerque Morning Journal*, 13 August 1919, 4.

"Stage and Screen." *Santa Ana Daily Register* (CA), 27 January 1926, 10.

"Stage Folk Hurt in Crash." *Los Angeles Times*, 11 July 1929, ii: 1, 20 [40].

"The Stage: Trouble for Eltinge." *Anaconda Standard* (MT), 28 August 1910, 11 [31].

Stanton, Donna, ed. *Discourses of Sexuality: From Aristotle to AIDS*. Ann Arbor: University of Michigan Press, 1992.

"Star Theater: Julian Eltinge." *Buffalo Enquirer*, 14 November 1916, 9.

Starr, Jimmy. "Weil Signs Stage Star." *Los Angeles Record*, 23 July 1929, 3.

Starr, Kevin. *California: A History*. New York: Modern Library, 2007.

States, Bert O. "The Dog on the Stage: Theater as Phenomenon." *New Literary History* 14, no. 2 (Winter 1983): 373–388.

Stein, Charles W., ed. *American Vaudeville as Seen by Its Contemporaries*. New York: Knopf, 1984.

Stoller, Robert J. *Perversion: The Erotic Form of Hatred*. London: Karnac, 1975.

Stoller, Robert J. "Transsexualism and Transvestism." *Psychiatric Annals* 1, no. 4 (1971): 60–72.

Sueyoshi, Amy. *Discriminating Sex: White Leisure and the Making of the American "Oriental."* Champaign: University of Illinois Press, 2018.

"Sunday Vaudeville Crusade." *New York Times*, 3 December 1908, 9.

"Supreme Court Decides Sunday Shows Illegal." *Variety*, 7 December 1907, 2.

Suthrell, Charlotte. *Unzipping Gender: Sex, Cross-Dressing, and Culture*. Oxford: Berg, 2004.

Swartz, Ronnie. "Social Work Values in an Age of Complexity." *Journal of Social Work Values and Ethics* 4, no. 3 (Winter 2007): 65–80.

338 SELECT BIBLIOGRAPHY

Sweetser, M. F. *King's Handbook of Newton Massachusetts*. Boston: Moses King Corp., 1889.

"Swordfish Stabs Julian Eltinge." *Okmulgee Daily Times* (OK), 17 October 1931, 1.

Tallqvist, K. G. "Behind Scene Views of Vaudeville's Man Vamp." *Arkansas Democrat*, 18 January 1922, 5.

Taylor, William R., ed. *Inventing Times Square: Commerce and Culture at the Crossroads of the World*. Baltimore: Johns Hopkins University Press, 1991.

"Theatre and Vaudeville Bills." *Lexington Herald* (KY), 25 June 1911, 3 [25].

"Theatre for A. H. Woods." *New York Times*, 15 August 1911, 9.

"Theatres Last Night: 'The Merry Shop Girls' Appear at Ford's Opera House." *The Sun—Baltimore*, 20 December 1904, 8.

"Theatrical News: Star Theatre." *Buffalo Commercial*, 5 October 1915, 14.

"Theatrical Notes: Julian Eltinge: 'The Fascinating Widow.'" *Shreveport Journal*, 1 January 1913, 3.

Themista [pen name of: Wilshire, Ida]. "He Fascinates the Women in His Feminine Finery." *Boston Globe*, 1 March 1901, 7.

Themista [pen name of: Wilshire, Ida]. "Julian Eltinge: The Woman Impersonator." *Daily Province* (Vancouver, BC), 29 January 1910, 11 [127].

Thirteenth Catalogue & A History of the Hasty Pudding Club. Riverside Press, 1907.

"This Man Is to Marry This Woman." *Pittsburgh Press*, 29 August 1908, 4.

Thornton, Tracy. "The Great Pretender." *Montana Standard*, 16 April 2000, C1.

Tighe, Dixie. "Mae West Fills Minor Role in Jury Picking." *Standard Union* (Brooklyn), 18 March 1930, 4.

Tinée, Mae. "Ask Me, Ask Me, Ask Me." *Chicago Sunday Tribune*, 12 January 1919, vii: 5 [36].

"To Fashionable Audience." *Boston Globe*, 11 May1904, 3.

Toll, Robert C. *On with the Show: The First Century of Show Business in America*. New York: Oxford University Press, 1976.

"'Tony' Pastor." *New York Clipper*, 5 September 1908, 722.

Tregelles, Frederick. "Difficult Art of Stage Makeup Described by an Expert." *Times-Democrat* (Lima, OH), 8 June 1907, 12 [6].

"The Truth about Tanguay." *Pittsburgh Post*, 5 May 1912, 8.

Tuchman, Barbara W. *The Proud Tower: A Portrait of the World before the War, 1890–1914*. New York: Random House, 2014. (Original work published 1962.)

Tucker, George. "In New York." *Monroe News-Star* (LA), 31 May 1940, 4.

Tucker, Sophie. *Some of These Days: The Autobiography of Sophie Tucker*. Garden City, NY: Garden City Publishing, 1946.

Ullman, Sharon R. "'The Twentieth Century Way': Female Impersonation and Sexual Practice in Turn-of-the-Century America." *Journal of the History of Sexuality* 5, no. 4 (April 1995): 573–600. https://www.jstor.org/stable/4617203.

Underhill, Harriette. "Julian Eltinge on Keeping One's Lines." *New York Tribune*, 2 December 1917, iv: 4 [32].

"United Booking Offices Cleans Up All 'Big Time.'" *Variety*, May 4, 1912, 5.

"United Managers in One Big Corporation." *Variety*, 22 June 1907, 14–19+.

US Bureau of the Census. *Historical Statistics of the Unites States, 1789 to 1945: A Supplement to the Statistical Abstract of the United States*. Washington, DC: US Government Printing Office, 1949.

SELECT BIBLIOGRAPHY 339

US Bureau of the Census. *Historical Statistics of the Unites States, Colonial Times to 1970, Bicentennial Edition, Part 2*. Washington, DC: US Government Printing Office, 1975.

US Department of Commerce. *Statistical Abstract of the United States*, no. 52, Washington, DC, 1930.

US Department of Labor and Commerce. *Statistical Abstract of the United States*, no. 32, Washington, DC, 1909.

Uyehara, Mari. "The Western Strategy." *Nation*, 23 August 2021, 17–81.

Van Duzer, Winifred. "Why 'Iron Mike' Became 'Miss Fluffy Ruffles.'" *Zanesville Times Signal* (OH), 11 October 1925, 38.

"Vaudeville of the Year." *Variety*, 10 December 1910, 20–21.

"The Vaudeville Stage." *New York Dramatic Mirror*, 29 February 1896, 19.

"Vaudeville's Clearing House." *New York Clipper*, 29 November 1913, 1.

"Victoria—My Lady." *New York Dramatic Mirror*, 23 February 1901, 16.

Von Blon, Katherine T. "Julian Eltinge Great Trouper." *Los Angeles Times*, 26 January 1936, iii: 2 [44].

Von Blon, Katherine T. "Julian Eltinge 'Straight.'" *Los Angeles Times*, 15 December 1935, iii: 2 [50].

Waitt, Ernest L. "Boston." *Variety*, 22 February 1908, 27.

Wallace, George. "Julian Eltinge, the Fascinating Widow." *Northport Journal*, 2 March 1995, 1+.

"The Week at Local Theaters: Chase's—Julian Eltinge: Gibson Girl Impersonator." *Washington Post*, 10 March 1907, 2 [19].

Welton, Charles. "This Man a Martyr to the Modiste." *Pittsburgh Press Illustrated Magazine Section*, 3 March 1918, 91.

West, Nathanael. *Miss Lonelyhearts* & *The Day of the Locust*. New York: New Directions, 1962. (Original work published 1933.)

"What Greater Vaudeville Promises This Winter." *New York Times*, 1 September 1907, vi: 2.

"When Girl-Boy Weds Boy-Girl, Who'll Be the Boss?" *St. Louis Post-Dispatch*, 18 August 1908, 2.

Who's Who in the Movies." *Goodwin's Weekly*, 8 September 1917, 12.

"Wichita Women Meet Eltinge." *Wichita Eagle* (KS), 16 November 1919, 6.

Wilkerson, Isabel. *Caste: The Origins of Our Discontents*. New York: Random House, 2020.

"Will Withdraw 'Salome.'" *New York Times*, 18 February 1909, 1.

"William Dalton Is Old Butte Boy." *Butte Inter Mountain* (MT), 26 January 1910, 2.

"William Morris." *Variety*, November 8, 1932, 31.

"William Morris Invades Pacific Coast." *New York Clipper*, 31 July, 1909, 635.

"Williams Goes with Keith." *Variety*, 16 February 1907, 2.

"Williams Sells Theatres." *New York Clipper*, 4 May 1912, 10.

Williams, Raymond. "Base and Superstructure in Marxist Cultural Theory." *New Left Review [NLR]* 82, no. 1 (November/December 1973): 3–16.

Williamson, Harold F., ed. *The Growth of the American Economy*. New York: Prentice-Hall, 1951.

Wilshire, Ida [see: Themista]. "Julian Eltinge: Then and Now—An Appreciation." *Daily Province, Vancouver, British Columbia*, 24 February 1923, 12.

Wilson, James F. "The Somewhat Different Diva: Impersonation, Ambivalence and the Musical Comedy Performances of Julian Eltinge." *Studies in Musical Theatre* 12, no. 1 (2018): 9–23.

"Wire Dancer Known as 'Eltinge of the Wire.'" *Paterson Morning Call* (NJ), 8 May 1922, 5.

340 SELECT BIBLIOGRAPHY

"Withdraw 'Salome' after Police Fiat." *New York Times*, 30 November 1910, 11.

Wolf, Rennold. "The Sort of Fellow Julian Eltinge Really Is." *The Green Book Magazine*, November 1913, 793–803.

"Woman Infatuated with Julian Eltinge Is Divorced." *San Francisco Chronicle*, 20 September 1922, 7.

"'Woman Is Only Ten Percent Nature, the Rest Is Art.'" *San Francisco Examiner*, 12 April 1914, 36.

"Womanly Photographs of a Manly, Athletic Harvard Grad, Who, When He Dons Skirts, Fools Even His Own Manager: Athlete in Gowns Stage Sensation." *St. Louis Post-Dispatch*, 5 July 1907, 16.

Wood, James Playstead. *The Story of Advertising*. New York: Ronald Press, 1958.

Wood, Robin. "Murnau's *Midnight* and *Sunrise*." *Film Comment* 12, no. 3 (May–June 1976): 4–19.

Woods, Leigh. "Sarah Bernhardt and the Refining of American Vaudeville." *Theatre Research International* 18 (Spring 1993): 16–25.

"World's Biggest Cosmetic User." *Andalusia Star* (Alabama), 29 May 1928, 1.

"World's Foremost Imitator of Women." *Spokesman-Review* (Spokane, WA), 30 June 1907, v1.

Wright, Chester W. *Economic History of the United States*. New York: McGraw-Hill Book Group, 1949.

"Yank, Second Julian Eltinge, to Appear in 'Chicken' Role." *Des Moines Register*, 12 June 1919, 7.

"Young Russian Female Impersonator May Tread Toes of Julian Eltinge." *Wichita Eagle* (KS), 23 July 1922, 29.

Zaretsky, Eli. *Political Freud: A History*. New York: Columbia University Press, 2015.

Zellers, Parker R. "The Cradle of Variety: The Concert Saloon." *Educational Theatre Journal* 20, no. 4 (December, 1968): 578–575. https://www.jstor.org/stable/3205001.

# # #

Archival Sources

Academy of Motion Picture Arts and Sciences Archive (Los Angeles, CA).

Anne Alison Barnet Collection (Boston, MA).

Butte–Silver Bow Public Archive.

Henry Ford [museum and research center] (Dearborn, MI).

Institute of the American Musical (Los Angeles, CA).

Keith-Albee Collection, University of Iowa Libraries, Special Collections.

New York Public Library for the Performing Arts, Billy Rose Theatre Collection.

Newton Archive (Newton, MA).

Northport Historical Society (Long Island, NY).

Shubert Archive (New York, NY).

# # #

Index

For the benefit of digital users, indexed terms that span two pages (e.g., 52–53) may, on occasion, appear on only one of those pages.

Figures are indicated by *f* following the page number

1492 (musical comedy). *See* Cadets organization

Adventuress, An. See Over the Rhine
Albee, Edward Franklin "E. F." 30–32, 81–82, 84–86. *See also* Keith vaudeville organization
Alger, Horatio 45, 58
American Tragedy, An (novel). *See* Dreiser, Theodore
Ames, Lionel E. "Iron Mike" 216–18, 217*f*
antigay, antiqueer, anti-trans. *See* reactionism
Armory. *See* Cadets organization
Australia 127, 152, 166, 190, 205–6
Austria. *See* Vienna

Babes in Toyland 37, 214
Baker, Juliana Edna. *See* Dalton, Julia
Balshofer, Fred 207–8, 209
Bank Officers' Association, Boston 57–58, 59, 66–67
Barnet, Robert Ayres 48*f*, 49–51, 54, 56–58, 66–67, 68, 74, 90–91
Barnum, Phineas Taylor "P. T." 12, 17–18
Baron Humbug 66–67
Barrymore, Ethel 55, 62–63, 81–82
Benham, Earl 111–12, 246
Berlin, Irving 68, 162, 195–96
Bernhardt, Sarah 113, 116, 164, 165*f*
Bible and its parts (e.g., Book of Deuteronomy). *See* religion
Black and White Revue. See Eltinge, Julian: cabaret and revue-style performances
Black Crook, The 53–54, 57, 68, 69–71

Black culture and persons in the United States 29–30, 46, 87–88, 105–6, 109. *See also* race and racism
Boston 1, 28–29, 30, 41–42, 43, 44, 46, 47, 48*f*, 49, 50, 54, 57–58, 59–60, 85, 96, 143–44. *See also* Bank Officers' Association, Boston; Cadets organization
boxing 10, 62–63, 94, 158, 160–62, 161*f*, 174–76, 190. athletic, outdoor and sporting activities of; Eltinge, Julian: masculinity, performances/ embodiments of
Brennan, Jay 8–9, 212–13, 238–39
Brice, Fanny 95, 115
Brinig, Myron 34, 35
Broadway theatrical district and business 63–64, 103–4, 110, 135, 136–37, 147–48, 153–54, 163–64, 166, 225–26, 235–36, 239–40, 242, 245. *See also* Eltinge, Julian: musical comedies, performances in; Woods, Aladore "Albert" Herman, aka "A. H."
Browne, Bothwell 12, 89–90, 166, 207–8
Buck on Leave, A 195–96
Burkan, Nathan 238–39
burlesque
 history of genre 53
 stereotypical qualities of 53, 54
 as term for subtype of female impersonation 9–10, 55–56
Burlingshaw, Aaron 91
Burnett, Frances Hodgson. *See* Fauntleroy, Little Lord

342 INDEX

Butler, Judith 23–24, 243–44, 253, 254–55
Butte, Montana 29, 34–35, 36–38, 39–40, 72–73, 130, 150–51

Cadets organization 48*f*, 49–50, 51, 53, 54–55, 56–57, 68, 74
cakewalking 46–47, 109, 120
California. *See also* Los Angeles and San Francisco
  environment and climate 211
  extractive and mining activities in 29–30
  politics 126–27, 241
  populations 123
  queer communities in 126–27, 198–99
  San Diego County (*see* Sierra Vista Rancho)
censorship 42–43, 86, 117, 235–36, 237, 238–39, 243–44. *See also* reactionism
Chaplin, Charlie 137–38, 186
Charley's Aunt 95
Chauncey, George 16–17
Chicago 42–43, 57, 63–66, 89–90, 133, 143–44, 149, 153–54, 243
Children of the Rich 242
"chorus girls," cultural phenomenon of 69–71, 72
Christian Science (First Church of Christ, Scientist). *See* Eddy, Mary Baker
Cibber, Colley 79, 80–81
Clever Mrs. Carfax, The 181*f*, 183
Cohan, George M. 104–5, 110, 112, 136–37, 225–26
Confederacy & United States' South. *See* race and racism: white supremacy in entertainment and politics
conservatism. *See* reactionism
consumerism, rise of and trends in 44–45, 67, 72–73, 74, 85, 148–49, 154–56, 158–60, 174, 179–80, 189
"coon" singers and songs 108–9, 112, 115, 226–27. *See also* minstrel acts and minstrelsy
copper. *See* mining: copper, gold, silver, and other metals and minerals
Corbett, James J. 160–62, 161*f*
Coreopsis 57–58, 60

corsets and corseting. *See* Eltinge, Julian: corseting
cosmetics, makeup, and skin preparations 27, 94, 112, 154–60, 155*f*. *See also* Eltinge, Julian: product endorsements and branded lines of merchandise *and* precision, professionalism, and technical mastery
Countess Charming, The 180–82, 181*f*, 185–86
Cousin Lucy 170–74, 173*f*, 175*f*, 176–77
Creole Fashion Plate, The. *See* Norman, Karyl
Crinoline Girl, The 167–70, 168*f*, 215
Crisp, Donald 182, 183

"double-voiced" artists 13
Dale, Alan 38
Dalton, Julia 28–29, 30, 31*f*, 39–40, 41–42, 91, 98–100, 99*f*, 102, 192, 198, 224–25, 228–29, 241–42, 246, 247–48. *See also* Eltinge, Julian: birth, childhood, and family of origin
Dalton, Michael Joseph "Joe" 28–30, 32, 33–34, 35, 36–37, 38, 41–42, 102, 152, 228. *See also* Eltinge, Julian: birth and family of origin
Dalton, William J "Billy". *See* Eltinge, Julian: nomenclature, pronunciation, and stage name of
"Dance of the Seven Veils". *See* Salome and "exotic" acts
Dartmouth College. *See* Mills, Halsey
Dawn, Hazel 147–48, 160, 239–40
Delsarte, François, method of 47–49
De Mille, Cecil B. 186–88, 197
De Mille, William C. 197
Derrida, Jacques 23
Dockstader, Lew 109, 219–20
Dos Passos, John 32–33, 110–11
Drag, The. See West, Mae
Dreiser, Theodore 25, 72, 254–55
D'Wolfe Greene, Malcolm 57

Eddy, Mary Baker 33
Edward VII, King 69–71, 93, 152

INDEX   343

Elizabethan England. *See* Great Britain: laws and codes

Ellis, Havelock 20–21, 167–70, 232–33. *See also* sexology and scientific thought

Eltinge, "Charles" and/or "Willie". *See* Eltinge, Julian: nomenclature, pronunciation, and stage name of

Eltinge, Julian

aspirations for legitimate acting 59, 69, 95, 133–35, 166, 167, 180, 201, 214, 220–21, 230, 242

athletic, outdoor and sporting activities of 11, 61–63, 66, 98–102, 116, 158, 160–62, 185–86, 190

audience responses to 3–4

birth, childhood, and family of origin 28–30, 31*f*, 33–34, 36–40, 41–42, 44, 109

cabaret and revue-style performances 96, 204–5, 210–11, 212–13, 218, 219–21, 228–29, 243–44, 245, 246

corseting 89–90, 124*f*, 126, 144, 154–56, 210–11, 246–47

dancing abilities of 47–49, 51, 59–60

death and funeral 246–48

educational fabrications of 60–63, 82–83, 116, 150–51, 184–85, 216

employment prior to show business 43, 44–45

estate (*see* death and funeral)

fashionable attire, display of 27, 45, 58–59, 72, 73, 91–92, 97*f*, 122–23, 146–47, 166, 170–71, 172, 173*f*, 174, 185–86, 201, 204, 209, 211, 219–20, 224–25, 228–29

health and medical issues 210–11, 213–14, 230–32, 246–47 (*see also* weight and bodily dimensions)

international tours 90–91, 93, 95, 102, 152, 166, 205–6

Julian Eltinge Magazine and Beauty Hints 158–62, 159*f*

Julian Eltinge Theatre, New York City 135, 153–54, 189–90, 225–26, 239–40, 245–46

legal battles and issues 213, 230–32, 238–39, 243–44

LGBTQ/"queer" icon, debate over role as 6–7, 252–53, 254

makeup (*see* precision, professionalism, and technical mastery)

marriage, issues related to 118–20, 160, 174–76, 190–92, 240

masculinity, performances/ embodiments of 10, 25, 38–39, 58, 93, 101–2, 110–11, 132, 133–35, 158, 159*f*, 160–62, 161*f*, 171*f*, 174–77, 183, 184–85, 190

misogynistic tendencies of 220–21, 240

motion pictures, employment in 176–77, 179–80, 181*f*, 185, 197–99, 202–4, 206, 208–9, 210, 230, 244–45

musical comedies, performances in 69, 139, 140–41, 143–25, 167, 170–72, 176–77, 207–8

nomenclature, pronunciation, and stage name of 12–13, 28, 30, 37, 58, 60–61, 69, 73–74, 138*f*, 223–24

patriotism & militarism (*see* politics and values of)

personality of 51, 87, 103, 148–49

politics and values of 6–7, 14–15, 110–11, 190, 198–99, 206, 237, 238, 240, 241, 243–44, 251

popular characters of 1–3, 9–10, 11, 93, 94–95, 104*f*, 112, 115–16, 119–20, 131, 132–33, 160, 166, 167, 204–5, 208*f*, 220–21, 254

precision, professionalism, and technical mastery 5–6, 7–8, 24, 27, 47–49, 94, 122–23, 189–90, 238

privacy and secrecy, apparent desires for 16–18, 28, 44–45, 184–85, 249–51, 250*f*

product endorsements and branded lines of merchandise 89–90, 144, 154–56, 155*f*, 157*f*, 158–60, 171*f*

radio, efforts in 214–15, 232–33

real estate: homes, residences, and other properties 97–102, 99*f*, 152, 186–91, 187*f*, 188*f*, 192, 225–26, 240–42 (*see also* Sierra Vista Rancho)

344 INDEX

Eltinge, Julian (*cont.*)
    rivals and imitators 7–8, 9–10, 12–
      13, 102–3
    salary and wealth 58, 69, 89, 90–91,
      102–3, 104–5, 129, 146–47, 152–
      54, 164–66, 172, 176–77, 185–86,
      198, 199, 202–3, 204, 225, 238–39,
      241, 247–48
    sexuality of 15, 17–18, 100, 119, 160–
      62, 174–76, 190–91, 192–93, 240–
      41, 251–53
    superlative judgments of 3–4, 11, 28,
      38, 40–41, 82–83, 87, 93, 94–95,
      143, 253
    theatrical clubs, memberships
      in 162–64
    vaudeville, success in 82–83, 88–89,
      90–91, 95, 102–3, 127–28, 199, 200*f*,
      204, 210
    vocal talent and qualities of 2, 47–49,
      51, 58, 96, 133, 198
    weight and bodily dimensions 15, 89–
      90, 116, 145–46, 150, 154–56, 167–
      70, 174, 198, 204, 220–21, 224–25,
      227–28, 245
Elusive Lady, The 214–15, 235–36
Eon, Chevalier d' 21
"eonism". *See* Eon, Chevalier d'
Errol, Bert 12
Evans, George "Honey Boy" 104–5, 107,
    109–10, 111–12, 162
Eytinge, Rose 37

Fads & Fancies of the Fair Sex. See Eltinge,
    Julian: cabaret and revue-style
    performances
Fairbanks, Douglas 137–38, 183
"fairy". *See* homosexuality: coded terms
    and epithets
Famous Players-Lasky movie studio 178,
    179–80, 197, 202–3
Farnum, Dustin 101–2, 136–37, 180
Fascinating Widow, The 140–41, 141*f*,
    142–46, 145*f*, 149, 151, 152–53, 159*f*,
    164, 166, 180–81, 199, 210, 213–14
fashion and couture design 27, 45, 72–73,
    74, 97*f*, 172–74, 204. *See also* Eltinge,
    Julian: fashionable attire, display of

Fauntleroy, Little Lord (character and also
    literary works) 30–32, 31*f*, 119
female impersonation. *See also* Eltinge,
    Julian: rivals and imitators
    Asian artists and their traditions of 13–
      14, 253
    blackface minstrelsy and 105–6, 107–9,
      112, 116, 253
college and university groups 45, 48*f*, 61,
    62–66, 126–27, 142–43, 151, 180–81,
    216–18, 251
    experts' concerns over its
      effects 45, 117
    history of 12, 13–14, 18–19, 74–81
homosexuality, association with 19–20,
    84, 212–13, 218, 227–28, 236, 237–39
men's clubs and fraternal organizations
    engaging in 40, 49–50, 54–55, 57, 59,
    63, 69–71, 74, 162–63, 180–81, 183–
    84, 198–99
    nomenclature and stage names in 12–
      13, 15
    popularity of 8–9, 11–12, 215–16
    salaries 13–14
    subspecialists in 13–15, 115
    vaudeville, in 81, 86, 102–3, 199–
      201, 218–19
    Western frontier and Great Plains,
      on 39–40
    World War I and 194–97, 208*f*
First Corps of Cadets of the Massachusetts
    Volunteer Militia. *See* Cadets
    organization
Fish, Mamie, aka Mrs. Stuyvesant Fish 9–
    10, 60
FitzGerald, Fred 192–93, 194–95, 198–99
"flappers" 1–2, 93–94, 218
Florodora 69–71
Fort Salonga, Long Island, New York. *See*
    Eltinge, Julian: real estate: homes,
    residences, and other properties
Fortescue, George 37, 68
Foucault, Michel 20, 252–53
Freud, Sigmund 17–18, 20, 21–22, 117,
    249. *See also* sexology and scientific
    thought
Friars Club 162
Fuller, Loie 90–91, 113

INDEX 345

Gaxton, William "Bill" 163–64, 246–47
gender constructionism and
    performativity 23–24. *See also*
    Butler, Judith
Gibson, Charles Dana. *See* Gibson Girl
Gibson Girl 1–2, 2*f*, 112, 119–20. *See also*
    Eltinge, Julian: popular characters of
Gilbert & Sullivan 85–86, 150
Glassey, Patrick Francis 13
Great Britain, kingdom as a whole and
    regions and cities. *See also* Edward
    VII, King; London and
  arts, culture, and literature 30–32,
    53, 77, 79
  female impersonation in 77–80, 115
  laws and codes 15–16, 18–19, 77–79
Greece and Rome, classical 75–76
Griffith, D. W. 178–79, 186

Hammerstein theatrical family (Oscar I,
    Oscar II, Willie), 63–64, 103–4, 113–
    15, 139, 179–80, 215
Hammerstein venues. *See* Hammerstein
    theatrical family
Harbach, Otto. *See* Hauerbach, Otto
Haresfoot Club, University of
    Wisconsin 63–64, 140, 216–18
Harvard University 29, 30–33, 43, 46–47,
    51, 56–57, 61–63, 64–66, 82–83, 116,
    120, 184–85, 216, 251. *See* also Hasty
    Pudding Club
Hasty Pudding Club 32–33, 61–64, 216
Hauerbach, Otto 101–2, 140, 167
Hearst, William Randolph, 237, 241
Held, Anna 108–9, 180
Henschel, Harris and family 100,
    101*f*, 102
heterosexuality and heteronormativity. *See*
    also masculinity
  concept and terminology, development
    of 15–17, 193–94, 218–19
  laws and norms reinforcing 15–16, 18–
    19, 74, 78–79, 160, 253–54
Hirschfeld, Magnus 21, 40–41, 167–70.
    See also sexology and scientific
    thought
Hoffman, Gertrude 113–15, 116,
    119, 146–47

Hollywood
  culture of 163–64, 184–86
  journalism 62–63, 184–85, 190–91,
    201, 230
  motion picture industry, development
    and growth 178–80, 182, 186, 197,
    199, 201, 202, 203, 210, 229, 230
  World War I and 206–9
homosexuality. *See also* heterosexuality
    and heteronormativity
  coded terms and epithets 10, 22, 54–55,
    57–58, 84, 110–11, 133–35, 174–76,
    193–94, 198–99, 212–13, 227–28,
    232–33, 236, 237–38, 243–44, 251–52
  historical and cultural development of,
    as a concept 16–17, 193–94, 251–52
  homophobia (*see* reactionism: antigay,
    antiqueer, anti-trans)
  in relation to female impersonation
    artists 7–9, 19–21, 57, 78, 119, 174–
    76, 218–19, 236, 237, 238–39, 251–52
    (*see also* reactionism)
  as site of knowledge and
    inquiry 251–53
  World War I and 193–94
homophobia. *See* reactionism: antigay,
    antiqueer, anti-trans

If I Had My Way 244–45
Ince, Thomas 180, 206–7
indigenous culture and persons in North
    America 29, 35, 39, 42
"inverts" and "inversion," use of terms 4–
    5, 20–21, 167–70, 193–94, 212–13,
    236. *See also* sexology and scientific
    thought
Ireland and Irish people in the United
    States 28–30
Isle of Love, The. See *Over the Rhine*
Ivy League colleges and universities. *See*
    individual institutions by name (e.g.,
    Dartmouth, Harvard, University of
    Pennsylvania, Yale, etc.)

Japan and Japanese people in the United
    States 26*f*, 40–41, 123–25, 126–27.
    See also Shima, Ko
Jessel, George 163–64, 251–52

346 INDEX

Jolly Mr. Wix of Wickham and the Merry Shopgirls. See Mr. Wix of Wickham
Jolson, Al 109, 225–26

Kaiser Wilhelm II of Germany 190, 191–92, 206, 207–8
Keith, Benjamin Franklin "B. F." 81–82, 84–86. *See also* Keith vaudeville organization
Keith vaudeville organization. *See also* female impersonation: vaudeville in
  Catholic church, ties to 84–86
  design and maintenance 1, 81–82
  growth of 81–82, 85–86, 87–88
  monopolistic practices of 86–87, 127, 128
  respectability and supposed moral cleanliness of 81–82, 84–85, 86, 117, 147–48, 237–38
  RKO merger/formation 229
  UBO (United Bookings Offices of America) 86–87, 102–3, 147–48, 235
  venues 1, 81–83, 93–95, 103, 108–10, 125, 179, 204, 229, 251
Kern, Jerome 73–74, 140, 170–71, 174, 215
Kingsley Commission. *See* censorship; reactionism: antigay, antiqueer, anti-trans / antitheatrical
Kingsley, Grace 224–25, 238–39
Klaw & Erlanger theatrical organization 82–83, 90–91, 128, 162
Klaw, Marc. *See* Klaw & Erlanger theatrical organization
Krafft-Ebing, Richard von 20, 218–19, 232–33. *See also* sexology and scientific thought
Kynaston, Edward 79–81

Lambs Club 162–64, 246–48
Lasky, Jesse. *See* Famous Players-Lasky movie studio
Lauder, Harry 127–29, 130–32
Laurie, Joe., Jr. 95, 251
Lawrence, John D. *See* Retter, Marvel
Lehr, Harry 9–10, 60
"Leon" 13. *See also* Glassey, Patrick Francis

Lind, aka "Lind?" aka. "?Lind?" 13
Little theatre movement 222, 242
London 57, 80–81, 90–91, 113–15, 117, 139, 152. *See also* Great Britain
Los Angeles 12, 40–41, 130, 185–88, 197, 199, 204, 225–26, 230–32, 243. *See also* Hollywood
Lusitania 152

Madame Behave 226–28
Maid to Order 230
makeup. *See* cosmetics, makeup, and skin preparations
Marx, Karl and Marxism 25, 43
masculinity. *See also* Eltinge, Julian: masculinity, performances/embodiments of
  athletics and sporting activities' relation to 25, 65*f*, 66, 98, 116, 160–62, 161*f*, 174–76
  clubs and organizations reinforcing/supporting 57, 63–64
  conventionally-assumed signs of 10, 58–59, 84, 93–94, 101–2, 110–11, 141–42, 144, 161*f*, 167–70, 190–91, 195–96, 198–99, 212–13, 223–24, 226–27
  national identity and 106
  Western frontier and its relation to 32, 39
  work and professions' relation to 24, 25–27, 38, 42, 45, 58, 218, 238
Mask & Wig. *See* female impersonation: college and university groups; Pennsylvania, University of
Massachusetts 28–29, 49–50, 56, 59
McClatchy, C. V. *See* reactionism: antiqueer, antigay, anti-trans
Megatharians of Malden organization 59–60
Mei Lan-Fang 13–14
Michigan, University of, Mimes troupe 63, 64–66, 216–18, 217*f*
Michigan Mimes. *See* Michigan, University of, Mimes troupe
Michigan Union Opera. *See* Michigan, University of, Mimes troupe

INDEX 347

Miladi & The Musketeer 49–51, 53, 54, 55–56, 59, 67, 118, 144
millinery profession 45, 91–92
Mills, Halsey 66, 251
mining: copper, gold, silver, and other metals and minerals 29–30, 34–35, 39–40, 41–42, 128–29, 130
minstrel acts and minstrelsy 13, 38, 46, 56–57, 104–9, 110–12, 115, 121, 125, 162, 226–27, 253
misogyny 67, 75, 76–78, 88, 93, 113, 115–16, 131, 144, 150, 154–62, 155*f*, 167–70, 218, 220–21. *See also* Eltinge, Julian: misogynistic tendencies of
Miss Simplicity 58–59
Mitchell, Julian 37
Montana 29, 32–33, 34–35. *See also* Butte, Montana
moral panics. *See* censorship; reactionism
Morris, William 127–29, 130, 199, 210
motion pictures. *See* Hollywood: motion picture industry, development and growth
Mr. Wix of Wickham 69–74, 70*f*
"musical comedy," origins of genre and term 68, 215
My Lady. See *Miladi & The Musketeer*

naturalism 74
Navy, United States 192–93, 194–95, 198–99. *See also* female impersonation: World War I and
New York Academy of Medicine 21
Newtonville, Newton, Massachusetts 29–30
Nez Percé people. *See* indigenous culture and persons in North America
Niblo, Fred 146–47, 162, 204–5
Norman, Karyl 13, 134*f*, 215–18

Order of the Eastern Star 96
Orpheum circuit. *See* Keith vaudeville organization
Over the Rhine 206–9
Overton, Ada 46

Paduzzi, Georgie. *See* Norman, Karyl
"pansy craze". *See* homosexuality: coded terms and epithets
Paramount Pictures. *See* Famous Players-Lasky movie studio
Paris
  as fashion and style inspiration 69, 91–92
  theatrical activity in 85, 90–91, 102, 152, 195–96
Parsons, Louella 186–88, 190–91, 230
Pastor, Tony 53, 84, 150
Pennington, Ann 226–27, 228
Pennsylvania, University of 61, 64–66
Pickford, Mary 60–61, 137–38, 186
Pierre, Jacques 111–12, 214, 246
Pleasure Man. *See* West, Mae
Psychoanalysis and psychiatry. *See also* Freud, Sigmund
  professions' views on crossdressing and homosexuality 21, 22, 243–44
Purviance, Edna 186

race and racism. *See also* female impersonation: blackface minstrelsy; minstrel acts and minstrelsy
  appropriation by whites of Black art and cultural forms 46, 106, 109
  frontier expansionism and globalization 32, 42
  in relation to norms of beauty and gender 4, 6–7, 105–6, 108–9, 112, 126–27, 154–56, 206–7, 208*f*, 223–24
  white supremacism in entertainment and politics 12, 62, 81–82, 84–85, 105–6, 109–10, 112, 125, 153, 162, 206–7, 210–11, 226–27
Ragged Dick. *See* Alger, Horatio
reactionism
  academics and professors as agents of 64–66, 77–78
  anti-Bolshevik, anticommunist, antisocialist, antiunion 14–15, 34, 110–11, 198–99
  antigay, antiqueer, anti-trans 8–9, 16–17, 21, 23, 40–41, 60–61, 64–66, 78–79, 80, 84, 117, 126–27, 132, 133–35,

348 INDEX

reactionism (*cont.*)
144, 167–70, 174–76, 193–94, 198–
201, 204, 213–14, 218–19, 232–35,
236, 238–39, 243–44, 249
antiimmigrant 14, 40–41, 117, 123–25,
126, 135–36
antitheatrical 77–79, 117, 185, 204,
236, 238, 243–44, 249
Red Cross organization 180–81, 183–84,
206–7, 208*f*
religion. *See also* reactionism:
antitheatrical
Christianity's role in influencing sex and
gender norms 18–19, 76–78
church involvement in popular
entertainment and vaudeville 84–
86, 117
decline of 19, 22–23
Republic Pictures. *See Over the Rhine*
retailing. *See* consumerism, rise of and
trends in
Retter, Marvel 240–41
Revue of Nineteen-Nineteen. See Eltinge,
Julian: cabaret and revue-style
performances
Rialto cinema. *See* Rothafel, S. L. "Roxy"
Rice, Edward E. 68–71, 72–74
Ring, Blanche 244–45, 246–47
RKO (Radio-Keith-Orpheum). *See*
Keith vaudeville organization: RKO
merger/formation
Rogers, Leonhardt & Curtis
organization 132–35
Rome. *See* Greece and Rome, classical
"roof garden" venues 103–4
Roosevelt, Teddy 17–18, 32–33, 34, 64,
82–83, 98–100, 116, 129, 193–94
Rothafel, S. L. "Roxy" 179–80, 182
Russell, Lillian 36, 38, 149–51
Russia and Russians 9–10, 14–15, 96, 125.
See also reactionism: anti-Bolshevik,
anticommunist, antisocialist,
antiunion

Sabbatarian League. *See* reactionism:
antitheatrical

Salome and "exotic" acts. *See also* Eltinge,
Julian: popular characters of
cultural fad 112–15, 121, 166
famous portrayers of 113–15, 114*f*, 116,
119, 120
moral panics related to 114*f*,
117–18
origins of 113
Salt Lake City 34
San Francisco 33–34, 40–41, 129, 130,
178, 194–95
Savoy, Bert 7–8, 39–40, 194, 212–13, 233–
35, 238–39, 251–52
Sears, Roebuck 17–18, 25–27, 81–82
"self-made man," myth of 29–30, 33, 84–
85, 135–36, 140–41
Senelick, Laurance 17, 254–55
"separate spheres" concept regarding the
sexes 33, 58–59, 88, 123, 183–84,
225, 238
Sex (stage play). *See* West, Mae
sexology and scientific thought 19–23,
94, 167–70, 193–94, 218–19, 232–33,
237–38, 243
Shakespeare, William 76–77, 80–81, 112,
133–35, 160, 180, 238–39
Shima, Ko 26*f*, 123–26, 124*f*, 127, 145–46,
199–201
Show Boat. See Kern, Jerome
"show girls". *See* "chorus girls," cultural
phenomenon of
Sierra Vista Rancho 222–25, 228, 240–41,
242, 246, 247–48
Silver Bow County, Utah. *See* Butte,
Montana
"sissy" and "cissie.". *See* homosexuality:
coded terms and epithets
Sister Carrie (novel). *See* Dreiser,
Theodore
sodomy 15–16, 80–81
St. Denis, Ruth 2
"sumptuary" codes and laws.
See heterosexuality and
heteronormativity: laws and norms
reinforcing
Swann, Dorsey 8–9

"talkies" or "talking motion pictures". *See* Hollywood: motion picture industry, development and growth

Tanguay, Eva 30–32, 67, 95, 113–15, 116, 118–21, 131, 146–47, 164–66, 190–91, 203, 235, 254

Toll, Robert 11–12, 251–52

"transvestism," invention and use of term and its derivatives 21, 22, 78–79, 167–70. *See also* Hirschfeld, Magnus

"travesty" and "*travesti*" 22, 54–55

Tremont Theatre 49, 54

Tucker, Sophie 6–8, 90, 108–9, 122–23, 128, 135–36, 226–27

Turner, Frederick Jackson 42–43

"two-spirit" people. *See* indigenous culture and persons in North America

UBO (United Booking Offices of America). *See* Keith vaudeville organization

Ulrichs, Karl Heinrich 19–20, 236

United Kingdom. *See* Great Britain

"Uranian" and "urning". *See* Ulrichs, Karl Heinrich

Valentino, Rudolph 209

vaudeville. *See also* Keith vaudeville organization *and. See also* female impersonation: vaudeville, in
- alcohol and tobacco banned from 84
- "big-time" vs. "small-time" 84–85, 86–87, 179
- burlesque, in contradistinction to 81–82
- corporatization of 25, 72–73, 81–82, 84–86, 147–48, 229
- decline of 229, 244–45
- ethnicity and 85, 108–9, 115, 123, 125, 128–29, 131, 143 (*see also* race and racism: white supremacy in entertainment and politics)
- etymology of term 86, 278–79n.47

gender and sexuality issues in 13, 84, 88, 115, 117, 119–20, 235
- history and origins of 81–85
- motion pictures and visual acts in 125, 178–79, 199
- rivalries in 116, 238–39
- salaries of players 89, 115, 127–28, 129, 229
- Salome (*see* Salome and "exotic" acts)
- statistics: industry as a whole: demographics, theatre size, ticket prices, etc. 87–89, 133
- structure of shows 87, 132–33
- women artists in 95, 115

Vienna 36, 90–91, 102, 152

Villa Capistrano. *See* Eltinge, Julian: real estate: homes, residences, and other properties

Walker, Ada Overton. *See* Overton, Ada

Weber, Max 17–18

Wenrich, Percy 101–2, 167, 170–71, 228–29

West, Mae 30–32, 118, 233–39, 234f, 242

Western frontier, myth and allure of 29–30, 32–33, 39, 42. *See also* masculinity: Western frontier and its relation to

white supremacism. *See* race and racism

widows and widowhood. See *Fascinating Widow, The*

Widow's Might, The 197–98, 201, 206

wigs, wearing and removal of 3, 89, 93, 96, 103–4, 112, 145–46, 185

Wilson, Woodrow 42–43, 83

"womanless weddings" 102, 183–84. *See also* female impersonation: men's clubs and fraternal organizations engaging in

Woods, Aladore "Albert" Herman, aka "A. H." 101–2, 133–40, 143–44, 146–49, 151, 152, 153–54, 158, 160–62, 164–66, 167, 170–71, 176, 225–26, 228–29, 239–40

World's Columbian Exposition of 1893 57, 62, 153

350 INDEX

World War I. *See* Eltinge, Julian: politics and values of; female impersonation: World War I and; Hollywood: World War I; homosexuality: World War I and
Wright, Thew, Dr. 213–14
Wyman, Lilla Viles 47–49, 57–58

Yale University 45, 46–47, 64–66, 69–71, 236

Young, Brigham 34, 40

Ziegfeld, Florenz 17–18, 32–33, 37, 42, 53–54, 72–73, 108–9, 113–15, 147–48, 151, 204–5, 210, 214, 226–27
Ziegfeld Follies. See Ziegfeld, Florenz
Zukor, Abraham. *See* Famous Players-Lasky movie studio